Exploring IBM e-business Software

Other Titles of Interest From Maximum Press

Exploring IBM Technology, Products, & Services, Fifth Edition: Hoskins, 1-885068-82-4

Exploring IBM @server pSeries, Eleventh Edition: Hoskins & Bluethman, 1-885068-81-6

Exploring IBM @server iSeries, Eleventh Edition: Hoskins & Dimmick, 1-885068-92-1

Exploring IBM @server xSeries, Twelfth Edition: Hoskins, Wilson & Winkel, 1-885068-83-2

Exploring IBM @server zSeries and S/390 Servers, Eighth Edition: Hoskins & Frank, 1-885068-91-3

Exploring IBM Network Stations: Ho, Lloyd, & Heracleous, 1-885068-32-8

Building Intranets With Lotus Notes and Domino 5.0, Third Edition: Krantz, 1-885068-41-7

Internet Marketing for Your Tourism Business: Sweeney, 1-885068-47-6

Marketing With E-Mail, Third Edition: Kinnard, 1-885068-68-9

Business-to-Business Internet Marketing, Fourth Edition: Silverstein, 1-885068-72-7

Marketing on the Internet, Sixth Edition: Zimmerman, 1-885068-80-8

101 Internet Businesses You Can Start From Home: Sweeney, 1-885068-59-X

The e-Business Formula for Success: Sweeney, 1-885068-60-3

101 Ways to Promote Your Web Site, Fourth Edition: Sweeney, 1-885068-90-5

Internet Marketing for Information Technology Companies, Second Edition: Silverstein, 1-885068-67-0

Internet Marketing for Less Than $500/Year, Second Edition: Yudkin, 1-885068-69-7

The Business Guide to Selling Through Internet Auctions: Hix, 1-885068-73-5

Exploring IBM e-business Software

Second Edition

Become an Instant Insider on IBM's Internet Business Tools

Casey Young

MAXIMUM PRESS
605 Silverthorn Road
Gulf Breeze, FL 32561
(850) 934-0819
www.maxpress.com

Publisher: Jim Hoskins

Manager of Finance/Administration: Joyce Reedy

Production Manager: Gina Cooke

Cover Designer: Lauren Smith

Copyeditor: Andy Potter

Proofreader: Jacquie Wallace

Indexer: Susan Olason

Printer: P.A. Hutchison

Library of Congress Cataloging-in-Publication Data

Young, Casey, 1951-

Exploring IBM e-business software / Casey Young.— 2nd ed.

p. cm.

ISBN 1-931644-00-4

1. Computer software. 2. IBM Personal Computer—Programming.
3. Electronic commerce. I. Title.

QA76.754.Y68 2003

005.365—dc21

2003001965

For Becky Goldstein and Richard Yevich,
whose lights went out far too early.

Acknowledgements

I'd like to thank my publisher, Jim Hoskins, for believing in this book in the first place. IBM has been very supportive of this book, especially my manager, Jerry Heglar and Data Management's General Manager, Janet Perna.

I'd also like to thank my intrepid IBM reviewers: Kirk Davis, Roger Miller, Curt Cotner, Jeff Josten, Betty Patterson, Francis Ricchio, Jason Aycock, Jackie Burhans, Scott Rau, Stephen Londergan, and Carlton Doe.

Thanks also to my son, Tony D'Elia, for his support, as well as that of my partner, Ken Dawes, who remains patient and understanding no matter how stressed I get.

Trademarks

The words contained in this text which are believed to be trademarked, service marked, or otherwise to hold proprietary rights have been designated as such by use of initial capitalization. No attempt has been made to designate as trademarked or service marked any personal computer words or terms in which proprietary rights might exist. Inclusion, exclusion, or definition of a word or term is not intended to affect, or to express judgment upon, the validity of legal status of any proprietary right which may be claimed for a specific word or term.

Foreword

In a world of constant change, reducing costs and improving productivity are the biggest challenges customers face in becoming on demand e-businesses. IBM is there for every step of the journey, delivering technology that is "always on," accessible from anywhere, and designed to stand the test of time.

IBM's software technology is the universal glue that helps businesses make this giant leap into the future and get to a much more efficient way of doing business. It's about making everything occur in a seamless flow: A customer places an order, the system checks inventory, delivery gets scheduled and inventory is replenished. It's about integrating applications to make them operate as if they're one. That's the e-business infrastructure.

We set out several years ago to change the face of the software industry by building an integrated portfolio of middleware brands that would help customers become e-businesses: DB2 for collecting, analyzing and securely distributing all forms of content; WebSphere for managing transactions and integrating new Web-based applications with existing ones; Lotus for messaging and collaboration solutions; Tivoli for security and storage management; and now Rational for software development.

This book provides an introduction to some of IBM's e-business software products, and describes the importance of having a standards-based, scalable infrastructure. In the e-business world, a single transaction can involve dozens of different applications flitting across hundreds of servers, routers and hubs in different states. How do you funnel this into one enterprise when your infrastructure is literally all over the map? The answer is through a serious software infrastructure. That's what IBM is committed to providing.

Donn Atkins
Vice President, Worldwide Sales and Marketing
IBM Software Group

Table of Contents

Introduction xvii
What This Book Is xviii
What This Book Is Not xix
How to Use This Book xix
Your "Members Only" Web Site xx

Chapter 1:
IBM and e-business 1

Why Is e-business Important? 2
e-business Integration and Infrastructure 3
What Is e-Commerce? 4
Business-to-Business (B2B) 5
Four Waves of Information Technology 6
IBM and Open Standards *8*
Integration *9*
Infrastructure *10*
Innovation *11*
Web Services 12
Grid Computing 14
IBM Autonomic Computing Initiative (aka Project eLiza) 14
e-business on demand 15
Concepts to Make an e-business Work 16
Tag Languages *18*
Java *20*
Extensions to Java *22*

Chapter 2:
Architectures That Pre-date e-business 24

Batch 25
VSAM 27
OLTP 28
Databases 31

Distributed Architectures 35
Object-Oriented Databases 37
Hybrid Database Management Systems 40
Component Broker Architecture 42
Business Intelligence 43
Applications 47

Chapter 3: Hardware Architectures and Operating Systems 49

Hardware 50
IBM's Hardware Series 54
Hardware Architectures 55
Operating Systems 56
Mainframe 56
Parallel Sysplex Technology 58
Non-Mainframe 59
The World Is Blending 60
Hardware, Operating Systems, and e-business on demand 61
Grid Computing 62
Autonomic Computing Initiative 62
Networks 63
Protocols 66

Chapter 4: WebSphere 69

Foundation and Tools 71
WebSphere Application Server 71
WebSphere Studio Product Family 77
WebSphere Homepage Builder 78
WebSphere Studio Site Developer 80
WebSphere Studio Application Developer 81
WebSphere Studio Application Developer Integration Edition 82
WebSphere Studio Enterprise Developer 82
WebSphere Studio Asset Analyzer for Multiplatforms 83
WebSphere Studio Application Monitor for z/OS and OS/390 83
WebSphere Studio Workload

Simulator for z/OS and OS/390 85
WebSphere Studio Device Developer (formerly VisualAge Micro Edition) 85
Macromedia ColdFusion MX for WebSphere 86
Versata Logic Suite for WebSphere 86
WebSphere Host Integration *86*
IBM Personal Communications 88
WebSphere Host On-Demand 88
IBM Screen Customizer 89
WebSphere Host Publisher 89
IBM Communications Server 90
Reach and User Experience 91
Portal Solutions *91*
WebSphere Portal for Multiplatforms *93*
WebSphere Portal Express *96*
WebSphere Personalization 96
Enterprise Information Portal (EIP) 98
Pervasive Solutions *100*
WebSphere Voice Server 100
WebSphere Voice Response with DirectTalk Technology 103
WebSphere Voice Server for Transcription 103
WebSphere Translation Server 104
Mobile Application Platforms *105*
WebSphere Everyplace Access *105*
WebSphere Everyplace Server, Service Provider Offering *107*
WebSphere Everyplace Suite Embedded Edition *109*
WebSphere Everyplace Connection Managers *110*
WebSphere Everyplace Subscription Manager *111*
WebSphere Transcoding Publisher *112*
WebSphere Custom Environment *115*
WebSphere Micro Environment *115*
WebSphere Business Integration 116
Process Integration 116
WebSphere MQSeries Workflow 118
IBM CrossWorlds 119
Holosofx Business Process Management Suite 120
Application Integration 121
WebSphere MQ (formerly MQSeries Messaging) *121*
WebSphere MQ Everyplace (formerly MQSeries Everyplace) 125

WebSphere MQ Event Broker 125
WebSphere MQ Integrator Broker (formerly MQSeries Integrator) 126
WebSphere Data Interchange 126
WebSphere Business Integration Adapters 127
WebSphere Foundation and Tools 128
Enterprise Modernization *128*
WebSphere Host Integration 128
CICS Transaction Gateway 130
Transaction Processing *130*
CICS Transaction Server 130
OS/390 C/C++ and z/OS C/C++ 131
TXSeries 131
Transaction Processing Facility (TPF) 133
COBOL 133
VisualAge for Java 133
VisualAge Generator 134
VisualAge Enterprise Suite 137
VisualAge Pacbase 137
VisualAge Smalltalk 138
Other WebSphere Products 138
WebSphere Business Components *138*
WebSphere Business Components Composer 140
WebSphere Business Components Studio 141
WebSphere Bank Teller Business Components 141
WebSphere Text Analyzer Business Components 141
WebSphere Order Capture Business Component 143
WebSphere Software MultiChannel Banking Solution ... 144
IBM SanFrancisco *145*
WebSphere Edge Server *145*
WebSphere Site Analyzer *146*
Footnotes 146

Chapter 5: DB2 147

IMS Family 148
IMS *148*
IMS Transaction Manager *155*
IMS Connect and IMS Connector for Java *155*
DB2 Universal Database 156

DB2 Universal Database for z/OS and OS/390 .... *161*
DB2 Server for VSE and VM *166*
DB2 Universal Database for Multiplatforms *167*
DB2 Universal Database for iSeries *171*
DB2 Everyplace *171*
DB2 Extenders 172
DB2 Content Management 173
DB2 Content Manager *173*
DB2 Content Manager VideoCharger 176
Electronic Media Management System 177
DB2 Content Manager Solutions 178
DB2 Content Manager CommonStore *179*
DB2 Content Manager OnDemand *179*
Informix 180
Informix Dynamic Server (IDS) *181*
Informix DataBlades *183*
OnLine Extended Edition *185*
Red Brick Warehouse *185*
Informix Extended Parallel Server (XPS) *186*
Informix Solutions *187*
U2 Product Family 188
UniData *188*
UniVerse *192*
RedBack *193*
SystemBuilder *194*
wIntegrate *195*
COBOL Direct Connect *196*
Information Movement and Access 196
DB2 Connect *196*
Informix Connect and Office Connect *197*
DataJoiner *197*
Informix Enterprise Gateway Manager and Informix Gateway with DRDA *198*
DB2 DataPropagator *199*
IMS DataPropagator *199*

Chapter 6: Managing Your e-business Application **201**

Security Software 201
Security Concepts *203*

Access Management *205*
Tivoli Access Manager for e-business 206
Tivoli Access Manager for Business Integration 207
Tivoli Access Manager for Operating Systems 208
Identity Management *208*
Tivoli Identity Manager 209
Threat Management *210*
Tivoli Risk Manager 210
Tivoli Intrusion Manager 212
Privacy Management *212*
Tivoli Policy Manager for e-business 214
Tivoli Solutions 214
Tivoli Identity Management Solution 214
VeriSign Managed Services 214
Tivoli Security Event Solution 216
Tivoli Enterprise Console *216*
Storage Software 217
Tivoli Storage Network Manager *217*
Tivoli Storage Manager *218*
Tivoli Storage Resource Manager *220*
Tivoli SANergy *221*
Tivoli Storage Solutions *221*
Performance and Availability Software 222
Tivoli Analyzer for Lotus Domino *222*
Tivoli Business Systems Manager *223*
Tivoli Monitoring *223*
Tivoli NetView *225*
Tivoli Switch Analyzer *226*
Tivoli Performance Modeler for z/OS *226*
Tivoli Service Level Advisor *227*
Tivoli System Automation for OS/390 ..... *227*
Tivoli Web Site Analyzer (formerly WebSphere Site Analyzer) *227*
IBM CICS Performance Monitor for OS/390 ..... *228*
WebSphere Studio Application Monitor for OS/390 and z/OS *228*
Tivoli Performance and Availability Management Solutions *229*
Configuration and Operations Management Software 229

Tivoli Configuration Manager 230
Tivoli License Manager 230
Tivoli Point-of-Sale Manager 230
Tivoli Remote Control 231
Tivoli Workload Scheduler 231
Tivoli Data Exchange 232
Tivoli Configuration and Operations Management Solutions 232

Chapter 7: Lotus **233**

Lotus Notes 233
Lotus Domino 235
Lotus Domino Server 236
Lotus Domino Everyplace 239
Domino Unified Communications Services 239
Lotus Sametime 241
Lotus Team Workplace (formerly QuickPlace) 242
IBM Mindspan Solutions and Lotus LearningSpace 243

Chapter 8: Application Accelerators **245**

WebSphere Commerce Solutions 246
WebSphere Commerce 247
WebSphere Commerce Professional Entry Edition 248
WebSphere Commerce Professional Edition 248
WebSphere Commerce Business Edition 248
WebSphere Catalog Manager 249
WebSphere Commerce Payments (formerly WebSphere Payment Manager) 250
WebSphere Commerce Analyzer Advanced Edition 254
WebSphere Commerce Portal 255
Patterns for e-business 255
e-business Partner Solutions 258
Business Solutions 260
Enterprise Resource Planning and Customer Relationship Management 260

Chapter 9:
An Approach to e-business 262

Where Do You Want to Go? 263
Where You Are 267
IBM Sales Team 269
IBM Web Sites 270
developerWorks 270
alphaWorks 271
Putting the Pieces Together 272

Appendix A: Rational Software 273
Appendix B: Glossary 276

Introduction

When I joined IBM about five years ago, I trained sales personnel in data management software. In doing that, I found that there was the same breadth of awareness of software solutions that I had discovered working as a consultant at many Fortune 500 companies. The knowledge ranged from the technician of many years who could competently talk bits and bites of data processing, but had no knowledge of how that area fit into the emerging world of Internet commerce, to the Web home page builder who could dazzle with a presentation of sound, movement, and color, but had no idea how to show any real information.

These people, who needed to talk to each other, did not speak the same language. This same lack of communication can cause problems when designing and building e-business systems. Both skills, plus all the combinations of skills in between, are necessary for a successful e-business system.

The idea of this book came from this experience. I believe that we need to find common ground if we are to continue to move the world's business (not to mention our lives) forward electronically. Of course, I am still in pursuit of the mythical four-day work week and the paperless society, so that already defines me as a dreamer. But seriously, communication and understanding is the key to great systems, and I hope this book provides you with the understanding.

While I was training salespeople, I discovered a book entitled Exploring IBM Technology, Products, and Services. It is an impressive book on the vision of IBM, its hardware offerings, and IBM Global Services, but I felt it did not do justice to IBM's impressive software portfolio. I offered to write such a book for the series, the proposal was accepted, and the first edition was published in 2001.

Since all things change, and software changes more frequently than most things, the need for a second edition became apparent in 2002. This edition captures the newest packaging and strategy of IBM software products, as well as the newer developments of its product lines.

What This Book Is

This book provides an introduction to some of IBM's e-business software products. I say "some of" because it would take a much longer book to catalog all of IBM's software items. Also, as the e-business marketplace emerges, IBM is responding to the marketplace and customer needs by creating offerings to meet current e-business requirements. However, this book will give you the basics you need to open the discussion with your IBM representative or do further research on the Web. Purchase of this book provides you with access to a "members only" Web site (described later), so you have an excellent starting point to get your questions answered—chapter by chapter.

My purpose in writing this book is to:

- Provide a fundamental understanding of IBM's e-business strategy, including "e-business on demand"
- Provide a historical framework for e-business that communicates how these new technologies must fit within the existing structure
- Describe significant IBM e-business software products within the IBM brands: WebSphere, DB2, Lotus, and Tivoli
- Describe processes that can be used to get started in e-business
- Provide the reader places to get more information about the products.

This book is intended to be a fundamental explanation of IBM's e-business software for the reader who is unfamiliar with many of IBM's e-business software products. Therefore, I use easy-to-understand language and provide background and definitions for technical terms and structures as they are introduced.

In addition, in the chapters about specific products (Chapters 4 through 7), I provide an introduction to Rational Software in Appendix A. Appendix B provides a glossary of important abbreviations or phrases that are used in this book.

What This Book Is Not

This book is not a comprehensive IBM product catalog or a technology encyclopedia. It is not intended to be an in-depth discussion of the technical bits and bites of each product or solution in the IBM software portfolio. On the other hand, it is not written at such a high level that you can't understand how the basic process works. As noted, not every bit of software is explained. In developing something that could be comprehended by someone relatively new to any portion of the software (someone being really smart about databases and not quite as smart about security, for example), I sometimes had to make choices about what to leave out. This book does not expect you to be an engineer, nor does it expect you to be able to install any of these products at the end. However, if you do pursue more information on these products, you will find many of them easier to install and use than you anticipated.

If I have not included your favorite e-business software product, let me know and perhaps it will be included in later editions of this book.

How to Use This Book

The first three chapters are background chapters. Chapter 1 defines IBM's e-business strategy based on presentations given by Lou Gerstner, former Chairman and CEO of IBM, and Sam Palmisano, current Chairman and CEO of IBM. Chapter 2 defines architectures that have historically affected system designs, such as online transaction processing (OLTP), business intelligence, relational theory, object theory, and the like. Chapter 3 looks at some of the heterogeneous elements that e-business architects need to look at when developing these types of applications: hardware architectures and operating systems.

Chapters 4 through 7 contain product information, with a chapter for each brand. The last two chapters focus on getting started in e-business and point to additional resources.

Chapter 8 connects the information about IBM software solutions and the reader's e-business challenge. In a discussion on how a company can begin or expand its e-business portfolio, there is information about some of IBM's application accelerators such as WebSphere Commerce Suite. Chapter 9 is the jumping-off point to get started in e-business development—what to plan for and where to get more information from IBM.

Your "Members Only" Web Site

The world of IBM technology and products changes every day. That is why there is a companion Web site associated with this book. On this site you will find news, expanded information on the topics covered in the book, and other resources of interest. The book refers to particular areas that will probably have updates or additional information in the near future.

However, you have to be a member of the "IBM Insiders Club" to gain access to this site. When you purchased this book, you automatically became a member. (In fact, that is the only way to join.) So you now have the full privileges of the IBM Insiders Club.

To get into the "Members Only" section of the companion Web site, go to the Maximum Press Web site located at *www.maxpress.com* and follow the links to the companion Web site for *Exploring IBM e-business Software*. When you try to enter, you will be asked for a User ID and Password. Type the following:

- For User ID: *ebizsw2e*
- For Password: *offside*

You will then be granted full access to the "Members Only" area. Visit the site often and enjoy the updates and resources with our compliments—and thanks again for buying the book. We ask that you not share the "User ID" and "Password" for this site with anyone else.

1

IBM and e-business

This is a book about software—specifically IBM's e-business software. Software is what makes the computing world work. Hardware—the physical box that sits on your desk or in a computer room—makes nothing more than a great doorstop if the software is not there. It is software that makes the computing world work, and better software makes it work better.

If all this sounds simple, look at the Internet. Originally developed by the U.S. Department of Defense in 1969 to promote networking research, the ARPANET, as it was called then, was little more than a collection of computers linked together by wires. There was software, but it was crude and rudimentary, and you really had to want to use it to invest the time it took to learn it. The first major change to the Internet was the development of a standard communications protocol (a standard software coding language) to handle communication between different components (computers and wires) on the Internet. This coding language was called TCP/IP (Transmission Control Protocol/Internet Protocol). The second major change, the change that really made the Internet a common appliance in every home, was the development of the World Wide Web and its common language—HTML (HyperText Markup Language). Both of these are software developments that will be discussed throughout this book.

And what is the world's largest software company? Well, if you stood IBM's software division on its own, it would be the world's largest software company. Used to thinking of IBM as a hardware company and Microsoft as the world's largest software company, many people are surprised by this fact. Not only is IBM the world's largest software company, it is also a software company committed to e-business.

This chapter focuses on discussions about IBM and e-business, including a working definition of e-business and some of its sub-components, a discussion of IBM's new initiative of e-business on demand and a discussion of the more common elements, such as Extended Markup Language (XML), that are components of most e-business solutions. First, we'll take a look at why e-business is important.

Why Is e-business Important?

In spite of the current economic difficulties, e-business continues to grow. Why? There are two main reasons companies are turning to e-business—the number of new people on the Internet and the efficiency of doing business on the Internet. Today there are, by some estimates, over 505 million people in the world attached to the Internet. This number is estimated to grow to close to a billion by the end of 2003. The significance of this is increased when you take a look at the amount of money changing hands via the Internet. In 2000, $657 billion changed hands, or about 8.6% of total worldwide sales. By 2004, that number is expected to grow tenfold to close to $6,790 billion, or close to 13% of the world's commerce spending.

The other significant advantage is the cost of a transaction over the Internet versus one that requires human interaction, even over the telephone. Banks determined the cost of an ATM transaction to be significantly less (about ten cents) than one involving a teller (about $1.25). Customers that only used ATMs for their transactions got better rates than those whose transactions require a teller. Banking is finally moving online in a serious manner as people become more and more accustomed to doing things over the Internet—particularly their profitable customers.

These items apply to wired e-business connections, but the Internet evolution continues to wireless devices. By 2004, IDC, an industry analysis firm, predicts that 1.4 billion people will access Web content from wireless devices. IDC estimates that 32.5% of the U.S. population use some form of wireless devices, with 52% of Europeans and 60% of Japanese doing so. Most significant to the business planner, however, is that by 2005, it is estimated that three-quarters of all Web transactions, totaling $200 billion, will take place over the air.

e-business Integration and Infrastructure

So what does any of this have to do with e-business? If you'll recall, the advanced stage of e-business requires integration of objects, networks, people, etc.—in short, everything in an enterprise. But let's take a look at where e-business has come from to be able to get to that point of excellence.

To many people the faces of e-business are the Web page and the media hype of fortunes made and lost by the "dot-com" businesses. The ability to buy and sell things on the Internet was fascinating. Surely people would rush to use this new technology to do their daily shopping. And for a while that seemed true—until the immutable business laws of supply and demand and return on investment (ROI) reared their collective heads and caused the tumble of many dot-coms in 2000, a trend that continues today as companies fold, consolidate, and rise up re-invented.

But this shakeup is only part of the picture. According to a speech given by Lou Gerstner, former chairman and CEO of IBM, at the e-business Conference Expo on December 12, 2000, this is what happens with transformational technologies. First there is wild enthusiasm, then a period of disillusionment, and, finally, reality. And what is this reality? The Internet is a tool—no more, no less. And if we treat e-business as a business and learn how to leverage the tool, we can do very well indeed.

According to Gerstner, two main things will be important for the emergence of an e-business founded on fundamentals: integration and infrastructure.

Integration is about the entire span of what happens with a business transaction, from the moment of the first click on the Web page to the final reckoning with the government tax bureau. These different business systems need to be able to interact with each other, securely passing information, massaging the information as needed, and getting the information where it needs to go when it needs to get there.

And that's the easy part.

Companies are traditionally built along business lines. Applications were built within these business pipelines. The order entry system was built separately from the supply chain system. Customer accounts were separate from sales opportunity tracking. And the business leaders of these units were separate from each other and frequently ran their line of business as if it were a separate company.

For e-business to work, companies that have invested in their pipeline organizational model are going to have to make significant change to become an integrated e-business. Handshakes between one pipeline and another are going to have to be fast, secure, and reliable.

Infrastructure is the second important aspect of e-business. Gerstner pointed out three items that were important for e-business infrastructure. The first is that e-business infrastructure is "end-to-end." This doesn't mean that clients connect with servers, but that front-end applications access applications within the firewall that access applications that are outside the firewall that return information back into the organization. It also means that all the new devices that are becoming front-end applications need to be considered. This goes beyond receiving stock quotes on your pager. It moves to the heart of "pervasive e-business," filled with devices that talk to each other to insure that your pacemaker keeps running, your car can send a positional distress signal if you're in trouble, and your refrigerator can remind you to pick up milk on the way home.

The second important aspect of infrastructure is open standards, which we will discuss later in this chapter.

The third important aspect of infrastructure is that it must be "self-healing." If there is a problem, be it hardware, software, or plain old human error, the software needs to be able to adapt to the problem and keep on going. If there is a spike in brokerage traffic on the day after an important economic announcement, the software needs to be able to balance that load and keep on going. If a hacker tries to break in and does some damage, the software needs to detect the break-in, heal the damage, and keep on going. According to Gerstner, we are not quite there yet, but within a few years this type of "self-healing" will be commonplace in all kinds of mainstream commercial applications.

Over the last few years, IBM has expanded this idea of end-to-end integration. But, before we get to the expansion of these ideas, let's look at a few more concepts.

What Is e-Commerce?

Essentially the front end of e-business, e-commerce is about buying and selling goods, services, and information to individuals electronically. L.L. Bean and Amazon.com are two well-known places to purchase goods.

Travel agencies such as American Express and auctioneers such as e-Bay expand the concepts of e-commerce beyond the selling of goods. Charles Schwab is a leading discount brokerage company that was one of the earliest brokers to offer the ability to access accounts and place trades from anywhere, 24 hours a day, over the Internet. At the end of the last century, almost anything imaginable (as well as some things that weren't) was available for purchase over the Web.

Then there are things on the Web that are less easily identified as commerce. The government puts massive amounts of information on the Web. It is probably cheaper than printing the little pamphlets that were available for order, but is it e-commerce? It is a stretch, but probably. You are just buying your information in a more circuitous manner—through your tax dollar. And what about those banner ads on the Web? Commerce? Definitely. Especially if you click through and buy something.

The future of e-commerce is good if a few fundamental practices are resolved. The first is that basic business processes must be adapted to the Web. As easy as it is to click and buy, it must be that easy to click and return, ask a question, or find what you are looking for. The second large e-commerce issue is privacy.

Ironically, as people have gotten more comfortable entering their credit card information over the Web, they've become less comfortable entering their personal information. Customers will put false information in the forms that are nicely presented on the Web. (How many customers named Mickey Mouse do you have in your database?) They do not trust that the company will respect their privacy and not abuse or sell their personal data. In order to combat this, companies are going to have to define clear, specific privacy policies and adhere to them. Chapter 6 reviews what IBM does about privacy.

Business-to-Business (B2B)

B2B is more about the back office applications that go beyond the company. It includes such things as supply chain management (SCM), customer relationship management (CRM), and enterprise resource planning (ERP). In addition, it provides the ability to interact with business partners and other outside agencies such as Dun and Bradstreet and the government. They include e-marketplaces where a company can get the supplies it needs "just in time" and at the best price. It can be as simple as a supplier of electrical parts selling them to a government contractor over a Web site on the Internet. It can be more complex, with transfer of data processing files from one company to another in order to provide information about services. For example, a package shipping company could send a file of information to a company indicating the whereabouts of all the packages they had picked up for delivery that day.

IBM is working with partners to produce solutions for e-business as well as provide products for those companies that wish to build their own. These partner offerings are solutions made up of multiple components that provide ready-to-run support for applications from 20,000 business partners, including nearly 9,000 independent software vendors (ISVs). In addition, for those who wish to build their own, IBM provides application accelerators such as WebSphere Commerce and Patterns for e-business to provide starting blocks with the tools and architectures needed to build these applications, yet based on open XML technology to allow companies to keep their options open for emerging technologies.

Four Waves of Information Technology

In 2002, Sam Palmisano, now CEO and Chairman of the IBM Board of Directors, gave a speech about the new computing model at IBM's PartnerWorld Briefing. He talked about entering "into the phase known as the e-business era. The e-business era is end-to-end integration." Using this type of integration, all systems are connected, legacy and Web, machines and humans.

IBM considers that there are four waves of information technology. The first, active in the 1960s and 1970s, was based on functional automation, and included batch, online transaction processing (OLTP) and COBOL systems. The second, active in the 1970s and 1980s, came with the advance of personal computers (PCs), relational databases, and networks. This second wave led to local empowerment of users and the birth of the client/server architecture. The third was based on network-based computing—the 1990s e-business. This wave saw the emergence of ERP, Internet, Java, e-commerce, business-to-business (B2B) integration, as well as connection and functional re-automation. The 21st century brings us process- and event-driven systems development, resulting in horizontal integration and the use of XML, Web services, Open Grid Services Architecture (OGSA) described later, and transactional middleware.

End-to-end integration is needed for process- and event-driven systems. IBM is supporting a model that provides integration from demand to delivery (Figure 1.1). However, based on a study of 33,000 companies (both IBM and non-IBM) that IBM conducted in early 2002, enterprises were at varying points along a continuum. These points break down into three main stages:

- An early stage, where companies are doing simple Web transactions such as publishing information or taking a simple order. These companies may still require you to phone or fax the actual order to them. About 42% of the companies that IBM surveyed were in this stage at the start of 2002.

- An integrating stage, where companies are beginning to integrate the Web into their business systems. This means they are taking the order from the Web and transferring the information to other departments involved in the production process. About 26% of companies were at this stage.

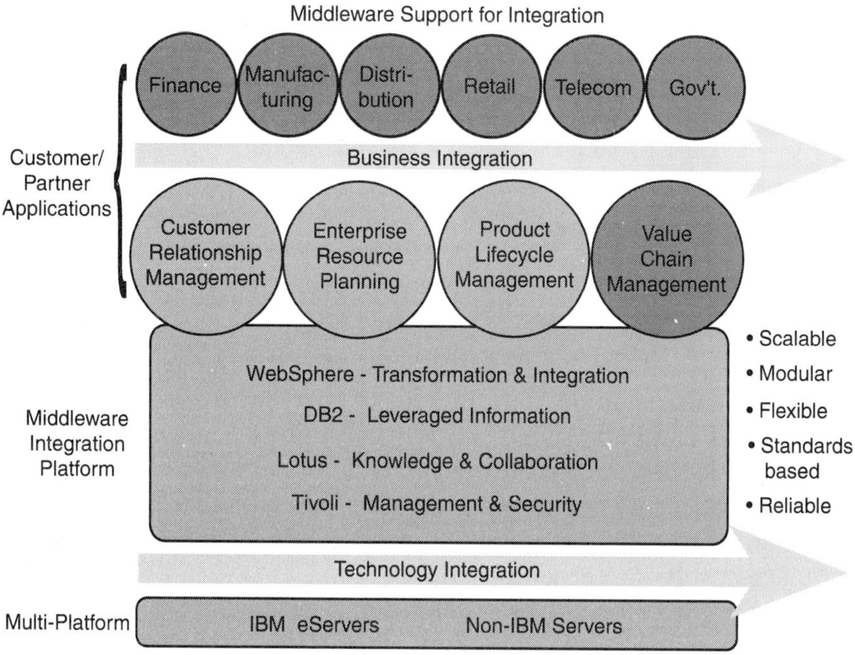

Figure 1.1. Integration from demand to delivery.

- An advanced stage, where companies are inventing new ways to do business with the new medium available, such as eBay's online auctions. A small percentage of the companies that IBM surveyed were at this stage at the start of 2002.

IBM's e-business software, along with its vision and e-business on demand initiative, is designed to help companies move along this continuum. IBM provides integration of business processes, applications, information, directory, and security; innovation, including patents, work with open source computing efforts such as Linux, and new initiatives such as autonomic computing; and the software that is the infrastructure of these initiatives (as well as this book): WebSphere, DB2, Tivoli, and Lotus.

According to statistics from Gartner Group, approximately 40% of information technology budgets are spent on integration. This is a huge amount of time, effort, and money to spend just to pull your information together. The best approach to this problem is to find a way to enable systems to use the newer technologies without having to be replaced. IBM delivers e-business software that addresses integration capabilities to allow you to leverage existing legacy investments and rapidly deploy new technology acquisitions. The key to this development is open standards. We'll take a look at IBM's commitment to open standards and then delve more deeply into the three components of IBM's software strategy: integration, infrastructure, and innovation.

IBM and Open Standards

IBM is committed to the idea of open standards because in order to make integration and end-to-end infrastructure work, components of e-business need to be able to communicate with each other in a standard manner, without a lot of adjustment. IBM has stated that the only reasonable way to avoid vendor lock-in and maintain the flexibility needed to introduce products and technologies based on value and not on proprietary constraints is through open standards. And they have demonstrated this commitment with their financial support and investment in software products.

The Linux operating system (described further in Chapter 3) is an open standards operating system with no ties to any one company. IBM invested in Linux and insured that the majority of IBM's software runs on Linux on any hardware platform, including zSeries. IBM also uses an open programming model based on Java.

XML (described later) is the software standard that is being used to communicate the meaning of all the information we pass around the globe. It is important to IBM that the XML standard remain an open standard and not become a proprietary portion of someone's software code. Again, XML has been incorporated into a majority of IBM's software products. IBM has also enabled its software portfolio to support the development, deployment, storage and management of Web services solutions (described later). Finally, IBM has made a $40 million contribution to the open systems community.

Integration

Businesses need to integrate their various systems and technologies in order to gain greater productivity and increased business value. They are being driven by competitive pressures, customer demands, and supplier demands. Problems they face include manual, sometimes undocumented, processes; application silos; islands of information; and diverse end user (customer, employee, business partner, etc.) needs.

Technology departments face these issues from a different direction. They need to improve their return on investment through improved efficiency, greater utilization, and faster time to value. These needs are based on line-of-business objectives, environmental complexity, and expense cutbacks. Their problems include distributed applications, increasing security threats, numerous security mechanisms to counter these threats, and varied storage types.

IBM addresses these integration problems in four main ways: experience, innovation, open standards and infrastructure products, and solutions. Although almost everyone would agree that IBM has been in business a long time, the strategy specifically points to more recent experience with e-business. This includes IBM Global Services (discussed in *Exploring IBM Technology, Products, and Services*), IBM Patterns for e-business (discussed in Chapter 8), and developerWorks (discussed in Chapter 9).

The specific needs of business and technology are addressed through IBM's software products (see Figures 1.2 and 1.3). Note that as IBM researches new technologies, acquires companies, and repackages software, the names of some of these products may change. The best way to

Integration Area	Capabilities	Products
Application	Application Connectivity	WebSphere MQ Integrator WebSphere MQ Crossworlds Connectors
	Build to Integrate	WebSphere Application Server WebSphere Studio Tools
Business Process Integration	Workflow	WebSphere Workflow Holosfx Modeling Tools Rational Software
	Broker Process Automation	WebSphere Business Integration Crossworlds Collaborations
	B2B Connectivity	WebSphere Business Connection
Integration of People	User Interaction	WebSphere Portal Lotus Notes
	Role-based Access	Tivoli Identity Manager
	Skills/Expertise Location	Lotus Discovery Server
	Advanced Collaboration	Lotus Sametime and Quickplace
Information	Federation	DB2 Universal Database
	XML for Integrated Information	DB2 Extenders Enterprise Information Portal
	Caching and Replication	DB2 Extenders Enterprise Information Portal
	Transformation and Analysis	DB2 Intelligent Miner

Figure 1.2. Addressing business-driven integration.

keep track of product names and packaging is to check the Companion Web Site (see page xx).

Infrastructure

If you'll recall from our earlier discussion, Gerstner said that e-business infrastructure must be end-to-end, open, and self-healing. These capacities, as well as the new ones discussed in "e-Business on demand" later

Integration Area	Capabilities	Products
Security	Correlation of threat information	Tivoli Risk Manager
	Web single sign-on Policy-based access control	Tivoli Access Manager
Operating Environments and Networks	Self-managing environments Self-configuration Self-healing Self-optimization Self-protection	Tivoli Configuration Manager Tivoli Monitoring Tivoli Service Level Advisor
	Horizontal Integration	Tivoli Workload Scheduler eWLM Developers Toolkit
Storage	Intelligent data movement	Tivoli Storage Manager
	Intelligent data storage	Tivoli Storage Manager
	Policy-based automation	Tivoli Storage Manager

Figure 1.3. Addressing technology-driven integration.

in this chapter, are being built into all the software components that IBM is building.

At the time of this writing, IBM Software Group has four key brands. (A fifth brand, Rational Software, was just announced. Check for details in Appendix A). They are WebSphere, DB2, Lotus, and Tivoli. These brands are foundation technologies to meet key information technology challenges. WebSphere is designed for transformation and integration, DB2 for leveraging information, Lotus for leveraging know-how, and Tivoli for managing technology. The bulk of this book (Chapters 4 through 7) delves into this technology in more depth.

Innovation

For a company that began making business machines in the late 1800s, IBM has spent much of its career re-inventing itself to take advantage of growing markets and changing times. Yet, as Lou Gerstner noted in the title of his book, *Who Says Elephants Can't Dance?,* IBM has intensely focused on innovation and change in the last decade. IBM also knows that the rules continue to change and will continue to change rapidly.

There are several different ways that this innovation can be noted. The most traditional of these is patented research. With 22,257 patents over the past decade IBM continues to outrank every other software company, including Microsoft. IBM is committed to and funds research at laboratories all over the world. Another area of innovation is IBM's work with other business partners. Using a strategy that moved it away from isolation; at the end of 2001, IBM was working with 64,000 ISVs, 4,500 systems integrators, 1,000 Web integrators, and 400 service providers, and had 77 strategic ISV alliances.

According to research, the revenue growth of the Linux operating system is projected to be the fastest of any operating system platform. IBM has made intensive investment in Linux, with more than 1,000 developers, extensive enablement of all four Linux brands, complete hardware server support of Linux, and Linux Development Centers for ISV development and porting.

Let's look a little closer at some other software innovations.

Web Services

Web services standards and technologies allow you to describe and deploy applications or services on a network in a consistent way so that they can be discovered and invoked in a secure and reliable manner. A Web service is an application that uses these standards and technologies. In a complete picture, it's likely that a particular Web service will be employed as part of a larger set of transactions or involved in a business process/workflow with many activities.

The model is based on three components: service provider, service broker, and service requester (Figure 1.4). A service provider provides e-business services and publishes these services through a registry. A service broker provides support for publishing and locating services, and a service requester finds the services from the service broker while binding to services via a service provider. The bottom line to this model is that information or services desired can be gathered from several places and provided to the application or person that needs it.

Three main technologies are required to make this happen: SOAP (Services-Oriented Architectural Protocol), UDDI (Universal Description, Discovery, Integration) and WSDL (Web Services Description Language).

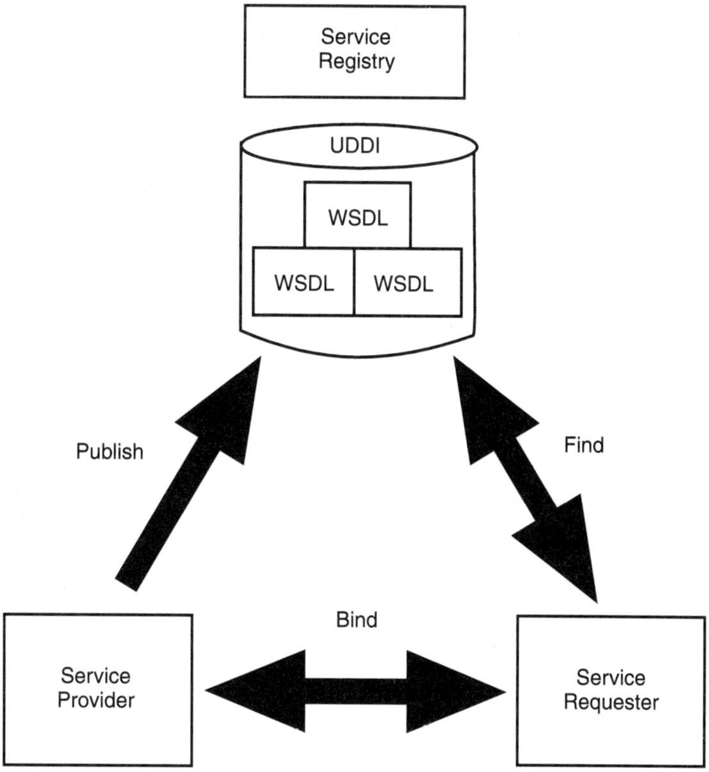

Figure 1.4. Web services.

The easiest component to understand is WSDL, an XML vocabulary that is used to describe service interfaces and is the common language between the components. SOAP wraps a message in a common technology for transference. In this way, the body of the message doesn't need to change in order to be transmitted. UDDI is a project to speed interoperability and adoption for Web services. This will provide the registry portion of the Web services model, allowing standards-based specifications for service descriptions, which makes them more easily discovered.

Web services is still in an early adoption phase. According to IDC, full implementation of Web services, meaning full dynamic search and use, will take place in the 2006 to 2008 time frame.

Grid Computing

In November 2001, Dr. Irving Wladawsky-Berger from IBM gave a presentation at the Kennedy Consulting Summit that discussed the next generation of "distributed computing." In that presentation he explored the concept that it will be possible some day to treat the Internet as a giant logical computer. This concept has been expanded to become grid computing.

With grid computing, new open standards and software will enable resource sharing, collaboration, and computing utilities on the Internet. Grid middleware will create virtual servers and storage from pools of servers, clients, and storage dispersed throughout the Internet. Grid computing utilities will then emerge and become like power utilities.

The intercompany project that is working to develop this theory into reality is the Globus Project (check the Companion Web Site on page xix). IBM has worked on the UK National Grid, an early prototype of grid computing. This grid allows the supercomputers at several major universities in the United Kingdom to be linked over high bandwidth and appear to users as a single virtual computer.

Eventually, grid computing will be integrated with Web services, resulting in Open Grid Services Architecture (OGSA), according to a Globus Project paper.

IBM Autonomic Computing Initiative (aka Project eLiza)

In order to make grid computing a reality, as well as improve existing systems, self-managing systems are a necessity. This is driven by improved price performance of hardware, new, more complex workloads, skills shortage, and requirements for high availability and quick adaptation to change.

The autonomic computing initiative (previously known as Project eLiza) is about technology used to fix technology. It's a project that transcends all the hardware servers in IBM's portfolio—zSeries, pSeries, iSeries, and xSeries. The goal is to smooth out glitches that might occur, to respond to capacity demands without human intervention, and to have servers automatically configure themselves when new hardware is added. The result of this goal is to allow companies to manage more complexity with fewer human resources.

There are four key focus areas within the project: self-configuration, self-healing, self-protection, and self-optimization. As new hardware and software are added to an infrastructure, a system that is self-configuring will be able to adapt to the additional components across the infrastructure. A system that is self-configuring will be able to manage this without human intervention.

Just as a salamander grows a new tail, a self-healing infrastructure must be able to "regrow" failed components. A self-healing system will identify, isolate, and fix the problem to allow continuous availability of systems.

A system that is self-protecting will maintain methods and procedures to allow people who should have access in and keep others out. Should some type of unauthorized access be attempted, the self-protecting system will report the intruder.

Workloads are never stable. They hit peaks and valleys of use—particularly e-business systems. An infrastructure that is self-optimizing will take these peaks and valleys in stride, allocating resources to provide the most throughput for the workload.

e-business on demand

In the fall of 2002, IBM announced "e-business on demand." This is in response to companies gearing up to meet the third phase of e-business described earlier. In this phase, if you'll recall, companies want to invent new ways to do business with the new medium available. In order to do this they need technology that provides end-to-end integration across the enterprise and with key partners, suppliers, and customers. This technology needs to help them respond with flexibility and speed to any customer demand, market opportunity, or external threat. This technology is what IBM calls "e-business on demand."

IBM has identified four necessary characteristics of an on-demand business:

- Responsive: These companies are capable of sensing changes in the environment and responding dynamically, whether to unpredictable fluctuations in supply or demand; emerging customer, partner, supplier, and employee needs; or unexpected moves by their competition.

- Variable: These companies can adapt cost structures and business processes flexibly, reducing risk and driving business performance at higher levels of productivity, cost control, capital efficiency, and financial predictability.

- Focused: These companies are committed to concentrating on core competencies, leveraging tightly integrated strategic partners to manage selected tasks ranging from manufacturing, logistics, and fulfillment to human resources (HR) and financial operations.
- Resilient: These businesses must be 24-hour-a-day operations. This model requires systems and processes that are robust and able to bounce back in real time, whatever the circumstances.

In order to have an on-demand business, you need an on-demand operating environment. This environment must have four essential characteristics.

- It is integrated.
- It is open.
- It is virtualized (grid computing).
- It is autonomic.

There are many software products within IBM that help companies on the road to e-business on demand. As time goes by, IBM will enhance others, integrate them, and connect them to the e-business on demand strategy. The September 2002 announcement pointed to Tivoli software as the first place to look to help you gain integrated system management, autonomic computing, best practices, and rapid deployment. When more information becomes available, links will appear on the Companion Web Site (see page xx).

Concepts to Make an e-business Work

The rest of this chapter is devoted to an exploration of e-business buzzwords, theories, and concepts. In order to create an e-business that can satisfy customers and provide the company the benefits that it needs, several requirements need to be satisfied: transaction persistence (the ability for the transaction to exist for more time than it takes to download it from the Internet), transaction security, scalability (the ability of an application to handle as many users as it needs to), content accuracy, and self-learning transactions (remembering the things that you have done previously in a transaction and being able to repeat them).

Persistence is a concept borrowed from the object world. It implies that an object exists in its current state after a user is done manipulating the object. For example, even though I am no longer connected to my online bank and I am done making entries to it, it will still exist in the state that I last left it—with money associated to the account. This becomes more critical when you are in the middle of an Internet transaction. Some sites don't remember much as you go through a transaction. For example, suppose you fill out a form describing in loving detail your great-aunt Harriet's crystal vase for an auction site and forget to fill in one of the required fields. You press Enter and the computer screen changes to an error message telling you that you did not fill in one of the required fields and to click the Back button to finish the transaction. You follow instructions and click the Back button, only to find out that the form is blank and your lovingly created description is gone. Had your description remained, then you would be dealing with persistence.

Transaction security applies to everything about a transaction—the content as it exists everywhere: the company's data storage, your computer, and all lines in between. It insures that the credit card number you enter onto a Web form is encrypted before it leaves the safety of your computer. It also insures that no unauthorized person can look at the information you provide. It also implies a level of trust that you have in the entity with which you are doing business—that they will not give your information to another group without your consent. Privacy, an off-shoot of security, is a large concern for everyone.

Scalability, while not strictly an e-business concept, is highly important to e-business, particularly Web sites. When a company is building an in-house system, some effort is normally made to gather information about how many users will be on the system at a particular point in time. No such research is available for the Internet. So most Web site developers are of two minds—please let everyone find my site and please don't all come at once! But, of course, they do and if you are unlucky, your system slows or crashes and they never come back. Another site is only a click away.

Content accuracy is contentious. Some of it is due to our own ability to confuse things. Take nicknames for example. It is easy for a computer software program to discern that Bill is William, but more difficult to understand that Casey, Carol, and Carol Ann are the same person. More than once I have found myself getting two copies of the same magazine after renewal—only to find that one of them has a slight variation of address. A friend of mine separates the source of his junk mail by using variations of his name for the different magazines to which he subscribes. For example, using D.P. Snow for his subscription to *Forbes* and Danny Snow for his subscription to *Outdoor Life*. This allows him to understand which magazine is selling its mailing lists. However, it doesn't help any company trying to understand customers by what they read. And then, of course, there is what the company does to mangle the information. One company found they had over a thousand customers with the same social security number. It seemed that when the data entry clerk could not find the social security number, she entered her own. This was bad enough when data was kept internally, but now that a user gets to see her data in all its living color, accuracy is becoming more of an issue.

Tag Languages

Tag languages communicate information about the data with which they are sent. They do this by associating tags with content to provide information about the content, either content meaning or how the content should be displayed. Keywords or characters are enclosed in angle brackets (<, >) that are sent from one place to another with the content. Parsers at either end of the transaction interpret the keyword or character in order to display or understand the data.

SGML (Standardized General Markup Language) is one of the oldest tag languages. It never caught on with the Web community because it is very difficult to master. It has, however, formed the basis for today's most popular tag languages: HTML and XML.

HTML provides users with a simple, easy-to-use language for creating Web sites and linking to other Web pages for simplified Web navigation. Released in 1986, it is now in its fourth version. HTML is the most widely used vehicle for delivering information over the Web. Most Web pages you see are stored and transmitted in HTML and are easily accessed by a browser that contains an HTML parser.

HTML tells the browser how that item is to be displayed on the screen. In the following

<b>$5.98</b>

<b> indicates that the price, $5.98, should be displayed on the screen in bold. It does not explain whether $5.98 is the cost of the item, the sale price of the item, or even if the price is in Canadian, U.S., or Australian dollars. Not only is that meaning unclear to humans, it is also unclear to search engines looking for the lowest price of a particular item. Because HTML only describes how content should be displayed, HTML documents are called unstructured documents.

This problem is compounded when companies try to transmit information to each other. Companies have been sending information to each other for many years using a format called Electronic Data Interchange (EDI). EDI is a powerful tool that has been used by a number of companies to exchange data. The companies agree to a pre-determined format with the appropriate headers and trailers giving number of records sent, date sent, etc. The receiving company could tell where the information they needed was in each record by its location and physical description (type, length, etc.). In addition to requiring extensive agreement to the format of the records, EDI transmissions could only be exchanged between companies with like hardware and operating systems. Company A could not send an EDI file created on OS/390 to Company B who wanted to receive it on a computer with an AIX operating system.

XML (eXtended Markup Language) is a markup language that can be used to create structured documents that are stored and transmitted over the Web. It separates the content and what it means from how the content is to be displayed. This means that the only thing that any two companies need to agree on to transfer data is the set of XML tags that will be used with the transmitted content. XML is also extensible because it allows the creation of new tags without having to have the tags approved by a standards board.

An example of an XML tag is:

<PRICE type="sale"unit ="US Dollar">$5.98</PRICE>

This tells us that $5.98 is the sale price in U.S. dollars, not suggested retail price in Canadian dollars. An XML-enabled search engine can interpret this tag when looking for the lowest price of a particular item.

XML extensions have proliferated, many of them defined by industry or function, such as cXML for catalog content. These extended tags used by a particular document are stored in a file called the document type definition (DTD). This file can reside on the same physical location as the XML document or on a different server accessed by multiple applications. Thus, if a chemical company and its associated suppliers have agreed upon a set of XML extensions, the companies only need to have one DTD apiece to enable them to parse the XML documents.

XSL (eXtensible Style Language) is an XML language for reformatting and presentation, similar in concept to HTML. Style sheets in XSL can be associated with a document as it is displayed on different devices or in different formats. For example, a retailer could develop a catalog page that can be used in a hard-copy paper catalog and also displayed on a Web page. He can then associate two different XSL style sheets. In addition to flexibility for the medium in which the sheet is displayed, the separation of style and content description allows the retailer the ability to change the price of an item in only one place—the original XML page—and have it readily available in multiple mediums.

IBM is developing and strongly supporting XML. In combination with TCP/IP as the universal connectivity protocol, connecting everything from mainframes to your washing machine, and Java as the "write once, run anywhere" programming language, XML extends the universality of e-business to content.

Java

Just as early bulletin boards, HTML, and the World Wide Web changed Internet computing, Java changed the ability of companies to take advantage of Web computing and transform their businesses into e-businesses. Prior to the Java computing model, computer programming was generally platform dependent. Different languages were developed for different operating systems (discussed further in Chapter 3). While there was some portability of languages to these operating systems, there was virtually no portability of a program from one platform to another. (In this context, platform means a combination of the operating system and the hardware on which it runs.) If a program was built and compiled on an S/390 mainframe, there was no way it was going to run on an IBM Personal Computer with a Windows operating system, much less on a cell phone.

Java changed all that. Java was developed by Sun Microsystems to enable companies to build software that can run on many different types of computers as well as pervasive devices. How does this work? Java runs on a piece of software called a Java Virtual Machine (JVM). It is virtual because the machine does not really exist, it just appears to exist. All Java programs are written as if they were running on this platform. The platform is then built into Web browsers, cell phones, and the like. This virtual machine is charged with translating the JVM platform instructions into instructions of the machine that the virtual machine is running on. So, if the Java program is running on zSeries hardware, the instructions are translated to z/OS operating system instructions. If it is running on Windows NT on an IBM Netfinity, the JVM translates the instructions into Windows NT operating system instructions, and so on. The idea is to "write once, run anywhere."

Java programs are called applets. An applet is a program that can be executed from another application, but not from an operating system. They are small in size, cross-platform compatible, and highly secure. An applet that runs on a Web application server is called a servlet. There is also a concept in Java called a Java Bean. What is a Java Bean?

A Java Bean is a piece of software code that can be used as a component in a Web application. A component is software code that performs a certain function, such as rotating an object on a Web page. Beans are developed with object-oriented theory in mind (more on object theory in Chapter 2). To that end, they share several object characteristics: introspection, customization, events, properties, and persistence.

Because a bean allows introspection, builder tools and programmatic interfaces can understand how a particular bean works. This allows the programmer to manipulate the bean as needed. To that end, a bean that rotates an object only needs to be told by the programmer that the object needs to rotate and to what degree. The programmer doesn't need to create the code to perform the rotation.

Customization allows a user to alter the appearance and behavior of a bean. In our rotating example, the bean can be changed from general rotation of an object to a rotation of an object 180 degrees. That means that every time the bean is used, the object with which it is used rotates 180 degrees, no more, no less. This is similar to the object concept of inheritance.

Events are like triggers in object theory. Beans can be recipients of events as well as have the ability to fire events. For our rotating bean, if a button on a Web page is pressed, the bean can automatically rotate an object 180 degrees. This rotation can fire an event that flips another object on a page that causes another object to stream across the page, etc.

Beans have properties. These properties are the hooks that allow the customization and manipulation of the bean. For example, the rotating bean has a property that dictates the number of degrees it is able to rotate an object. Prior to customization, the programmer supplied that number. After customization, it was, in our example, set to 180 degrees.

Finally, persistence allows the bean that has been customized to have the state of the bean saved and restored. This allows the developer to use the bean as originally built and at the same time use the customized bean.

Extensions to Java

The Java language has grown beyond JavaBeans and server pages to include other services that can be utilized to develop e-business applications. IBM has incorporated many of these extensions in products such as WebSphere Application Server (discussed in Chapter 4). The next few paragraphs will provide some background in these extensions.

Java 2, Enterprise Edition (J2EE) is a standard for multi-tiered programming built on the Java programming base and developed by a consortium of software vendors. It's a specification built around three main concepts: components, containers, and connectors. Application development is focused on building the component. Different containers can "wrap" the component, providing security, transaction management, and other system requirements that are unrelated to business logic. Connectors can connect different components together by providing a single application programming interface (API) that can be accessed by a variety of connectors from different vendors.

Enterprise JavaBeans (EJBs) are one of the components of J2EE. EJBs are similar to JavaBeans, but can be held inside a construct called a container. The container provides management and control functions, such as security, for the EJB. This further isolates the business logic from having to deal with any underlying technical changes. For example, if we have a tape of the Beatles' "Yellow Submarine" and a CD of the same music, we can't use the same mechanism to play the music. But if we had a container that held all the bits of the music that could be wrapped in a plastic tape cartridge or enclosed in a CD, depending on where it needed to be played, that would serve a similar function to the container of EJBs.

J2EE Connector Architecture (JCA) defines a standard programming interface, similar to Java Database Connectivity (JDBC), that can be used to connect Java applications to different types of systems, including non-relational databases such as IMS (see Chapter 5) or transaction managers such as CICS (see Chapter 2). JCA has two basic components. The Common Client Interface (CCI) manages the flow of data between the application and the connected system without being aware of any business logic on the application server or within a container. The system-specific services are developed by each vendor to use the CCI.

Java Messaging Service (JMS) is another component of the J2EE platform. Its purpose is to implement the transfer of asynchronous messages among J2EE components and legacy applications that allow messaging, such as IBM WebSphere MQ (described in Chapter 4). Based on an EJB structure, JMS listens for the arrival of a message on a queue, performs a task, and can then send a return message. (This is part of the J2EE 1.3, EJB 2.0 Message-Driven Beans specification.)

The Java Authorization Service is another standard that can be used to allow different authorization schemes to "play nice" together. With standardized authorization communication, customers can use heterogeneous authorization solutions in their applications, as long as these authorization solutions conform to the standard.

Java Management Extensions (JMX) provide the ability to build tools that manage and monitor Java applications. JMX is also part of the J2EE standard that records and logs statistics on usage and resources. These statistics can then be picked up and used by system monitors and management products, such as those from Tivoli. (Tivoli products are described in Chapter 6.)

2

Architectures That Pre-date e-business

In Chapter 1, we discussed how IBM is positioned to handle e-business. An important part of e-business is the ability to access external systems, particularly legacy systems. Someone once described legacy systems as application systems that are working. To some extent that is true. However, the legacy systems that really keep people awake at night are the ones that involve older data stores such as VSAM (Virtual Storage Access Method) and older programming methods such as pre-Internet COBOL (COmmon Business Oriented Language). But what if these systems contain your most important information? Companies do not have the luxury or the funds to rewrite these systems, yet they need to make these applications available to the Web.

In order to take advantage of existing systems that are important to e-business, it is important to understand some of the architectures of the past that have influenced and maintained our current computing applications. There have been paradigm shifts from process-oriented design to data-oriented design and back again. Centralization has come into vogue and gone out again with the waves of decentralization. Our existing business processes reflect these shifts. We have distributed processes, proprietary processes, and open processes. We have redundancy in many places. We have incomplete information and incorrect information, and it is all visible to the world.

This chapter is devoted to taking a historical look at these architectural influences and exploring how they can be made accessible to our e-business structures. We will not only be exploring application architectures, we will delve into some of the data architectures that influenced the topography of our current systems. Most notably these include the IBM-developed relational architecture that underpins DB2 Universal Database, Oracle, and SQLServer, but also the object-oriented architecture that had a great influence on component application architectures.

So return with us now to those thrilling days of yesteryear.

Batch

Although it seems as if changes in computer technology are coming at a rate that is faster than the proverbial speeding bullet, original change proceeded at a more leisurely pace. Close to 20 years passed between the time the first computer (ENIAC—Electronic Numerical Integrator And Computer) was activated in 1946 to the general use of punch cards in the late 1960s. College students of the 1960s, used to protesting everything, protested the use of punch cards in their lives as well. The phrase, "I am a human being, do not fold, spindle, or mutilate," came directly from the phrase printed on the bottom of the punch cards that identified each individual college student.

Punch cards only had room for 80 characters, since that was what the technology of the time supported. Base 16 numbers were used to represent the characters. (Base 16 numbers include 0–9 and A–F, with A–F representing the numbers 10–15.) The data was printed in human readable form on the top of the card, and holes were made in the card for the machine to read. Those initial holes were called bits. Punch cards were used to capture machine instructions or content. Cards were read and manipulated by the computer one at a time. A lot of information needed to be kept on one card. Because of this, data was encrypted into codes. Years were not even in two-digit format, only the last digit was kept. Because of the physical medium used, information was positional. If you didn't know what number column the data was in, you couldn't find what you were looking for. If you didn't know what the codes meant, you couldn't understand the data you had.

Batch jobs got their name from the manual procedure of "batching" groups of documents to give to different clerks so they could write the information on paper forms. The name carried over to early computer programs using the punched cards that were batched together. After a batch of 80-character punch cards was produced, it was put in the middle of a job deck of similarly punched cards that contained machine instructions. If you were really lucky and did not drop a box full of these cards on the way, you loaded them into the computer card reader. The job was started, the cards were read, and output was produced. It was only after you ran the job that you knew whether or not it worked. Additionally, while the computer had the punch cards, you could not access them to read them or change them. They were unavailable.

Computers grew up a little, and electronic file structures, called flat files, became available. Due to their history and the programs used, these files were 80 characters wide, and data was still positional and encoded. The advantage was that you could enter the information using a keyboard and a "dumb" terminal rather than a punch-card machine. Each iteration of information was called a record, and each piece of data within a record was called a field. For example, an individual student schedule was called a record. The area on the card that contained the student's name was a field. Each number or letter in the field was a character. All the records together were called a file.

Eventually, people became adventurous and new programs were written that could handle variable-length records with variable-length fields. The advantage of variable-length fields was that they only needed to be large enough to store the data they contained. The length of a name field could change with the length of the name. SMITH needed five characters; WORKOWSKI needed nine characters. A fixed-length field needed to be as large as the largest possible entry (for example, nine characters). For names that were shorter than the fixed length, blanks were padded at the end of the name to fill the entire field. The disadvantage of variable fields was, and still is, increased complexity in programming. Also, a difference of field types can still cause problems when merging systems or externalizing data for e-business applications.

Due to the legacy of batch programs and the longevity and compatibility of the mainframe operating systems, some older flat file structures are still with us. Sometimes these files are accessed by programs that understand the positions and the codes, but are not maintainable because no one can decipher the program and the source code has been lost.

With the move to electronic files, batch jobs could more easily massage the data and output another flat file or report. Depending on the type of flat file, the data might be available for read processing while the batch process was running. In order to insure that data was correct (data integrity) companies tended to keep the files locked during the batch process so no one could read them while they were being updated. In fact, companies often insisted that the only way anyone could review the data was through the batch process. Most batch processes were only run on a daily, weekly, monthly, quarterly, or yearly basis. Otherwise, the data was unavailable.

VSAM

None of the files discussed so far had indexes. Indexes are a quick way to get to a specific record in a file or database. They generally contain a piece of key data and a physical pointer to the rest of their associated data. Prior to indexes if you wanted to find a record, you had to read through the file until you found it, even if it was the last record in the file. Several access methods were developed that used indexes to get a more direct hit on needed information. The one that is still with us is VSAM. Indexing made access quicker, but VSAM data stores were, at the time they were developed, still constrained by the expense of storage. Codes and abbreviations were still necessary. Changing the VSAM structure was cumbersome and took a long time with little tangible business benefits. As a result, many fields in VSAM files were "reused," leading to poor data quality. For example, a field that was documented to contain gender codes (male or female) might be reused to contain values indicating marital status (married female, divorced female, single male, etc.). Knowing about these types of reuse becomes important if these VSAM data stores are subsequently used for business analysis or made available via the Web.

Almost any sizable company that has been in business for the last 25 years has VSAM data stores on mainframe computers and active systems that use them. In order to move forward in an e-business world, data quality must be verified and Web access must be provided to this storage. IBM recognizes this need. It has worked with business partners to provide tools to analyze and improve data quality. It has also developed, and continues to develop, products that can access and integrate VSAM data into e-business applications. The majority of these products are discussed in the WebSphere chapter, Chapter 4.

VSAM files were accessed through batch applications initially. Odd as it may seem, new batch programs are written for new systems fairly frequently. They are an effective way to get through a lot of data quickly. With today's capacity to split and execute batch jobs in parallel using a high level of processing power, batch jobs can be very quick indeed. These batch programs are often run unattended, often at night, in a time referred to as a "batch window." Since these jobs can make data unavailable, the challenge for a company trying to implement an e-business application that's available 24 hours a day, seven days a week, is to reduce, or, better still, eliminate the batch window. This does not mean that the batch jobs can't run. It just means that the data needs to be available while they do it.

OLTP

Batch processes were a definite improvement over manual processes, but there was a growing impatience with the 24-hour turnaround required to get answers to most questions. People wanted to read and change data from their terminals, preferably without having to maneuver through computer gibberish to get to the data. The next great challenge was to produce an online transaction processing system. In this case, "online" didn't necessarily mean what we today think of as "online"—doing all our interactions via a terminal, either a client or a Web server. Instead, it meant that a file could be read or manipulated in some manner other than a batch job.

Initially, simple online processes were developed to allow users to read and edit VSAM and flat files online. Early screens to allow users to edit files were crude and had one major drawback—only one user could edit a file at a time. Each time a particular user read or edited a particular file, it was called a transaction. Only one record could be accessed at a time. Otherwise, the data was unavailable.

What was required was a transaction manager, a piece of software that could play transaction traffic cop. Transaction managers can handle the start, running, and completion of transactions for many concurrent users. The most prevalent transaction management system in the earlier years of computing was the Customer Information Control System (CICS), originally developed for the utility industry.

CICS provided interaction for the user through a terminal screen. The user typed in a transaction code on the terminal to access the process to be executed. Based on the code that was entered, a CICS program would be executed and screen images would be returned as a form for input or to display results. Multiple people could use the same CICS program and the CICS program could read the same data stores at the same time. However, only one CICS transaction could perform an update to a file at the same time until a syncpoint was reached. The syncpoint signaled the end of a unit of work (see Unit of Work sidebar).

CICS also kept track of changes made through a process called journaling. Journaling kept a copy of before and after images of a changed record in a data store called a journal. Later data management products adopted this process and termed it logging.

Requests for account information were common processes that used a CICS transaction model. If you were to call your bank (remember this is pre-Internet and ATMs) for information about your accounts, the clerk who answered your call could type in a CICS transaction code on

LOGICAL UNIT OF WORK

A logical unit of work (sometimes abbreviated LUW, sometimes UOW) is described more from its beginning and ending points than the things that occur in the middle. The point is that both the beginning and the end points should leave the data in a state that is acceptable to the business or the customer (data integrity). The most common example of a logical unit of work is that of a transfer between a savings and checking account.

The unit of work begins with a balanced set of accounts. The customer initiates the transfer of $100 from savings to checking. This actually provokes two processes; the deletion of $100 from savings and the addition of $100 to checking. The unit of work does not end until the addition of $100 to savings takes place. If a problem occurs anywhere in between, the application must roll back to the start of the unit of work to insure that the accounts are balanced.

a "green screen" to access the account information. The CICS transaction would start and display an electronic form (often called a map) for the clerk. The clerk would then enter your account number to access the information. The CICS transaction program would take the information, parse it, and use it to access the data store. The results would then be mapped back to a screen format and displayed on the terminal.

CICS has evolved over the years to take advantage of the growing complexity of computer system architectures, including Internet-based architectures, but its fundamental function to allow reliable, concurrent access and manipulation of data has been maintained. It takes the information fed to it from some source (a terminal, another CICS program, a data queue in memory, WebSphere MQ, and the like) and works with it in a programmatic manner to achieve the desired results. Syncpoints can now be coordinated between CICS and the programs it calls to access the data in the Information Management System (IMS) database or the DB2 Universal Database. In short, CICS, particularly Distributed CICS, can be an important part of an e-business architecture. (CICS is also discussed in Chapter 4.)

Another transaction manager that is important in OLTP processing is IMS Transaction Manager, which was created for IMS but can also be used with DB2 Universal Database. IMS Transaction Manager has similar characteristics as CICS, among them the ability to finalize a unit of work and the capacity to log changes. (IMS and IMS Transaction Manager are discussed in Chapter 5.)

Both batch applications and OLTP applications are important parts of any company's application portfolio. They rapidly process repetitive actions such as bank transactions that support the basic business. Both play a role in e-business applications as well. As we go through this chapter, you will see the role that batch processes take in business intelligence and distributed applications. Business intelligence applications gather the data needed for business analysis to insure that companies are going in the right direction—to apply the business rules of return on investment. OLTP transactions can also be accessed by external services of Web application servers, externalizing their data to Web pages. In this way, customers can do such things as view their own account information without requiring a company to change its existing OLTP application. Figure 2.1 shows how existing systems can be incorporated into a Web application system. The Hypertext Transfer Protocol (HTTP) server accepts requests from a customer to access his or her account information. The request is passed to the Web application server so the

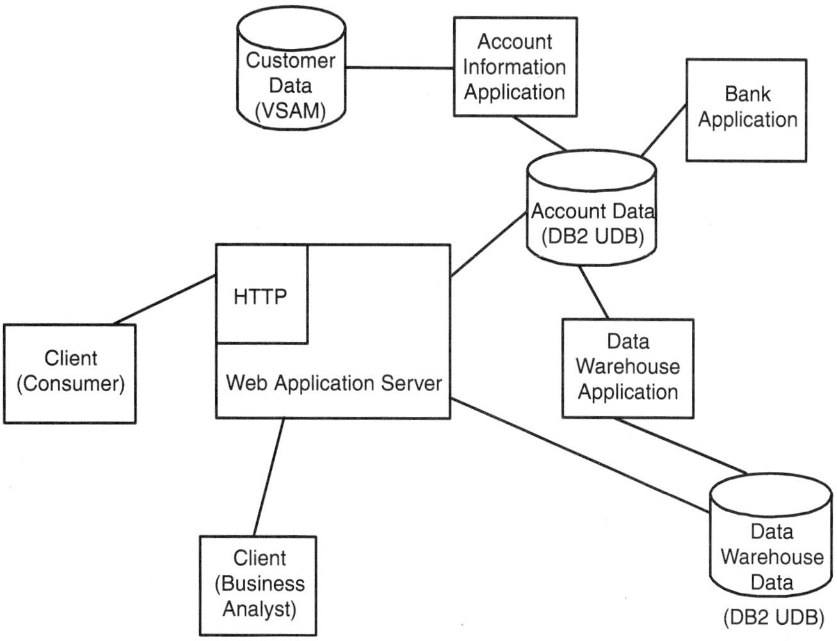

Figure 2.1. A sample Web application.

server can obtain the information using external services. Bank information is also added to the DB2 Universal Database, extracted to a data warehouse data store. This data warehouse information is made available to the bank employee via the Web application server.

Databases

At the same time as CICS and other transaction monitors were making OLTP possible, a parallel effort was under development to improve the ability of companies to understand, consolidate, and use their information more effectively. Several data architectures were developed: network, hierarchical, and relational.

Network architectures were built on the idea that each segment of data had a relationship to another segment. A segment, just like a file, has a structure that represents a particular thing. Within each segment there are multiple instances of the segment type. For example, a class segment would have a segment instance for each class in a university. Segments are smaller in scope than the record of a flat file or VSAM data store. In those data stores a record could contain student name and address as well as the class code and description. With a network database that information would be broken into two segments—class and student. Relationships were expressed in terms of pointers from one segment to any other segment to which it bore a relationship. No segment was parent to the other; all existed in the same plane. In Figure 2.2 an instructor has a class that has a student who has a class that has an instructor. It is important to note that each class has a pointer to all the students in that class. If Tom Jones is taking five classes, there will be five pointers attached to the Tom Jones record. There will be multiple pointers on the class records to the possible instructors, as well as pointers to all the students in the class. As you can see, getting data in and out of a network structure can be very complex indeed.

Network databases have waned in popularity, although there are some still out there. In order to use one in an e-business application, it is important to understand how to access the data—either by providing a shell to the existing data store or extracting the data and moving it to another data store (think batch job).

Hierarchical databases were also developed during this time period. IBM's hierarchical database, IMS, is still with us and enabled for

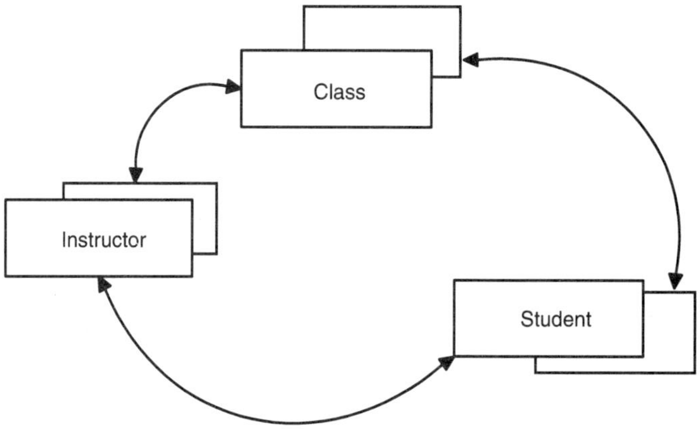

Figure 2.2. Network database example.

e-business. A hierarchical database also has data segments, but there is a definite expression of parent–child relationship. Segments are built in the same manner as a networked database and relationships are still maintained by pointers. In Figure 2.3 a class has an instructor and also has a student. A hierarchical database is meant to be traversed in both directions—parents to children and children to parents. However, the starting place (the root segment) is always at the top of the structure. In this case the root would be class. There are no loops. Only a segment that had a parent could have a pointer back to that parent.

Hierarchical databases are extremely effective for OLTP or batch transactions that are repetitive in nature, with little or no variance in request. IMS is effectively used for high-volume transactions such as ATM machines and manufacturing.

In 1970 Dr. E. F. Codd, a mathematician at IBM Research, developed a paper on relational database theory. It proposed that databases could be structured as relations that resembled tables. Each table required at least one unique key, and these keys formed the basis for relationships between the tables. Selection of information from one or many tables always resulted in a result set that looked like another table. There were many other rules about how the tables related, how unknown values were to be represented, and how result sets were to be obtained. IBM used this work to develop a prototype relational database called System R. From this foundation DB2, as well as other relational databases, was born.

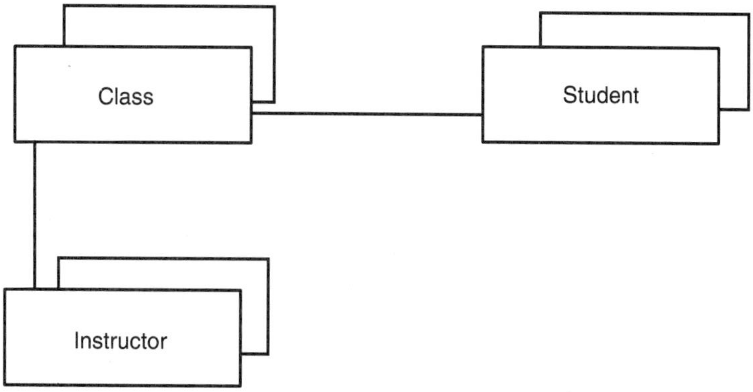

Figure 2.3. Hierarchical database example.

In Figure 2.4 we have tables of our familiar classes, instructors, and students. Conceptually, you can relate a table to the idea of a segment in a hierarchical or network database. Each instance of a class, instructor, or student is a row in the table. Each table has a key: class number for the class table, instructor identifier for the instructor, and student identifier for the student. There are no pointers. In order to understand how one table relates to another, database designers add in intersection tables such as class–instructor and class–student. Each row in these intersection tables only contains the keys from its parent tables, not the other information. This way classes can be taught by multiple instructors, instructors can teach multiple classes, classes can have many students, and students can have many classes. In order to develop a list of classes for a student, three tables—class, student, and class–student—would have to be used.

DB2 (now named DB2 Universal Database) is a powerful database used for e-business transactions as well as OLTP transactions and business intelligence applications. It has been extended to include some of the features developed for object-oriented databases and, of course, en-

Class Table

Class Number	Class Name
101	Sociology
102	Math
103	English Literature

Instructor Table

Instructor Number	Instructor Name
924	A. Einstein
925	O. Wilde
926	M. Mead

Class-Student Table

Class Number	Student Number
101	1054
102	1055
103	1056

Student Table

Student Number	Student Name
1054	C. Dion
1055	M. Gibson
1056	J. Oliver

Figure 2.4. Relational database example.

abled for e-business. It also provides the underlying structure for a number of IBM's other e-business products such as Content Management (Chapter 5). It also provides data stores for Web application products such as Web Application Server, discussed in Chapter 4. DB2 Universal Database will be described in more depth in Chapter 5.

Distributed Architectures

Up until this point in time—sometime in the mid-1980s—processing and data storage were two separate notions. Predominant architectures included batch and OLTP processes with data stored in VSAM, IMS, and DB2 as well as some other data storage products. User interfaces, while better than a keypunch machine, were rudimentary. The mainframe was king: if you wanted data, you had to go to a centralized location to get it. Personal computers (PCs) were beginning to become more common in the workplace, and the Apple concept of communicating to the computer through icons was catching on.

Just as businesses go through cycles of centralization and decentralization, processes go through a cycle of consolidation and distribution. Hardware was still expensive in the 1980s, so the thought of cheaper PC processors was appealing. In 1986 IBM launched the AIX (Advanced Interactive eXecutive) operating system for hardware smaller than mainframes. AS/400 hardware also became popular during this time period. In short, the smaller world of computing appealed to a wider world of companies.

Pressure was on IBM, as well as other companies, to provide the ability to distribute its software. Databases were broken into smaller pieces and located closer to where they were used. For example, regional data was moved to computers closer to their associated office—London's data in London and San Francisco's data in San Francisco. Applications were replicated and stored with the regional computers. This worked reasonably well unless a company-wide report or process was needed. Then information had to be gathered from all the different locations (usually through a batch job) and put into a new data store. Company-wide reports could then be run from this corporate database. Alternatively, the application could access the data from the different locations as it ran, using distributed processes that could access the data in each location.

There were a few problems with this scenario. One was latency, or how much time passed from the time the data first existed in a distributed environment to the time it got to the corporate data store. The second problem was the time it could take to compile a report that required data from more than one location. These problems are still with us, although to a much lesser degree. A lot of IBM software and hardware solutions are intended to alleviate these problems in distributed architecture.

At the same time, new developments ushered in something called client/server architecture. This architecture was founded on the belief that there were three main pieces to a system: the data store, the application, and how the information was presented to the user. These pieces were defined as the data layer, the application layer, and the presentation layer.

Like most computing techniques we take for granted now, client/server architectures were crude in the beginning as companies tried to determine the best way to implement the new structure. In most cases multiple client machines contained both the presentation and the application layers and connected to the server to obtain the data from the data layer. These clients were initially called "fat" clients, although many other names have evolved. Presentation layers were built using GUI (Graphical User Interface) and "screen scraper" technology that copied the contents of mainframe reports to show on client machines.

There were (and still are) a few significant challenges with the original client/server setup. Since each client had a copy of the application, every time the application changed new copies had to be sent to each machine. Often this was done through "sneaker net"—a clerk delivered disks with new software to each person who had a copy of that application on their client machine. Today (yes, these structures still exist) changes to applications for these types of client/server setups can be handled through an automated deployment mechanism.

A second challenge was the amount of data that needed to be sent through the pipeline. Since the application did most of the filtering and sorting of the data, the request sent to get the data was broad—"get all the account information for Sally Smith," when all Sally wanted to look at were her last three savings account transactions. As these architectures emerged and combined with distributed architectures, systems of applications could become quite convoluted (Figure 2.5). And if Sally moved from Boston to London, access could get even more difficult. The bulk of the application code began to move from the clients to a

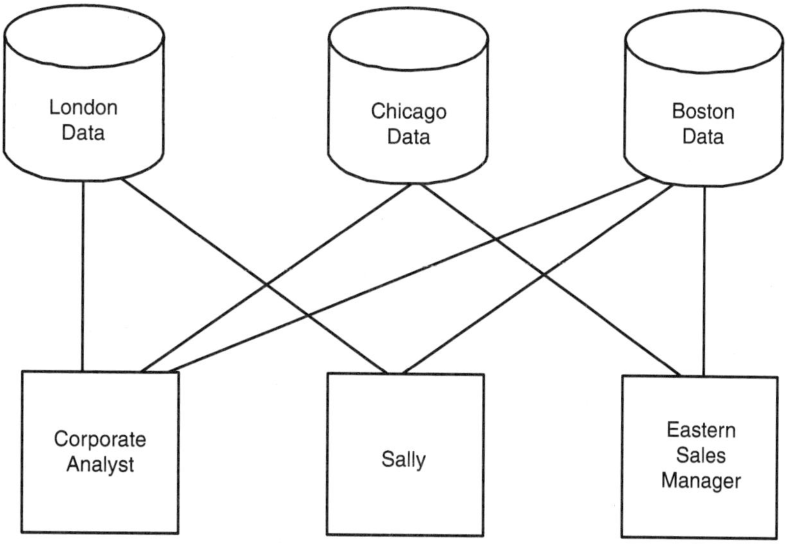

Figure 2.5. Distributed application.

central server—or tier—and three-tier client/server architecture came into being. The presentation layer stayed on the client, the data server was kept separate, and the application moved to an application server in the middle. Eventually, this evolved to an n-tier architecture with multiple application servers and multiple data servers available to multiple clients. The shift of the application off the client and to an application server enabled the development of a "thin" client, a client that only contains the presentation layer. With the advent of the World Wide Web, the ultimate "thin" client was born.

Object-Oriented Databases

About the same time as client/server was being developed, companies began to realize the tremendous investment they were making in developing new applications. In addition, companies found that relational databases were proliferating as each department or division created a new one and coded applications that served their portion of the business without regard to the business as a whole. With dissimilar data structures, multiple database vendors, and dissimilar ways of retrieving data, managers of two departments frequently got two reports that were supposed to have data commonalities, but instead had data discrepancies. Days (and tempers!) could be lost while the two teams that developed the two reports determined why there was a difference.

As the demand for reuse of application code and data stores increased, there also began to be a demand for storage of complex data types. Complex data types are required for objects that cannot be stored in traditional character data. As an example, libraries of pictures, three-dimensional objects, film clips, text objects, and reports needed to be stored using complex data types.

Because of the demand for reuse of code and storage of complex data types, object-oriented (OO) programming and databases became a popular concept for many companies. The promise of reuse was attractive, and many books were written about the theory. Pure object-oriented databases have not replaced relational databases in business, but have had a profound impact on their development. The next few paragraphs describe the design concepts of OO programming and indicate at a general level how these concepts have been integrated into relational databases as well as other e-business components.

The premise of object-oriented design is that content (objects) should have certain properties that are always true and cannot be changed by anyone but the object owner (encapsulation). These objects can only be accessed in a certain way (method). Therefore, if an object, such as square, was developed, it could be encapsulated with certain properties: four lines of equal length connected by four right angles. Methods that would be allowed on the object could include resizing or changing the lengths of the sides equally. A method that tried to change the length of only two of the lines would be rejected.

Objects are further defined by their class. Classes of objects are similar in concept to the biological classes of species. There is a major grouping, such as the equus (or horse-like) class, that has certain characteristics: four legs, hooves, mane, tail, etc. There can also be subclasses of equus, dividing the major horse group into breeds such as Appaloosa, Arabian, and the like. These classes "inherit" the characteristics of the main class, such as four legs, hooves, mane, and tail, but have additional characteristics, such as the spotted rump of the Appaloosa and small head of the Arabian, that set them apart from the main class and each other. There can be instances of each subclass; for example, Walter Farley's Black Stallion as an instance of the subclass Arabian. A particular instance of a class is an object. Therefore, the Black Stallion is an object.

To look at our original example, the class (sometimes called the parent or superclass) would be rectangle, the subclass would be square, and a particular square would be the object. A program interfaces with an object's methods by sending messages to invoke them. Suppose a person was building a presentation and had created the object, square. By using a mouse pointer, the person drags a corner of the square to resize it. The mouse drag sends a message to invoke the method that will resize the square. The method allows the object to grow, but it always remains a square; it never becomes a circle. There are a few more important concepts regarding objects: object identity, object complexity, and persistence.

Object identity states that each object has an identity that is independent of its data values. It has a unique identifier, and that is the only thing that makes it unique. So if we are building a presentation and decide to create two one-inch squares, each square (object) is regarded as a unique thing with a unique number, even though they have the exact same components (four lines, each two inches long, connected by four right angles).

An object can be complex in that it can treat multiple pieces of data as one data type. For example, the employee object can store the employee's name, address, gender, birth date, and employee number as one retrievable data type. This concept flies in the face of relational theories that require a data type to contain an atomic (single) piece of information. Using relational theory, the employee name, address, gender, birth date, and employee number are each separate data types.

Persistence dictates that the information about an object remain in some retrievable state—for example, stored within an object database. Whether or not an object has persistence is based on how the object is initially designed. If it is designated as persistent, then an individual object will be stored. Otherwise, it's gone when the application is gone. Think of persistence as pressing the Save icon on your word processing screen. If you haven't saved the text and the application has a problem, you will lose any data that hasn't been saved. The unsaved data is not persistent.

These concepts appealed to many companies. The idea that they could agree on and set in stone their corporate data and business rules once and for all meant the days of recoding applications might be at an end. But, like all of technology's silver bullets (relational theory, client/server, distributed architecture, etc.), object theory didn't provide the total answer that information systems was looking for.

Hybrid Database Management Systems

Object databases became hot commodities, and soon many companies were building applications that used these new techniques. Along with cries that the mainframe was dead, there were noises that relational databases were dead. (Both ideas proved to be false.) Pure object applications had two main failings: they did not scale well enough to meet the needs of large applications, and they did not interface well with existing applications—including relational applications. Since the idea of object theory was reuse of code, not building new applications, companies did not want to rebuild all their applications using object-oriented databases. To meet this need, relational database vendors, including IBM, searched for ways to incorporate benefits of object-oriented theory into their databases.

In the 1980s IBM developed a research prototype called Starburst that was designed to include object concepts in a relational Database Management System (DBMS) in order to create an extended relational DBMS. IBM incorporated the results of this research into its products, primarily DB2 Universal Database. The following is a list of items that might be included in an object-relational extension. With each version of DB2 Universal Database, IBM has enhanced these object-relational extensions in the product.

- User-Defined Types (UDTs): UDTs are data types that can be defined by the user based on a pre-existing data type. For example, a UDT called dollar can be defined using a decimal data type. The advantage of defining a UDT is that like can only be compared to like. You can't compare a dollar data type to a French franc data type. This enforces the object idea that objects have only certain allowable methods. If you define both currencies as decimal, a program could inadvertently add French francs and dollars.

- User-Defined Functions (UDFs): UDFs are similar to methods in that they are defined on a particular object, such as employee.

They are built on functions that were previously defined within the database, and with each release of DB2 have been extended to give more flexibility in their creation. An example of a function would be "area." This function could be defined as returning the area of a rectangle, given a particular rectangle.

- Large Objects: Most relational databases allow large objects (LOBs) to be stored in columns. Large objects are those items that do not fit nicely into constrained numeric or character columns. These types of objects include text, video segments, audio segments, etc.

- Stored Procedures: Stored procedures are similar to methods in that they can be called to access particular sets of data. Stored procedures are small programs that can be written in many programming languages. They are called by other programs to perform certain functions.

- Constraints: Constraints are allowed on columns and restrict the values that can be contained in the column. For example, the only values that are allowed in a marital status column could be those for single, married, partnered, divorced, or widowed: S, M, P, D, or W. Constraints do not restrict valid operations on a column, however, as data encapsulation would. So an operation could change a value from M to S since S is an allowed value, even though the business rule states that a value of M can only be changed to D or W.

- Triggers: Triggers are similar to methods because they can be used to enforce behavior. Triggers are also small programs that are executed (fired) when some other action occurs. For example, if an inventory for a particular store falls below a certain threshold, a trigger could be fired that sends a notice to the distribution center to send more of the item. Triggers aren't perceived as being part of the table, however, so object purists don't consider them true data encapsulation objects.

Hybrid databases can be referred to as relational databases or object-relational databases. It is important when developing a design for e-business (discussed in Chapter 9) that the architect understand how to take advantage of all the features of databases in order to improve performance, maintain data consistency, and encourage reuse of data and programming alike.

Component Broker Architecture

By the end of the 1980s, several factors were converging to move computing away from the traditional disciplines of application development. The lines between applications and data storage were no longer clear. Applications and data were distributed, and clients could have all of the application logic, none of the application logic, or some of the application logic. While some reuse was possible, neither client/server nor object theory had solved the backlog of applications that needed to be built.

Distributed architectures moved away from strict client/server with the influence of OO theory. The idea of components began to surface. Components were discreet pieces of code or code and data that served a specific function. There could be components that sent the client request to the application and others that received the request on the application server, edited the request for correctness, returned error messages to the client, ran the request through the corporate business rules, accessed data as needed, and the like. These components, or objects, could then be reused as needed within a new application. An important key to this thought was that the objects needed to have a standard way of communicating with each other. And so the war of the standards began.

The Object Management Group (OMG) defined a reference object model (CORBA) that put in place OMG's standards for distributed object architectures. Another set of standards proposed for a distributed component architecture was the Distributed Common Object Model (DCOM). There was SOM (System Object Model) and DSOM (Distributed System Object Model), OLE (Object Linking and Embedding) and ODBC (Open Database Connectivity). As time has gone on, some of these standards, such as OLE, have become de facto standards. Others have faded away. IBM complies with standards established by standards boards as well as incorporating other common de facto standards that its customers require to do business.

Because of these architectural models, design principles began to change: application development was less focused on separating data from process and began to look at data access as another component of the architecture. In this way, data access components could theoretically be changed from accessing data in one store to accessing data in another store. In practice, at least in the early days of this architecture, the theory worked better as a theory than in practice. Data access components were not always easily changed from one data store to another (all SQL [Structured Query Language] is not the same). Sometimes companies made their components so small that performance of these initial CORBA applications suffered.

But as the architectures matured, so did their performance and their ability to handle the high volumes typical of OLTP systems. In today's world these component architectures have formed the basis for the e-business architectures discussed in Chapter 1.

Business Intelligence

As the further distribution of data and processes began to occur, companies' business analysts began to realize that they had a great deal of information in the data that was being scattered all over the digital infrastructure. In the mid-1980s, companies began to develop information centers to try to understand the information in their OLTP systems. These efforts began with fourth-generation languages such as Focus and Ramis, created to stem the tide of demands from the business community for information. DB2 Universal Database was commonly used at this time to build the first data warehouses, even though they were not called that at the time. Information from VSAM and flat file systems was imported into DB2 tables and then business analysts were able to create reports with the information that they needed. At this time, they also began to discover strange discrepancies in their data as programmers' creative field use began to come to light.

Information center data stores grew into a concept called data warehouses. Designs began to appear for these data warehouses that included a plan to architect this type of database. These designs revolved around a central question: How do we get the data from the condition it is in into a condition that is useful for the business analyst? Data warehouses are still with us and are an important part of an e-business structure, so let's take a look at how some of these theories played out.

When determining the data structures for the data warehouse, designers looked at how often the data needed to be moved, where it needed to come from, and if it needed to be summarized. There were all types of summarization—lightly summarized, moderately summarized, and heavily summarized. In the beginning, it was taken for granted that people using the data warehouse wouldn't look at detailed data. (This is no longer an assumption for data warehouses.)

For example, if you are looking at sales data for Annie's Iced Teas it can be summarized by week, month, quarter, or year for each store. That would be lightly summarized data. Moving up, the data can be moderately summarized by the same time slices for district, region, or country, producing time slices of sales for Annie's Iced Teas across all the company's stores. For corporate reporting, the data would probably be heavily summarized.

A balance needed to be achieved between the time taken to load the data, how frequently it was refreshed (its latency), and how long it took the business analysts to get their questions answered. Many of these analysts' questions were complex, requiring a long time and a lot of processing resources to answer the question. Companies found that they needed to move data warehouse applications and data to different servers from OLTP applications in order to relieve the strain on the OLTP applications. All this business of moving data from one place to another, from OLTP to data warehouse stores, from detail to summarization, is termed replication.

As database designers looked at the data warehouse systems they built, they began to see a trend emerge from their designs. There was generally a large table that contained various degrees of summarized data surrounded by smaller tables that contained further information about the factors used to summarize the information (Figure 2.6). The central table was termed a "fact" table, the surrounding tables were called the dimension tables, and the star schema was born. Later, complexities were added where dimension tables were built upon dimension tables and the snowflake schema was created, but in general, it is the star schema that is most often used.

Another aspect of business intelligence or data warehouse applications that began to emerge was the need to understand what data meant and the formulas that were used to derive it. Metadata is a term that means data about data. Metadata can be the physical characteristics about data, for example, if the data is fixed or variable length, how long it is, what type of data it is (alphabetic, large object, numeric), and any other physical characteristics that might be important such as decimal

Dimension Table

Country Code	Country Name
US	USA
CN	Canada

Dimension Table

Region Number	Region Name
1	US East
5	US West

Dimension Table

District Number	District Name
1	Bergan County
99	Santa Cruz

Fact Table

Country	Region	District	Store	Product	1	2	3	4	5	6	7	8	9	10	11	12	2001 Total
US	1	1	200	3598	200	300	400	300	200	100	100	50	50	100	200	300	2100
US	1	1	200	3600	1	1	1	5	6	1	5	5	5	5	5	5	45
US	5	99	601	3598	700	700	700	700	700	700	700	700	700	700	700	700	8400

Dimension Table

Store Number	Store Name
200	Mahwah
601	Westside

Dimension Table

Product SKU	Product Name
3598	Annie's Green Tea
3600	Annie's Gourmet Dog Biscuits

Figure 2.6. Star schema.

points. Metadata can also include what a data object means. For example, is $5.95 the price of the tie, its cost to manufacture, or the commission paid to the salesperson for selling the tie?

XML, which we discussed in Chapter 1, is the cornerstone of the current thinking on metadata. This tag language ties the metadata to the object so that wherever the object goes, the metadata goes.

Because systems grew up in the 1970s and 1980s in isolated silos, there were often conflicting values and codes. This causes a great deal of the work that occurs with the development of data warehouse-type applications. For example, some applications may contain state values with postal abbreviations, such as NJ and CA for New Jersey and California respectively. Other applications may assign numbers to the states so that 07 stands for New Jersey and 03 stands for California. When it is time to merge these applications for a data warehouse project, one of the application's codes needs to be changed. This change is called transformation.

Remember how we talked about data that wasn't quite right—where programmers "reused" fields when the original use of these fields was no longer useful to the company? When data was moved to data warehouses, these problems surfaced and people needed to fix them. Fixing the data is called cleansing the data. If you don't believe that your company has "dirty" data, think again.

Most data warehouse users are analysts who don't want to learn how to code. As a result, many companies built front-ends for their data warehouse products so that the intricacies of the database design could be hidden from the user. IBM did not choose to do this. Rather, they partnered with several "presentation layer" companies. Data warehouse presentation layers, like others, are moving to the Web, making the data warehouse available to analysts on the intranet and customers on the Internet.

As businesses realized the value of the information they gained from their data warehouses, they wanted more data, summarized in many ways. They also wanted detailed data. Data warehouses grew, the storage they needed grew, and the batch window needed to replicate the data from OLTP systems to data warehouses grew. There are probably as many different ways to build and feed a data warehouse as there are data warehouse consultants. The principles, however, remain the same as we have already discussed.

Business analysts, particularly financial analysts, love spreadsheets. Data warehouses were great, except most analysts moved the data a second time, from the warehouse into a spreadsheet product, so they could twist and turn the data in every which way, trying to figure out how to read the crystal ball correctly. Eventually, someone figured it was possible to build a data warehouse that could store data in a cube-like manner that analysts could spin to their heart's content. This database was called an OLAP (OnLine Analytic Process) database. Dr. Codd wrote rules about what defined an OLAP database, and a new industry was born.

While OLAP databases are effective at processing cube-like information patterns, they tend not to be able to process large amounts of data, mainly because the data has to be visible in so many different ways. In order to make these databases viable, data is often summarized before being loaded into an OLAP database. If analysts want detail data, they generally go back to the original source data—either a data warehouse or an OLTP system.

Data warehouses and OLAP databases were good if you knew what information you were looking for, but what if you didn't? For example, suppose you want to keep the most profitable customers in your store. These are the customers who spend a lot of money every time they come in to shop. If you were using a data warehouse, you could produce a list of what customers purchased what (based on the correlation of their store loyalty card with their purchases), but analyzing trends month after month would take a very long time. Data mining tools can solve this problem.

Data mining tools, such as IBM's Intelligent Miner, search through mounds of data looking for patterns and trends. Using the tool, business analysts can review these patterns to answer questions such as determining the purchases of the most profitable customers. These are sophisticated tools that review mounds of data to determine their trends. In the e-business world, these data mining tools are being used via the Web to provide greater access to the dynamic information they can produce. (By the way, the most profitable customers of the grocery store? They were the ones who bought the stinkiest kind of cheese!)

Applications

One final trend needs to be reviewed before we leave this chapter. In the mid-1990s companies such as SAP began to develop and sell applications. The first of these applications were for systems such as ERP (Enterprise Resource Planning). These applications were complex, distributed systems that required extensive changes in how people worked. They were firmly based in client/server architecture and have incorporated the Web into their architectures. IBM has partnered with several of these ERP application vendors, as well as CRM (Customer Relationship Management) application vendors, to provide support for their e-business architectures. IBM provides databases for their data storage, Web application server software for their runtime environments, and Tivoli management software for the security of their applications. We will take a look at some of these applications in Chapter 8.

3

Hardware Architectures and Operating Systems

Why are hardware and software important to e-business? Just think of your company. If you are in a large company, you might have one or many mainframe machines, possibly even tied together in a Parallel Sysplex environment. Every employee has a personal computer (PC) on his or her desktop—generally with some variation of a Windows operating system. Then there are the server farms composed of mid-tier machines running every flavor of the UNIX operating system imaginable. If you are in a smaller company, your systems might be limited to a UNIX server, a cluster of Windows 2000 machines, or a few AS/400 machines.

Think about the location of your systems. The systems that you want to use for your e-business process are located on almost every piece of hardware that you possess. While software processes are needed to speed up transactions to e-businesses, hardware processes can have a big impact as well.

Finally, this chapter attempts to clear up common confusion over the word "platform." Platform is used liberally to mean operating system, hardware, or a combination of the two. We will avoid the use of that word in this chapter.

In addition to the physical boxes and the operating systems that run them, this chapter covers some basic concepts of network systems. These concepts are important because the king (or queen) of e-business is bandwidth. If you doubt that, think about how long it takes to download something using a telephone line in comparison to using a Digital Subscriber Line (DSL).

Hardware

Hardware is the physical box that sits on your desk or in a computer room. (For more specific information on hardware, please see *Exploring IBM Technology, Products, and Services*, as well as its companion books on specific types of hardware in this series.) IBM was originally a hardware company (International Business Machines) and still has a significant presence in the hardware market—particularly at the high end of mainframe servers. IBM has just refocused its branding of its hardware into different series: zSeries, xSeries, iSeries, and pSeries. The zSeries hardware is the 64-bit version (that means it has more power) of the System/390 (S/390) computer line. It will support the z/VM (formerly VM/VSE [Virtual Machine/Virtual Storage Extended], z/OS (formerly OS/390), and Linux for zSeries operating systems. The xSeries computers are designed for high-end Windows operating systems. The pSeries is designed for UNIX operating systems. The iSeries is for OS/400 operating systems.

It is important to look at hardware in the context of software. Why? Because all software must fit into an existing hardware architecture. Some software runs on some hardware platforms and not on others. The ability of computers to "speak" to one another is an important aspect of today's architectures. In addition, some of the performance gains that are necessary for e-business performance and availability are made at the hardware level. This is possible because hardware—including disk storage, routers, input/output (I/O) mechanisms, and the computer itself—comes with bits of software code, frequently called microcode, in it.

In 1946, ENIAC (Electronic Numerical Integrator And Computer), the world's first electronic, large-scale, general-purpose computer, was activated at the University of Pennsylvania. During the following decade, IBM helped shape the fledgling computer industry with a line of computers based on vacuum tubes. These early computers were supplanted in 1964 by a revolutionary new set of computers, the IBM System/360 (S/360) family. These computers were a breakthrough because of the speed with which they could compute. Through the 1970s and early 1980s, these computers evolved to many models of the System/370 (S/370) architectures. Major changes in technology, including faster communication channels and the ability to couple computers together to perform large tasks, resulted in the introduction of the Enterprise System Architecture/390 (ESA/390) in 1990. These types of computers (along with IBM competitor models, such as Hitachi's line of large computers) are generically referred to as mainframes. These are the computers that have evolved into IBM's zSeries.

Mainframes were, and still are, important to large corporations who had large amounts of work that they needed to do in a short amount of time. Most of them were used in early batch processes, crunching thousands of numbers to produce large stacks of paper. The government, master of number crunching, was also an early user of the new processing power. However, as with any new technology, the general public was suspicious of the new computing power, believing (perhaps with cause) that someday the government would know too much about them. Universities were always willing to experiment, and they adapted the technology eagerly. However, there were several parallel hardware revolutions taking place both within and without IBM, threatening the power of the mainframe.

As noted, mainframes were generally used by the government, universities, and large companies. But there were many small to medium-sized companies, as well as departments within the giants, that needed smaller scale computing power. So, in 1969 IBM introduced the System/3 computer. This was the predecessor to a series of S/3x computers that took advantage of technology that made it possible to put more hardware circuitry in a smaller space. These types of computers were enhanced over the next two decades, ending with the last introduced S/3x model in 1987. These computers formed the foundation for the AS/400 family that combined ease of use with advanced architecture and productivity. Businesses that heavily used AS/400 computers rarely switched to any other platform. AS/400s have evolved into the iSeries of computers.

In 1975 IBM began work on a project to develop a computer that simplified the range of instructions used to perform tasks and optimize the computer to efficiently execute these instructions. This approach was called RISC (Reduced Instruction Set Computing). Scientific communities needed a fast computer that could crunch through their calculations repetitively as they explored their "what if" scenarios, eliminating possibilities and finding right answers. IBM introduced the first computer to use RISC technology in 1986. These machines evolved into the RS/6000 series of computers through the last decade. Today they are part of the xSeries of computers.

In 1976 another significant event occurred: Apple Computer was started by Steven Wozniak and Steven Jobs. Apples soon popped up in classrooms and other early computing sites. Over the next few years, the company took off and the idea of a personal computer for every home began to be a reality. Eventually, Apples evolved into colorful Macintosh computers. We will come back to Apple and its impact on operating systems later in this chapter.

In 1981, IBM introduced its own version of the personal computer, the IBM PC. This technology is based on the use of Intel microprocessors (chips). As Intel and other microprocessor manufacturers have been able to put more and more computer instructions on their silicon chips, the speed of computers has improved. An important concept in the hardware aspect of computing is that the shorter the distance an instruction to the hardware needs to go, the faster the overall speed of the computer. By being able to put more instructions on the physical microprocessor itself, chip manufacturers cut down on the need for the chip to get an instruction from another location off the chip. As instructions are executed more quickly, the speed of the processor goes up, and users can do more work. Today, laptops possess more computing power than ENIAC did.

IBM's PC family has branched into several different brands designed for different types of customers. In addition, other companies, such as Dell, Gateway, and the like, have built "IBM-compatible" computers. The term "IBM compatible" is used to distinguish the type of computer from an Apple or Macintosh. This in turn is meant to identify the type of operating system that can run on the hardware and hence the software that could run on the computer. With the proliferation of operating systems that can take advantage of any type of computer hardware (predominantly Linux) and the cross-pollination of the Windows and Macintosh operating systems, these lines are not as clearly drawn as they used to be.

With all the alternatives, the computing industry outside of IBM proclaimed the mainframe dead or dying toward the end of the 1980s. Distributed (or network or workstation or whatever name someone happened to call computers that weren't mainframe computers) computing was the new paradigm. There were a number of reasons why companies thought that moving away from mainframes would be a good idea. The first was a perceived sense of cost. A non-mainframe server was cheaper than the mainframe and appeared to have the same number of processors. However, in many cases, companies discovered that the processors on their servers were not as powerful as the processors on the mainframe. They had to buy lots of servers to make up for the loss of the mainframe.

The other reason people wanted to get away from mainframes was the proprietary nature of the mainframe. In the 1980s the interfaces to the operating systems and the software that used the mainframe were not made public to anyone but the most trusted business partners. There were very few standards and many different ways of doing things. If you wrote software, you had to play by the rules of the company that made any software with which you interfaced. Companies wanted to get away from costly, proprietary systems. They moved away from the mainframe and declared its demise. Then three things happened.

The first was the ability of IBM to provide cheaper and smaller hardware for mainframe computing. The CMOS (Complementary Metal Oxide Semiconductor) technology was introduced as a building block for very large computers. These computers could be coupled together or networked with distributed types of computers to provide incredible computing power. This power was extended in 2000 with the announcement of the zSeries family of computers.

The second significant event was the exponential growth of the Internet. The Internet generated large numbers of users with unpredictable use patterns and a large amount of data that needed to be stored somewhere. While mid-range computing systems, such as RISC, can handle much of the traffic, especially if networked together, the high-end computing needs of the Internet business made many people revisit their prediction of the death of the traditional "IBM" mainframe.

The third thing that happened was that management began to realize that there was a certain amount of expense involved with managing multiple servers. Applications had to be copied from place to place and kept in sync. Now, instead of just one place that had to be primed for backup and recovery, there were many—large server farms that were more complex to manage than the mainframe. While the pendulum has not swung all the way back to centralization, it is certainly closer than five years ago.

There is a group of terms that are important when understanding how operating systems and applications interact with hardware: system processors, memory (or storage), and I/O processors.

System processors control what happens within the computer system. They make up the part of the computer that actually processes the instructions and does all mathematical calculations. For each of the hardware architectures discussed above, the system processor architectures can be different and are known by different acronyms such as CPs (Central Processors), CPUs (Central Processing Units), microprocessors, and the like.

Memory is like an internal worksheet for the system processor. The processor will temporarily store data it is using for calculations or other logical instructions in the memory area. Different types of memory have different characteristics, but primarily they are high-speed storage areas easily accessed by the system processor. Memory, dependent on type of hardware, also has different names such as central storage, main storage, RAM (Random Access Memory), cache, and the like.

I/O processors control the computer's interaction with devices external to the computer, such as data storage, communications, workstations, etc. As with system processors and memory, the construct and name of the device varies from hardware platform to hardware platform.

IBM's Hardware Series

In October 2000, IBM aligned its hardware into a set of e-servers—the zSeries, the xSeries, the pSeries, and the iSeries. Within each of these series, there are different models.

The xSeries is designed for Intel processors and small servers for business. The iSeries is designed for the integrated solution of the AS/400 environment.

The pSeries grew from the RS/6000 line of processors. They come in SMP (Symmetric Multi-processor) models (see "Hardware Architectures") that are designed for large e-business applications. Most pSeries systems are based on a 64-bit architecture for faster access to larger amounts of data. The zSeries 900 is designed and optimized for the high-performance data and transaction service requirements of high-end e-business applications. The zSeries implements 64-bit architecture for the mainframe end of the business.

To whet your appetite for things to come, IBM is working with the U.S. Department of Energy to develop the world's largest supercomputer. The hope is to have a peak theoretical performance of up to 467 trillion calculations per second (teraflops), more than the combined processing power of all 500 top supercomputers. Wow!

Hardware Architectures

Sometimes you will hear terms like shared-something, shared-nothing, and clusters. These refer to hardware architectures that are the basis of most of the hardware we have already discussed. Just to clarify, though, here are some of the terms that you will hear and an explanation of their architectures.

The microprocessor, or CPU, is the heart of the computer. It contains the instructions that are needed to run the computer. The more instructions can be put on the microprocessor, the faster the computer will run. That is the essence of the speed gains that we have made over the last few decades—putting faster and faster computing in smaller and smaller devices.

If you have one microprocessor, you have uniprocessing. Many home computers have uniprocessing. If you have more than one microprocessor, you have multiprocessing. The most common multiprocessing is SMP. SMP distributes the computer's workload among the multiple microprocessors. Computers employing SMP architecture share resources such as I/O subsystems and memory. SMP architecture can be found in PCs such as Netfinity, mid-tier servers such as AS/400 and RS/6000.

SP (Scalable POWER parallel) can also be referred to as shared-nothing or MPP (Massively Parallel Processing). The essence of this architecture is that the multiple processors within the system do not share memory or I/O, but communicate with each other via a communication vehicle called a bus. These multiple processors are actually each a computer that can stand on its own—either an SMP or a uniprocessor. Each one of these processors is called a node. Because they do not have to share any part of the computer architecture, this type of architecture scales as the business grows, by adding new nodes to the complex. Some models of RS/6000 support this type of architecture.

The term "clusters" can refer to a group of computers loosely coupled together over a network such as the Internet or as a group working together in a closely coupled environment such as the Parallel Sysplex architecture described later.

But it is still just a box unless you have an operating system.

Operating Systems

Mainframe

The first operating systems (OSs) were designed for mainframe hardware systems. Among the earliest OS produced by IBM that has been retrofitted for e-business is the VM (Virtual Machine) operating system. VM was designed for a large number of interactive users—each having his or her separate "virtual" session with the hardware. This virtual session simulates the existence of a real machine with dedicated processor functions, storage and I/O devices. Think of it as everyone having his or her own "personal computer" within a larger machine.

VM is still used today, particularly in Europe. Initially it was combined with CMS (Conversational Monitor System) to be deployed on the 43xx and 30xx series of computers. CMS is still in use with VM today, but VM has also been expanded to other hardware architectures to enable its use on S/390 hardware. VM can also run other operating systems under its umbrella operating system, allowing virtual machines to exist under its control. VM can be a standalone operating system or interact with z/OS, Linux for S/390, Linux for z/OS, OS/390, Transaction Processing Facility (TPF), VSE/ESA, or CMS, or with another z/VM operating system. (These operating systems are described later in this chapter.)

As of this writing, VM/ESA is in its fourth release, with the announcement of z/VM on the IBM software pages as the successor to VM/ESA. The announced release can run on z/Architecture or S/390 (ESA/390) servers. This version of VM can take advantage of the 64-bit architecture of the zSeries hardware.

z/VM also has improved its TCP/IP (Transmission Control Protocol/Internet Protocol) connectivity, including improved security with the inclusion of an SSL (Secure Sockets Layer) server. (Security is discussed in Chapter 6.) In direct support for e-business, z/VM has improved data transfer performance—speeding data over the network means faster data to the Web.

The VSE (Virtual Storage Extended) operating system has also been around since the mid-1960s. It evolved from DOS (Disk Operating System) and was developed for the smaller models of the System/360 computer architecture. Like VM, VSE also used the concept of a virtual machine, only in this case, the objective was to enhance the use of storage, giving the user the illusion that there is more storage available than there actually is. VSE is still alive today (VSE/ESA), being enhanced for e-business by allowing connections to the WebSphere Application Server (see Chapter 4) and TCP/IP.

Another mainframe operating system heavily in use today was originally designated MVS (Multiple Virtual Storage). MVS has morphed through MVS/ESA and OS/390 to become z/OS. The incarnation of this family of operating systems contains a base control program (BCP) that includes both MVS and an OS/390 UNIX Systems Services Kernel. The configuration of the operating system allows the operation of traditionally S/390 architected applications, but also provides the ability to run UNIX applications and exploit object-type applications such as those running Java.

The z/OS operating system handles the basic structures that are required for applications, including memory management and I/O calls. With today's focus on security, z/OS contains the components needed to serve a robust e-business enterprise. This includes technologies such as LDAP (Lightweight Directory Access Protocol), SSL, Kerberos, and PKI (Public Key Infrastructure). Integrated Cryptographic Service Facility (ICSF) provides cryptographic functions for data security, data integrity, personal identification, digital signatures, and the management of cryptographic keys. Several of its components handle other required operations in today's e-business world, controlling access to I/O devices and communications, and enabling other components to interact with the z/OS operating system.

An important feature of the OS/390 and z/OS operating systems is Workload Manager (WLM). With WLM you define performance goals and assign a business importance to each goal. WLM monitors the system and decides how much resource, such as CPU and storage, is given to each process in order to meet the defined goals. WLM integrates with many of the other OS/390 and z/OS software components to enable quick e-business development with limited human resources.

The z/OS operating system lets the OS/390 operating system take advantage of the 64-bit architecture of the zSeries servers. Both the hardware and the operating system software are intended to supply the e-business user with the ability to manage large applications with a minimum of fuss.

z/OS takes advantage of expanded central storage in the same manner as z/VM. Improvements to WLM and Parallel Sysplex architecture increase the performance and availability of the mainframe systems.

Parallel Sysplex Technology

Parallel Sysplex is the ability to have multiple computers, or sections of computers called Logical Partitions (LPARs), provide maximum availability. Each computer or LPAR is considered a member of the Sysplex configuration. The Sysplex uses a separate computer or LPAR for a Coupling Facility (CF). This facility manages the coordination of resources among multiple members. In case one of the members of the Sysplex is taken offline for maintenance or has a problem, the other members of the Sysplex can take over its work.

The Parallel Sysplex technology provides special-purpose clustering hardware to support Coupling Facilities and Sysplex Timers. This zSeries hardware was built in conjunction with Parallel Sysplex software development to insure that the hardware was designed for multisystem shared-disk clusters. Within the z/OS operating system a special component, XCF/XES (cross-systems communication facility/cross-systems extended services), provides a robust set of clustering services including "group management," intersystem messaging, interaction with coupling facilities, and recovery management.

The Coupling Facility contains information about read/write interest (locking) information for all members, as well as a shared cache called a group buffer pool. Parallel Sysplex uses CPU-synchronous processing to communicate this read/write interest and buffer pool contents to the Coupling Facility, thus making it a fast type of processing. As mentioned earlier, the XCF/XES provides the services needed for this communication at a high speed. Due to this speed, there is the additional benefit of keeping the application information available in the CPU cache, avoiding the necessity of having to re-retrieve it. Because hardware and operating system components are the foundation of the Parallel Sysplex architecture, the performance and small amount of overhead of this type of clustering architecture is impressive.

The very nature of Parallel Sysplex architecture lends itself to failover processing. If several CPUs can access the same information, transactions against the data can be rerouted to another CPU. In terms of availability, Parallel Sysplex allows you to add maintenance to one member at a time to keep your systems up and running while keeping up to date on service. The technology of Parallel Sysplex allows you to roll in a new release, one member at a time. You can keep your data sharing group running with an outage of only a few minutes—even across a release migration.

Non-Mainframe

While there are many operating systems for non-mainframe hardware (Macintosh, Windows flavors, UNIX flavors, etc.), IBM has only produced three: OS/2 Warp for PCs, OS/400 for the AS/400, and AIX (Advanced Interactive eXecutive) for the RS/6000. OS/2 and AIX operating systems can be used on machines that function as either clients or servers in a network.

Aficionados of OS/2 feel that it is a superior operating system for a PC, but market share has fallen to competitors, primarily Microsoft. Nonetheless, IBM has continued to support and enhance this operating system. OS/2 is a full-functioned operating system, handling systems management and communication to other environments via TCP/IP, Java capability, and interoperability with WebSphere. Based on the OS/2 Strategy for 2000 White Paper, there are indications that IBM may be moving away from support of OS/2. (Given the pace of technology, statements regarding IBM's future direction and intent are subject to change or withdrawal without notice, and represent goals and objectives only.) The recommendations in this paper indicate that customers should do future development with Java, Domino, and WebSphere rather than OS/2.

AIX was launched in 1986. It is a 64-bit version of the UNIX operating system and was designed to run on computers ranging from smaller personal computers to larger S/370 computers. More commonly now, it is available on the entire range of RS/6000 hardware, and it is available on RISC-compatible hardware as well.

Developed to be part of the open systems software, AIX conforms to standards (programming interfaces, communications protocols, etc.) defined by independent standards groups. This operating system provides the facilities required to interact with RISC hardware and provides security and storage management. It also provides interaction with device drivers (small programs that are resident on the hardware) as well as external storage devices and the network. It is designed to work on both

Symmetric Processors (SPs) and High Availability Cluster Multi-Processing (HACMP) systems. AIX is also evolving, as are IBM's other operating systems, from the necessity of entering cryptic commands to get things done, to graphical interface, and finally to a Web-based technology.

The hallmark of an AS/400 (iSeries) is the tight integration of its software and hardware. Many products, separately licensed on other machines, are included with the AS/400. In the AS/400, the operating system also interfaces with the System Licensed Internal Code (SLIC) layer. SLIC is a set of highly specialized programs embedded deep within the computing hardware that are never directly accessed by the user. Within AS/400, the SLIC layer is particularly rich, including a built-in DB2 database, single-level storage, and object-oriented architecture.

OS/400 provides all of the normal housekeeping functions of an operating system in a single product. The OS/400 contains all operating system functions—whether or not the user actually needs them. These include components to support an Open Software Foundation (OSF) Distributed Computer Environment (DCE), DB2 for AS/400, support for Java and support for the WebSphere Application Server.

The World Is Blending

If you aren't sufficiently confused by the multitude of operating systems and hardware systems, there will be more changes as these operating systems are enhanced and evolve to provide similar functions across all lines of hardware, using the same software components. Java heralded this change with the concept of "write once, deploy anywhere." All IBM operating systems are Java-enabled. They all have TCP/IP connections to speed up network connections according to standard protocol. Also, in line with component architecture, functions that were contained in operating systems are moving to separate products that exist on all lines of hardware and software. For example, the Tivoli family of products is used to manage applications, systems and security in a uniform manner. WebSphere Application Server is being integrated with all these operating systems, making scalability a reality from the tiniest handheld to the largest mainframes coupled together in a Parallel Sysplex configuration.

IBM has also embraced Linux. Linux is a free UNIX-type operating system that was created by Linus Torvalds. Originally the province of small systems development in very back corners of computer rooms, the operating system has evolved to be an answer to Microsoft's hold on the non-mainframe operating systems world. IBM has ported Linux to many hardware systems, including Netfinity and the S/390. It is a statement of their support of open standards. Operating systems on these platforms, such as AIX and z/OS, are being enhanced to include the ability to communicate with Linux. This allows both Linux and non-Linux applications to be run on the same machine.

Linux is a genuinely open system. There are a wealth of applications written for Linux that can be migrated to another hardware platform with a simple recompile in most cases. Why is this important? The ability to move applications from one place to another gives users the flexibility to choose where they want to build and deploy their applications without being limited by extensive rewrites for each hardware platform. Users can also rapidly move to a new hardware platform in order to scale up an application (adding more concurrent users, more data and more parallel processes).

Why move Linux to the S/390? The majority of corporate data resides on S/390 systems. Running Linux on an S/390 gives users the advantage of Linux applications accessing enterprise data where it's stored, improving performance. Linux for zSeries supports the 64-bit architecture in real and virtual mode on zSeries servers. It is based on the open source Linux 2.4 kernel.

The S/390 Virtual Image Facility for Linux allows multiple Linux systems on one S/390 processor. It can operate within an LPAR on the S/390, or within an undivided S/390 (native S/390). As of this writing, IBM intends to provide HiperSockets for Linux for zSeries and Linux for S/390. HiperSockets provides high-speed memory-to-memory TCP/IP communication across LPARs. This speeds up communication between LPARs, always a benefit for e-business.

Hardware, Operating Systems, and e-business on demand

If you will recall from Chapter 1, the four necessary characteristics of an on-demand business were given as responsiveness, variability (flexibility), focus, and resilience. The requirements for an on-demand operating environment were that it be integrated, open, virtualized, and autonomic. Within IBM's operating systems and hardware development organizations, two main concepts have emerged to support this type of environment: grid computing and autonomic systems.

Grid Computing

A grid is a collection of distributed computing resources available over a LAN (Local Area Network) or WAN (Wide Area Network). The end user perceives the grid as one large virtual computing system. The vision is to create virtual dynamic organizations through secure, coordinated resource sharing among individuals, institutions, and resources. Grid computing is an approach to distributed computing that spans not only locations but also organizations, machine architectures, and software boundaries to provide unlimited power, collaboration, and information access to everyone connected to a grid. Grid computing provides the ability for a computing system to be responsive to the changes in the environment.

Grid computing is the natural progression from the clustering and Parallel Sysplex coupling of computers that has occurred over the last decade. This movement will continue from further resource aggregation (powerful computers splitting work and completing it in shorter amounts of time), to data sharing (as is done with Parallel Sysplex today), to collaboration. Today grids are primarily being used by universities and research labs for projects that require high-performance computing applications. These projects require a large amount of computer processing power or access to large amounts of data.

Grid computing is an initiative that is taken as a design point for development work that has been done and continues to be done on IBM hardware, operating systems and software such as WebSphere (see Chapter 4) and DB2 (see Chapter 5).

Autonomic Computing Initiative

Formerly called eLiza, the autonomic computing initiative promotes the idea of self-managed systems, always responsive and resilient. IBM's eServer products have been designed and continue to be designed to incorporate capabilities that are self-configuring, self-healing, self-optimizing, and self-protecting.

Self-configuring systems require that any new hardware can be seamlessly integrated into an existing operating system. These systems should be able to configure and reconfigure themselves as needed without human intervention. Additionally, self-configuring systems adjust automatically to changes in the environment to meet preset business goals. For example, if the business goal is that access through the company Web site be maintained at a subsecond response time and a spike of users doubles the capacity requirement of a server, the system should automatically adjust, adding new resources as needed.

Self-healing systems need to do exactly that. In case a problem arises, the system must contain the problem and recover from it with minimal or no impact on the operating system or workloads. It should be able to do this without calling out the troops, as well.

Self-optimizing capabilities allow computing systems to autonomously measure the performance or usage of resources and then tune the configuration of hardware resources using their self-configuring abilities. Self-protecting allows the system to dynamically react to internal and external threats to the integrity and privacy of applications and data, whether or not the specific threat has been pre-programmed into the system.

Networks

Networks, to most people, represent a black box—well, maybe not even a black box, but a bunch of black wires that mysteriously carry information from one place to another. Network administrators talk in numbers and letters to each other, and sometimes, trying to get a simple answer is more than you can bear. So here we go—taking a look at networks from the 20,000-foot level—to determine what we need to know for an e-business system.

The point of a network is to get data from one point to another—from a source to a target. There can be many points in between the originating source and final target, using items such as switches and routers, but each movement segment (sometimes called a "hop"), at some level, takes place between a source and a target. It might be helpful to view sources and targets as stacks of possibilities (see Figure 3.1). For the sake of simplicity, we will look at the process as it flows from top to bottom and assume the information isn't altered between the source and the target. Then we will look at variations.

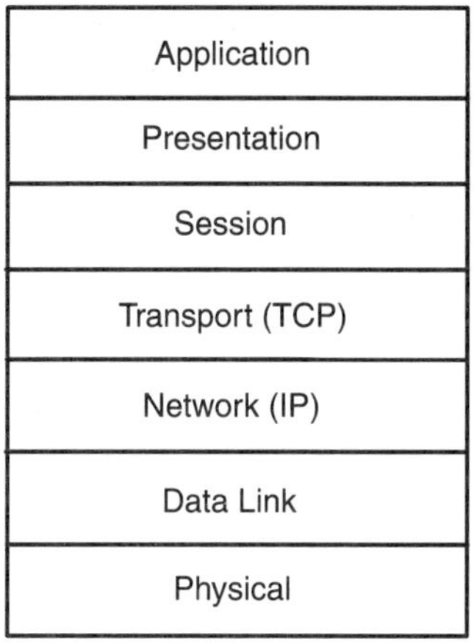

Figure 3.1. Communication stack.

The highest level in the stack is the application that wants to transfer the data. This can be a file transfer program such as FTP or TELNET, or an application with a distributed protocol, such as DB2 Universal Database. A protocol is like a language. If communication is to occur, both people speaking need to have a common language. Only when parties at both ends of a communication network know the language and the rules for speaking does it work. Let us imagine that your DB2 Universal Database program needs to get data from the server in Los Angeles to the server in New York to answer a request from the New York program. If the application network environment is TCP/IP, then the application will open up a socket to transfer its request through the layers to send the information.

The second and third highest levels are generally not used, so the request to send data goes directly to the transport level, home of Transmission Control Protocol (TCP). TCP wraps the data from the DB2 Universal Database request to be transported. If the data stream is large, it could break the data into segments and wrap each segment in TCP information.

The TCP segments are received at the network level, the Internet Protocol (IP) level. At this point, the data is put into packets and associated with headers and trailers that contain further information about the data, such as the number of bytes being transferred.

The next level down is the data link level. This level provides point-to-point communication between a source and a target. This is not end-to-end communication (from the original source to final destination), but rather a low level of data transfer. At this level, technologies exist to perform rapid transfer of data, but there is very little meaning associated with the data—only enough to get it from one place to another. This level takes the wrapped packet and further wraps it in something called a frame (Figure 3.2).

At the lowest level, the physical level, is the actual wire connection from one place to another. It is rather like your telephone wire—if it is not plugged into your phone, you don't have a connection, no matter how many fancy services your telephone company has promised to provide you.

Once the package has been wrapped, it needs to be sent on its way. It can go to its destination over a LAN, a WAN, the Internet, or an intranet network. Each has certain characteristics and methods to move data from one place to another. A local area network can have different formats, speeds, and methods for moving data. The most familiar are Ethernet, Token Ring, FDDI (Fiber Distributed Data Interface), and Gigabit Ethernet. These move data along using slightly different methods, at different speeds.

Within a company, an intranet can run over a LAN or a WAN, or, like the Internet, use telephone wires to move from place to place. (The latter is not recommended!)

Now what about those intermediary stops along the way? Networks of any type can be connected by pieces of software and hardware commonly known as switches and routers. Switches are used within LANs and have the ability to keep track of the devices connected to ports on the switch and move data very quickly between those ports. When a piece of data is moved from one port to another within the LAN, the switch reads the address of the target and immediately routes the data to that target. It is not a very complex process. It is like the postal sorter

Frame Header	IP Header	TCP Header	Data	Frame Trailer

Figure 3.2. Communication frame.

that reads the zip code from the front of an envelope and shoots it to the correct bin.

Another type of routing mechanism used with LANs is hub, or shared, routing. This mechanism accepts data from any of its connected ports and shares the message with all the devices until the message is accepted by the intended recipient.

Frame relay types of routers accept the data from the data link level and are only concerned with the frames that surround the data. Without unwrapping any of the enveloping processes, the frame relay sends the packet to the next stop in the relay. We will change our analogy here to the Pony Express—those guys just changed saddle bags, never really caring what the contents were, and sent them to the next relay station.

Finally, routers have a little more intelligence built in and therefore require more sophisticated software within the router and sometimes add a little to the performance overhead to pay for their time to open the envelope, check the TCP/IP information, and send it along to the correct target.

Your e-business infrastructure will be built from any number of these network components. Some will be in your control and some won't. However, because there is so much you don't have control over, you do need to understand how well your internal network is configured and its performance.

Protocols

TCP/IP contains the protocols that most people have a passing familiarity with—they've at least heard the name and associate it with the Internet. However, there are other protocols that exist, and have existed for many years. The following discussion will give you a little bit of background in these protocols. This knowledge is important when trying to understand the communication server software offered by IBM.

TCP/IP, which was used in the description of networks above, is a connectivity protocol that allows dissimilar devices to communicate with each other. It's based on connection-oriented transport riding on top of a dynamically routable delivery mechanism, allowing individual parts of the transmission to travel over different paths before being linked together at the receiving end of the transmission. Sometimes this works really well and the transmission is fast, and sometimes it doesn't. We all know days when the Internet just seems to be crawling, despite the snazziest DSL we have in our house. Part of this problem is based in the very flexibility that enables TCP/IP to route information efficiently. Because there are no predefined routes from source to target, it is difficult to insure that the speed of transmission is consistent and there are no congested areas on the network or that the chosen route is not the most clogged one on the network.

SNA (Systems Network Architecture) is a set of network protocols that was introduced in 1974 to support system communication. SNA is a connection-oriented transport. This means that there are previously defined networks for each connection to take. In addition, the protocol has a hierarchical flavor. With SNA there is a central node that controls the establishment of connections or conversations between two endpoints in the network.

To give an example, look at Figure 3.3. Suppose you want to get information from the source to the target; regard A, B, C, D, and E as nodes (stopping points along the way). The connections from A to C, A to B, C to E, E to the target, and C to the target are broadband connections. The path from A to B to the target is faster, but the SNA path has been configured from A to C to E to the target, so the transaction can

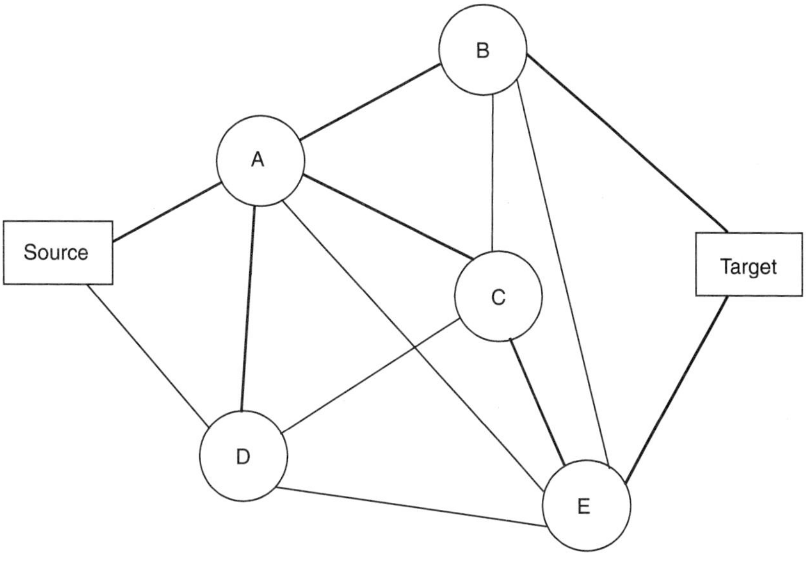

Figure 3.3. Connections and nodes.

only use that route until it is manually changed. As a connection-oriented, but routeable connectionless transporter, TCP/IP can choose any path from the source to the target, and can go A–C–E–Target or A–B–Target. Depending on the path chosen, your response time can vary.

APPN (Advanced Peer-to-Peer Networking) was introduced by IBM in 1987 for SNA client/server applications. Moving away from the central host concept, APPN defines two types of nodes—an end node and a network node. This provides more flexibility in routing communications, but the pre-existing physical connections are still required, much like TCP/IP. The routing is based on knowledge of the service level commitment or transmission priority of the transaction and thus limits the routes that the transaction can take. So, in our example, a transaction using APPN protocol could take either the A–B–Target route or the A–C–E–Target route as long as they both finished within the time limit specified and all the nodes maintained connection during the entire transference. The other benefit of APPN is that a central node does not participate in the establishment of communications between two peer-to-peer endpoints.

HPR (High Performance Routing), a more recent APPN development, streamlined the protocol and made significant performance improvements as well as adding more flexibility. The two main components of HPR are ANR (Automatic Network Routing) and RTP (Routing Transport Protocol). ANR provides a connectionless routing mechanism for moving packets through the network on a predetermined path. The difference is that the packet contains the information about its route. A node doesn't need to make the connection to the next node until it's received the packet. RTP is the mechanism used by the nodes to establish a connection as needed. This connection is often called a "transport pipe." RTP is then responsible for handling the error detection and recovery, speed of data through the pipe, and data integrity until the packet is received by the next node.

4

WebSphere

In order to run and manage an e-business, you have to build and deploy it. This chapter focuses on the WebSphere brand of products that enables you to do these things as well as grow your application. Because WebSphere products allow you to build components, you can reuse the building blocks you create, either in a different application or as extensions to your application to different presentation devices. Because IBM believes in standards, these building blocks can be easily used with each other and with non-IBM products that conform to standards. Security and manageability are important aspects of systems to IBM. WebSphere components have interfaces that enable them to the security and management functions that Tivoli provides.

Components form multiple pieces of the application, each performing a specific, discrete business function. Portions of them may reside on the enterprise data server, Web application server, or client; on multiple Web application and data servers; or within the Web browser itself. The design and management of this complexity is probably the most difficult task in an e-business world. If the design is solid, the application is easier to implement and the reuse of components can actually occur.

The current WebSphere Software Platform (Figure 4.1) changes and extends the previous WebSphere Software Platform to allow you to functionally divide the products into categories to use as needed. The changes

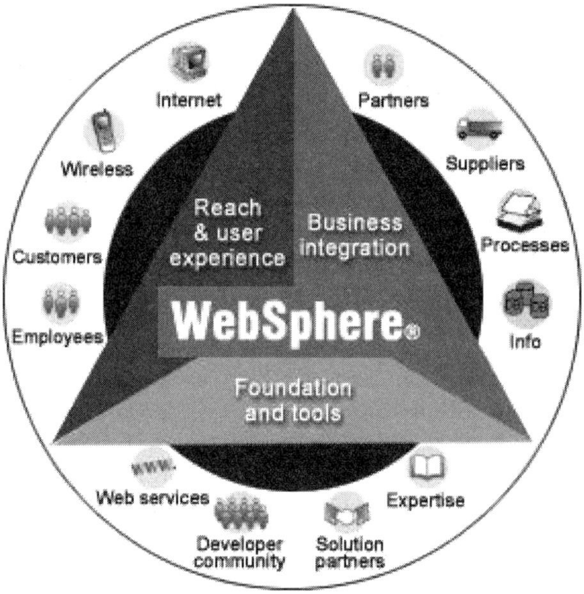

Figure 4.1. Websphere software platform.

in the platform structure reflect the way that e-business has evolved in the last few years. There are four groups within the WebSphere Software Platform: Foundation and Tools, Reach and User Experience, Business Integration, and Transaction Servers and Tools. Some WebSphere products cross category lines because of their multifunctionality.

The Foundation and Tools group includes products that prepare existing applications for e-business, including exploitation of the latest technologies, such as Web services. Following a component structure, applications are integrated into automated, connected processes.

The Reach and User Experience group covers the software that allows you to customize your user interface, whether that interface is to a Web page user or a pervasive device.

The Business Integration group provides products to help you integrate your internal and external business processes.

The Transaction Servers and Tools group provides products to help you maintain and integrate your legacy systems with your current application development.

Foundation and Tools

WebSphere products are built on a foundation of open standards with facilities that enable you to reach into your legacy applications and incorporate them into your e-business processes. These open standards include Java and Web services, and Extended Markup Language (XML). The foundation of the WebSphere Software Platform is WebSphere Application Server (WAS), an application deployment environment that includes the capability to securely manage transactions in a heterogeneous environment with the performance and scalability you need to achieve 24×7 availability. WAS is extended with the Host Integration Offering that enables you to access your legacy systems and incorporate them into a structure of components that can be used to build and publish new e-business applications.

WebSphere Application Server

WAS contains all the components required to receive requests, execute functions, and interface with other components external to WAS (see Figure 4.2). By providing a basic runtime environment for business applications, WAS supports the component applications that you can build or buy. WAS's component features allow networked applications to use, coordinate, store, translate, and sort information from disparate existing or new applications and back-end systems. WAS is compliant with the J2EE standard, allowing it to extend to other components built on the same standard. (While the functionality extensions may vary, the basic core functionality remains the same.)

WAS combines data storage with an application runtime environment as well as connections that allow it to get information from relational databases, legacy systems such as CICS (Customer Information Control System) and IMS (Information Management System) and other application servers such as Lotus Domino.

The essence of WAS is to provide a structure that allows access to content from multiple client types (personal computers, browsers, or pervasive devices) or dynamic content services (HTML [Hypertext Markup Language], XML, etc.) using different types of runtime and connection services. These services are viewed as components that can be integrated as various building blocks. This architecture allows you to integrate existing business processes with Web applications using Web

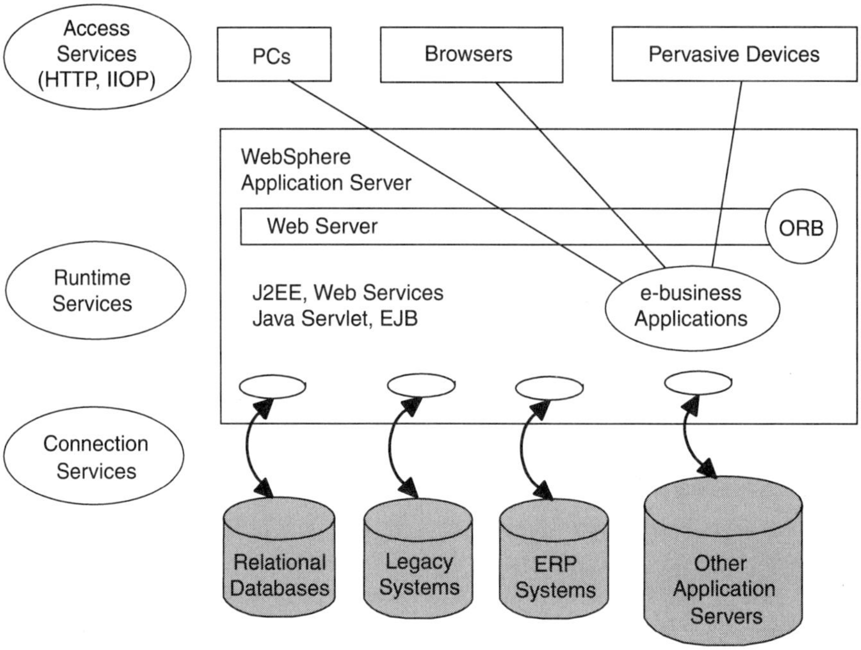

Figure 4.2. WebSphere Application Server (WAS).

services, with little understanding of the old technology required. Based on open standards, WAS has the flexibility to last in the world of continual change and integrate with other components to form end-to-end chains of e-business applications.

Before spending time on the WAS components, let's review the general components of a Web server application to demonstrate where WAS fits in. Users issue a request using their Web browser for an HTML page at the beginning of their session. The request is sent to an HTTP (HyperText Transfer Protocol) server for the page. The page can be retrieved from a Web Container or built via a Common Gateway Interface (CGI) script. If there is no further information required, the transaction ends after the form is displayed by the user's browser. If further logic is required, the Business Logic Container executes the business logic required, retrieves whatever additional information is required from a database server, and returns the information to the Web Container. The page is built and sent back through the HTTP server to the user's browser.

The Web Container can contain Java Servlet Pages (JSPs), servlets, or XML to produce the Web page. The Business Logic Container can contain Enterprise JavaBeans (EJBs) or Web services. Communication with the database server would be via tools such as Java Database Connectivity (JDBC). The database server can contain, in addition to data, Java servlets or stored procedures to complete the work. WAS contains the persistence and communication components to perform all these functions.

WebSphere applications can be accessed using a wide variety of client technologies such as personal computers (PCs), Web browsers, or pervasive devices. Specifically, WAS can be accessed by devices that support HTML, XML, Web services, SSL (Secure Sockets Layer), or JSPs. In WAS terminology, these are considered dynamic content services made accessible by the access services of HTTP, HTTPS (HyperText Transfer Protocol Secure), or Internet IIOP (Inter-Orb Protocol) engines. In addition, WAS enables dynamic application interaction through the Java Messaging Service (JMS). A JMS listener, running in the background, pulls messages arriving in an inbound queue and passes the content to a message bean. The message bean invokes the appropriate business logic bean.

After these clients access WAS, the request is handed to the object request broker (ORB) or Web services. This Java-based ORB provides support for CORBA (Common Object Request Broker Architecture)-compliant objects using RMI (Remote Method Interface) over IIOP.

Business logic beans are found within e-business applications on WAS. Rules can be written to derive values, classify situations based on input values, and execute scripts. Business rules can be encapsulated within business rule beans, allowing you to change how your business works without changing your entire application. These components can take advantage of dynamic application services, including the ability to expand your business beyond U.S. borders. While WAS won't translate English to German for you (although WebSphere Translation Server, described later, will), it provides the methodology to include the language translation as well as adjust for time zone and currency differences within your business logic.

Information can be shared dynamically using shared work areas. Shared work areas are like virtual scratch pads that allow you to read and write information. This information is attached to the execution of an application, providing up-to-date information. This interactive format of data capture makes the information more maintainable than if you were to issue a remote call to retrieve the information or access a persistent storage.

However, persistent storage is an important part of WAS technology. EJB components can be stored in DB2 Universal Database, Oracle, Sybase, Microsoft SQLServer (through Merant support), or Informix databases. A limited license of DB2 Universal Database comes with WAS.

WAS applications can be executed with a choice of runtime environments. TXSeries provides a traditional, procedural programming model, and Component Broker (part of WAS Enterprise Edition) supports the CORBA distributed object programming model. TXSeries is a high-performance distributed transaction processing environment that uses Distributed CICS or Encina for C++ applications.

Connection Services include Java, Java Connector Architecture (JCA), EJB, and transactional APIs (Application Programming Interfaces). Component Broker is a CORBA runtime object capable of supporting both CORBA and EJB objects that can coexist in a shared transactional environment. Component Broker can serve as a master in the coordination of resource managers, like those supported by Connection Services, helping insure data and transactional integrity. Java classes can also be made available to ActiveX using J2EE through an ActiveX bridge.

Because it is a component architecture, multiple WAS servers can be coupled together, providing the following possible connections from one server to another:

- Servlet to servlet
- Java to C++ applications using JNI (Java Native Interface)
- JavaBeans to JavaBeans
- EJBs to EJBs using RMI over IIOP
- ORB to ORB using IIOP.

These component servers can be managed by WAS, providing high availability and workload distribution. After a request is received, WAS uses these Connection Services to access the information it needs to complete the request. WAS can support the relational databases, legacy systems, Enterprise Resource Planning (ERP) applications, and other data stores. WAS can also access data using distributed database transactions across heterogeneous DB2 Universal Database servers or Oracle servers.

There are several tools in the WebSphere Studio family available to build an e-business application using WAS as the application server. WebSphere Studio Site Developer can be used to design pages, Java applets, scripts, etc. The Web and business logic containers can be built by either WebSphere Studio Site Developer or WebSphere Studio Application Developer (or a combination of both) and stored on WAS. WebSphere Studio Site Developer or WebSphere Studio Application Developer can also be used to build stored procedures to access DB2 Universal Databases. WAS provides full support of Web services, XML and J2EE technology (Chapter 1).

WAS can be used to insure security controls for application access protection. Applications can interact with the WebSEAL component of Tivoli Access Manager (Chapter 6). This allows WAS to redirect a transaction request from a Web server residing outside a firewall or within a secure zone between firewalls to a WAS inside a firewall within an intranet environment. In 2002, IBM announced that there would be tighter security integration in WebSphere Application Server Version 5. Version 5 will have an embedded version of Tivoli Access Manager. This further security extension allows WAS to support WS-Security and security available in Tivoli Access Manager. The security defines a standard set of SOAP extensions to provide integrity and confidentiality in Web services applications.

For internal WAS security, access control lists can be set up at a group or individual level. The group function allows for easier maintenance of security because the group can be allowed to perform certain functions. A person can be attached or detached to the group as needed without affecting the group's accesses. In addition, WAS allows use of LDAP-based user directories such as those found in Lotus Domino, IBM Directory Server, Sun ONE Directory Server (formerly iPlanet) and Microsoft Windows 2000 Active Directory. Version 5 extends security authentication to include Kerberos tokens.

Finally, WAS security takes advantage of Java extensions to authenticate and enforce access controls on users. WAS Version 5 includes four new authorization and authentication capabilities:

- Common Security Interoperability (CSI) for EJB component and CORBA application security.

- Java Authentication and Authorization Service (JAAS), the latest development in the Java Security Architecture. This provides building blocks for developers to code security external to their applications, and keeps them from inadvertently leaving "holes" in the security.
- Java Cryptography Extension (JCE) provides a framework and building blocks for encryption technology.
- Web Services Gateways filters Web services' access to registries and other applications.

WebSphere and Lotus Domino work closely with each other, including the ability to share services. For example, WebSphere and Lotus Domino can share a common list of users/groups from a Lotus Domino directory using LDAP. WAS can be installed onto a Domino server in order to use the HTTP stack on that server. In addition, Lotus Domino can use the WebSphere Servlet Engine to provide more robust servlet support.

WAS can take advantage of clustering, allowing you to scale your applications as you need to as well as providing workload balancing and failover capacity. The cluster itself can be across nodes (a node being a CPU [Central Processing Unit] and its attendant software and hardware) within a single box, or several computers loosely coupled together. Each JVM (Java Virtual Machine) and its Java applications are cloned across the clusters. In addition, WAS allows you the ability to perform JVM and connection pooling. JVM pooling allows you to create and drop JVMs dynamically, providing the ability to react to changing workloads. Connection pooling follows the same concept, only the connection refers to the connection to the relational database. Connection pooling allows the threads to float from one application to another on a disconnect or commit boundary, allowing maximum throughput. With Version 5, clusters can be managed by an XML-based administrator client that works over HTTP.

Knowing when you need to add another server or tighten performance is important when managing software applications. Statistics gathering is a basis for understanding an application and determining when change is necessary. Version 5 includes support for Java Management Extensions (JMX). JMX records and logs statistics on usage and resources. This information can be passed to management software such as Tivoli, to enable adaptation to changing conditions. Tivoli Performance Viewer, which allows auto-tuning of WAS, is included in the product. Auto-tuning software is an important component in IBM's e-business on demand, described in Chapter 1.

WAS comes in four flavors: WebSphere Application Server, WebSphere Application Server for Developers, WebSphere Application Server Network Deployment, and WebSphere Application Server Enterprise Edition. Network Deployment is a full configuration edition that is geared to those that need to build applications requiring high transaction rates with distributed security and remote administration. The WebSphere Application Server flavor has the same J2EE and Web services support as Network Deployment, but has simplified administration. It is aimed at departments and medium-sized businesses that don't require multiserver (clustering) management. The WebSphere Application Server for Developers is aimed at developers of a WAS application.

WebSphere Application Server Enterprise Edition extends the capabilities of WAS to the following services:

- Business rule beans
- Internationalization service
- Bidirectional CORBA connectivity
- Shared work areas
- C++ CORBA software development kit
- ActiveX bridge
- TXSeries
- A scaled down version of WebSphere MQ.

WebSphere Application Server–Express was recently introduced. It provides the ability to begin your J2EE development and deployment with simple servlet or JSP components.

WebSphere Studio Product Family

Developing a Web application—particularly an application that uses multiple hardware and software platforms to do its work—can be a time-consuming process, especially for people who are new to Web application development. The WebSphere Studio product family brings together several products to build Web applications, from a small set of pages to provide a simple image on the Internet to complex applications (see Figure 4.3).

WebSphere Studio provides the ability to modernize systems that have been built over the last 30 years and integrate them within an open Web services environment. This means that you can develop Java-based Web services based on legacy code written in languages such as COBOL and PL/I. It also can coordinate the back-end applications to complete cross-enterprise business transactions with Web services.

WebSphere Studio uses the WebSphere Studio Workbench as a development platform. This platform is based on Project Eclipse. Eclipse allows developers to use different tools from multiple vendors in an integrated, portal-like environment. This allows developers to move through all states of development and testing, using their favorite tools, from a single user interface.

WebSphere Homepage Builder

Everyone wants a home page! But how do you build a home page? More important, how do you build a page that is dynamic, attractive,

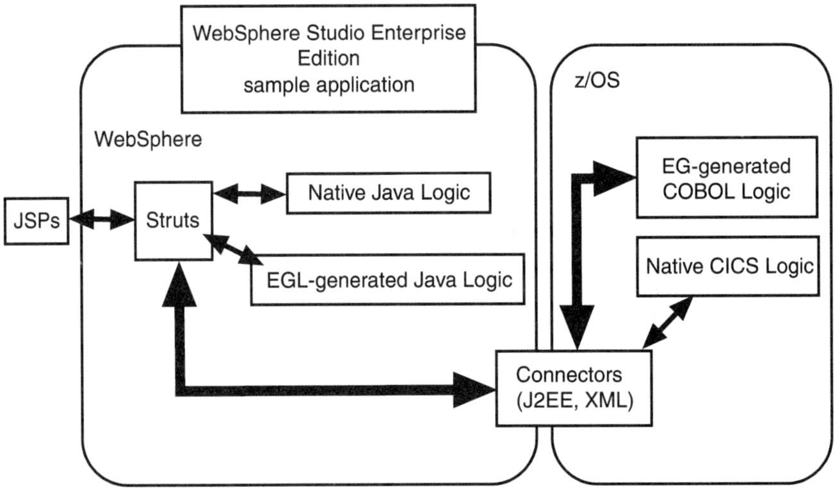

Figure 4.3. WebSphere Studio Enterprise Edition.

and easily updatable (a home page that never changes never gets revisited). A static home page might be all right for Aunt Martha's description of her exploits during World War II, but it is death if your home page needs to support your business.

WebSphere Homepage Builder is a group of related components that allows for easy development of Web pages. The Page Editor Homepage Builder component performs functions that are necessary to any Web page development using a WYSIWYG (What You See Is What You Get) form of editing with HTML and Cascading Style Sheet (CSS) support. CSS insures that your pages will have a similar style throughout your site. The editor allows you to edit multiple pages at a time and preview these pages using multiple Web browsers so you can insure that what you see is indeed what you get, no matter what presentation mode you use. It contains a full text implementation (font manipulation, etc.), page presentation properties (backgrounds, etc.), linking abilities (to other URLs, etc.), table creation, and modification (including format as well as content manipulation). There are wizards to help you create motion on the page. (For a link to demonstrations of this ability, check out this book's Companion Web Site on page xx. Motion doesn't translate well to the printed page.)

The Page Editor Template Wizard provides over 2,000 templates to create pages quickly. This Wizard also includes over 5,000 sample files that provide images, sounds, applets, etc. In order to incorporate these objects into your page, they are simply dragged and dropped to the page being built in the Homepage Builder.

The Image Tools enable users who have gotten past the drag and drop stage to create a more customized Web page. The WebArt Designer tool makes it possible to create objects such as logos, buttons, or rollover images. It works conceptually like the effects available in your word processing program. You create the text for the image that you want and then create a design effect that is associated with that text. However, this time instead of changing font colors and sizes, you are modifying the text to act as a button, logo, or rollover image on your page as it is displayed through the Web browser.

Like the word processor program, the Image Tools can be used to manipulate the size, shape, and orientation of the image. This includes being able to paste images from TWAIN 32-compliant devices such as digital cameras and scanners. (TWAIN is an interface standard for scanners.) Image conversion from one type of file to another, such as GIF (Graphics Interchange Format) to JPEG (Joint Photographic Experts Group) and vice versa, is also available through this tool.

The Web Animator image tool (Animated GIF Designer) expands on this basic image manipulation to create animated GIFs and banners. These images can be manipulated to wipe, scroll, mosaic, blur, or fade into your pages as the seconds roll by.

The Site Management/Site Gallery View provides management of the various pages of a Web application. One of the most annoying things is to get the dreaded 404 error, indicating that a page has moved or the Web site has gone to the graveyard of dead Web sites just when you think you have honed in on the information you are looking for. This tool automatically finds broken pages or data links and corrects them. The Site Style Wizard component of this tool allows you to enforce a uniform appearance throughout your site. Finally, to make pages friendly to users with impaired hearing or vision, the tool automatically checks the pages for accessibility by these types of users.

The File Transfer component of this tool allows you to manipulate files on the Web server as if they were on your PC. It is just one more set of files available from your computer system.

Video editing features are also included in this product. This allows users to manipulate video clips and insert them into a page. The product supports video files (AVI MPEG1, MOV), audio files (WAV, AIFF) and image files (GIF, JPEG, PNG, MIF, DCM, WMF).

In combination with IBM i-Photo Builder (which is bundled with it) WebSphere Homepage Builder can be used to build images at a size suitable for display on the screen of an I-mode cellular phone or WorkPad device.

WebSphere Studio Site Developer

WebSphere Studio Site Developer builds on WebSphere Studio Homepage Builder by providing a passage to WebSphere Studio J2EE application development, including servlets and JSPs. It provides everything a developer needs to create, manage, and maintain dynamic Web pages using Java technology. In a nutshell, the product moves you beyond the creative home page to an interactive site. So if Aunt Martha decides that she wants to charge money for her mothballed World War II memories, she can use this product to help her.

With the developer, you can use the same tools embedded in the homepage builder product to create your super Web site to dazzle and amaze. As with many of the other WebSphere products, WebSphere Studio Site Developer has been enhanced to enable development of applications that can use Web services. These tools include a few wizards—Web Services Client, Web Services DADX (Document Access Definition Extension) Group Configuration, and a plain old Web services wizard. Using the IBM UDDI Explorer, you can search the Web for existing Web services that you might want to incorporate. These services can be existing objects, such as a URL that publishes a form to collect information from the applicant. The wizards help you "wrap" the object to send to the service in a language format they can understand, such as SOAP services. Once you have the configuration that you want, you can deploy the application into WAS to test and eventually publish your own services to the UDDI Business Registry.

If Aunt Martha extends her memories to her fellow generation members, she can take advantage of the XML development environment in WebSphere Studio Site Developer. This will allow her to develop a way to analyze the documents, reference them, and find out whose memories conflict. If she decides to let Uncle Bob in on her project, she can use the integrated team environment. That way, Uncle Bob can listen to the sports and smoke cigars in the comfort of his den, while she can have dry martinis and listen to jazz. When they are done with their work they can feed their changes to a "team stream," that will ultimately enable them to integrate their work into the existing application.

WebSphere Studio Application Developer

WebSphere Studio Homepage Builder allowed you to start with the basics. WebSphere Studio Site Developer allowed you to incorporate Web services in an integrated Web development environment to develop an interactive site. WebSphere Studio Application Developer builds on WebSphere Studio Site Developer to give you the ability to build a full-fledged application integrated with your other systems.

Based on the Eclipse open source platform, WebSphere Studio Application Developer builds on VisualAge for Java functions in a J2EE development environment as well as the Web development environment used in WebSphere Studio Site Developer. The J2EE development environment allows you to build, test and deploy server-side (servlets, JavaBeans, EJBs) and client-side (HTML, JSPs) components for Web applications. The J2EE environment also provides support for SQLJ or JDBC languages. This flexibility allows you to determine which language provides the best development and performance for your application. Using perspectives (described later), you can use Web, Java, or XML development environments as well.

The product includes the teaming structures described earlier, but also supplies robust testing and debugging tools required for a more intricate application. These tools allow you to check the performance of your application (Aunt Martha's friends don't have all day to wait for an answer) as well as monitor it on an ongoing basis to fix problems before they become major.

In addition to application support, the product provides support for database connectivity. This allows you to import and map database schemas to your application as well as handle connections from EJBs. The product includes a copy of Rational ClearCase LT for relational database design. Relational databases that are supported for this development include DB2 Universal Database, Oracle, Sybase, MySQL, Informix, and Microsoft SQL Server.

WebSphere Studio Application Developer contains a series of perspectives that are tailored for specific roles or tasks. Perspectives are made up of views and editors. Views are windows with information about resources and editors (such as HTML and JSP) that are available to create and modify code.

WebSphere Studio Application Developer Integration Edition

The WebSphere Studio Application Developer Integration Edition is a beefed up version of WebSphere Studio Application Developer. As the product title suggests, the additional components provide an easier way to integrate your new applications with your current back-end systems. The product does this by providing tools to build application adapters—the links to your current systems. WebSphere Studio Application Developer Integration Edition leverages the J2EE Connector Architecture (JCA).

Once these adapters are built, you can use the product's visual interface to architect the flow between the various components of your business applications like EJBs, or Web services.

Pulling some components from WebSphere Studio Enterprise Developer (described next), the product also includes the ability to construct Business Rules Beans, work areas for additional integration and internationalization capabilities.

WebSphere Studio Enterprise Developer

WebSphere Studio Enterprise Developer provides the ability to develop Web applications in a similar manner to WebSphere Studio Application

Developer. However, using this product, installable on Windows platforms, allows you to deploy these objects to a z/OS operating system.

It does this by using a component-based development environment based on "Struts," an open source implementation of the model-view-controller (MVC) architecture. This tool allows the developer to access editors and wizards needed to create JSPs, as well as to access Enterprise Generation Language (EGL) Java logic and native Java logic. EGL, in turn, allows the developer to create COBOL transactions to access native systems on z/OS or to develop Web Java applications. The main benefit of this tool is that it leverages the skills in a company, retaining the investment already made in mainframe systems (see Figure 4.3 on page 78).

In addition to leveraging these skills, WebSphere Studio Enterprise Developer contains all the attributes already described in WebSphere Studio Application Developer.

WebSphere Studio Asset Analyzer for Multiplatforms

WebSphere Studio Asset Analyzer for Multiplatforms (Figure 4.4) helps you understand the legacy applications that you have on the mainframe and determine how best to bring this information forward into the e-business era. Using a Web interface, the user can have the application take an inventory and push the results into a DB2 Universal Database for z/OS. The database can then be used to obtain information about existing applications, including asking "what if" types of questions when determining a change.

The inventory process investigates the artifacts (artifacts are pieces of an application, such as a program module or data structure) on the z/OS system for basic information such as programming language and then determines the relationships between the artifacts. It places this information in the database. The user can then access the database to determine what will happen if certain aspects of the artifacts, such as data accessed or program called, are changed (impact analysis). The connector information required to position a z/OS system in an n-tier architecture can be analyzed by the Connector Builder Component of the product. Finally, the user can explore the contents of the database to glean the information compiled by the inventory process.

WebSphere Studio Application Monitor for z/OS and OS/390

WebSphere Studio Application Monitor for z/OS and OS/390 provides the ability to monitor J2EE applications using WAS on the mainframe

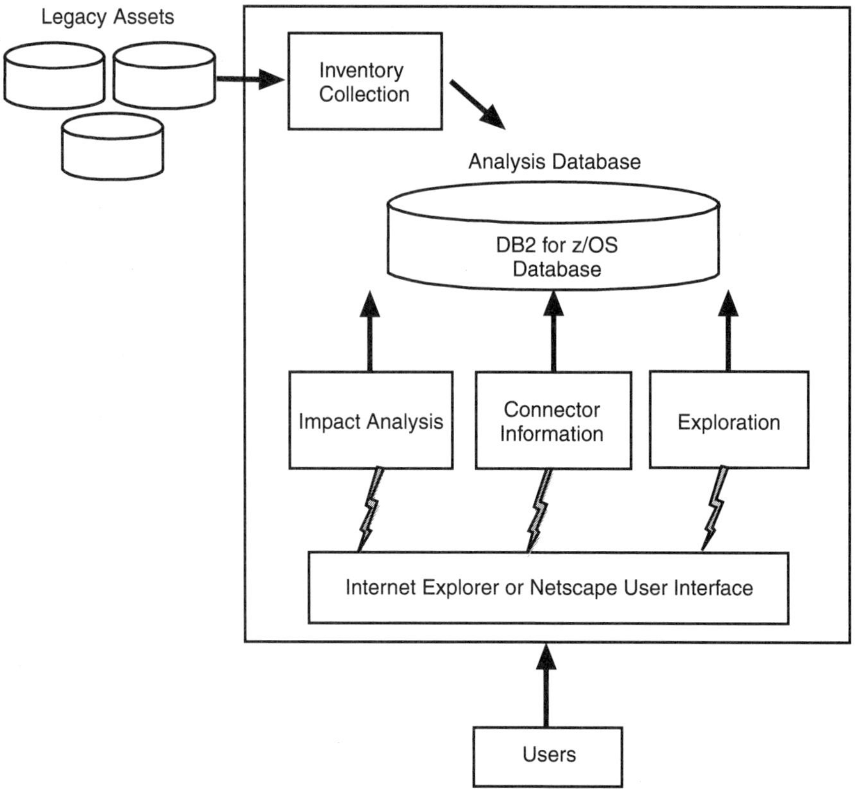

Figure 4.4. WebSphere Studio Asset Analyzer.

to insure optimum throughput and minimum downtime. The product consists of two components: a data collector and a managing device. The data collector gathers information on J2EE applications, and the managing device displays the information using a Web browser.

The display can consolidate application information for monitoring, yet also provides a drill-down technique. If you see a problem with one of the groupings, you can then search through the application activity details screens to find the source of your problem. Like many monitoring tools, the product can produce reports for analysis, so you can anticipate a problem, such as a long-running SQL statement or disk-space shortage, before it arises. In addition, should a problem occur and the necessity arise to cancel a thread, the product facilitates that process.

WebSphere Studio Workload Simulator for z/OS and OS/390

WebSphere Studio Workload Simulator for z/OS and OS/390 provides load testing and performance testing for applications that anticipate a lot of Web traffic. And who doesn't want that?

The product simulates large numbers of virtual users and generates their virtual Web traffic so you can determine how your Web application will react when all those potential customers come to see your new site. Will it stay up? Or will it crash and burn?

Although the product runs on z/OS or OS/390, it only uses the mainframe to drive the simulated users. The simulator engines can then drive the transactions across the network to an application on any server, such as AIX or Windows. As with most simulator tools, the WebSphere Studio Workload Simulator for z/OS and OS/390 captures the process that a real user initiates on the Web site and plays that back as directed through a controller. The tester can vary the number of users and the speed at which they "click through" the Web site, or sit and think for a while. Once the test is run, the product produces reports for analysis.

WebSphere Studio Device Developer (formerly VisualAge Micro Edition)

From the very large to the very small—the WebSphere Studio Device Developer is a development environment that allows you to build applications that are to be deployed on hand-held devices such as PDAs and the newest generation of cellular telephones.

Rather than using a J2EE environment, the product supports a WebSphere Micro Environment (an extension of the WebSphere Software Platform for cellular telephones, PDAs, and hand-held computers) for developing J2ME (Java2 MicroEdition) applications. If you'll recall, the main problem with porting applications to these smaller environments is insuring that the "footprint," the amount of resources used, is reduced to the minimum. WebSphere Studio Device Developer helps you by taking existing applications and optimizing them to insure efficient use of memory on small devices. The product also employs just-in-time (JIT) and ahead-of-time (AOT) compilation. This type of compilation is common in Java applications and is used to preserve the portability of the applications to various devices as well as minimize the footprint.

WebSphere Micro Environment contains messaging capabilities of MQe (Message Queue Everyplace) and the data management capabilities of DB2 Everyplace. The WebSphere Custom Environment, also contained in the product, provides the runtime environment for these small applications.

Macromedia ColdFusion MX for WebSphere

Macromedia ColdFusion MX for WebSphere runs on the WebSphere Application Server to provide the runtime services for ColdFusion applications. These runtime services include connectivity to databases, Internet protocols and components, a Web services engine, and resource management features such as database connection pooling, thread management, and security.

Macromedia ColdFusion MX itself is a server scripting product that contains integrated search and charting capabilities. The product is designed for rapid application development.

Versata Logic Suite for WebSphere

What are business rules? Why are they important? Applications depend on business rules, as do databases. Business rules are the underlying structure of any business application, as much as those of us in the business would like to believe otherwise. But the cantankerous part of business rules is they aren't stable. They change as business people try to adjust to a changing environment around them. Of course, that does keep information technology in business as they rewrite systems to adopt the changed rules.

But what if business rules could be more simply captured and changed? This ideal is the function of software such as Versata Logic Suite for WebSphere. This application software allows a business user to create business rules, even nesting business rules, that can then be encapsulated in an EJB. In addition, the product maintains the logical integration of the rules, even as they change, so that application code conflicts can be resolved during the business rule definition.

WebSphere Host Integration

WebSphere Host Integration solution is yet another way to "e-" your legacy applications. This solution fits in between your legacy host applications and the Web application server, providing external services.

It enables you to accomplish tasks such as giving your host applications a Web look and feel without programming or integrating multiple legacy applications into a single Web page without requiring any changes to the existing applications themselves. This solution can be used both for applications that are internal to your organization and for applications that reach beyond the firewall to your customers, suppliers, and partners.

WebSphere Host Integration Solution works with WebSphere Application Server and WebSphere Studio to create and deploy applications that access the host. WebSphere Studio provides the ability to develop applications, WebSphere Application Server provides the runtime environment, and WebSphere Host Integration Solution products provide the ability to deploy dynamic host content using Java servlets, JSPs, XML, or EJB components. The solution can access data on IBM iSeries and zSeries hardware as well as data on operating systems such as UNIX and Microsoft Windows.

Six products compose this integrated offering:

- IBM Personal Communications
- WebSphere Host On-Demand
- IBM Screen Customizer
- WebSphere Host Publisher
- A version of WebSphere Application Server
- IBM Communications Server.

In terms of security, WebSphere Host Integration Solution supports SSL authentication and encryption as well as using host security systems such as RACF (Resource Access Control Facility). Support for a digital certificate is included in the WebSphere Host On-Demand component. As with other WebSphere solutions, WebSphere Host On-Demand can integrate with Tivoli SecureWay to take advantage of public key infrastructure (PKI) methods.

Using the IBM Firewall and Communications Server, you can build a virtual private network (VPN) to connect remote users and business partners. A VPN extends your enterprise's private intranet across a public network, such as the Internet, using a secure connection known as an encrypted tunnel.

All of the WebSphere Host Integration Solution products contain a comprehensive set of APIs, including Host Access Class Libraries (HACLs). HACLs provide access to 3270, 5250, and VT (Virtual Terminal) data streams. The solution also provides the ability to develop Host Access Beans for Java. These beans can be used to access information on the host and reused in other WebSphere Software Platform components as your e-business changes. HACLs, Host Access Beans for Java, and ActiveX, as well as other host integration programming technologies, can be used to deliver dynamic host content using Java servlets, JSPs, XML, and EJB components.

IBM Personal Communications

Green screens haven't totally left us. They lurk in the bowels of "native" development rooms and the cold refrigerators where the servers hide. Today, however, you don't need to put on your overcoat and go into these rooms. Instead, you can use a piece of software called an emulation package to bring that green screen to your office. IBM Personal Communications is such a piece of software.

The software is a host communication and terminal emulation package. It supports 3270, 5250, and VT "green screens" as well as SNA and TCP/IP connectivity. The SNA connectivity is enhanced through use of Advanced Program-to-Program Communications (APPC) and HPR, which were discussed in Chapter 3. An extensive API set offers HACLs, Emulator High-Level Language Applications Programming Interface (EHLLAPI) and Windows High-Level Language Applications Programming Interface (WinHLLAPI) through programming languages such as C++, VBScript, and Java technology. These APIs come with the TCP/IP support in IBM Personal Communications.

Other protocols available with IBM Personal Communications are ISDN and HPR.

WebSphere Host On-Demand

WebSphere Host On-Demand provides a single interface to 3270, 5250, VT, and CICS applications. Although its purpose is the same as IBM Personal Communications, its implementation is different. IBM Personal Communications provides a method of accessing the host that requires its installation on the client. In contrast, WebSphere Host On-Demand uses a Web browser-based access that doesn't require software installation on the client.

From the browser, the user can click a hyperlink to launch the WebSphere Host On-Demand Java applet. This provides a secure connection that provides a single interface to TN3270E, TN5250, VT52, VT100, VT220, VT320, VT420, and CICS Transaction Gateway access. A default GUI simplifies the experience for users unfamiliar with "green screens."

Once the Java applet is served to the client, the user can connect directly to any standard Telnet server that provides the best access to the required data. Configuration information is provided by an HTML file or through the WebSphere Host On-Demand configuration server. The configuration server normally stores its data locally on the WebSphere Host On-Demand server, although it can be configured to use LDAP, an industry standard, instead.

WebSphere Host On-Demand provides a rich Java tool set, including Host Access Beans for Java, HACL API, Host On-Demand Connector, and JavaScript API. Host Access Beans for Java provides host connectivity and emulator functions through component-based development tools such as WebSphere Studio. With the JavaScript API, WebSphere Host On-Demand sessions can be integrated with a Web page.

IBM Screen Customizer

IBM Screen Customizer converts 3270 and 5250 host screens into graphical presentations, which are easy to customize without programming. It consists of three components: Administrator, which captures host screens from an active host session and saves them as maps; Customization Studio, which customizes host screens that were captured in the administrator; and Client Runtime, which allows end users to view screens customized in the Customization Studio. Using the customization studio on the screens captured by the administrator allows you to add new objects, change fonts and colors, apply templates, hide host fields, reorder workflow, and combine data to improve screens.

WebSphere Host Publisher

WebSphere Host Publisher is another method you can use to leverage your legacy applications and move them into the e-business software environment. It provides more complexity and integration features than any of the products discussed earlier.

The product consists of two major components: WebSphere Host Publisher Studio and WebSphere Host Publisher Server. The first component allows you to create objects that can be used to dynamically access back-end data sources. WebSphere Host Publisher Server provides the runtime environment to execute these objects. The created objects are based on JavaBeans and can be accessed by other Java applications. The results from WebSphere Host Publisher Studio creation are fully customizable HTML output with embedded JSP tags.

WebSphere Host Publisher Studio can also be used to create new Web services by generating new Java technology-based methods that help optimize network performance and response time when deploying legacy services across a wide area network (WAN).

Once the objects are created, WebSphere Host Publisher Server is used as a runtime environment. This environment supports applications running on host systems, such as 3270, 5250, and VT. Using JDBC, the application can also connect to databases with JDBC connectivity, such as DB2 Universal Database (discussed in Chapter 5).

IBM Communications Server

IBM Communications Server software allows interconnection of people and applications, even when platforms and network configurations are diverse. Network protocols and routing were discussed in Chapter 3, and it might be a good thing to reread that section before trying to understand what IBM Communications Server gives you.

Essentially, the server is a multiprotocol gateway that connects SNA and TCP/IP networks, enabling SNA and sockets applications on any platform and from any vendor to be transported across interconnected SNA and TCP/IP networks. SNA applications have full support for APPN, which provides dynamic routing for applications written using APPC or CPI-C, including the 5250 and 3270 protocols, which are common with legacy applications. The server also allows an extensive range of connectivity options for local area networks (LANs) and WANs.

IBM Communications Server converts Telnet client traffic, such as that coming in from a Web server, to SNA protocol to access legacy systems. It can also convert these protocols to a TCP/IP protocol. It does this by using MultiProtocol Transport Networking (MPTN), which works at the API layer. For example it can convert the sockets interface to use SNA protocols instead of TCP/IP, or, alternatively, it can convert the APPC/CPI-C interface to use TCP/IP protocols instead of SNA. MPTN incorporates compensation mechanisms to handle the differences between SNA and TCP/IP, regardless of which backbone it uses to get across the network.

Reach and User Experience

While Foundation and Tools allows you to build a foundation infrastructure and access your legacy information, Reach and User Experience covers the software that presents your face to your customer. These include tools that allow your users to customize their Web sites (personalization and portals) or get the application to any device (pervasive solutions, mobile connections, and voice solutions). WebSphere Studio Device Developer, described earlier, is also part of the Reach and User Experience. The group also includes WebSphere Commerce Solutions, which are application accelerators. These solutions are discussed in Chapter 8.

Portal Solutions

A portal is an old-fashioned word for doorway. The dictionary traces it back to the Latin *porta*, a gate. This being the 21st century, every vendor has one or wants one. And why not? In 2002 IDC announced that the portal market will reach more than $3.1 billion by 2006, from $550 million in 2001. And Forrester Research says that nearly 60% of companies will have a portal initiative underway by the end of 2002. But what, exactly, is a portal?

Since every vendor makes sure the definition of a term matches the product it is selling, we will stick with IBM's definition—which is actually a pretty good one. A portal is a method to provide a single, secure access to a proliferation of information stored in many formats. The portal can then be personalized to provide only the information the user wants in the manner he or she wants it. Think of the portal as an extension to Xerox PARC's original windowing scheme (used by Apple, Macintosh, and Microsoft Windows), except that each window on your computer is backed by coordinated information that makes sense to you. Each window is not a separate portal, but a separate use of the portal. My set of portal windows will look different from yours, and yours will look different from others. The "windows" are actually areas of Web pages.

IBM differentiates between a corporate portal and a public portal. The former is enabled for collaborative effort between different portions of the organization, with information flowing in multiple directions. The public portal has a unidirectional view from the portal creators to the viewers.

Within corporate portals, IBM defines four types:

- Enterprise Information Portals connect people with information by organizing large collections of content on the basis of subjects or themes within the content.

- Collaborative Portals enable teams of users to establish virtual project areas or communities along with tools for collaboration for their use.

- Expertise Portals link people together based on their skills or expertise as well as their information needs.

- Knowledge Portals do everything the first three portals do, plus an unspecified something "more."

WebSphere Portal for MultiPlatforms was delivered in 2001 with a major enhancement delivered in 2002. This portal provides state-of-the-art navigation, categorization, search, information and application access, syndicated content access, personalization, customization, and user administration. The portal framework provides the common services (connectivity, integration, administration, and presentation). Connectivity services give you access to internal data, such as enterprise data, as well as external data such as newsfeeds or your business partners' applications. Presentation services allow you to personalize your desktop. The flow and display of information is controlled by portlets running within WebSphere Portal. The framework can be extended through use of a portlet API that conforms to open standards.

WebSphere Portal makes use of the WebSphere Personalization product, which is also described in this chapter.

WebSphere Portal for Multiplatforms

WebSphere Portal for Multiplatforms is the primary implementation of the portal product. It is designed to help build business-to-employee (B2E), employee-to-employee (E2E), business-to-business (B2B) and business-to-customer (B2C) portals. It also supports a wide variety of pervasive devices, such as PDAs (see Figure 4.5).

WebSphere Portal Enable helps build scalable portals to simplify a user's access to personalized information and applications. Two personalization technologies are used in this product. The first is a rules-based filter that determines which Web content is displayed for a particular user. The second allows you to take advantage of statistical models and matching techniques. Based on information gathered about visitor behavior and trends, you can tailor displayed content to individual users and groups. Also included is a search facility (from IBM Research) that provides accurate search results dedicated to small and mid-size collections of Web pages. This facility efficiently applies state-

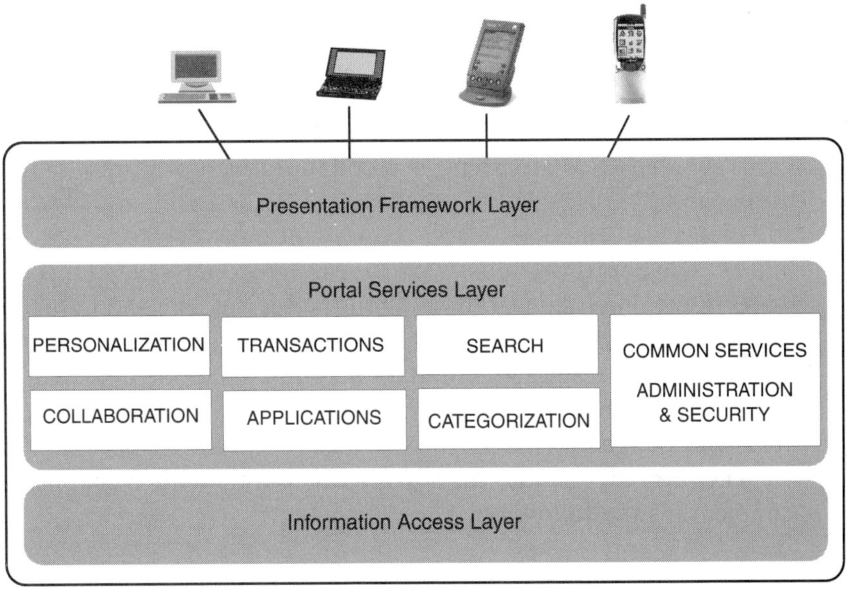

Figure 4.5. WebSphere Portal Server.

of-the-art search algorithms and improved search precision by incorporating lexical affinities.

Connectivity and integration with internal and external applications and data sources are handled by this product, as well as presentation and administration. This allows you to access prebuilt ERP, CRM (Customer Relationship Management) and SCM (Supply Chain Management) applications such as SAP and Siebel through your portal. The administration component also allows you to control security using an LDAP directory.

The product includes the following software in addition to the portal toolkit:

- WebSphere Application Server Advanced Edition
- Tivoli SecureWay Directory
- WebSphere Personalization
- DB2 Universal Database for Multiplatforms
- WebSphere Studio Application Developer
- Web Content Publisher.

WebSphere Portal Extend is a collaborative portal that contains all the capabilities of the Enable package as well as an integrated team room and messaging, extended search, community, and Web site analysis capabilities. The portal will allow you to search through several types of data stores (DB2 Universal Database, Lotus Notes, Oracle, and Lotus Domino databases, several Web search engines, and text or HTML documents) and handle the resulting compilation of information. The collaborative portion of WebSphere Portal Extend allows you to develop virtual team areas and designate workflow as well as collaborative development.

The product includes the software available with WebSphere Portal Enable, plus the following:

- Lotus Collaborative Places
- Lotus Collaborative Components

- Lotus Extended Search
- Tivoli Web Site Analyzer
- A limited (to portal use only) version of Lotus Sametime
- A limited (to portal use only) version of Lotus Quickplace.

WebSphere Portal Experience includes everything in the Extend offering and also includes the ability to develop e-meetings, application sharing, and enterprise content management as well as enhanced security features. This offering extends the collaborative team room and allows you to capture the applied structure and knowledge of a workspace as a reusable asset that can be shared throughout your organization. By including DB2 Content Manager, the product provides a repository that allows you to index, store, search, and distribute varied types of digital content, including HTML and XML Web content, document images, electronic office documents, and rich media such as digital audio and video. The product also moves security to a more robust level, in that it protects Web resources including Internet addresses, scripts, and data accessed by traditional Web browsers and WAP (Wireless Application Protocol)–enabled devices.

The product includes the software available with WebSphere Portal Extend, plus the following:

- A full version of Lotus Sametime
- A full version of Lotus Quickplace
- DB2 Content Manager
- Tivoli Access Manager—formerly Tivoli Policy Director
- Enterprise Information Portal.

Web Content Publisher provides a browser-based interface that allows nontechnical users to create, contribute, and manage content on portals and Web sites. The tool provides template management, workflow management, versioning, and access control of documents.

WebSphere Portal Express

WebSphere Portal Express is designed for small and medium-size business portal development. It offers full support for portal personalization, campaign management, single sign-on across applications, authentication, authorization, and communication between portlets.

WebSphere Portal Express Plus contains the same functionality as WebSphere Portal Express but includes instant messaging, online "people-awareness" and chat, virtual team rooms, group calendaring, task management, document libraries, and document sharing and revision capabilities.

The premise of this tool is ease of installation and development for small and medium-size business users as well as easy interoperability with tools that they already have. For example, the product comes with SecureWay LDAP Directory, but also allows you to access user profile information stored in a Domino Directory or Microsoft Active Directory.

The ease of development is provided through use of tools and frameworks. There's a toolkit for portal development. The portal framework can be used to integrate the portal with applications or data sources. Users can use the portal interface to organize their portal pages, select the applications that will appear on them, and choose the visual appearance that they like best.

WebSphere Personalization

Personalization of a Web site is about selecting the content that best matches the needs and interests of each site visitor. About 41% of companies that have Web sites are doing some type of personalization. Personalization is both the welcome messages and the recommended purchases you see on Web sites such as Amazon.com. It is used to attract and retain site visitors. Personalization can also benefit non-e-commerce sites, such as B2B, intranets, and non-intranet Internet (extranet) sites by giving information as needed. For example, as members of a particular department sign on to the company intranet, they can be reminded of the department meeting that morning. WebSphere Personalization is included with all WebSphere Portal offerings: Enable, Extend, and Experience.

In order to personalize a Web site, several functions are required. First, the visitor must be identified, either by a cookie or a user logon. Second, the profile that contains information about the visitor's interests, role in an organization, or other data about the visitor must be retrieved. Third, based on the profile, a decision must be made about the content to be displayed. This is called matchmaking. Finally, the Web page must be assembled.

Profiles can be developed from data captured on the site via explicit questionnaires or data collected from third party sources. Sometimes profiles can be extracted from information that already exists within the company's legacy business systems—particularly in the case of intranet applications.

There are two broad categories of matchmaking technologies—business rule engines and recommendation engines. Business rule engines, as is not surprising, use a company's business rules to determine what to display to a site visitor. Recommendation engines, on the other hand, base their recommendations on statistical techniques using information about other sites that visitors have viewed.

Business rules can be divided into three varieties: classifier, action, and binding. A classifier rule determines what category a site visitor falls into. Sample visitor categories could be browser, customer, or deadbeat customer. The business owner of the site defines the categories. An action rule determines what content should be selected. Action rules could be such things as display sales, display news and member information, or list suggestions for members. A binding rule combines the classifier rule with the action rule to determine what content should be displayed. For example, a suggestion for a deadbeat customer could be "Please contact our Account Department regarding your overdue account for $739." Rules are entered using the Rule Editor of the Personalization Toolkit, inside of WebSphere Studio Application Developer.

When a visitor requests a page from a site hosted on WebSphere Application Server, a JSP is called either directly or indirectly. The JSP can contain JavaBeans that have conditional logic that can determine what content is returned to the site visitor based on the visitor's stored preferences. For example, as the baby boomer generation ages, large type on Internet pages could be something in a site visitor's list of preferences. This allows a certain amount of customization with WebSphere Application Server alone.

By adding WebSphere Personalization to WebSphere Application Server, a matchmaking engine (a business rule or recommendation) can be used to determine content. The Resource Engine of WebSphere Personalization manages access to the profiles and content in order to provide the personalized pages. It does this by allowing site developers to query multiple databases of content and profiles with a set of Java interfaces using JavaBeans or EJBs. The beans can be created with VisualAge for Java or WebSphere Studio Advanced Edition.

The Resource Engine allows the user to build groups to target information effectively at a segment of the population. Grouping profiles in this manner can save computation time by not having to evaluate a classifier rule for every category of visitor segment. After all, there is no use in having personalization if it makes the retrieved page come back more slowly.

WebSphere Personalization can be integrated with Tivoli Web Site Analyzer for reporting on the effectiveness of your site's campaigns and business rules in achieving your business objectives. It can also work with Integrate Interwoven TeamSite, Enterprise Information Portal (described below), and LDAP.

Enterprise Information Portal (EIP)

IBM first introduced Enterprise Information Portal (EIP) in November 1999. EIP is a federated search gateway that provides a rich development environment for the composite of mass customized applications or views. Two of the services of the WebSphere Portal Experience offering are actually handled by EIP: Search and Categorize. In addition, the function of the Information Access Layer is handled by EIP.

The design of EIP allows a user to coordinate information from disparate sources into one cohesive view of life. All forms of data can be searched and delivered to the user in response to a single question, such as all the information about a pending house sale: loan documents, house pictures, inspection report, etc. EIP supports intranet and Internet Web crawling as well as information mining. This enables new applications that support categorization and summarization of document information. Search results can also be categorized and summarized. Metadata stored in DB2 Warehouse Manager may be accessed through the IBM Business Intelligence Information Catalog. This information is passed to the actual portal presentation layer for display to the user.

How is this done? In order to access different data stores on different data platforms, including the 85% of data that is unstructured, access pipes (like plumbing to a water supply) need to be constructed.

IBM calls these pipes data access connectors. Each of these connectors accesses different types of data stores. IBM has pre-built several of these—mainly to its own products. Several of the connectors access unstructured data stored in the DB2 Content Manager products, the relational data stored in DB2 Universal Database, and the Lotus data stored at Lotus Domino.Doc. They have also built connectors to non-IBM relational databases such as Oracle and others that support ODBC (Open Database Connectivity) or JDBC connections. These connectors can also access company intranets or external Internet sources such as Web search sites and syndicated content such as Dun and Bradstreet using Web crawler technology. The Web crawler can access data in local file systems and in File Transfer Protocol (FTP) collections, as well as Lotus Notes (Chapter 7). EIP can also access DB2 DataJoiner for access to even more data stores.

In addition, IBM provides the capability for users to develop their own custom data connectors. IBM provides the Unified Content API for portal development. Using popular Web development interfaces such as Java, JavaBeans, C++, and ActiveX, the developer can integrate EIP with existing applications. These APIs and a guide published on the EIP Web site allow third parties to write connectors to plug into the framework. These access methods are the Information Access Layer of portal architecture.

The search capability is developed by mapping different connectors to a search algorithm. A data store can be configured as a standalone data store or as part of a federation. These federated data stores can be composed from any number of data stores, including other federated data stores. This allows the search engine to view the entire group as one object, manipulating and returning content from that viewpoint.

Categorization is done accessing information stored in the DB2 Information Catalog. This catalog is based on the Common Warehouse Metadata Interchange (CWMI) standard. Categorization can also be done by the Web crawler. This crawler will find, index, and monitor what you need on the Internet or in your intranet. Information Mining can group related documents based on their content, without requiring predefined classes. These documents can then be assigned to one or more user-defined categories. A summary can also be provided from the document's key information. Security is provided by LDAP support (Tivoli SecureWay Policy Director and Microsoft Active Directory) with single sign-on capability.

All this is complex to manage, so the product is managed by a workflow service. The EIP Advanced Workflow service is integrated with the WebSphere MQ Workflow engine as well as DB2 Content Manager capabilities. The workflow provides decision points to automate decision making based on user interactions or user- or system-defined data containers. The routing provides the flow to the crawling, as well as a collection point, to wait until external events occur before moving on to other data collection routines.

Pervasive Solutions

Pervasive solutions are applications that enable delivery of information over any network using any device. It is computing power that goes beyond the desktop to reach to wireless hand-held devices, automobile telematics systems, home appliances, and commercial tools of the trade. The software products covered by this general term include some from other branches of the WebSphere Software Platform as well as those with a specific focus to enabling pervasive solutions: voice technologies, mobile application platforms, and mobile solutions.

As was noted in Chapter 1, the future of e-business is not only in wired connections to the Internet—it involves wireless connections to pervasive devices as well. Remember that some estimates state that by the end of 2002 we will see more wireless subscribers capable of Internet access than wired users. Close to 1.3 billion people worldwide will probably be plugged in to Web-capable phones by 2004, compared to just 700 million people with ordinary Net connections.

The primary development tool for pervasive products is WebSphere Studio Device Developer.

WebSphere Voice Server

As blessed as many are to be able to see and type, there are many in this world who cannot do one or the other. For them, the fancy videos and pictures on the World Wide Web do not make sense. In addition, there are people for whom the written word is far more cumbersome than the spoken word, for example, people with dyslexia. Even if these two situations do not apply to you, there are times when access to the Web is not possible because you do not (gasp!) have anyplace to plug in your laptop, the batteries on your cell phone have died, or you aren't in a place that has converted to wireless technology. Then there are those times when using a regular phone is just plain nice. Enter WebSphere Voice Server (see Figure 4.6).

WebSphere Voice Server provides technology to develop and deploy conversational e-business solutions. There are four key elements that make up the product:

- A speech recognition engine that recognizes through one or more application-specific grammars and converts the speech to text. This component can interact with a variety of telephony platforms: WebSphere Voice Response, Intel Dialogic, and Cisco Voice over Internet Protocol (VoIP).

- A TTS (Text-To-Speech) engine that produces speech from text. There are three TTS offerings: format, which provides unlimited vocabularies with synthesized voices; concatenative, which provides unlimited vocabularies using human voices; and phrase splicing, which provides limited vocabularies using prerecorded

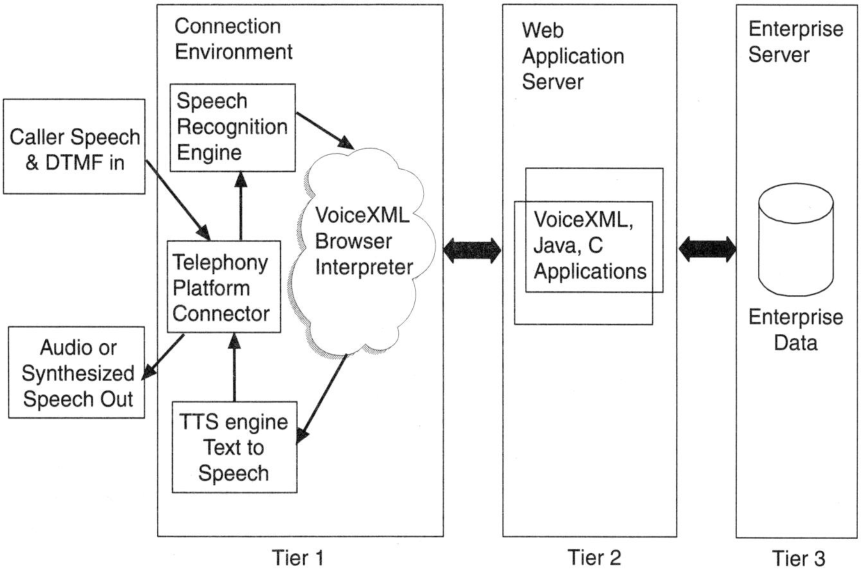

Figure 4.6. WebSphere Voice Server.

human voices. This component can interact with the same telephony platforms as the speech recognition engine.

- Voice application development tools that support applications written in VoiceXML, JavaBeans, or C:
  - WebSphere Voice Toolkit, which helps developers build voice applications by providing grammar and VoiceXML editors as well as a pronunciation builder so that application developers do not need to know the internals of voice technology. It is built on Eclipse and is part of the WebSphere Studio family.
  - WebSphere Voice Server SDK, which uses VoiceXML technology to allow developers to create voice-enabled applications and test them on a desktop workstation.
- Telephony platform connector, the runtime platform for speech applications that connects the voice audio streams from the public telephone network or VoIP to the speech recognition and TTS engines.

There are two main ways of accessing the telephony platforms. Using the first, you can speak into a telephone or microphone and the system recognizes the speech patterns and translates them into client to the Web application server. The second type of presentation is the use of DTMF (Dual Tone MultiFrequency), which is the use of number keys on the telephone, commonly called Touch-Tone. The telephony platform itself is not a part of WebSphere Voice Server, but is a separate product. WebSphere Voice Server contains connectors that interact with WebSphere Voice Response (described below), Intel Dialogic, and Cisco VoIP.

The telephony product can generally deal with the DTMF types of applications. However, to fully implement voice applications, the speech recognition and TTS engines are required to translate the voice input to text and vice versa. This text is then used as input to applications written in VoiceXML, JavaBeans, or C that can interact with new e-business applications or legacy systems. Business logic can be embedded in server pages, servlets, or server pages.

The WebSphere Voice Server includes entry-level editions of WebSphere Application Server and WebSphere Studio, both described earlier.

WebSphere Voice Response with DirectTalk Technology

WebSphere Voice Response with DirectTalk Technology is an interactive voice response (IVR) product that provides a telephony component to run self-service applications. It can support simple to complex applications. Developers using the tool can develop applications using the native telephony development environment or using standards-based development tools for Java or VoiceXML.

The product works by allowing the user to present a request by providing verbal responses to a "form" that is presented orally. For example, to request additional insurance forms, an employee can dial an 800 number. The voice system instructs the employee to fill out the "form" by punching the employee number out on the telephone keypad and pressing the pound sign. The disembodied voice then asks how many copies of the form are needed. Since the employee number provides the name and address of the employee, that is all the information the employee needs to give.

In addition to the automated attendant (the technical term for the disembodied voice), WebSphere Voice Response can send faxes, page someone, or provide support for dinnertime telemarketing calls. It can run multiple applications at the same time. Disembodied voice responses can be stored in a relational database such as DB2 Universal Database and accessed as required, in a fashion similar to retrieving graphics for an HTML page.

There are technical requirements to be able to hook this software application into a telephone system, be it a local telephone exchange, or PABX (Private Automatic Branch Exchange) system. It supports two types of common channel signaling protocol: ISDN and Signaling System #7 (SS7). A piece of hardware called the DTXA (Digital Trunk Extended Adapter) was developed to connect the IBM pSeries family to the telephony network. Up to four of them can be installed, giving up to 16 T1 or E1 trunk lines to a pSeries Server.

WebSphere Voice Server for Transcription

I know most of you have been in a doctor's or lawyer's office recently. Have you ever looked at the volumes of documentation each must keep on every office visit? Back before computers existed, people tried to make sense out of scribbled notes in a process called transcription. Dictaphones were the first technical device: a transcriptionist stepped repeatedly on a pedal to pour the professional's words into her head (they were generally women) and flush them out to typed words on a piece of paper. While this situation still exists today, another technology has emerged.

WebSphere Voice Server for Transcription allows multiple users to dictate audio text from various locations and devices such as microphones, hand-held recorders, and telephones. Transcription can convert recorded audio, using a user's personalized voice model, into standard text files. It uses the speech recognition component that was discussed in WebSphere Voice Server, but adds a level of sophistication because it can recognize particular user voices and associate them with information captured in the database.

In addition, the WebSphere Voice Server for Transcription can participate in a workflow application. Once the user dictates the information, it is sent to the transcription server to enable speech recognition as well as personal information. The text is then sent to the workflow management application. This application keeps the original audio, the transcribed text, and the edited text in a data store. Once the text file is generated, the workflow application sends the audio stream and text to a human to insure that proper edits have taken place. The result is stored in the workflow data store.

WebSphere Translation Server

Ever since the Tower of Babel, people have been searching for easy communication. (Sometimes it's difficult even when you both speak the same language.) While WebSphere Translation Server doesn't solve the communication problem totally, it is certainly a step in the right direction.

The WebSphere Translation Server translates Web pages, e-mail messages, and chat conversations to multiple languages in real time at a rate of 500 words per second. The supported languages include a bidirectional translation for American English to/from French, Italian, German, Spanish, Japanese and Chinese (traditional and simplified), as well as American English to Korean and American English to Brazilian Portuguese. (These last two are not bidirectional.) The product also allows you to define specific words and corporate terminology to expand on the basic language translation.

The WebSphere Translation Server consists of four parts that can be run on the same hardware platform (if run on a Windows NT or Windows 2000 system) or on different hardware platforms: User Dictionary

Manager (UDM), WebSphere Translation Server for Multiplatforms, Web server plug-ins or application filters, and language pair machine translation engines.

To insure maximum scalability, WebSphere Translation Server can run on a dedicated server using RMI and Java protocol to communicate with WebSphere Application Server, Lotus Domino, or Lotus Sametime applications. Web page HTML content can be translation-enabled to support HTTP servers from Netscape, Apache, Microsoft, or IBM.

Mobile Application Platforms

Pervasive computing means that computers are everywhere. Moving beyond the computer functions of our cell phone, pager, and those annoying computer chips in our car, we are moving into a world where the refrigerator in our home can send our grocery order to the store, or page us to let us know to pick up milk on the way home.

The pervasive computing environment means the need to access both personal and corporate information from a spectrum of devices, products that are intuitive, and network access that is invisible to the end user. These products are part of the WebSphere Everyplace Products.

WebSphere Everyplace Access

WebSphere Everyplace Access (see Figure 4.7) provides mobile employees with access to productivity data and enterprise applications from virtually anywhere, at any time. It supports multiple pervasive devices such as PDAs and smartphones from a single platform. It is an entry-level product for wireless application support. When you consider that close to 1.3 billion people worldwide will probably be plugged in to Web-capable phones by 2004, compared to just 700 million people with ordinary Net connections, the ability to port applications to wireless devices becomes essential.

Most enterprises have a variety of applications in their portfolio, including developed applications, purchased applications, software package mixes, e-mail applications, and personal information management (PIM) applications. WebSphere Everyplace Access bridges the gap between these types of applications and the wireless device. It does this by providing the following services:

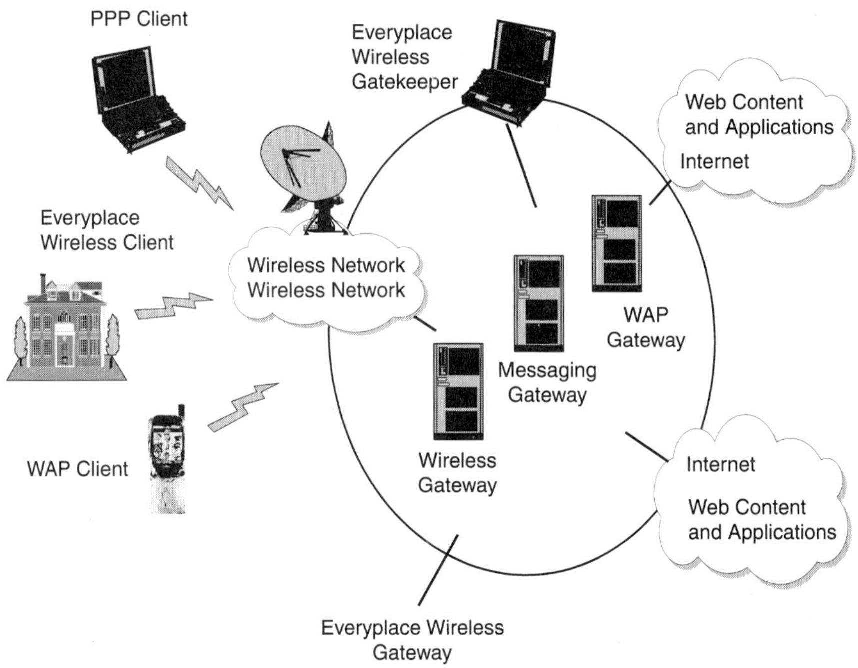

Figure 4.7. IBM Everyplace Wireless Gateway.

- Synchronization services that use open standard SyncML technology to support synchronization of e-mail, PIM applications, and business data between a mobile device and the server.

- Content adaption services using transcoding technology that supports content conversion to target device markup languages. These device markup languages include Wireless Markup Language (WML) from the WAP forum; compact HTML (cHTML), used primarily for iMode in Japan; and eXtended Hypertext Markup Language (XHTML), used on the Web and in Version 2 of WAP. Two aspects of content adaptation are:

  - Automated content conversion, which uses transcoding techniques to automatically determine the transformation needed for the target device and delivers it that way. This means that the content you see on your mobile screen actually fits on your mobile screen.

- Managed content conversion, which uses text clipping instructions created by the developer to do the adaption.

- Prepackaged portlet applications. (Portlets, a subclass of Java's HTTP Servlet class, are small Web applications typically seen as a box within a Web page or portal.)
- Offline Web content browsing that allows you to select the Web content that is sent to the device. The content can be refreshed as needed by the user.
- Common services such as user identification and authorization services, administration services, and customization services.

WebSphere Everyplace Access also contains the WebSphere Everyplace Toolkit, which is a plug-in to the WebSphere Studio Developer Device. The toolkit is built as a plug-in to extend the WebSphere Studio development environment to allow users to create new mobile applications or extend existing enterprise applications into the mobile environment. The tool includes portal and portlet integrated development environment (IDE) capabilities, content creation and adaptation, and sample applications.

WebSphere Everyplace Server, Service Provider Offering

WebSphere Everyplace Server, Service Provider Offering provides the infrastructure to connect, adapt, manage, transform, and scale existing Web applications and business data into pervasive applications. It provides security-rich and wireless connectivity from communications networks such as cellular networks (e.g., GSM, CDMA, TDMA, PDC, PHS, iDEN, AMPS), packet radio networks (e.g., GPRS, CDPD, DataTAC Mobilex), and satellite networks to the appropriate application servers. The gateway can also provide connectivity to the application server for Wireline environments including DSL (Digital Subscriber Lines), cable modem, Internet Service Provider (ISP), ISDN, Dial, and LAN networks.

Not only can the gateway receive information from the devices, it can also push information out to the devices. This is how you receive your stock quotes on your pager without having to issue a request for them.

The product can integrate with an existing gateway, or use the wireless gateway that includes a messaging gateway with Short Messaging Support (SMS) push proxy. A proxy server assumes the responsibility of retrieving Internet data for multiple browsers. Instead of going directly to the server with its request, the browser goes through the proxy server and the application server sees the address of the proxy server, not the original requester. In this process, the proxy server can be configured to keep pages in cache, thus making them available for any other browser that might need them.

In terms of performance, WebSphere Everyplace Server clients and gateway provide wireless performance optimization for standard IP communications. WebSphere Everyplace Connection Manager also provides optimization by the use of compression of the IP packet to speed transmission, reduction of the TCP header size, and reduction in the number of retransmissions allowed—particularly important when there is high traffic over a link. Short hold mode, another component of the gateway, allows retention of a logical link, but lets go of a physical link, thereby reducing air traffic.

WebSphere Transcoding Publisher (described later) is used for content adaption, as are WebSphere MQSeries Everyplace (described later), Lotus Domino Everyplace, and IBM Everyplace Synchronization Manager. This last piece of software enables pervasive devices to operate applications "offline" and synchronize the results of their activities with the server when connection is reestablished. The nice part about this manager is that it can synchronize any relational database directly with an ODBC database without the need to synchronize via a PC. It also allows direct synchronization between Lotus Notes and Microsoft Exchange servers; Palm OS or Microsoft Windows CE and Symbian EPOC devices; and synchronization to almost any ODBC-compliant database, such as DB2 Everyplace. The product also integrates the capabilities of WebSphere Voice Server (described earlier).

Security with WebSphere Everyplace Server depends on concepts of logon IDs and password identification, although these aren't necessarily typed in by a human—they can also be encoded in the device. WebSphere Everyplace Server security also depends on digital certificates, a concept that will be explained in more depth in Chapter 6. Briefly, a digital certificate contains information about the device that is registered with a group that is a trusted authority. It guarantees that the device is who it says it is and the server it is accessing is who it says it is. It does this through using public and private keys that allow both parties to encrypt and decrypt transmitted messages.

Windows and Windows CE security for clients is provided by bidirectional authentication with key distribution in a protocol called Two-Party Key Distribution Protocol (2PKDP). PPP (Point-to-Point Protocol) clients use password authentication protocol (PAP) or challenge-handshake authentication protocol (CHAP) user identification and password authentication. In addition, WebSphere Everyplace Server, Server Provider Offering provides support for Tivoli Access Manager.

Management services are done by Tivoli Personalized Service Manager. The product provides a central LDAP directory that contains runtime information about active sessions, users, devices, and networks. Everyplace Suite Manager allows an administrator to register users and devices, define logging and tracing controls, etc.

WebSphere Everyplace Suite contains the components that are required to extend e-business to pervasive devices, providing connectivity, performance optimization, security, and management services for these types of applications. If you will, they provide the presentation layer of the application to these devices.

WebSphere Everyplace Suite Embedded Edition

WebSphere Everyplace Suite Embedded Edition integrates essential software for device manufacturers, developers, and service providers. It's designed to provide the device-side "client" for WebSphere Everyplace Server, Service Provider Offering (described earlier). WebSphere Everyplace Suite Embedded Edition provides the software to interact and manage information coming from all the chips that exist in the various devices and allows them to "talk" to back-end systems that can pass along the information to whoever (or whatever) needs it and reply back to the chip.

Take, for example, the organic milk you bought yesterday. Imagine that the container has a "chip" that will measure the level of the milk that goes down and send off a message when it gets to a half-full point. That message triggers a delivery of milk to your house. WebSphere Everyplace Suite Embedded Edition helps make this happen.

The product contains an open standards-compliant real-time operating system (RTOS) such as QNX Neutrino. These types of operating systems support multiple hardware platforms, allowing the user to port the developed product almost anywhere. WebSphere Everyplace Suite Embedded Edition has software to manage input from a large number and variety of network-connected devices (imagine all that organic milk!) within a secure environment. (You don't want just anyone's milk.)

To develop the milk application, the product provides the IBM Service Management Framework (SMF), a standards-based architecture that is designed to be compliant with specifications developed by the Open Services Gateway Initiative (OSGi). SMF provides the lifecycle management of network delivered applications. The product also comes with a copy of WebSphere Studio Device Developer (described earlier).

To receive information from the "chip," the product includes an HTTP Server/Proxy, DNS (Domain Name Service), and SSL, that can be tuned to user specifications. IBM ViaVoice Embedded for Multiplatforms is included as well. This product supports a variety of RTOSs and microprocessors, allowing the development of "talking" software. So, instead of the embedded chip making the request for more milk, you can leave a message from your cell phone to get more milk delivered.

WebSphere Everyplace Connection Managers

WebSphere Everyplace Connection Manager[1] is a communications platform that supports secure data access for WAP and non-WAP clients. It can integrate data from wireless as well as wired networks for mobile users. The components that make up this product are Everyplace Wireless Gatekeeper and Everyplace Wireless Client (see Figure 4.7).

The Everyplace Wireless Gatekeeper serves as the Java-based administration console. This allows you to define and configure wireless gateways, register users and mobile devices, and perform other routine administrative tasks. The generated data is stored in an LDAP directory.

The client software runs locally on the mobile devices to provide a full function interface to the gatekeeper. Once the mobile device is authenticated to the gateway, you can assign an intranet or Internet IP address to it. IP applications can run on a wireless network using the standard TCP/IP provided by the operating system on the mobile device. WebSphere Everyplace Connection Manager (WECM) then supports standard IP routing through an encrypted tunnel, even over non-IP wireless bearer networks. This helps greatly to insure unbroken, end-to-end TCP sessions between mobile devices and application servers, providing greater data integrity and application availability. WECM supports applications using sockets programming interfaces.

The gateway software serves as a translator for the mobile language to the server language. For example, it supports WAP Wireless Session Protocol (WSP) to link cellular phones and PDAs to your application. As a WAP gateway, it receives messages from WAP clients, translates the WSP into HTTP requests, and then forwards them to an HTTP proxy. The gateway handles traffic going in the reverse order as well—translating HTTP into WSP and forwarding it to the WAP client.

Alternatively, you can configure the WebSphere Everyplace Connection Manager to be a messaging gateway. In this case, the Web application server sends messages to a mobile client, such as a pager or a phone. It supports several types of messaging modes, including SMS, e-mail, and SNPP.

To adapt to the reliability, availability, and scalability required of today's 24×7 applications, the gateway can be a principal or subordinate node in a cluster of wireless gateways. This allows load balancing and failover support.

WebSphere Everyplace Subscription Manager

WebSphere Everyplace Subscription Manager replaces Tivoli Internet Services Manager. The product creates and manages service offerings for multiple service providers. For each hosted provider, WESM contains the necessary functions and features to enroll, authenticate, service, and support up to 20 million subscribers.

WESM provides services over broadband using Point-to-Point Protocol over Ethernet (PPPoE) or dial-up access. Subscribers to the service can choose their own ISPs and can subscribe to multiple service offerings, either as individual services or as part of predefined bundles. The subscriber can do this either over the Web or by calling into a customer service representative.

The product also supplies support for network storage services, SoHo Web hosting, and other services, such as on-demand video.

Virtual service provider support for wholesale business models is included, providing customizable interfaces and data elements to support virtual ISP/wholesale business models. Every significant event in WESM can generate a provisioning transaction, which can help insure that external systems are synchronized with the WESM database.

In order to provide authentication of inbound dialers, WESM includes Remote Authentication Dial-In User Service (RADIUS) with two-way proxy capability and user definable authentication exits.

One of the advantages of standardization and open systems initiatives is that you can integrate many products together, allowing you to mix and match to achieve the result that you want. WESM integrates with several products, allowing you to support the many subscribers to your (hopefully) successful business. It can integrate with Portal Intranet billing and CyberSource credit card authorization, LDAP, Tivoli Access Manager, and WebSphere Portal (described earlier), as well as provide flexible programming toolkits so you can integrate with your existing systems and processes.

WebSphere Transcoding Publisher

Wireless connections include new formats for transmission and display, new operating systems, new markup languages, and, of course, new devices. The majority of Web content today is in HTML format and to some degree XML. However, the pervasive devices require different markup languages. The purpose of WebSphere Transcoding Publisher is to adapt, reformat, and filter content to make it suited for pervasive computing.

WebSphere Transcoding Publisher consists of several interrelated components that provide a platform to adapt Web data to a pervasive computing environment. This enables you to take content that you have developed for existing Web applications, particularly images, and reuse them for other devices. For example, an image of your company logo that sits on your Web site can be easily copied for reproduction on a cell phone screen.

The primary components of WebSphere Transcoding Publisher (Figure 4.8) include a set of standard content transformers as well as a pluggable infrastructure that lets you integrate new transcoders for the constant parade of newly invented devices. An administration console provides the ability to add, enable, and change transcoders and other objects.

Finally, there's a developer's toolkit to help you add or build custom transcoding solutions. The application server plug-in adapter is provided by WebSphere Application Server (described earlier), and the EdgeServer plug-in adapter is provided by WebSphere Edge Server (described later).

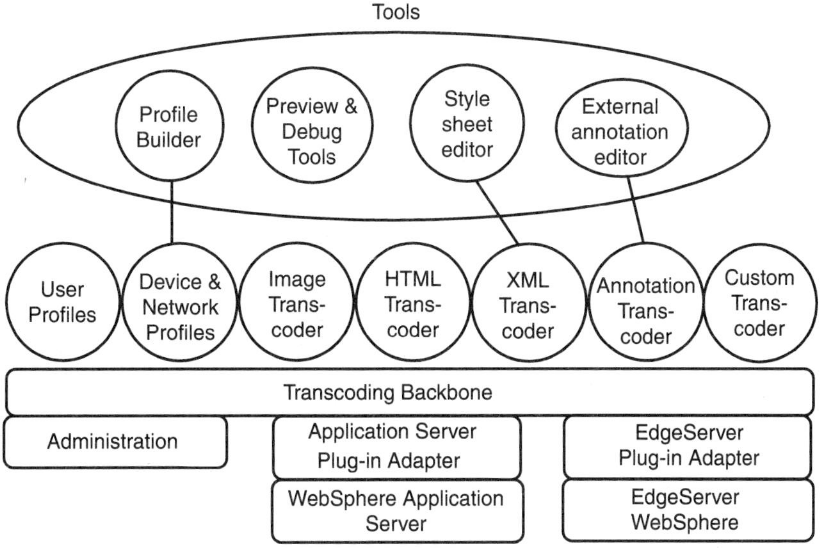

Figure 4.8. WebSphere Transcoding Publisher Components.

Existing HTML- and XML-based content can be translated by bridging several markup languages with standard text transcoders.

As many of us have already discovered, moving data across networks, or even the air waves, can be the most time-consuming portion of an application. In order to circumvent this problem, WebSphere Transcoding Publisher streamlines content before it is sent across the network. This allows the device to receive the information efficiently. Some of the techniques that WebSphere Transcoding Publisher uses are converting HTML to simplified HTML, images to links to retrieve images, and simple tables to bulleted lists. The reason to use simplified HTML is fairly self-evident. The fewer tags you have describing the content, the quicker the information can be transmitted and displayed. Given the size of the screen of cell phones, the amount of gee-whiz features you need is limited. Rather than displaying an image automatically, WebSphere Transcoding Publisher can provide a link so that the user can download the image or not. A table similar to one that you would develop using a spreadsheet tool also doesn't make sense on a cell phone screen. WebSphere Transcoding Publisher deconstructs the table and creates bulleted lists that are much more suitable for a small screen. The beauty of this technology is that it is already built into the WebSphere Transcoding Publisher software and doesn't have to be developed by the company.

WebSphere Transcoding Publisher removes features, such as JavaScript or applets of Shockware files, that cannot be handled by the device. If images are required, WebSphere Transcoding Publisher can convert, reduce, or eliminate images to match display capabilities and optimize delivery to constrained devices. Smaller image files are faster to send over wireless networks. These smaller files render more quickly on small-screen devices, particularly gray-scale devices.

Before downloading data to the device, the WebSphere Transcoding Publisher deck fragmentation transcoder dynamically subdivides content into smaller pieces. This allows complex Web content to be altered to match the physical constraints of Internet-enabled phones. The deck fragmentation is available for WML, HDML, and iMode languages.

Content can be delivered to the device through annotation or text clipping. Annotation is the ability to put comments on the original page that contain instructions for selecting and tailoring content. It is done through an XML-compliant annotation language rather than programming. Text clipping is the ability to extract (clip) specific content to be delivered. It requires some Java programming to tailor content.

WebSphere Transcoding Publisher includes a standard set of device and network profiles containing configuration and capability information for the networks or devices. Devices can include PDAs, RIM BlackBerry Pagers, WAP-enabled phones, and HDML-based phones, used in North America, as well as iMode phones, used in Japan. WebSphere Transcoding Publisher also contains transformation capabilities for voice-only phones. When processing Web content, WebSphere Transcoding Publisher dynamically selects a network profile and a device profile to apply to the document.

Deployment of WebSphere Transcoding Publisher content can be done in several ways, providing increased flexibility—for example, standalone proxy server, caching proxy, reverse proxy, WebSphere Application Server servlet, or JavaBeans can be used for deployment. As part of its standard implementation, WebSphere Transcoding Publisher uses an LDAP directory to store monitoring and management configuration information. Multiple WebSphere Transcoding Publisher servers can share this directory.

WebSphere Custom Environment

Do you own a "smart car?" A smart car can transmit its location and trouble to its home base. But how does a smart car become smart? It does so by the use of miniature computers and transmission systems under your dashboard. These types of applications need a specialized runtime environment. Enter WebSphere Custom Environment.

WebSphere Custom Environment is a complete runtime environment for the deployment of embedded applications to real-time control systems, and automotive telematics systems. This runtime environment supports the tiniest of virtual machine environments: IBM J9 Virtual Machine. J9 has been optimized for each of its supported reference platforms—critical when every byte of memory is tracked and the need for application performance is required.

This environment includes a full set of class libraries (Xtreme, Core, Gateway, and Max) to provide maximum flexibility without sacrificing the small footprint essential to these types of applications. Designers can use SmartLinker technology to eliminate up to 30% of unneeded classes, methods, and fields from the application and runtime class libraries.

Through IBM and business partners, WebSphere Custom Environment is available on over 35 reference platform implementations such as QNX, Hard Hat Linux, OSE, ITRON, PocketPC, and Palm OS.

WebSphere Custom Environment is the follow-on product to the Custom Class Libraries shipped with VisualAge Micro Edition. It is built on the Eclipse open platform described earlier, and the functions are available through WebSphere Studio Device Developer.

WebSphere Micro Environment

WebSphere Micro Environment is an extension of the WebSphere Software Platform to cellular telephones, PDAs, and hand-held computers. It is designed for developers and engineers who require a J2ME "Java-powered" platform on which to host multiple applications. It can be integrated to take advantage of messaging (MQe) and database (DB2 Everyplace).

The product contains a production-ready Java-powered runtime environment. This environment has been tested and certified to meet J2ME specifications as laid out by the Java Community Process.

WebSphere Business Integration

Business integration has been a goal for close to a decade, ever since the phrase "business reengineering" was coined. The fact that it is still a goal speaks to its importance to business and the fact that it is more difficult to do than to say. Business integration provides the ability to integrate data, applications, processes, and people. Companies that have a high degree of business integration interact with people and groups more easily than their competitors do. This includes the ability to collaborate with supply chain partners, leverage intelligence within and without the company walls, and enhance customer relationship management.

The third portion of the WebSphere Software Platform is WebSphere Business Integration, a series of products and methods designed to help customers get closer to the goal of business integration. These products allow you to leverage capital investments by integrating your current applications instead of installing all new ones.

Process Integration

Business integration requires a Business Process Management (BPM) solution (Figure 4.9) to be effective. This solution is a collection of instruments that allows you to model your enterprise business processes, cost them, simulate the processes, and deploy them. IBM uses three main products to accomplish this process: WebSphere MQSeries Workflow, IBM Crossroads, and Holosofx BPM (Business Process Management) Suite.

Separating business process logic from business process implementation provides process independence, just as separating logical data modeling from physical data implementation provided data independence. Business process logic defines what needs to be done, when, and why, and how it is done, by whom or by which application.

Process and workflow management integrates and manages high-level business processes that involve many people and applications across functional areas. WebSphere MQ Workflow provides capabilities to design, document, execute, control, improve, and optimize business processes. Holosofx enables you to rapidly define and model business processes as well as execute processes across people, departments, and

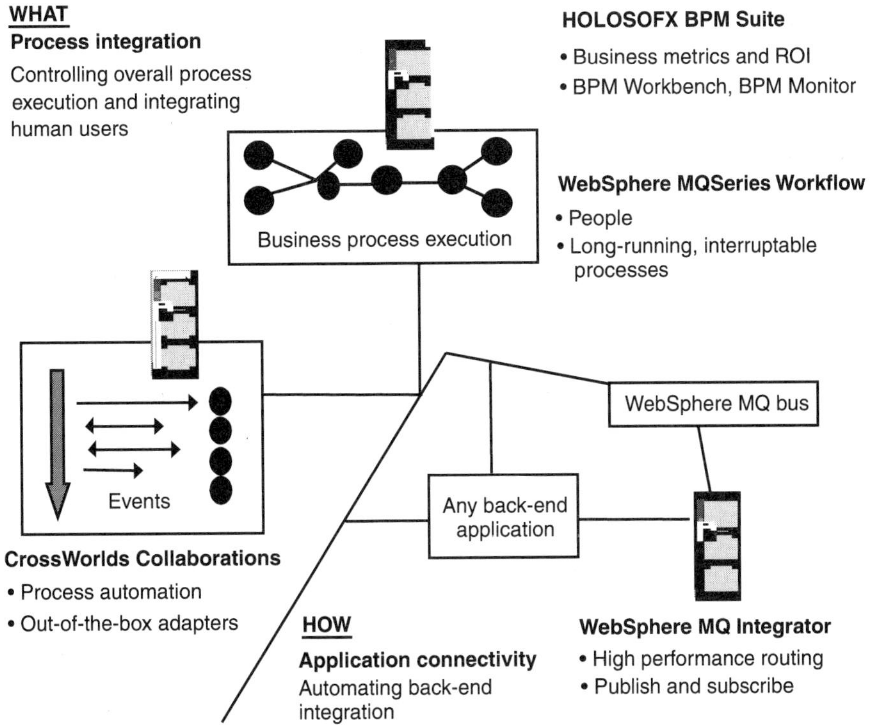

Figure 4.9. Business Process Management.

systems. Process automation helps automate distinct steps within a broader enterprise process. IBM CrossWorlds provides business object management and process automation capabilities, allowing you to quickly automate process steps. The integration of the three provides business process management.

Holosofx BPM Workbench will help define, simulate, and analyze business processes. These process definitions can be deployed to WebSphere MQSeries Workflow for automation. Holosofx BPM monitor gives you the ability to do real-time monitoring and iterative analysis of business process execution. BPM solution implementation will tell you which back-end systems need to be integrated into the whole in order to fulfill the business process you are modeling. The integration can be achieved through WebSphere MQ software or IBM CrossWorlds.

WebSphere MQSeries Workflow

WebSphere MQSeries Workflow is the process engine at the core of IBM's BPM solutions. The challenge of storing structured data has been solved with the advent of DB2 Universal Database and other relational databases. The challenge of storing unstructured data is being solved with products such as DB2 Content Manager. The next great challenge is the storage and automated use of complex business rules. One solution to this challenge has been the development of workflow management systems.

Workflow management systems are based on a set of user-defined business rules that state what happens in particular situations, primarily exceptions to the normal process. For example, in order to streamline loan applications, banks run the application through a series of criteria to see if it meets certain standards. Clear-cut cases are either accepted or denied based on these criteria. Cases with exceptions such as missing information, close to the edges of criteria, etc., would be handed to the workflow management system. Based on the type of exception, the system would send the application to the correct employee for resolution.

A group of companies, including IBM, are working together to develop specifications to allow different companies' workflow products to interoperate with each other. This group is called the Workflow Management Coalition (WfMC), and it has developed a reference model for these specifications. WebSphere MQSeries Workflow is a workflow management product that uses this reference model.

WebSphere MQSeries Workflow has the ability to capture and use knowledge about business processes to help define, document, test, control, execute, improve, and integrate business processes. It uses WebSphere MQSeries Messaging (described later) to deliver information and DB2 Universal Database for its data store. It can also send MQSeries messages using the MQSeries Integrator (described later).

Business processes can be defined to WebSphere MQSeries Workflow via a graphical editor with icons representing business processes and data. Connectors can join activities. These connectors can be data connections (where does the data come from or go to) or control connections (what is the next step in the process). Once the processes are defined, WebSphere MQSeries Workflow then generates Flow Definition Language (FDL), which is translated for execution by the runtime server. At execution time the runtime server distributes the activities to the clients of the designated persons or groups. The server provides information about the applications to be invoked and about relevant operational data.

APIs to support customized clients are provided in several programming languages such as C, C++, and VisualBasic. Workflow solutions for any Web browser can be created by using Java and JavaBean APIs. For OS/390, a native integration of CICS/IMS transactions is available.

IBM CrossWorlds

IBM purchased CrossWorlds in 2001. The product family consists of the IBM CrossWorlds InterChange Server, numerous application and technology connectors, pre-built collaborations composed of generalized business objects, and a collection of development and monitoring tools. This group of products allows you to reengineer your business products and select from a variety of components to easily automate and maintain this system. Because of the modularity and connector functions, reengineered systems can be plugged into existing architectures or matched with application packages such as Siebel and SAP.

IBM CrossWorlds InterChange Server is a process automation server for managing several discrete business applications as if they were one. Similar to a runtime server, it provides multithreaded and concurrent business logic execution with assurance of data integrity. The user has the ability to manage the system and configuration from one central location.

IBM CrossWorlds Connectors help customers integrate their businesses by accessing and exchanging information between different applications and data sources that support business processes. They come in several different flavors.

Application Connectors extend one or more of your group's applications to other divisions within your company or to trading partners over the Internet. There are connectors for BroadVision, Clarify, i2 Active Data Warehouse, MetaSolv TBS, Oracle, PeopleSoft 7, PeopleSoft 8, Portal Intranet, SAP R/3, Siebel, and Vantive. Many of these provide real-time, bidirectional integration from these packaged applications to your legacy data.

Connectors for e-business streamline your processes across functional boundaries within the company or across the Internet. There are e-business connectors for Web Services, EDI (Electronic Data Interchange) data, XML data, Access Framework, Access Framework for Enterprise Java

Beans, J2EE for CrossRoads InterChange Server, and trading profiles. There are also serverless connectors for e-business.

Mainframe connectors are exactly that—connections to mainframe software products such as ADABAS, CICS, DB2 Universal Database, IMS, and VSAM. In addition, there are technology connectors that provide a way to automate mainframe business processes. These connectors interface with e-mail, FIX messages, JDBC, JMS, Jtext, WebSphere MQ, WebSphere MQ Workflow, SWIFT's FIN network, and XML.

IBM CrossWorlds Collaborations provide pre-built solutions for business process automation. This allows you to graphically define end-to-end business processes that make sense for your business. Integration and business rules can be encapsulated to provide consistent enforcement of these essential business components. The collaborations are available for several businesses: automotive, electronics, insurance, retail, telecommunications and general e-business.

Holosofx Business Process Management Suite

The Holosofx Business Process Management (BPM) Suite helps define, integrate, automate, monitor, and administer business processes. The products are built on a component-based architecture using Java, XML, and other standards-based technologies. The suite provides three components—Workbench, Monitor, and Server—as well as the ability to monitor business process execution using WebSphere MQ Workflow.

Holosofx BPM Workbench lets you visually specify business process models using the properties of process activities, their costs, their timings, their data, the applications to be used, and work assignment rules for staff, if required. After process definition, the simulation engine indicates how the process might meet your business goals in a production environment. You can use the workbench to play "what if" and come up with the solution that meets your needs. These definitions can be registered with WebSphere MQSeries Workflow.

On the other end of the process, Holosofx BPM Monitor uses the WebSphere MQ Workflow to track the triggered transactions as well as the resources required to complete the process. This allows you to understand which activities have been completed and which haven't. Then you can further optimize your business processes, identifying bottlenecks and improving productivity.

Holosofx BPM Server provides repository management and Web publishing capabilities. This allows you to collaborate on business design and provides instant Web access to business process models, policies and procedures, and business rules.

Application Integration

IBM has rebranded IBM MQSeries to make it part of the WebSphere family. The function of the products hasn't changed, however. This set of products is designed to connect applications and systems to improve the flow of information without human involvement. These links need to be flexible enough to accommodate the inevitable changes to systems.

There are six major product areas under the application integration umbrella: WebSphere MQ, WebSphere MQ Everyplace, WebSphere MQ Integration Broker, WebSphere MQ Event Broker, WebSphere Data Interchange, and WebSphere connectors and adaptors.

WebSphere MQ (formerly MQSeries Messaging)

WebSphere MQ (MQ stands for Message Queue) was announced in 1993 during initial client/server development for many companies. It is part of a generic group of software called Message Oriented Middleware (MOM). Because of the security of its services and ease of development, MQ was rapidly adopted, to the point that three out of four customers who buy inter-application messaging systems buy WebSphere MQ—including one company that uses it to transmit over 250 million messages per day. More than two-thirds of the top 100 North American and European banks use WebSphere MQ, and over 10,000 customer sites use the product.

Conceptually, WebSphere MQ takes a piece of information, or message, encapsulates it in a secure wrapper, and sends it to its destination, ensuring one-time delivery in spite of any network disruptions that may occur. WebSphere MQ does this by handling the communication from one program to another using APIs. These APIs can communicate across different operating systems and networks.

The structure of WebSphere MQ is based on an object-oriented philosophy, but is not a pure object-oriented technology. Messages and other components of the product are referred to as objects, but the processes that act on these objects can be done with a procedural or object interface. These are the two essential pieces to WebSphere MQ—the message and the process that manages the message.

If you have ever been to Great Britain and waited for a bus, you know what a queue is! "Waiting" in British English is queuing and the line you are standing in is a queue. Since the development site of WebSphere MQ is in England, this language has been adopted for the product. Think of WebSphere MQ as a message queue, one message at a time waiting its turn to go through the queue. Just as new people come to the end of the queue to get on the next bus, new messages arrive all the time at the end of the message queue to get on the next delivery.

The Queue Manager component dispatches the buses to pick up the messages. It polls for messages from either a client or server environment. When it finds a message for delivery, it arranges for the safe delivery of that message to its target—WebSphere MQ. Setup for WebSphere MQ requires at least one Queue Manager per instance (copy) of MQ. Each Queue Manager can communicate with Queue Managers from other instances to insure all passengers get where they are going—just as a bus dispatcher can communicate to bus dispatchers in other towns to insure people get to where they need to go.

Multiple queues can be set up for a WebSphere MQ application. In the simplest setup, there is one queue and one Queue Manager on a server. The programs putting messages on the queue are on the same server and connected to the same Queue Manager. In Figure 4.10, Program A puts a message on the queue using a command called MQPUT. Program B gets the message using MQGET. If only the world were this simple.

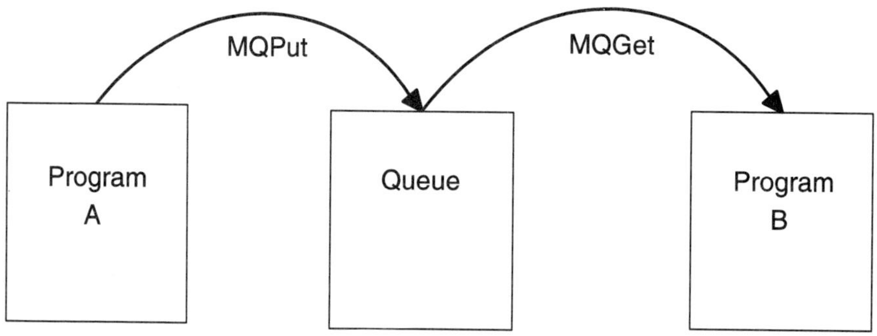

Figure 4.10. WebSphere MQ on a single server.

In Figure 4.11 Programs A and B are on different servers, connected to different Queue Managers. For message distribution to take place there must be communication between the two Queue Managers. This is accomplished via a communication channel between the two Queue Managers. Communication through this channel is done—you guessed it—by use of a queue. In this case it is called a transmission queue.

The Queue Manager is in charge of WebSphere MQ resources such as queues, channels, listeners, etc. It insures that changes to WebSphere MQ objects such as queues are logged and images of persistent messages are kept. (Types of messages are described later in this section.) This type of tracking can be done at the individual message level, or messages can be grouped to form a unit of work. WebSphere MQ calls this grouping transactional messaging. Transactional messaging can be coordinated with other types of transactional work such as database updates, insuring data integrity across system components.

Security is important when sending messages and WebSphere MQ can handle security on a number of different levels. For example, a restriction can be placed on who can create queues and managers. To insure that messages securely make it from one Queue Manager to another, security can be added to exit points on the channel connection between servers for encryption and other security checking. A WebSphere MQ component called the Message Queuing Interface (MQI) provides facilities for applications to identify themselves to the Queue Manager

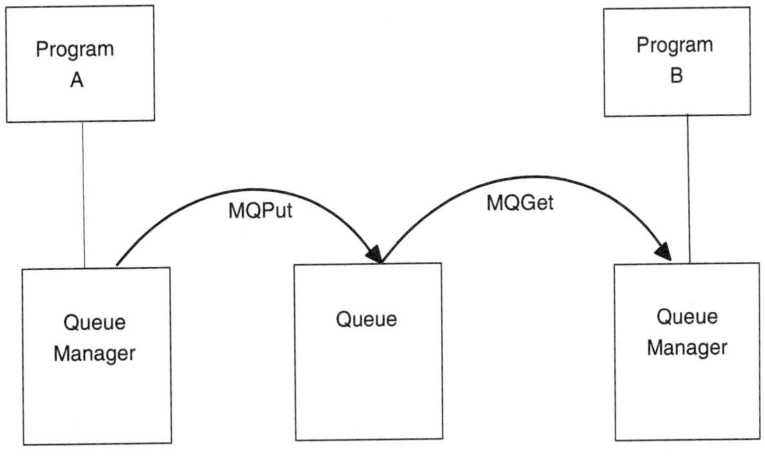

Figure 4.11. WebSphere MQ on multiple servers.

to insure that messages are only retrieved by the programs that are meant to receive them. On z/OS security can be linked to an external security manager such as RACF.

With the latest release of WebSphere MQ on all platforms, Queue Manager Clusters were introduced. Clusters are named collections of Queue Managers that provide dynamic workload distribution, public queue support, simplified channel and queue definitions, and automatic hot backup across WebSphere MQ networks, allowing the user to create multiple copies of the same queue with more than one Queue Manager, each of which can be on a separate machine. Each separate Queue Manager can see all the different queues available on the system. The Queue Managers communicate with each other to insure that the workload is balanced and throughput is maximized. Since this is done internally, the WebSphere MQ Messaging administrator actually has less work to do than if he or she were trying to handle a distributed system set up for workload balancing.

The second process that WebSphere MQ handles is done via the application. The application programmer works with one of three application programming interfaces: MQIs, Application Messaging Interface (AMI), or JMS. MQI is the original programming interface and was developed on a procedure-based architecture. It is the most complete and complex API. AMI is easier to use because it is more abstract in nature than MQI, but it provides less flexibility because not all features available through MQI are available in AMI. JMS provides functionality similar to that of MQI but is based on an object-oriented rather than a procedural interface.

The MQI and JMS interfaces can perform several tasks:

- Establish connection with a Queue Manager
- Open a WebSphere MQSeries object
- Put and get messages
- Set properties for the WebSphere MQ object
- Inquire about a WebSphere MQ object's properties
- Close a WebSphere MQ object

- Disconnect from the Queue Manager
- Establish unit-of-work boundaries that include WebSphere transactions and possibly other object transactions, such as database transactions.

The AMI interface does these same processes, but it considers them from a different viewpoint. The programmer generally only has to deal with three concepts:

- The message
- How the message is to be handled (the policy)
- Where the message is going to or coming from (the service).

WebSphere MQ Everyplace (formerly MQSeries Everyplace)

WebSphere MQ Everyplace is a small-footprint version of WebSphere MQ that supports pervasive devices such as PDAs, laptops, phones, or any other unattended device. It extends the original MQSeries Messaging to include the ability to create and send messages from all types of new networked appliances. WebSphere MQ Everyplace offers a choice of languages, APIs, and environments including Java, C, JMS, and J2ME. These devices communicate with a PC-based gateway on Windows platforms, Linux, HP-UX, AIX, or SUN Solaris. The gateway then handles the communication to any other WebSphere MQ Messaging application in the same manner described previously.

WebSphere MQ Event Broker

Web Services imply a publish and subscribe model described in Chapter 1. WebSphere MQ Event Broker allows businesses to publish information to specific subscribers. The product delivers real-time, personalized information across an internal network, the Internet, or pervasive devices. Integrated with WebSphere MQ, MQSeries Everyplace, Telemetry Integration, and IP transports, WebSphere MQ Event Broker provides a class service based on the content of the message. The underlying structure that supports this model is based on an event model. Event models provide an extension of the IF-THEN-ELSE construct. The graphical development environment helps you to visualize information flows.

WebSphere MQ Integrator Broker (formerly MQSeries Integrator)

The purpose of WebSphere MQ Integrator Broker is to help you process messages while they are on their way to their destination. Thus, WebSphere MQ Integrator Broker functions as a Message Broker, processing, transforming, and distributing messages. If you will recall our discussion of WebSphere MQ in a complex environment, Program A and Program B were on separate servers with separate Queue Managers. Communication between the two took place on a queue between the two Queue Managers. Imagine the complexity that evolves if every server needs to be connected with every other server just on the chance that they may need to talk with each other. WebSphere MQ Integrator Broker provides a hub that can be connected to any WebSphere MQ at any location, thereby facilitating the transmission.

After a message gets to the hub, if its instructions indicate, it can be transformed by WebSphere MQ Integrator Broker functions. The chief function, if you will, is the message broker function. This function calls nodes that perform required functions, can access data outside the message if necessary, and can even add an additional message to a message queue. These nodes can be linked together by connectors to create a complete workflow upon receipt of a message.

WebSphere Data Interchange

As discussed in Chapter 1, EDI was the original method used to communicate data between companies. In order to update these processes to XML, Web services, and other e-business formats, massive human intervention was required. WebSphere Data Interchange provides a method of making the transference without requiring human intervention. The product integrates EDI into the WebSphere business process, messaging, and Internet-based B2B capabilities. It supports optimized "any-to-any" transformation of EDI, XML, and record-oriented application data formats to a WebSphere implementation. To insure data integrity, there is a standards-compliant function to support transformation to industry-leading formats such as HIPAA, ANSI X12, and embedded HL7. XML DTDs (Document Type Definitions), either industry- or user-defined, can be used for mapping and translation. Like the other WebSphere products, transformations can be developed using a GUI screen.

WebSphere Business Integration Adapters

In addition to the CrossWorlds adapters discussed earlier, WebSphere provides products that allow you to create integrated processes that exchange information between ERP, HR (Human Resources), CRM, and SCM systems. These come in several flavors:

- WebSphere Business Integration Adapter Development Kit is an integrated-development toolkit that provides the framework for development of custom adapters. The kit provides programming interfaces in both Java and C++. These interfaces can then be used to standardize metadata exchange with WebSphere MQ Integration Broker and to exchange runtime data with the broker.

- WebSphere Business Integration Application Adapters extract data and transaction information from packaged applications, allowing access via APIs where possible. The adapters include interfaces to BroadVision Commerce, Clarify CRM, i2 Active Data Warehouse, MetaSolv TBS, mySAP.com, Nightfire, Oracle, PeopleSoft, Portal Intranet, Siebel e-business, Vantive, and WebSphere Commerce.

- WebSphere e-business Adapters securely connect over the firewall to customers' desktops, trading partners' internal applications, and online marketplaces and exchanges. These adapters include e-mail, JCA Connection to ICS (Internet Connection Sharing), JMS, Web Services, EDI, XML, TPI Solo, and TPI Trading Networks.

- Mainframe Adapters allow you to access application data in OS/390 and z/OS systems as well as provide connectivity approaches to AS/400. These adapters include ADABAS, CICS, DB2 Universal Database, IMS, and VSAM.

- WebSphere Business Integration Technology Adapters provide the ability to access other types of information and technologies that you need to complete your e-business system. These adapters include FIX Protocol, JDBC, Jtext, WebSphere MQ, WebSphere MQ Integrator, WebSphere MQ Workflow, SWIFT, and XML.

WebSphere Foundation and Tools

Over the past forty years, billions of dollars have been spent to develop business systems, using many of the technologies discussed in Chapter 2. The challenge of the past decade has been to integrate these existing (or legacy) systems into an e-business application as simply as possible. The people expense in changing systems is higher than the software or hardware costs, assuming you can still find people who can code in these languages.

WebSphere Foundation and Tools provides a mechanism to leverage these investments and still move forward into the e-business era.

Enterprise Modernization

Enterprise Modernization offers tools and services to update your existing systems and leverage the applications by transforming them into e-business components, which can then be built into a new integration-ready e-business solution. These products allow for rapid development and increased communication between disparate systems, enabling skills development as a by-product.

In addition to the products described below, Enterprise Modernization includes the WebSphere Studio Enterprise Developer and WebSphere Asset Analyzer described earlier. It also contains WebSphere Studio Developer for iSeries, part of the WebSphere Studio Product Family described earlier.

WebSphere Host Integration

WebSphere Host Integration Solution is yet another way to "e-" your legacy applications. The solution fits in between your legacy host applications and the Web application server, providing external services, enabling you to accomplish tasks such as giving your host applications a

Web look and feel without programming or integrating multiple legacy applications into a single Web page without requiring any changes to the existing applications themselves. This solution can be used both for applications that are internal to your organization and for applications that reach beyond the firewall to your customers, suppliers, and partners.

WebSphere Host Integration Solution works with WebSphere Application Server and WebSphere Studio to create and deploy applications that access the host. WebSphere Studio provides the ability to develop applications, WebSphere Application Server provides the runtime environment, and WebSphere Host Integration Solution provides the ability to deploy dynamic host content using Java servlets, JSPs, XML, or EJB components. This product also works with WebSphere Transcoding Publisher to enable the delivery of host data to client devices such as cell phones or PDAs.

This solution is really a group of software communication clients and servers that work together to provide integration of your legacy system into your e-business application by extending the reach of SNA and TCP/IP networks. These components include:

- WebSphere Host On-Demand
- WebSphere Host Publisher
- Personal Communications
- Screen Customizer
- Communications Server
- WebSphere Application Server
- WebSphere Studio
- WebSphere Transcoding Publisher.

In terms of security, WebSphere Host Integration Solution supports SSL authentication and encryption and also uses host security systems such as RACF. Support for a digital certificate is included in the WebSphere Host On-Demand component. As with other WebSphere solutions, WebSphere Host On-Demand can integrate with Tivoli SecureWay to take advantage of PKI methods.

Using the IBM Communications Server, you can build a VPN to connect remote users and business partners. A VPN extends your enterprise's private intranet across a public network, such as the Internet, using a secure connection known as an encrypted tunnel.

All of the WebSphere Host Integration Solution products contain a comprehensive set of APIs, including Host Access Class Libraries (HACLs). HACLs provide access to 3270, 5250, and VT data streams. The solution also provides the ability to develop Host Access Beans for Java. These beans can be used to access information on the host and reused in other WebSphere Software Platform components as your e-business changes. HACLs, Host Access Beans for Java, and ActiveX, as well as other host integration programming technologies, can be used to deliver dynamic host content using Java servlets, JSPs, XML, and EJB components.

CICS Transaction Gateway

CICS was one of the legacy transaction management systems described in Chapter 2. CICS Transaction Gateway is part of the software portfolio that IBM has developed to leverage existing applications that are integral to the running of your business. This product is IBM's strategic connector for connection to CICS, supporting J2EE for connectivity between the WebSphere Software Platform and existing CICS applications. The product includes the ability to authenticate and authorize users and processes for a secure environment. The application provides implementation of the J2EE Connector Architecture on all supported platforms and allows two-phase commit with WebSphere for z/OS and OS/390.

Transaction Processing

Transaction managers handle the start, running, and completion of transactions for many concurrent users. The development and use of these managers is described in Chapter 2.

CICS Transaction Server

Similar to older IBM software products such as DB2 Universal Database and IMS, CICS has maintained its development to insure its viability as an e-business component. To maintain accessibility to modern programming methods like Java, CICS supports Java SDK and supports the J2EE Enterprise JavaBeans programming model for session beans. Applications that use CICS can be written in COBOL, PL/I, C, C++ and other languages, which strengthens application development capability, allowing reuse of 3270 (green screen) applications. Applications can also manipulate XML directly from CICS.

CICS has improved its exploitation of TCP/IP services, supporting external call interface (ECI) over TCP/IP and support for the VTAM LU (Logical Unit) alias facility.

Applications that support e-business have to be available 24 hours a day, seven days a week. Systems that were built prior to the e-business need to be upgraded to be able handle this availability. CICS was previously enhanced to take advantage of Parallel Sysplex hardware, with CICSPlex system management to integrate with Workload Manager to insure correct business priorities and 24×7 availability.

OS/390 C/C++ and z/OS C/C++

C/C++ for OS/390 and z/OS provides the ability to develop C/C++ applications on the OS/390 and z/OS platforms. This product supports object-oriented technology and exploits the C/C++ runtime environment and library services available with the OS/390 or z/OS Language environment.

TXSeries

TXSeries (Figure 4.12) is actually a bundling of three separate products that perform different aspects of transaction computing. It provides a high-performance distributed transaction processing environment that supports operations with DB2 Universal Database and the Oracle, Informix, Sybase, and SQL Server databases; MQSeries messaging software; and programming languages including C, C++, COBOL, and PL/I. TXSeries includes support for object-oriented programming models such as Java and CORBA as well as interoperability with mainframe systems such as CICS and IMS.

TXSeries supports multiple programming models and open standards using two transaction-processing monitor environments: CICS and Encina.

The Encina product family builds upon basic services supplied by the Open Software Foundation (OSF)'s Distributed Computing Envi-

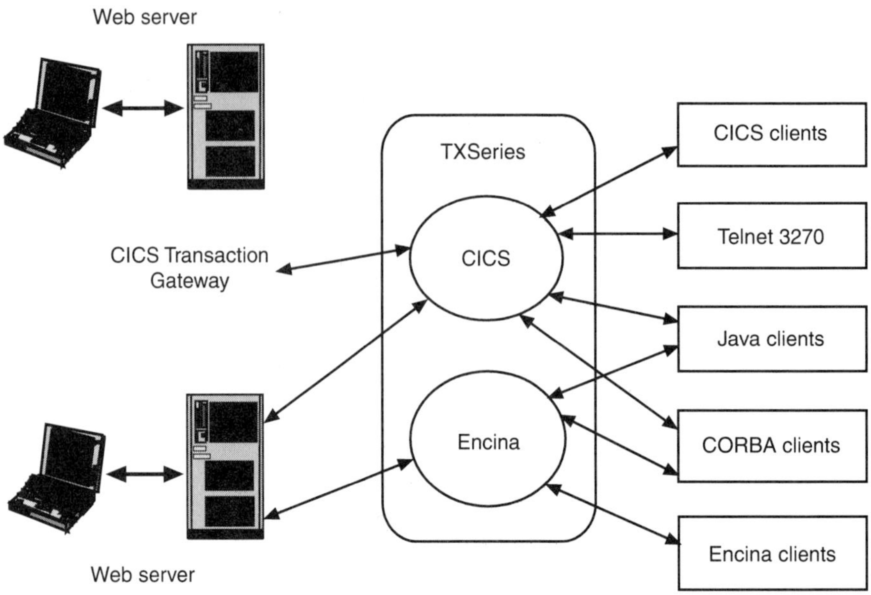

Figure 4.12. TXSeries.

ronment (DCE). The Encina "toolkit" implements the fundamental services for executing distributed transactions and managing recoverable data. This extends the CICS concept of transaction management beyond a single platform and preserves the notion of open standards.

The first role that TXSeries fills is as a transaction server, connecting end users and client applications. The second role of TXSeries is as a transaction server running on an intermediate tier in a multitier environment. In this case IMS transaction processing, alternate CICS processing, or another TXSeries can connect with the middle-tier TXSeries. The third role for TXSeries is as a transactional integration point for data and messaging. In this case any variation of an SQL database can communicate with TXSeries components and services via XA and CICS or Encina applications via SQL. WebSphere MQ can also communication to TXSeries components and services via XA, but uses MQI to communicate with CICS or Encina applications. Clients and other transaction management systems also communicate with TXSeries.

Transaction Processing Facility (TPF)

Transaction Processing Facility (TPF) is an operating system that works with application programs to process transactions for customers in a real-time environment. This system can be used for transaction processing, network switching, and front-end processing of large online transaction processing (OLTP) volumes and networks.

TPF is a message-driven system. Each query the system receives is called a message. The transaction consists of the message pairs (input/reply) required for a unit of work. The number of message pairs required to insure data consistency depends on the application design and the complexity of the transaction. Depending on the configuration, you can achieve scalability of more than 5,000 messages per second. The typical TPF system processes several hundred messages per second; a loosely coupled TPF system is required to achieve the higher scalability. Response time is usually less than three seconds from the time the user sends a message to the time the user receives a response to the message.

In accordance with IBM's drive to promote high availability for e-business, the loosely coupled TPF system can achieve undetectable failover. If one member of the complex fails, another member simply picks up the message, leaving the end user unaware of the failure.

Further information on these tools can be found by visiting the TPF Web site. The link is available via the Companion Web Site (see page xx).

COBOL

COBOL (COmmon Business Oriented Language) has been around for decades, and a large proportion of the world's largest companies run their applications using the COBOL language. While some of the newer languages and options, such as Java, appeal to programmers who want to be on the cutting edge of design, COBOL serves a fundamental structural purpose and will be with us for another set of decades.

IBM continues to enhance the language and port it to platforms beyond the mainframe, such as Windows NT and AIX.

VisualAge for Java

VisualAge for Java has been replaced by WebSphere Studio Application Developer (March 19, 2002). WebSphere Studio for Linux and

Windows (March 19, 2002), WebSphere Studio Application Developer Integration Edition (March 5, 2002) and WebSphere Studio Enterprise Developer (September 24, 2002). All of these products were described earlier.

VisualAge Generator

VisualAge (VA) Generator (see Figure 4.13) allows developers with little or no Java experience to implement e-business systems that can build an application that can access database and middleware products. Once the application is written, it can be generated for its target environment on operating systems from Windows NT to OS/390. The types of communications middleware it can employ are WebSphere MQ, CICS, IMS Transaction Manager, DCE, APPC, TCP/IP, and CA/400. Not only can it access DB2 Universal Database, it can access IMS, VSAM, Oracle, and other relational databases via ODBC. These applications can be built from either a traditional server point of view or a more stateless Web point of view.

If you will recall, we briefly discussed transaction management systems such as CICS and IMS Transaction Manager in Chapter 2. These

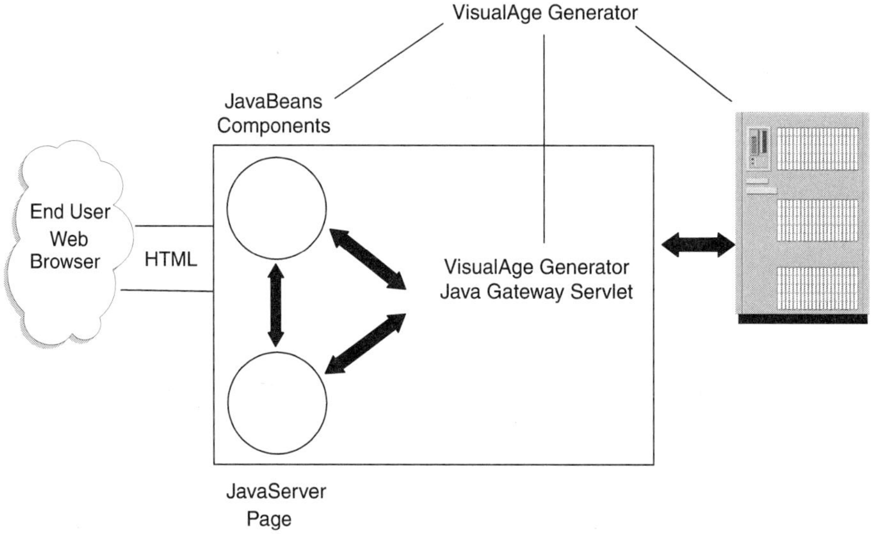

Figure 4.13. VisualAge Generator.

managers captured user input from "green screens" and performed an action. This was a transaction. At the end of the completed transaction, the connection to the program and the database was broken. When the user entered new input, the process began again. Caching techniques on the mainframe could be used to retain information already input by the user, such as account number. In order to use and change existing transaction management systems, an understanding of these techniques was necessary.

VA Generator leverages that structure. Using the tool, the developer can step through the inputs that are needed to complete the entire business transaction. VA Generator then retains all the input information and notes where the transaction program stopped, still utilizing the original IMS or CICS transaction code. In object terms, it retains the state of the transaction, allowing persistence. When the user presses a function key for the application, the function key is automatically changed into a transaction request, and VisualAge Generator picks from the data and continues the program from its last point. VisualAge Generator handles all required data access calls as well as completed units of work to insure data integrity.

Alternatively, VisualAge Generator can handle applications that do not need to keep information from one transaction to the next on the server. These are similar to browsing through Web pages, alternatively linking to another page using an HTML link or using the Back and Forward buttons of the browser to find the page that is cached on the client.

There are three components that come with VisualAge Generator—the developer program, the server program, and the templates customizer program. Programmers use the templates customizer program to develop the bulk of the application required to:

- Access and manipulate stored data while providing concurrency for multiple users.
- Display the information to the client device while managing navigation among multiple windows and session states.
- Provide housekeeping for items such as error conditions, online help, and the like.

This data driven framework builds the information of how the data is to be accessed and displayed. After it is complete, the developer can use the developer program to add the business process logic to the application. For example, suppose a user wants to move money from savings to checking. The data elements accessed or displayed in this process would include the account number, amount in savings, amount to be moved, and amount in checking. The template specifies what to get, how to display it, and how to retrieve an error message and where to put it on the client screen. If there is a business process that states you can't move money from savings if there is only $10 left, that is put into the application via the developer program.

These inputs are managed in a business logic manner, rather than in a programming language model, enabling developers unfamiliar with programming logic to determine how the process should run, rather than worrying about programming syntax. VisualAge Generator takes care of that.

One of the methods that VisualAge Generator uses to control data is called a User Interface record.The client accesses the Interaction Controller to get information from Command Beans. The Interaction Controller could use the User Interface Logic component to communicate with the Command Bean. VisualAge Generator uses a construct called a User Interface (UI) record that can be used by the User Interface Logic Component. VisualAge Generator's UI record can be used by the developer to define the format and edit criteria of information going to and coming from the client.

VisualAge Generator takes the user interface record and automatically generates JavaBeans and JSPs that contain the format and edit criteria for the input and output associated with the business application. Using WebSphere Studio tools or the VisualAge Generator Templates Customizer program, the developer of the user interface logic and user interface components can determine the way to accept and display the information on the client device—be it a Web page, cell phone, pervasive device, or any other client device.

Within the WebSphere Application Server, there is a servlet called a Gateway Servlet. It is used in conjunction with VisualAge Generator beans, JSPs, and user interface records to provide key functions for the runtime environment, such as:

- Interfaces to external services such as IMS and CICS
- Interfaces between the user interface record and the generated beans

- Serving the appropriate JSP to the application at run time.

Once the user interface record, JavaBeans, and JSPs are created, the developer can use the Interactive Test Facility integrated with the development facilities to fully test the system without having to deploy it in a production environment. After testing of the business logic functionality is complete, VisualAge Generator can transform the logic into COBOL, C++, or Java source code that can be compiled and run under the control of TXSeries, CICS/ESA, and IMS TM transaction managers. VisualAge Generator systems can also take advantage of MOM technologies using the WebSphere MQ rapid application development facilities.

VisualAge Enterprise Suite

VisualAge Enterprise Suite is a group of development products that are bundled together. It includes:

- WebSphere Studio Application Developer Integration Edition
- VisualAge Generator Developer
- VisualAge COBOL
- VisualAge PL/I
- Versata Studio Client.

VisualAge Pacbase

VisualAge Pacbase is a modeling tool that enables Rapid Application Development (RAD) from analysis and design to production of all types of B2B, B2C, and B2E applications. These applications are built using UML (Unified Modeling Language) component modeling techniques where the goal is to maximize reusability.

The developer workbench provides a Java-based interface to build applications. The product is administered via a Java-based workstation.

VisualAge Pacbase includes a high degree of integration to allow users to integrate COBOL applications, server components testing, and support for EJB session components. An interface with the Rational Rose environment is also supported.

VisualAge Smalltalk

VisualAge Smalltalk enables software developers to create highly portable, scaleable, multitier business applications using object-oriented technology. Smalltalk is very much alive; for example, VisualAge Smalltalk recently added support for XML schema and now runs on Red Hat Linux, Windows XP, and Windows ME. It also provides tools for integrating existing legacy applications.

One of the primary differentiators between this product and a product such as VisualAge Generator is that this product includes support for Web services and other standards-based components such as SOAP. It also includes a WebSphere OSE plug-in to allow Smalltalk code to integrate with anyone on the Internet.

The Web services support allows the developer to build applications that are self-contained, self-describing modular components that use standard protocols. This includes a one-step deployment of proxy services based upon the WSDL, a pluggable transport mechanism, the ability to host Web services, and an ability to wrap existing business objects and expose them as Web services.

Security is an important feature of VisualAge Smalltalk. SSL enables Smalltalk applications to use Open SSL to heighten security for any transactions running over Socket Communication Interface (SCI).

Other WebSphere Products

At the time of this writing, a few WebSphere products had not yet found their slot in the new WebSphere Software Platform. The following products were discussed in the last edition of this book and are included here for completeness.

WebSphere Business Components

As companies developed their umpteenth customer name and address application, they began to realize the need for prepackaged software. They soon realized that, much as companies like to identify their differences, there are some things that basically work the same almost everywhere you go. Hence the growth in companies that prepackage large applications such as SAP and Siebel. However, there are still areas where the applications are different from company to company, but some of the basic components (for example, needing to check credit history, credit, and debit an account) are required. This is where WebSphere Business Components (see Figure 4.14) comes in handy.

WebSphere Business Components provides pre-built, tested components in line with object-oriented design principles. The product contains a number of software components that package a related group of functions. Each component package specifies the services it provides as well as the services it requires. Component implementation details are encapsulated and kept separate from interface details.

The building blocks are in the WebSphere Business Components Composer, which provides transaction components and infrastructure Java components. Components are also combined into solutions for particular industries, such as banking.

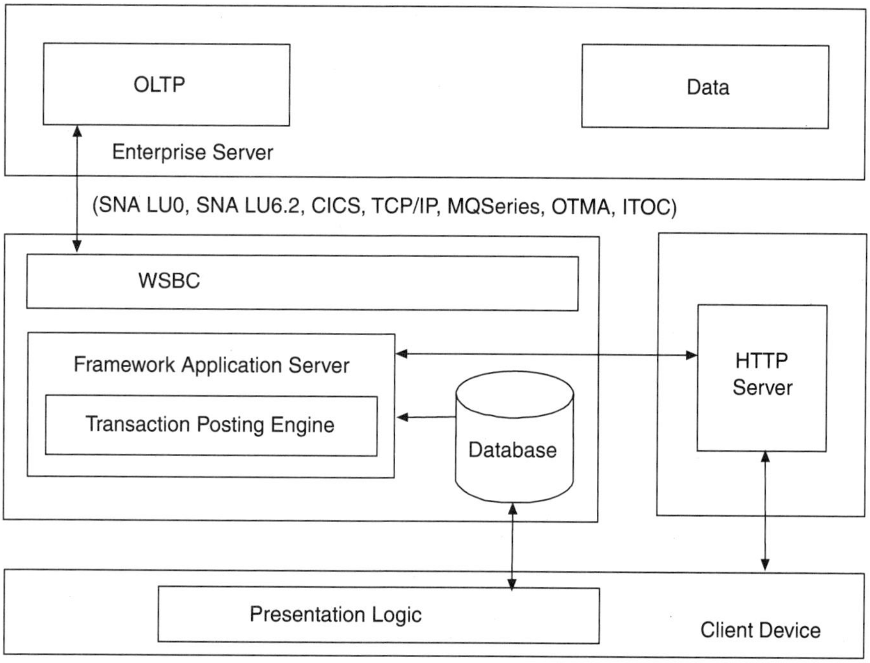

Figure 4.14. WebSphere Business Components.

WebSphere Business Components Composer

WebSphere Business Components Composer (WSBCC) is designed to provide components for Web-based financial services applications and retail delivery channels. These channels include Internet banking, call centers, standalone kiosks, automated teller machines, and mobile access terminals such as WAP cellular phones. Since many banking firms have already existing OLTP systems, WSBCC provides components to interface with these systems directly. These include components to access CICS and IMS transaction managers.

Application development for WebSphere Business Components Composer is done using a development workbench. This workbench provides the nontechnical user with the ability to define and store business processes and data in the WebSphere Business Components Composer Development Workbench Repository using development wizards. The components generator utility can encapsulate a set of composer operations to create advanced components and then generate the necessary Java source code and XML framework. The development workbench supports the application development framework as a plug-in to WebSphere Studio Application Developer.

The WebSphere Business Components Composer architecture is based on a three-tier model: back-end enterprise server, middle-tier application server, and workstation client. As noted before, many financial institutions have existing OLTP business data and logic on an enterprise server, frequently an S/390 mainframe.

Because of the component architecture, interface components can be used to access this data without changing the underlying data. Communication to the back-end enterprise server can be done by SNA (LUA interfaces), CICS, TCP/IP, WebSphere MQ, OTMA (Open Transaction Management Access), and ITOC. The middle-tier server is designed to be a WebSphere Application Server.

WebSphere Business Components Composer runs on the application server. Clients contain only presentation logic. Clients can use Java, HTML, XML, or WML (Wireless Markup Language) to interface with WebSphere Business Components Composer. For Java clients WebSphere Business Components Composer provides a set of GUI JavaBeans to create the client–user interface and support client navigation.

WebSphere Business Components are divided into base components and advanced components. Base components are typically of smaller size and scope than advanced components. They are considered "white box" components—in other words, their internals can be viewed and they can be modified by typical object-oriented techniques such as subclassing and class replacement. Advanced components are considered to be "black box" because their internals cannot be viewed and they must be modified only by configuration mechanisms.

WebSphere Business Components Studio

The WebSphere Business Components Studio provides tools for creating applications using WebSphere Business Components. It includes essential tools, components, and deployment support needed to develop EJB applications and component-based solutions. It is essentially a starter set of pre-built components that enables you to build applications quickly and then expand on those applications to enrich your e-business solution. Like the Bank Teller Business Components, they can be run using WAS. Some of the subcomponents of this studio are the Customer Profile Component, used to create and maintain persistent customer information for a provider, and the Product Catalog Component, used to store information about the products offered by an institution.

Because it is a starter set, The WebSphere Business Components Studio also provides examples, samples, and documentation of how to create and deploy these component types of applications. This product is a prerequisite for development with the Text Analyzer and Order Capture components.

WebSphere Bank Teller Business Components

WebSphere Bank Teller Business Components (Figure 4.15) support multiple standard branch devices such as passbook printers, card swipes, MICR readers, etc. to integrate with existing host systems to provide complete banking transactions. It is designed to enhance banking applications that were developed using WSBCC by providing additional components applicable to bank teller functions. Like other components developed on WSBCC, these components are developed using a development workbench and using a WAS runtime environment.

WebSphere Text Analyzer Business Components

The WebSphere Text Analyzer Business Components perform fast (20 to 40 messages per second) and accurate text document categorization.

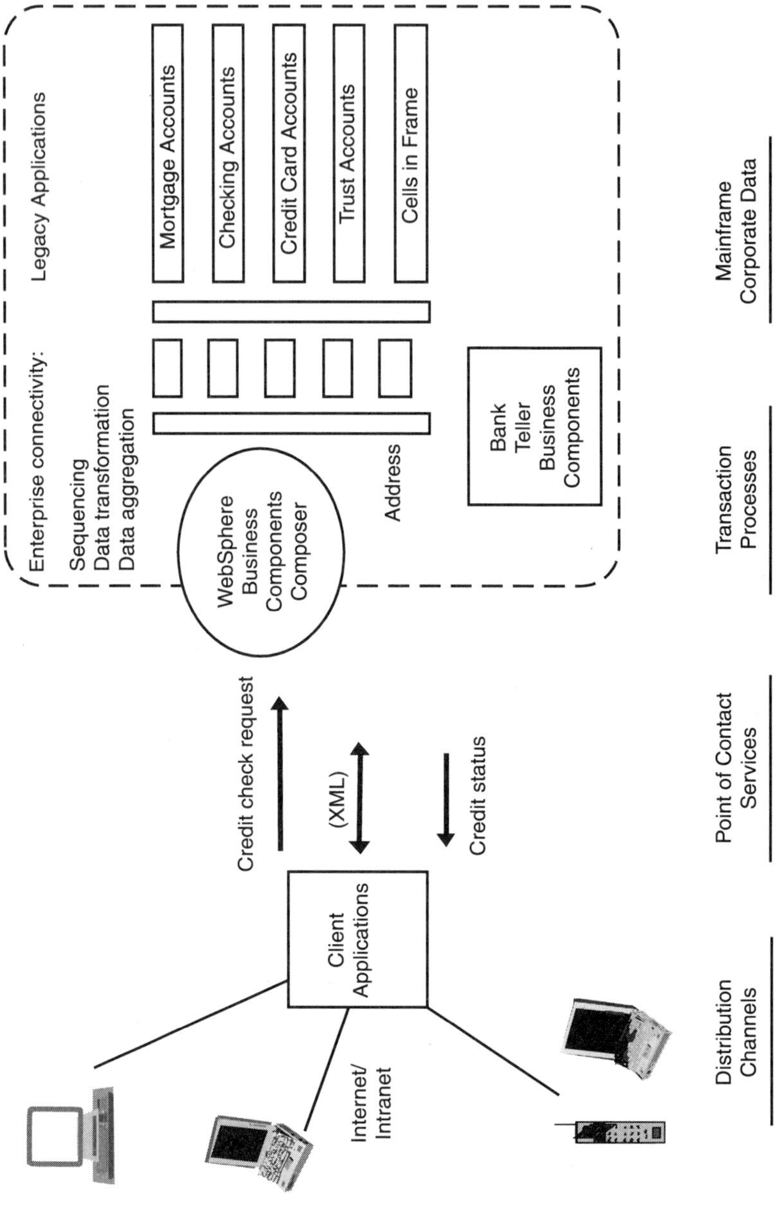

Figure 4.15. WebSphere software multichannel banking solutions.

This means that the component can be used to review any information in an electronic text character file (including scanned document images) and then group these documents according to some common features. The Text Analyzer has two major subcomponents: the Training Tool and the Categorization Engine. The Training Tool is used to create the categorization rules that are used by the Categorization Engine. The Categorization Engine does the actual categorization. A client application submits documents to the Categorization Engine and then accepts the returned categorization results.

WebSphere Order Capture Business Component

WebSphere Order Capture Business Component is considered an advanced component. The purpose of the Order Capture Component is to serve in between the sales channels and internal corporate systems to provide a single means to capture and maintain order information originating from the customer. It can then interface with any existing back-end order fulfillment system to provide the order. It provides the mechanisms to:

- Create, modify, and delete sales orders and sales order line items
- Query sales orders and sales order line items
- Provide pricing and discount functions
- Integrate inventory availability and credit availability checking functions
- Integrate with an existing fulfillment system.

There are four groups of external interfaces that are part of Order Capture. The members of these interfaces conform to the Open Applications Group Interface Specification (OAGIS), which defines a standard way of passing data in and out of applications using an XML format. These external interface groups are:

- The Maintenance Function Group, which is used by administrative personnel and peer applications to set up and maintain the structural data and parameters required to create or validate orders.

- The Order Capture Function Group, which is used by a client that is creating or maintaining the sales order on behalf of the customer.
- The Credit Function Group, which allows Order Capture to communicate with a credit management function to find out if the party placing the order has sufficient available credit.
- The Fulfillment Function Group, which provides the interface between Order Capture and an existing fulfillment function.

These components fulfill the functions of e-business architectures for the future. They conform to open standards, so they are able to integrate with other software that conforms to the same standard, even from other companies. They are component driven, providing building blocks for ever-changing businesses, yet providing the basic business functions that have been with us for the last century. By providing an interface between old and new, they provide a method for companies to integrate existing structures with the new face of e-business.

WebSphere Software MultiChannel Banking Solution

WebSphere Software MultiChannel Banking Solution (see Figure 4.15) provides the ability to develop multichannel retail banking applications that exploit J2EE, EJB, and XML technology in a component development environment. These applications support banking by allowing you to build applications that support branch renewal, CRM, sales enablement, and pervasive banking.

The product contains a copy of WebSphere Business Components Composer as well as an IFX (Interactive Financial Exchange) connector. This connector is an industry-standard specification for data formatting, connectivity, and security that manages IFX messages by an IFX server. The connector receives the messages from the client, handles the requested transactions and makes the appropriate IFX response to the client.

While DB2 Universal Database is the preferred database for JDBC services, the solution also comes with an Oracle plug-in. Security is enhanced by use of Tivoli Systems Management (see Chapter 6). You can also integrate this solution with Siebel eFinance to provide branch transformation solutions.

IBM SanFrancisco

IBM is no longer marketing IBM SanFrancisco. The capabilities of the product have been folded into WebSphere Business Components Studio Version.

WebSphere Edge Server

WebSphere Edge Server provides an integrated solution for LAN and WAN load balancing, content-based quality of service routing, and Web content filtering and caching for multivendor Web server environments. WebSphere Edge Server sits in front of client access to Web application servers, providing these services to improve performance from client to server. It does this by performing the following:

- Providing an application offload component that can decompose an e-business application and redistribute the components on the edge server closest to the required need.
- Providing enhanced proxy caching by offloading back-end servers and peering links as a forward, reverse (surrogate), or transparent proxy.
- Providing a load balancing component that receives incoming requests and directs them to the server that will process them the quickest.
  - Providing security via Tivoli Access Manager
  - Providing a method of prioritizing workloads through Transaction Quality of Service software.

WebSphere Site Analyzer

This product has been rebranded Tivoli Web Site Analyzer and will be discussed in Chapter 6.

Footnotes

1."WECM renames and reprices IBM Everyplace Wireless Gateway. These actions simplify the pricing structure and help to more closely align this product with other offerings in the WebSphere Everyplace family of products. WECM is functionally the same as Everyplace Wireless Gateway." from announcement letter 202-289.

5

DB2

We now begin discussion of the Data Management (DB2) brand of IBM software. This brand includes the flagship DB2 database products as well as content management products and Informix database products. (IBM purchased Informix in 2001.) This chapter also contains information on some of the granddaddies of IBM software—including the hierarchical database, IMS, developed in the 1970s.

Both Oracle and Microsoft tend to have tightly coupled offerings—selling their customers on suites and applications rather than the parts to build them. IBM's strategy has an open systems, plug-and-play flavor. This allows them to build components that meet industry standards that can interact with any other component that meets those standards. For example, DB2 Universal Database is Microsoft Back Office certified. This strategy also allows IBM to reuse products that they develop in several different product suites—providing the ultimate flexibility for its customers.

The DB2 strategy for e-business includes working toward an integrated multi-tier application development and runtime environment built on the work that has been done for WebSphere (Chapter 4) and Tivoli (Chapter 6). DB2 is also committed to evolving a complete system management framework into a self-managing/self-healing environment (e-business on demand) through SMART initiatives.

Data storage and management is an important factor for both small and large companies. Customer information, product information, and employee information all must be stored and maintained. The growth of data that is stored is a result both of the amount of data captured (firms that have hundreds of thousands of customers and those that capture information from anyone who touches their Web site) and the size of data captured (pictures, video streams, etc.). The software that is required to store data, move data, and manage data is in this group. Data storage begins with a discussion of IMS and DB2 Universal Database, followed by Informix, U2, and Content Management. IBM business solution software that applies to DB2 software will also be covered.

IMS is a workhorse piece of software that underlies many everyday applications, including automated teller machines (ATMs) and travel reservation systems. IBM has continually enhanced IMS, insuring its availability for e-business. DB2 Universal Database, IBM's relational database, is also a staple of every Fortune 500 company. In addition, IBM uses DB2 Universal Database to underpin many of its other software products such as Content Manager and WebSphere Application Server. Informix was acquired by IBM to fill a niche that had a strong customer base—the mid-size data storage and data warehouse market. U2 is designed for embedding in vertical applications. Content Manager is primarily used for storing unstructured data such as document images, PC-created documents, photos, and videos.

This chapter discusses data movement software as well as software needed to assure connectivity between applications and the data they need.

In 2000, IBM split its DB2 software tools from its DB2 software products.

IMS Family

The next few pages cover software that is part of the IMS (Information Management System) family of products.

IMS

IMS (Information Management System) is integrated into our daily lives. Over 95% of the Fortune 1000 companies use IMS. Aggregated, over 220 million users interact with some form of IMS, accessing and changing over 15 billion gigabytes of data. IMS processes over 50 billion transactions every day. Around for several decades, it supports much of our legacy processing, yet is enhanced to take advantage of new technologies such as Java and Extended Markup Language (XML). What follows is a basic description of its operation.

A hierarchical database such as IMS supports many complex tree structures (Figure 5.1). Each tree structure, termed a database, is composed of segments. The segments represent the parents and children of a hierarchical database, with the root segment being the highest level segment. A segment, other than the root or last child, can be both a parent and a child segment.

Each segment (or record) is defined as a distinct type. For example, a store segment might be 80 bytes long and contain a store identifier, store name, and store address. There can be many segments of the same type, and a segment can be of a fixed or variable length. The store type in our example will have a segment that is constructed in the same manner for each store and contains data peculiar to the store. Each unique store segment is referred to as an instance of the same segment. Within each segment specific fields are defined in a positional manner. In our example, the store segment has a store identifier, store name, and store address. A segment may only relate to one segment above it in the hierarchical tree, but a segment may relate to many records below it. (In hierarchical terms [only!] a child may have only one parent, but a parent can have many children.) In our example, one district may have

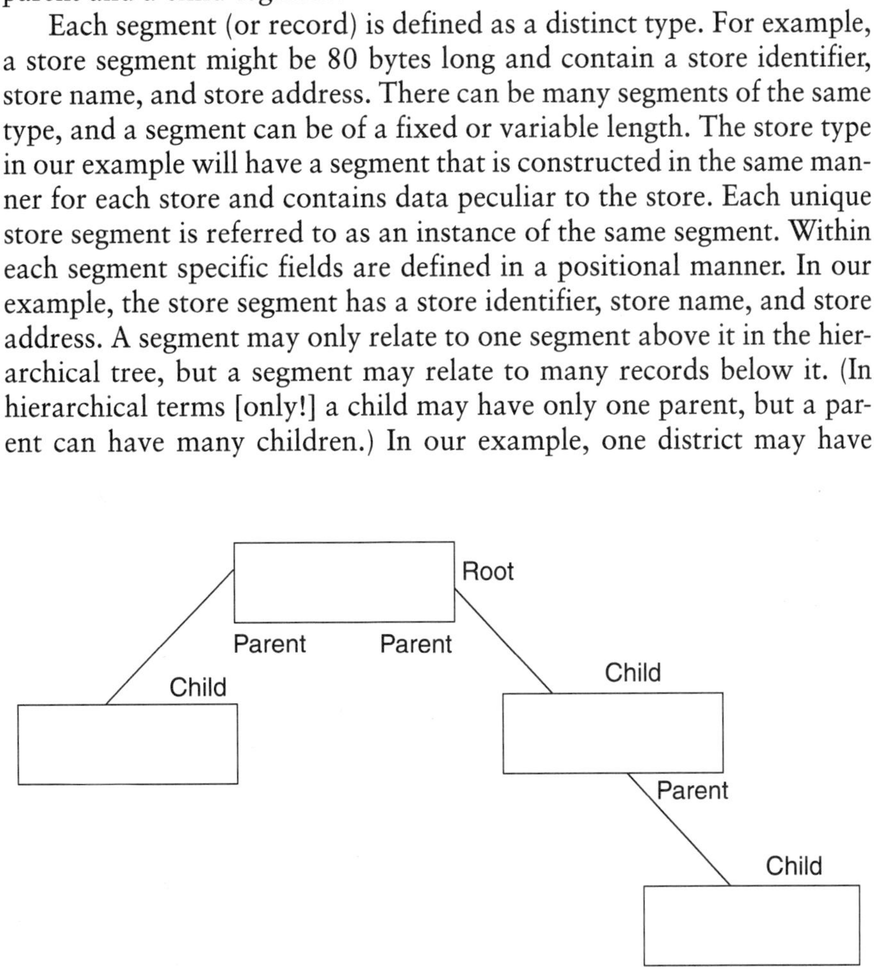

Figure 5.1. IMS tree structure.

many stores related to it, but a store may only relate to one district. If the business rules require that a child have multiple parents, the child instance would have to be carried redundantly in every parent. In Figure 5.2, the product Kate's Herbal Iced Tea would need to be carried as a segment under each of Brown's stores in which it was sold.

The structure in our example is a logical structure depicting how the segments are related to each other. It does not reflect how the data is stored physically in IMS. In order for a program to navigate through an IMS tree structure, it must be able to reflect both the logical and physical aspects of the database. This is done through Program Specification Blocks (PSBs) and Database Descriptors (DBDs). PSBs represent the logical view, and DBDs represent the physical view.

Access of IMS data is closely related to its physical storage. This means that changing the structure of the database to reflect changing business needs can be difficult. It is made more challenging by the different methods that can store and access the data. They are:

HSAM: Hierarchical Sequential

HISAM: Hierarchical Indexed Sequential

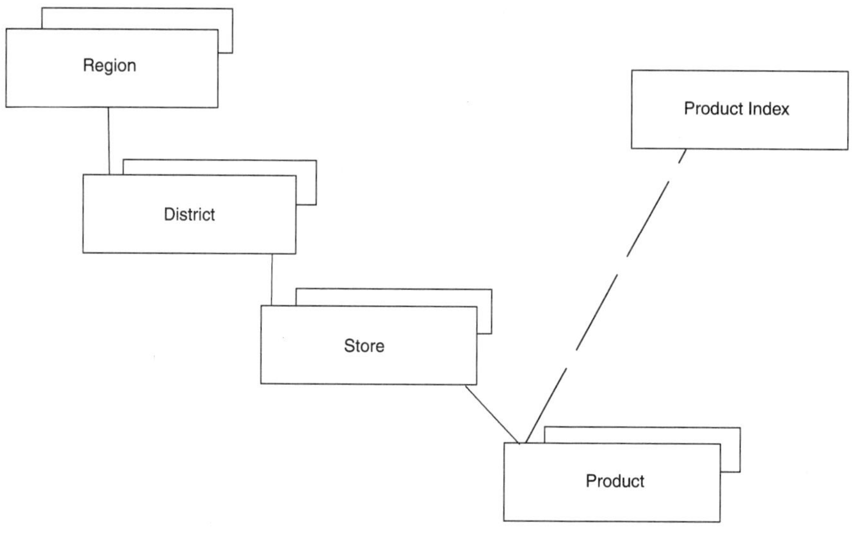

Figure 5.2. Brown's stores in an IMS structure.

HDAM: Hierarchical Direct

HIDAM: Hierarchical Indexed Direct.

IMS also has a structure known as a Data Entry Database (DEDB), sometimes called a Fast Path database, although Fast Path is the type of access and not the database.

The good news is that these access methods are transparent to the program. The program only needs to follow the hierarchical logical tree represented by the PSB and IMS makes the translation to the appropriate access by using the physical view stored in the DBD.

There are two main types of storage noted above—sequential and direct. The physical segments in a sequential structure are related by physical adjacency. In order to obtain data, IMS reads through the hierarchical levels sequentially. On the other hand, physical pointers relate segments in a direct structure. IMS only has to traverse an index to find the information it needs and then follow the direct pointer to the required segment. Some of the storage types also allow secondary indexes.

A secondary index allows alternate access to the data. Rather than having to traverse from district to store to product segments for each instance to develop a report indicating how much of Kate's Herbal Iced Tea the company has left, an index built on product (Figure 5.2) allows access directly to the product segments.

Application programming languages are supported directly out of IMS dependent regions. COBOL, PL/I, Assember, Pascal, or Java can be defined in the PSB definition. If the application is built using the IBM Language Environment, then a language is not specified in the PSB. Instead, any valid language supported by the IBM Language Environment (such as C) is supported by IMS. Alternatively, if IMS data is accessed through a DB2 stored procedure or WebSphere ODBA (Open Database Access) interface, IMS doesn't care what the programming language is as long as the application can invoke the callable interface. Data Language/One (DL/I) is the interface between the application program and the database.

Underlying the database and programs is the architectural structure of IMS, the elements that enforce its reliability, availability, and security. The architecture of IMS depends on regions carved from the MVS operating system memory that manage the various components of IMS. The regions also manage interactions between IMS and other MVS architectural components, such as data storage devices. Important from the availability standpoint, these regions also manage the transaction logging of IMS.

Transaction logging captures images of segments before they are changed by a transaction and after they are changed by the transaction. This is important because logging provides a method to recover information in a database in case of some type of failure. These failures can be mechanical, such as storage failure, or human, such as an application program bug that inserts incorrect data into an IMS database. The IMS restart capabilities use the log to restore data that has been lost in some manner. After the information is captured in the daily logs, the logs can be run through a log archive utility to consolidate the changes. This utility produces both System Log Data Sets, which contain data from one or more daily logs, and Recovery Log Data Sets, which contain only the log records that are needed for database recovery. Log information (time covered, data set name, status, etc.) is tracked by the Database Recovery Control region and stored in RECON data sets.

This structure gives IMS the deserved reputation it has for high availability. With the information maintained in various logs, IMS can be rapidly brought up in case of a failure. Logs are also available for other programs, such as data replication programs, to capture changes and copy them to other, distributed, data stores. The high availability of IMS can also be enhanced through the use of disk mirroring (making a hardware copy of data) and use of Sysplex technology, which is explained later in this chapter.

In order to insure that two users are not trying to update the same data at the same time, IMS, as well as DB2 Universal Database, employs a technique called locking. Locks allow for two people to read data at the same time, but control if data can be read during an update to the data. (Update is a catch-all term that means the insertion, deletion, or changing of specific data.) Updates to the same data at the same time are not allowed. Both IMS and DB2 Universal Database take advantage of the IRLM (IBM Resource Lock Manager) address space to control locking. IRLM is not really part of IMS, but works with it.

Chapter 2 discussed the concept of unit of work (UOW). At the end of a unit of work, both IMS and DB2 Universal Database perform what is called a commit. This commit lets the database know that the user really wants to complete this transaction. The database can be notified in a few different ways that the commit is to take place. If another agent, such as a transaction manager, is involved in the transaction, both parties have to agree that they are really, really ready to commit.

Similar to a dialogue between two people who are debating whether or not to marry, the two-phase (or coordinated) commit process involves a lot of "Are you ready?" dialogue. IMS supports two-phase commit with the IMS Transaction Manager (described below).

With the Batch Resource Recovery Service, IMS allows batch programs that use WebSphere MQ to coordinate a commit with DB2 Universal Database as well as IMS. This support allows disparate database management systems to be included in a single unit of work.

Java applications running on WebSphere Application Server on OS/390 or z/OS and CICS (Customer Information Control System) Transaction Server can access IMS using Java Database Connectivity (JDBC). DB2 Universal Database for z/OS and OS/390 can also access IMS using Java Stored Procedures.

Fast Path is a particular type of IMS database access using a DEDB. A DEDB is an HDAM-like database structure. It has two types of segments in addition to the root segment: sequential dependent and direct dependent. The direct dependent segment is similar to segments described earlier. Sequential dependent segments allow for very fast insert and delete processing as well as efficient mass retrieval of information. Secondary indexes are not allowed on DEDB structures.

DEDB databases allow for partitions called areas. Areas are separate physical areas of the same logical database. Going back to Figure 5.2, it might be nice to physically partition the database to allow each region to be in a separate physical space on a separate disk. Should one disk have a hardware problem, it will only affect one region. Also, requests for information, such as reports about all stores by region, can be run in parallel, providing faster throughput. IMS allows up to 2,048 areas, or partitions, per database.

IMS has a high degree of security at several levels. The following can be secured:

- Terminals, passwords, user ID sign-on verification
- Transactions
- Logical and physical databases
- Commands.

By using these security aspects, companies can protect themselves from unauthorized access to the database or transactions that use the database. They can also prevent unauthorized (or unknowledgeable!) people from using commands such as those that start and stop IMS.

As noted above, IMS can be enhanced by the use of Sysplex technology, a facility that allows multiple application programs in different IMS, CICS, or DB2 Universal Database subsystems to concurrently process requests against common IMS or DB2 Universal Database databases with full integrity. The description of Sysplex data sharing is found in the DB2 Universal Database section of this chapter.

IMS has been enhanced to enable its use for the high-traffic and Web access requirements of e-business. Some of these enhancements are included above, but here are a few more that extend IMS into the e-business world.

Availability, always a hallmark of IMS, has been enhanced and extended to embrace DB2 Universal Database. IMS/DB2 Coordinated Disaster Recovery extends the IMS Remote Site Recovery function to provide support for coordinated IMS and DB2 Universal Database disaster recovery. It does this by working with the eXtended Remote Copy (XRC) product that is available for moving information from DB2 Universal Database logs to a remote site. (The function of DB2 Universal Database logs is described later.) The result is that IMS and DB2 Universal Database applications can be automatically synchronized at a remote site in case of a disaster.

Hooks are provided into IMS for several other enhancements to improve communication with e-business infrastructures and make IMS data available to these structures. The Open Transaction Management Access (OTMA) facility is the part of IMS that provides the ability to communicate with IBM connectors such as WebSphere MQ and take advantage of Transmission Control Protocol/Internet Protocol (TCP/IP). OTMA also provides an application programming interface (API) that makes IMS accessible to C or C++ programs as well as Common Object Request Broker Architecture (CORBA). IMS can also be accessed by Open Database Access (ODBA)-compliant programs. IMS, like most IBM software products, has support for Java.

The Java support allows the flexibility of "write once, run anywhere" to extend to IMS. Java Dependent Regions allow IMS to take advantage of persistent, reusable Java Virtual Machines (JVMs). New region types for message-driven and non-message-driven IMS Java applications are also provided. Recent versions of IMS have enhanced their Java code to comply with Java standards.

IMS Transaction Manager

In order to provide high-volume, rapid response transaction management processing for application programs that access IMS (and DB2 Universal Database) databases, IMS provides IMS Transaction Manager (IMS/TM). IMS/TM uses dependent regions (portions of MVS memory that are dependent on the main IMS address spaces) to do its work. There can be up to 999 of these dependent regions.

XML support allows IMS/TM to send and receive messages as XML documents.

IMS Connect and IMS Connector for Java

IMS also provides, through associated products, the ability to communicate across a vast network of IMS systems. These tools also provide the ability for client/server architectures to access IMS directly. For example, IMS Connect provides communication and workload balancing between workstations and IMS using TCP/IP, supporting multiple TCP/IP clients that access multiple IMS systems. When used with IMS Connector for Java, IMS Connect provides the ability to access IMS data from the Internet. Studies have shown that IMS Connect is capable of handling almost 6,000 transactions per second (TPS).

IMS Connect interfaces with IMS using the MVS Cross Coupling Facility (XCF) and the OTMA interface. It provides connectivity to IMS TM from any TCP/IP or client application running on OS/390 or z/OS. IMS Connect can also access IMS from applications running on Linux for zSeries.

External services called connectors are software components that provide linkage between the Web application server and the services it needs via application specific protocols. IMS Connector for Java serves this purpose for IMS by providing a way to create Java applets or servlets to run on a Web server. These applets or servlets can access existing and/or new IMS transactions by using IMS Connect to invoke IMS transactions. Servlets accessing IMS can also be created through the WebSphere Studio. All these external services can be deployed via the WebSphere Application Server (Chapter 4).

Recent enhancements to IMS Connect and IMS Connector for Java include:

- Local support for non-TCP/IP communication between a Web-serving application and IMS
- Unicode support (Chapter 1)
- WebSphere adapter support provided through IMS Connector for Java 2 Enterprise Edition (J2EE) runtime support.

IMS Connect and IMS Connector for Java are important building blocks to allow you to access your legacy data from the world of e-business without having to rearchitect your entire system.

DB2 Universal Database

DB2 Universal Database is a relational database with extensions. Relational database theory was covered in Chapter 2 and will not be reviewed here. Relational data, be it in Oracle, Microsoft SQLServer, or DB2 Universal Database, is accessed using a structured query language (SQL). (A good place to look for DB2 Universal Database information is the DB2 Developer Domain, which you can access through the Companion Web Site listed on page xx).

DB2 Universal Database has been in existence since the early 1980s. As object theory moved more into the mainstream, DB2 Universal Database was enhanced with triggers, stored procedures, check constraints, XML, and object-oriented extensions. With the explosion of the Internet, DB2 Universal Database has been reengineered to allow it to act as an e-business foundation.

DB2 Universal Database runs on many hardware platforms, including iSeries, pSeries, xSeries, and zSeries, many non-IBM hardware platforms such as SUN and HP, and mobile devices. It works well with the underlying operating systems because while the basic DB2 Universal Database structure is primarily the same, the code is enhanced to take advantage of the operating system on which DB2 Universal Database is running. There are three main branches of DB2 Universal Database—DB2 Universal Database for z/OS and OS/390, DB2 Universal Database for Linux, Windows, and UNIX (DB2 Universal Database for Multiplatforms), and DB2 Universal Database for iSeries. These three branches of DB2 Universal Database were developed separately and are still slightly different, but predominantly their functionality is the same. First, we will discuss the common components of DB2 Universal Database and then differentiate between the main branches. Then we will briefly discuss DB2 Server for VSE and VM and DB2 Everyplace.

Tables are the foundational structure of DB2 Universal Database. They are complemented by index structures that provide direct access. In Figure 5.3 you can see the information about Brown's stores from a DB2 Universal Database perspective rather than an IMS perspective. The arrows are not implemented physically, but rather by carrying the primary key of one table in the table of its logical child.

Tables are contained in physical structures called table spaces. Indexes are built from the table data and contain pointers to specific rows in the tables. Within DB2 Universal Database they can be used to enforce uniqueness and provide performance benefits.

SQL is used to access DB2 Universal Database data. SQL can be embedded within other languages such as COBOL, C++, and Java. The American National Standards Institute (ANSI) and the Interna-

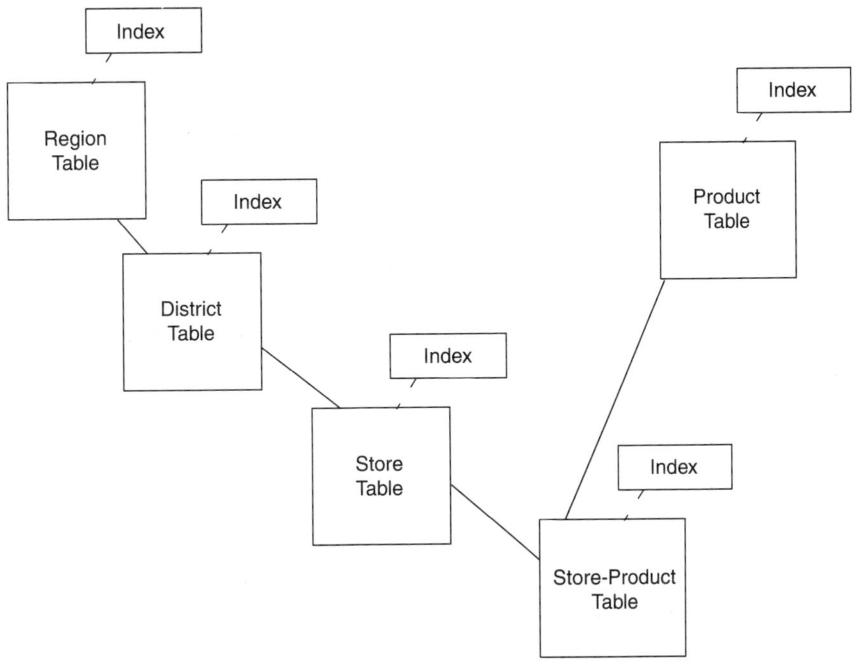

Figure 5.3. Brown's stores (DB2) with indexes.

tional Organization for Standardization (ISO) govern the format of this language with different SQL standards containing different features. DB2 Universal Database conforms to a subset of the most recent standard for SQL (ANSI/ISO/IEC 9075-1:199 144 Database Language SQL). This standard, known as SQL99, has two levels of conformance: Core SQL and Enhanced SQL Support. DB2 Universal Database conforms to a subset of SQL99 Core, and additionally has implemented some of the Enhanced SQL support of SQL99. IBM strives to comply with this standard as well as allowing extensions to the standard to enable customers to do the types of things that they need to do, particularly with e-business.

SQL to access the DB2 Universal Database tables can be invoked in many different ways. It can be embedded into batch programs, CICS transactions, stored procedures, and the like, or simply become part of Java constructs such as applets and beans. The following lists several ways these programs can then be invoked. Obviously, these are just a few of the ways to access DB2 Universal Database.

- The program can be invoked as a batch job scheduled to run at particular times during a day, month or year.
- A CICS transaction can be invoked from a terminal.
- A stored procedure can be called from a DB2 Universal Database client or WebSphere Application Server using DB2 Connect.
- A stored procedure can publish information as part of a Web services transaction.
- A Java applet can be started from the Internet using a Java-enabled Web browser.

There are also two ways an application program can interact with DB2 Universal Database: static SQL or dynamic SQL. With static SQL, the programmer must know exactly what SQL statements are needed and must write them within the program exactly how they are to be used. If the program is used to get data for more than one function, or even return the same data sorted in multiple ways, the programmer will have to code SQL in each of the possible ways it could be invoked.

However, because static SQL is known prior to execution, DB2 Universal Database can set up an access path prior to its use. An access path is the method by which DB2 Universal Database is going to get the data. Prior to retrieval, DB2 Universal Database determines if it will use an index, which index or indexes it will use, or if it will simply read the table without an index, among other things. SQLJ is the static version of SQL to use with Java. Static SQL provides a slightly higher performance edge than dynamic SQL, which, in most cases, needs to determine its access path every time it is run.

On the other hand, dynamic SQL can contain variables for the different portions of an SQL statement. Depending on the request, the variables can be inserted into the SQL statement and the statement compiled and run. For certain types of application architectures including e-business, dynamic SQL is the best way to access the data. IBM has also worked to reduce the number of times the access path needs to be determined for a dynamic SQL by providing portions of the memory (called cache) within the DB2 Universal Database address space to improve performance.

DB2 Universal Database provides several facilities for handling dynamic SQL statements: Deferred Embedded SQL, Call Level Interface (CLI), Open Database Connectivity (ODBC), and Java Database Connectivity (JDBC). CLI is discussed further under the DB2 Universal Database for non-zSeries platforms section later in this chapter.

Deferred Embedded SQL is similar to embedded static SQL because it can be surrounded by a host application program and run via normal application interfaces. The difference is that the access path for the dynamic SQL is determined when the program is run.

ODBC is an API in which functions are provided to the application programs to process SQL statements. The application calls a C or C++ function at execution time to connect, issue SQL, and get returned data and status. No precompile is necessary, so the application can go against any DB2 Universal Database without having to be recompiled. (Note that there are sometimes differences in SQL coding between DB2 Universal Database for z/OS and OS/390 and DB2 Universal Database for pSeries, iSeries, or DB2 Everyplace.)

The JDBC facility allows DB2 Universal Database to work with Java. It is a dynamic SQL interface for use with the Java programming language and supports the same types of functional details as noted for CLI. JDBC can also be used to create Java applets that access the database. These

JDBC applets can be invoked by any Java-enabled Web browser, allowing any authorized user on the World Wide Web to access your data.

SQLJ is an API that provides support to embedded static SQL in Java applications. SQLJ provides a simple mechanism that can be used to switch back and forth between JDBC and SQLJ on a single database connection, but they are logically different APIs.

As with IMS, DB2 Universal Database has a logging capability to be used in the event of damage to the data, as well as to give the user the ability to go back to a certain point in time, in case a corruption has occurred due to a programming flaw.

Security is available at the table level as well as at a subset of the table known as a view. The creator of a table is the owner of the table and can grant use of the table's data to users. Alternatively, a program or stored procedure can be created to access the table and grant use of that program or stored procedure to users. With newer releases of DB2 Universal Database, security can be extended to the row level, providing a greater degree of granularity.

Data integrity is insured by these security measures as well as a system of locking and transaction management. While a user or program is updating a particular row, limited access is provided to that row until the program processes a commit statement or ends its processing successfully. The commit statement releases the lock and insures that the changes are written to disk. The size of the lock (how much data is locked) and the duration (the time the lock is held) depend on the locking structure (table-, page-, or row-level locking) and the type of access that the holder of the lock wants. The type of access ranges from uncommitted read (it does not matter if an updater has completed its transaction) to repeatable read (no one else can change the data until the reader commits) with variations in between. The important point is that DB2 Universal Database insures data integrity from the beginning of a unit of work until the end. Like IMS, DB2 Universal Database for z/OS and OS/390 uses IRLM (IBM Resource Lock Manager) to enforce this locking process, as well as using some internal locking processes.

The optimizer within DB2 Universal Database is the portion of code that determines how DB2 Universal Database will access the data. It does that by viewing the various ways that the data can be accessed and comparing the relative cost of the access paths to determine the most efficient one. Thus it is called a cost-based optimizer.

There are actually two different optimizers within DB2 Universal Database, depending on the platform used. The original DB2 Universal

Database optimizer, developed from the System R research based on a paper written by Pat Selinger in 1979, is used in DB2 Universal Database for z/OS. The second, developed from Starburst optimizer research, is used in DB2 Universal Database for the non-zSeries operating systems. The goal of IBM is to keep the abilities of these two optimizers in close sync, but because of the different basis, as well as inherent differences in platforms, the two have never been totally the same. This may mean that there are times when the ability to do something on DB2 Universal Database on non-zSeries operating systems is not available on DB2 Universal Database for z/OS until a different release.

If you want to create applications for the entire DB2 Universal Database family, the IBM DB2 Universal Database SQL Reference for Cross-Platform Development will help you do that. The book covers all three branches of the DB2 family. The book describes the rules and limits for preparing portable programs for specific versions of these DB2 databases. Later releases of DB2 Universal Database will continue to bring the SQL code together. Check the Companion Web Site (see page xx).

As e-business technology has matured, the basic concepts have been incorporated into all of IBM's software. DB2 Universal Database is no exception. In addition to the Java extensions discussed, Web Services and XML are incorporated into these products. IBM's recently announced direction of e-business on demand, will mean key components of self-management that are already available within the software will be expanded.

The following sections describe some of the basic architecture of various types of DB2 Universal Databases.

DB2 Universal Database for z/OS and OS/390

The first relational database from IBM was written for the System/38. A few others evolved from that one, but the relational database that became DB2 Universal Database for z/OS and OS/390 came out in 1983, which makes it the oldest DB2 database. (Future releases will convert to the name DB2 for z/OS, so we will use that name for the rest of the chapter.) Although it was built for both transactions and query, the product was initially positioned for the information center, precursor to the data warehouses and business intelligence of today. Companies would extract data from their VSAM or flat files, load the data into DB2 for z/OS tables, and submit a query.

The user community liked the product, but was disappointed by its performance. With each succeeding release, IBM has improved performance of the product. Reliability, availability, and security, hallmarks of IBM databases, are found in DB2 for z/OS.

DB2 for z/OS has a modular structure built of subcomponents that interact with each other. These subcomponents are divided into four groups: system services, database services, lock services, and distributed data services. Each service has its own address space on z/OS. Combined together, these services compose a DB2 for z/OS subsystem. These address spaces interact together to manage the tables and indexes, insuring that data is recoverable, that users do not try to update the same data at the same time, and that users get answers in a reasonable amount of time. Address spaces also exist to keep track of distributed computing. Stored procedures also have their own address space.

As stated earlier, differences within the DB2 databases reflect the platform: hardware and operating system. These differences include optimization. Recalling the discussion in Chapter 3 about hardware architectures, the z/OS operating system runs on a Symmetric Multiprocessor (SMP) shared system, with the ability to pass information from one memory address space to another. A zSeries machine can be logically broken up into logical partitioning regions (LPARs). Each LPAR contains a division of the z/OS operating system and can contain multiple DB2 for z/OS subsystems.

Each DB2 for z/OS subsystem can have different configuration parameters, set in a structure called DSNZPARM. These parameters control things such as the number of users that can access a table at the same time, the frequency with which changes are forced to disk storage, etc. This allows users to configure each subsystem for its purpose. For example, if you want to have a DB2 for z/OS for test and a separate DB2 for z/OS for production (a wise idea!), you can set different parameters for each DB2 for z/OS.

Within a DB2 for z/OS subsystem, separate databases can be set up. Databases can be used to provide default parameters (such as which volumes to use for storage) for all dependent DB2 for z/OS objects. Other than that, they are more a logical conception than a physical structure. Beneath databases are structures called table spaces (Figure 5.4). Table spaces are the actual physical structures that are used to store data in tables. There can be multiple tables in a table space.

Alternatively, table spaces with one table can be partitioned. Table space partitions are physical breakdowns of a table insuring that differ-

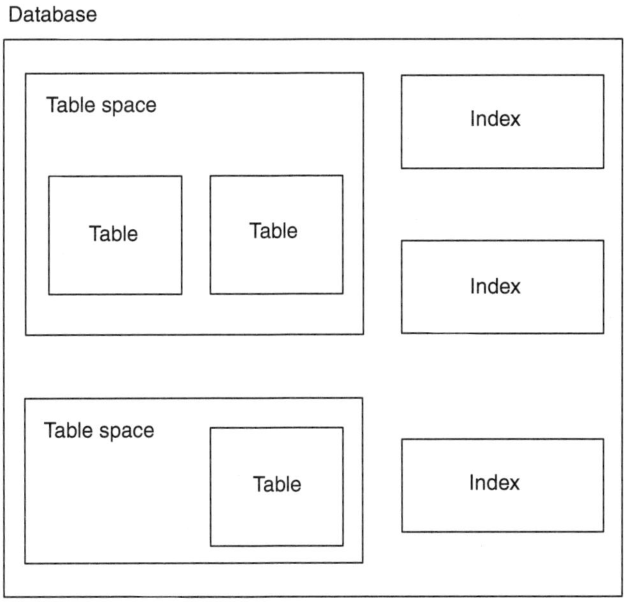

Figure 5.4. DB2 object structure.

ent portions of the data can be accessed in parallel. In Figure 5.5, Brown's stores break down their sales database into 24 partitions—12 months from the previous year and 12 months from the current year. Each partition contains one month's worth of sales data.

A query accessing a partitioned table space can be divided by DB2 for z/OS by using parallelism to break up the query and bring information back more quickly. This is the same concept as hiring four painters rather than just one to paint a house. By breaking up the work, the house gets painted more quickly. Just like hiring multiple painters, however, parallelism requires a bit of supervision overhead to insure that two painters are not trying to paint the same wall. Referring again to Figure 5.5, a query looking for the sales trend of Kate's Herbal Iced Tea over the last two years could be broken into twelve subqueries, each looking at two partitions to gather the data needed in parallel.

Table space partitioning also insures that a single portion of the data can be isolated in case of a problem or to perform maintenance, bringing the increased availability required in an e-business world. RAID

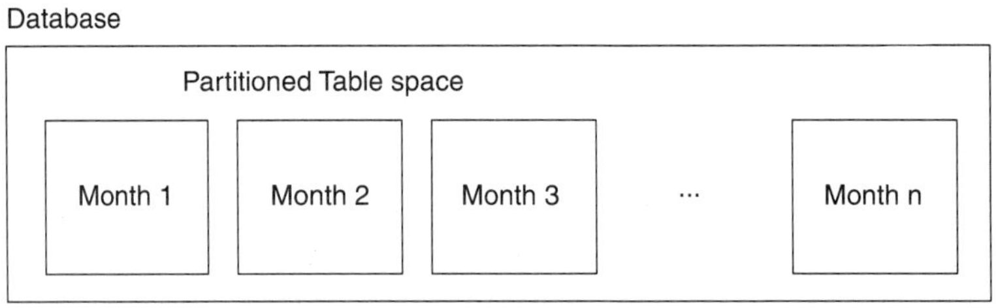

Figure 5.5. Partitioned table space.

(Redundant Array of Independent [or Inexpensive] Disks) storage devices provide the ability to insure data availability.

Physically, indexes are not kept in the table spaces with the tables. Table spaces can be partitioned at the table space level. Any additional index to the partitioned table space is termed a non-partitioned index (NPI). While these indexes can be broken into physical pieces, adding multiple NPIs to a partitioned table space hinders performance of inserts, updates, and deletes. Another index construct that allows more flexibility with partitioned table spaces is under development for a future release.

In addition to partitioned and non-partitioned table spaces (segmented table spaces), there are a few other types of table spaces within DB2 for z/OS. Some of these are used to store temporary information within a process. Some are used to store actual large object (LOB) data. In this second case, a type pointer is kept in the main table to facilitate access to the large object. The advantage of this construct is to avoid manipulation of large objects until it is determined that they are required for processing. For example, if a hospital wants all the x-rays for Sam Jones sorted in ascending date order, the rows can be accessed and sorted without having the megabytes associated with the x-rays involved in the sort. The x-rays can then be retrieved as needed.

Information about DB2 for z/OS objects (tables, indexes, and the like) is kept in a system catalog. DB2 for z/OS uses information about tables, indexes, and columns to help determine the fastest access path for a query. The catalogs also contain information about backups and other utilities (REORGs, LOADs, etc.) for system recovery. There is one system catalog per DB2 for z/OS subsystem.

An important consideration with any data store is recoverability of the data in case of a problem. As noted earlier, DB2 for z/OS has the ability to log changes as they are made to the database. Logs are kept at the subsystem level—one set of logs for all the tables in the DB2 for z/OS subsystem. As each change is made to the table, a before and after image of the change is kept, as well as information about the type of change. Logs continually grow, and are archived by the system periodically to keep the data set manageable.

Of course, in the case of an error, it would probably not be a good idea to go back to the beginning of time and apply all the log changes to the database in order to bring it up to date. DB2 for z/OS provides the ability to make periodic copies of tables (called image copies) and coordinate those copies with the changes captured in the log file to correct any data integrity problems.

DB2 for z/OS, like IMS and CICS, can take advantage of a Sysplex data sharing architecture (Figure 5.6). A data sharing structure is built using multiple LPARs of a single machine or multiple machines to access the same data. Integrity control of the data accessed by different DB2 for z/OS members is managed through locks communicated through a high-speed bus to the Coupling Facility. The Coupling Facility con-

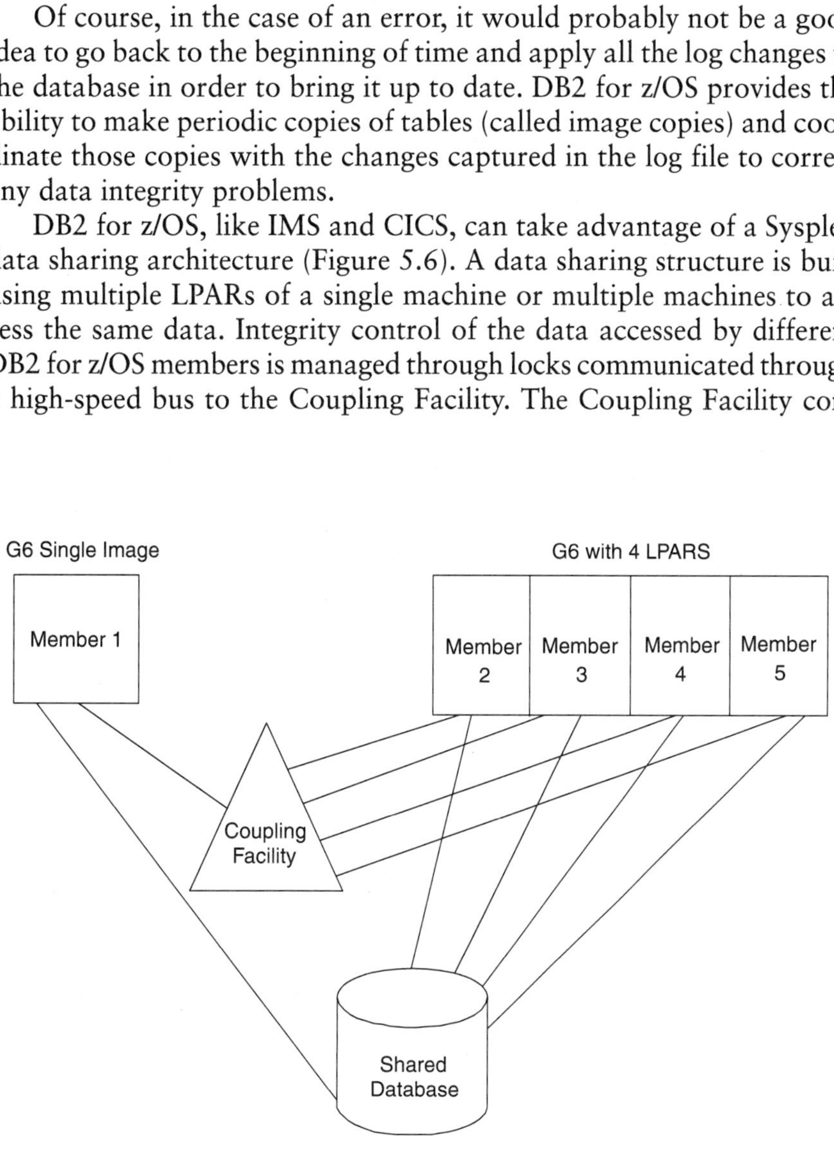

Figure 5.6. Parallel Sysplex.

tains all the information DB2 for z/OS needs to insure data integrity across a common database.

Parallel Sysplex dramatically increases DB2 for z/OS availability. The use of multiple members to access the same data allows you to roll out maintenance without experiencing significant application downtime. Should a situation arise that brings down one of the members of a Parallel Sysplex configuration, the other members can take over the work, keeping the application running—essential in an e-business application. For companies with a requirement to handle large amounts of data, transactions, or increased concurrency, such as that required for high-volume Internet transactions, Sysplex data sharing is an excellent way to achieve this objective.

Part of the z/OS operating system, Workload Manager (WLM) allows increased manageability of transactions using an automated facility. This allows you to set goals for different applications (both DB2 for z/OS and non-DB2 for z/OS) so that some applications take priority over others. This can be critical in an environment that allows both short online transactions such as an Internet logon and longer transactions such as an Internet search. With WLM, the load can be balanced by giving the different types of applications different performance goals. WLM then governs the resources given to each type of application to insure these performance goals are met. DB2 for z/OS uses operating system facilities extensively to provide improved synergy with zSeries hardware and the z/OS operating system. Dispatching is one example where the z/OS component WLM has been enhanced a number of times to do a better job of managing the diverse requests and meet the customer service level agreement.

Security is an important issue for any application and is discussed in Chapter 6. However, it is important to note that DB2 for z/OS has both its own internal security as well as the ability to use external security such as RACF (Resource Access Control Facility) and Top Secret. This internal security can be configured to allow certain users to use certain programs and tables to be accessed only by authorized users or programs. This security can also be configured to interface with existing security procedures and software.

DB2 Server for VSE and VM

DB2 Server for VSE and VM is the DB2 database implementation on the VM and VSE operating systems. It has also been around since the 1980s and has kept up with the implementation necessary to function in an e-business world. Like DB2 for z/OS, it can be accessed using the DRDA (Distributed Relational Database Architecture) protocol found in DB2 Connect over SNA (Systems Network Architecture) or TCP/IP networks.

DataPropagational Relational Capture allows users to pull information from DB2 Server for VSE and VM databases and distribute it to multiple locations across the enterprise. This product will be discussed further in the data movement section of this chapter.

DB2 Universal Database for Multiplatforms

In 1988, IBM expanded support for the DB2 database to the AS/400 platform. Subsequently, the DB2 database was released for AIX in 1993 and DB2 for Common Servers (including Windows, UNIX, and OS/2) in 1995. At about this same time, DB2 for Parallel Edition was launched to take advantage of shared nothing or MPP (massively parallel processor) hardware architectures discussed in Chapter 2. DB2 for Common Servers and DB2 for Parallel Edition were merged in the late 1990s to become DB2 Universal Database. As new types of operating systems have been introduced, particularly under the UNIX umbrella, the DB2 database has been made available for these operating systems, including the growing Linux platform. (Linux has also been ported to zSeries machines and can access DB2 for z/OS as well as DB2 for Linux for zSeries.) Again, checking the latest announcement letters for the DB2 database is the best way to understand which platforms are supported.

DB2 Universal Database comes in six main packages for different client/server set-ups. Two of them are developer's editions. The others are Personal Edition, Workgroup Edition, Enterprise Edition, and Extended Enterprise Edition.

DB2 Universal Database Personal Edition (PE) is designed for an individual setup where the client and server occupy the same SMP machine. It does not support multiple users. It can be used for small companies that need to design an application using a relational database or for initial development to be ported to a larger system.

DB2 Universal Database Workgroup Edition (WE) allows clients to be separated from the database kept on a server. The server can be on an SMP machine with no more than four processors. Clients communicate over a LAN (Local Area Network) to the server using Client Application Enablers (CAEs). The Workgroup Edition does not contain code for communication to other DB2 database servers.

The code required to access DB2 for z/OS from a DB2 database client is based on a DRDA protocol. DRDA has two parts: an application requester and an application server. The application requester is required on a client or server that needs to communicate to another server that acts as the Application Server. (This includes all servers in the DB2 database family.) The application requester functionality of DRDA is included in the following two DB2 Universal Database packages, as well as in DB2 Connect.

DB2 Universal Database Extended Edition (EE) is designed to support multiple clients accessing a database server on an SMP machine. In this case, the SMP machine can have more than four processors. The extended edition can also access other DB2 databases since they contain the DRDA application requestor protocol.

DB2 Universal Database Enterprise Extended Edition (EEE) is designed to support multiple clients accessing database servers built on a shared-nothing hardware architecture. For example, there may be multiple SMP machines, each with its own copy of DB2 Universal Database EEE (Figure 5.7). A network or high-speed switch connects these machines to each other. Each one of these machines may "own" a piece, or partition of the database. When a query accesses the data, the master processor divides the work and gives each DB2 Universal Database EEE a portion of the query, thereby executing the query in parallel—much faster than serial processing. (This is known as Inter-Partition Parallelism.)

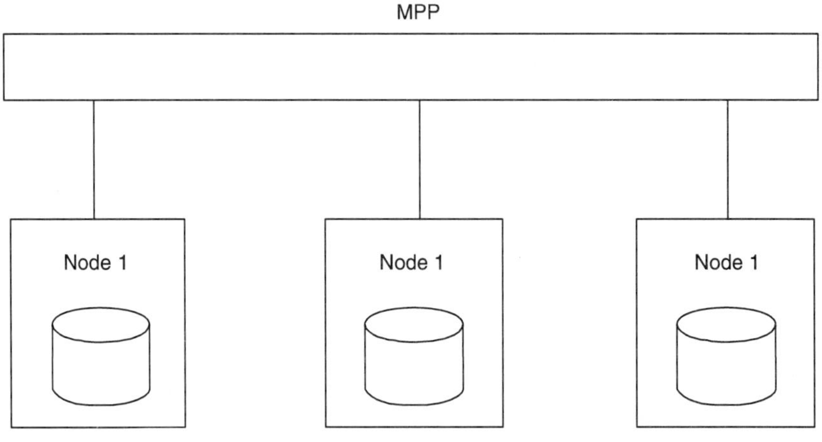

Figure 5.7. DB2 Universal Database.

To clarify between Sysplex data sharing discussed with DB2 for z/OS and the MPP structure of DB2 Universal Database EEE, note that data sharing allows all members of the Sysplex to access the data. With Inter-Partition Parallelism on an MPP, each computer can only access the data assigned to it.

Intra-Partition Parallelism is similar in concept to table space partitioning described in DB2 for z/OS. Partitions of the data exist in separate physical storage areas, but are "owned" by only one DB2 Universal Database (as opposed to *Inter*-Partition Parallelism). The DB2 Universal Database optimizer can split a query into parallel threads and access the data in parallel. Either type of partitioning also has the benefits of partitions in DB2 for z/OS. With physically separate pieces of data, any outage will affect only a small portion of the data. Data can be stored on mirrored disks in this structure as well, allowing for a hardware recovery if there is a problem.

While DB2 Universal Database has a structure that is similar to DB2 for z/OS, it has differences based on its development past as well as the operating systems on which it runs (z/OS vs. Windows and the various flavors of UNIX). DB2 Universal Database has the same code base across any operating system for about 90% of the code, with about 10% of the code changing per operating system (Linux, AIX, Windows 2000, etc.) to insure maximum performance by taking advantage of operating system differences.

Multiple copies of a DB2 Universal Database can run on the same physical machine if the operating system is UNIX or Linux, but not Windows NT or OS/2. Each copy is called an instance of DB2 Universal Database. Conceptually, this corresponds to the DB2 subsystem on DB2 for z/OS. Again the reason for using multiple instances of DB2 Universal Database is to allow the setup of different instances with different characteristics for different functions: test, stress test, data warehouse, online storefront, etc. The database manager configuration parameters contain the knobs for setting up different characteristics for each instance.

Each DB2 Universal Database instance can contain one or more databases, just like DB2 for z/OS. Within the databases, there are table spaces. These table spaces are associated with containers. (This is different from the OS/390 platform in that DB2 for z/OS doesn't support this construct.) A container can be a directory in the machine's file system, a physical file, or a device such as a hard disk. A table space can be associated with one or multiple containers. Like z/OS, there can be multiple tables within a table space. Indexes are kept in a separate table space.

Like DB2 for z/OS, there can be separate table spaces for large objects with pointers from the main table. Temporary tables are also available in DB2 Universal Database for Multiplatforms.

The concept of partitioning in DB2 Universal Database for Multiplatforms is somewhat different from the concept on the zSeries. If you recall, DB2 for z/OS allows a table space to be physically divided into different pieces. Each piece can be in different physical storage and accessed by different processors. Only one table can be in a partitioned table space.

In DB2 Universal Database the partitioning is done at the database level. Each table in the database may have some of its rows in each partition. Each partition has its own set of indexes that relate only to that partition.

Like DB2 for z/OS, DB2 Universal Database for Multiplatforms keeps log records of changes. It also has the ability to make copies of the tables, but in this case a copy is called a backup rather than an image copy.

Much of the management of DB2 Universal Database is done via a facility called the Control Center. The Control Center is a graphical tool for administering all DB2 databases, including DB2 for z/OS. It provides the ability to control several of them on different machines. The Control Center can run on the same server on which DB2 Universal Database for Windows is installed. However, DB2 Universal Database on a UNIX-type operating system must be controlled remotely from a Control Center on a Windows server.

As noted earlier, SQL is used to access the data on DB2 Universal Database. As with DB2 for z/OS, DB2 Universal Database has both static and dynamic SQL. Several facilities for handling dynamic SQL statements are available. These are CLI, ODBC, JDBC, and Deferred Embedded SQL.

Deferred Embedded SQL, ODBC, and JDBC were discussed in the DB2 for z/OS section. CLI is an interface that an application program can use to submit SQL statements for processing. The SQL is wrapped in a CLI function call. This function handles the details needed to connect to the database, get results, and define the unit of work, similar to the CICS transaction manager discussed earlier.

Security for DB2 Universal Database is similar to DB2 for z/OS—available at the object level (table, view, etc.), the user profile level, and the program level.

DB2 Universal Database for iSeries

The DB2 database that was incorporated into the AS/400 in 1988 has grown to become DB2 Universal Database for iSeries. DB2 Universal Database for iSeries contains most of the technology that makes DB2 Universal Database a robust relational database. However, it is optimized to run on the iSeries platform.

Over the past several years, DB2 Universal Database for iSeries has focused on four key areas of improvement and growth: open standards, performance, usability, and flexibility/extension. Open standards has produced increased support for the SQL standards, including their implementation for stored procedures, triggers, Java support through JDBC, and Java User Defined Functions (UDFs).

Attention to performance has paid off. DB2 Universal Database for iSeries leads or is in the top set of industry accepted benchmarks such as TPC-C, SAP's Two-Tier Sales and Distribution, and the Java based SPECjBB2000. Internal tests have shown that performance improvements apply to all facets of database management, including the ability to back up over 2.6 terabytes of data an hour.

DB2 Universal Database for iSeries is unique among the DB2 Universal Databases, because the AS/400 architecture allows the system itself to perform many of the tasks that require a Database Administrator in other environments. As in the other data management products, tools and utilities fill in the gaps.

The database also provides the ability to store, manage, index, and control all forms of information, ranging from traditional database data to documents and multimedia formats, providing the flexibility that is required in an e-business world.

DB2 Everyplace

DB2 Everyplace is the small footprint, high-performance, multiplatform, enterprise ready, relational database and synchronization architecture for mobile, wireless, or embedded computing member of the DB2 database family. It allows applications to be extended to mobile devices such as PDAs and smart phones. DB2 Everyplace can work remotely or as a client to a server if the two are connected.

There are three components to DB2 Everyplace. The DB2 Everyplace Database is the relational database that runs on the mobile device. DB2 Everyplace Sync Server handles data synchronization, and the DB2

Everyplace Mobile Application Builder provides the tools to create the application.

The DB2 Everyplace Sync Server securely exchanges data between enterprise data sources and mobile devices and also allows real-time queries to be performed. The DB2 Everyplace solution provides a Java2 MicroEdition (J2ME) Sync Client. With a very small footprint, the J2ME Sync Client uses the mobile information device profile (MIDP) for a standard platform for device-side development. The client can then provide a standard and secure interface to synchronize J2ME MIDP application data with enterprise data sources.

Because of its small footprint, this database can be embedded into things like cars and washing machines, allowing them to "phone home" in time of need.

DB2 Extenders

DB2 Extenders add to the relational database construct by giving you the capability to add and manipulate different data types. Because these extenders are designed for these data types, they can add more function and performance than simply cramming these data types into the existing DB2 database.

The following extenders are available:

- Net Search Extender allows you to index and search text files, both in memory and in the documents themselves.
- Text Information Extender and Text Extender were the initial products developed to index and search text files, but are not planned as a strategic releases in the future. Their functionality is incorporated into Net Search Extender.
- DB2 AIV (Audio, Image, Video) Extenders are a suite of three products. DB2 Audio Extender works on audio data types; DB2 Image Extender works on still images; and DB2 Video Extender works on video clips.
- DB2 XML Extender allows users to store and access XML documents.

- DB2 Spatial Extender allows users to store and access spatial data (information about the location of geographic features).

DB2 Content Management

The world of e-business is not only about traditional content such as numbers and letters, but must also include a full spectrum of digital information. This content can be scanned images, word processing documents, rich media, computer-coded data, or spreadsheets. Industry estimates suggest that 80% of a company's information is unstructured information that's usually in paper form (if you are lucky it's in a filing cabinet), on microfilm/microfiche archives, or in personally digitized content, rather than in a central repository. IBM's Content Management group of products is the software that IBM has developed to work with this hodgepodge of information.

DB2 Content Manager

DB2 Content Manager is an unstructured content management system optimized for large collections of large objects. Like many IBM software products, DB2 Content Manager uses a robust XML-ready physical data model that is implemented in a relational database (either DB2 Universal Database or Oracle) to store its information. Within this product family there are many solutions and products. The main DB2 Content Manager flavors are:

- DB2 Content Manager for Multiplatforms (AIX, Windows and SUN Solaris)
- DB2 Content Manager for OS/390
- DB2 Content Manager for AS/400.

These products provide similar functions and differ mainly to take advantage of underlying operating systems to improve performance.

The function of Content Manager is to enable management, sharing, storage and retrieval of digitally-stored objects such as images, word processing documents, spreadsheets, voice clips, video, HyperText Markup Language (HTML-) and XML-based Web content and Electronic Data Interchange (EDI). In order to do that, DB2 Content Manager contains two types of servers—a library server and an object server. The library server catalogs the objects, providing a common repository of indexes for easy search and retrieval. The actual digitally-stored objects are stored in one or many object servers. These servers can be centrally located, or decentralized to place the content close to the user. Content can be classified by content and document type (index classes) for searches by indexed keywords.

Workflow is supported by document routing capabilities. These capabilities include predefined flows with branching capability, user exits for work node entry, exit and overload handling, collection points to wait for one or more items before proceeding and worklists that let users work from one or more work nodes simultaneously.

The DB2 Content Manager library server is the single point of control for the system. In addition to holding the index information, the library server handles the requests from the clients, and then directs the appropriate object server to accept new objects or to send the object to the client. The library server is also in charge of security. Access to index classes can be controlled by content and document type, workbaskets, and advanced workflow processes. An administrator sets up security by granting access of these objects to users or groups of users.

The DB2 Content Manager solution also takes advantage of a mid-tier server which is a Web-exploiting broker that mediates between the client and the library server. It can also manage connections to the resource managers. Resource managers are specialized repositories optimized for managing storage, retrieval and archiving of enterprise content.

Incoming documents and multimedia are stored on magnetic storage during their active life cycle. To reduce costs, less active documents may be automatically migrated to optical storage or tape when the retrieval frequency is much lower. To aid the process for the multiplatforms edition, DB2 Content Manager uses Tivoli Storage Manager. On OS/390 the Object Access Method, a component of the Data Facility Storage Management System, is used to provide similar services. As noted earlier, the object servers can be centralized or distributed. The library server manages the traffic to the distributed servers. Distributed servers aid horizontal scalability because additional servers can be added as needed.

Vertical scalability can also be maintained by moving to a larger library server. Library server and object server platforms such as AIX, NT, and OS/390 can be mixed and matched with an implementation.

There are two types of DB2 Content Manager clients: a browser-based thin client called eClient and a desktop client that runs on Windows. Both clients have a GUI interface that provides functionality to the user by point-and-click operations. From the client, users can perform searches and work with documents or folders that have been routed to them. They can annotate images with a wide range of markups, such as highlighting, "type on" text, post-it notes, circles, squares, lines, arrows, or easily customized stamps. Free-form text comments can also be added to a note log that is associated with each document and folder. Folders can be nested, one within the other. In order to take advantage of workflow processes, you can use the DB2 Content Manager workflow components, which provide routing on serial paths, or integrate DB2 Content Manager with WebSphere MQ Workflow for more sophisticated process management.

In order to find the document needed, the user can take advantage of the basic search capability that allows users to query the system at a document or folder level and retrieve documents and folders. There is also an advanced search capability that allows the creation of complex SQL queries that can be saved as templates for future re-use. After the object is retrieved, the user has two approaches for viewing objects: retrieving and displaying objects in the DB2 Content Manager client or launching native applications for the retrieved document.

For example, with a word processing document, the word processor can be launched automatically, display the document and allow the user to edit and then restore the document.

DB2 Content Manager works with a number of industry-standard, high-performance fax solutions such as MessagePlus/Open. Incoming faxes are captured at the fax server and then automatically imported into DB2 Content Manager. Alternatively, users can select documents from the DB2 Content Manager client to fax out. All Content Manager clients can capture documents with desktop scanners or by importing files directly into DB2 Content Manager. After they are scanned, documents can be routed to an appropriate workbasket (queue) for indexing.

For higher volume scanning, a batch capture subsystem is usually implemented such as Kofax Ascent Capture and Action Point's Input Accel. These production-level document capture applications integrate high-performance batch scanning, image processing, Optical Character Recognition (OCR), Intelligent Character Recognition (ICR), and document indexing into a single package that significantly lowers the cost of capturing large quantities of documents into DB2 Content Manager.

If none of these tools meet your needs, the DB2 Content Manager client provides an extensive number of application programming interfaces and function calls. Supported APIs include Java, JavaBeans, C++ and ActiveX. This modular architecture is fully Unicode-enabled and embodies the open systems style of IBM software. The latest industry standards and Internet protocols, including HyperText Transfer Protocol (HTTP), File Transfer Protocol (FTP), RTSP, JDBC, ODMA and SQL are supported.

So how do you get all this great content to the Web? The IBM Enterprise Information Portal (EIP) technologies complement Content Manager. The IBM EIP Client Kit for DB2 Content Manager provides a client for access to content in DB2 Content Manager. The kit also includes a wide variety of APIs, including JavaBeans, C++ Object Oriented APIs, and ActiveX components for Content Manager solution development and integration. DB2 Content Manager OnDemand and DB2 Content Manager VideoCharger, described below, are optional features.

DB2 Content Manager ImagePlus for OS/390 is designed to manage very large volumes of document-based information in high-transaction rate applications needing content management services. One key component is the Folder Application Facility which provides library, folder, workflow and application functions. Another is the Object Distribution Manager which manages the movement of objects among storage locations (Direct Access Storage Device [DASD], optical and tape). It works with the System Managed Storage (SMS) capabilities of the zSeries hardware. The Object Access Method manages the storage of these images on magnetic and optical devices. This lets you keep the most frequently accessed images on the fastest (and generally most expensive) devices, while moving less frequently accessed documents to slower (and generally cheaper) devices.

DB2 Content Manager VideoCharger

DB2 Content Manager VideoCharger provides an integrated desktop player for realtime video delivery of multiple file types. This means that you don't have to be a technical guru to look at a video clip that someone has sent you or you have found on the Web. The solution can be used with DB2 Content Manager to provide corporate communications, distance learning, merchandising, video on demand, and enhanced customer service so you can show someone inserting Tab A into Slot B instead of hoping they understand from the drawings.

Like other IBM products, DB2 Content Manager VideoCharger was developed in a modular format, enabling customized applications using open systems architectures. It comes with a Software Development Kit (SDK) so you can easily integrate streaming video into your applications. The solution supports many multimedia formats, including MPEG-1, MPEG-2, MPEG-4, Apple QuickTime 5, AVI, HotMedia, MP3 and WAV.

Electronic Media Management System

The Electronic Media Management Systems (EMMS) is a suite of seven software components that interact to provide a method to manage and secure online content. These seven components (Figure 5.8) are:

- EMMS Content Preparation Software Development Kit which allows you to package content with associated rules of permitted use into secure containers. These containers can then be distributed.

- EMMS Content Mastering Program provides music content owners the ability to package and secure asset usage only by authorized users.

- EMMS Web Commerce Enabler allows you to integrate content into existing Web applications.

- EMMS Clearinghouse Program facilitates enforcement of content controls and prevents unauthorized use.

- EMMS Content Hosting Program stores digital content.

- EMMS Multi-Device Server facilitates the secure transfer of digital content to devices such as mobile handsets or kiosks.

- EMMS Client Software Development Kit allows you to develop industry-specific client applications that download, stream and use content in a tamper-resistant environment according to the usage rights specified by content owners.

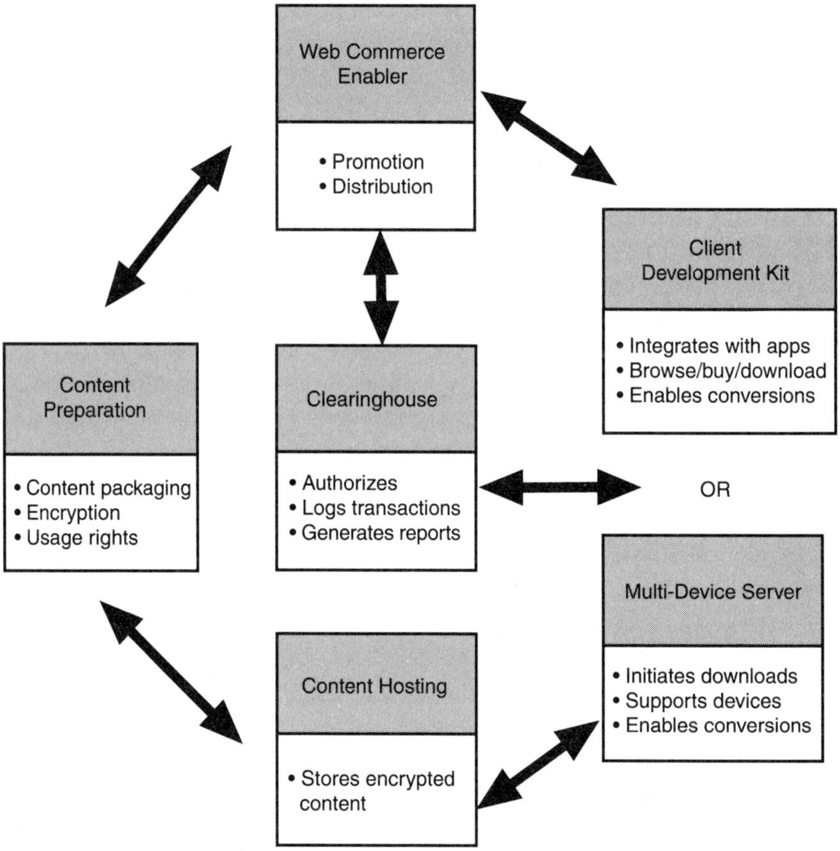

Figure 5.8. IBM EMMS Software Suite.

DB2 Content Manager Solutions

DB2 Content Manager can be purchased as part of the following integrated solutions:

- DB2 Content Manager can be integrated with WebSphere Portal (discussed in Chapter 4) to provide a content-rich portal solution.

- Enterprise Customer Service for Call Centers integrates DB2 Content Manager and DB2 Content Manager OnDemand with Siebel customer relationship management (CRM) solutions.

- IBM eRecords Solution integrates DB2 Content Manager and Tarian eRecords engine to provide management for electronic records such as Lotus Notes (Chapter 7) e-mail.

- MessagePlus/Open is an enterprise messaging solution capable of handling all incoming and outgoing communications of many types. This is a new version of FaxPlus/Open that works with DB2 Content Manager as described earlier.

- DB2 Content Manager for Financial Institutions is a portfolio of products that enables financial institutions to integrate and share information created in a variety of formats. It includes DB2 Content Manager, DB2 Content Manager OnDemand, Enterprise Information Portal, DB2 Content Manager CommonStore, DB2 Content Manager VideoCharger, WebSphere MQ Workflow and Lotus Domino.Doc.

DB2 Content Manager CommonStore

DB2 Content Manager CommonStore is a content manager solution designed to manage Microsoft Outlook (DB2 Content Manager CommonStore for Exchange Server), SAP documents (DB2 Content Manager CommonStore for SAP) and Lotus Notes documents (DB2 Content Manager CommonStore for Lotus Domino). The product allows you to externally archive e-mail or documents for long-term storage. To the every day user, the archived document looks like their normal document and they can call up the archived data through embedded links in the document.

These solutions can be enhanced by developing archiving policies for different types of documents and using the DB2 Content Manager CommonStore to implement these policies. These stored documents can then be moved to cheaper and cheaper storage as they age through the incorporated use of DB2 Content Manager OnDemand technology.

DB2 Content Manager OnDemand

DB2 Content Manager OnDemand provides a way to capture and manage large objects, including e-mail, electronic reports and scanned documents. The product allows you to automatically organize and store any printed output.

The OnDemand Capture System component of Content Manager OnDemand reads through reports to extract index information. This index information is used to build logical segments that allow you to have direct access to different sections of a report, rather than retrieve and browse the whole thing in order to find what you are looking for.

The product also provides a retrieval mechanism that allows you to have a "fill-in-the-blank" screen for queries. This generates a list of documents from which the user can choose reports to view, annotate, print or fax. Built-in security features enable administrators to control access to the system and its archived documents. Accessing this list can be done via the web, as well as local retrieval.

Support for multiple print datastreams is provided. This includes AFP, Metacode and PCL for the Multiplatforms version of Content Manager OnDemand.

Documents can be managed across magnetic, optical and tape devices. Depending on the version of OnDemand used (Multiplatforms; iSeries; OS/390 and z/OS), the substructure that manages the migration varies.

Informix

In July 2001, the Informix database business became part of the IBM DB2 portfolio. IBM has issued several statements of direction, each a little more detailed than the previous. In general, IBM is committed to supporting and enhancing the Informix product line at regular intervals for as long as customers are using them. They have also stated that there will be no forced migrations from Informix to DB2 databases.

At the same time, IBM DB2 has stated that the DB2 database is the technology base for IBM's future information infrastructure, so any new applications you are building should consider using that as a foundation, rather than the Informix products. Technology that is unique to Informix will be migrated into the DB2 database family. To ease the transition, future DB2 database releases will emphasize two general areas: native Informix connectivity and portability enhancements in the server.

Specifically, IBM only plans to support operating system updates for the Informix Standard Engine (SE) database server. IBM also has said that they have no future releases planned for Informix C-ISAM.

Informix Dynamic Server (IDS)

Informix Dynamic Server (IDS) is commonly used for On-line Transaction Processing (OLTP), decision support, CRM, enterprise resource planning (ERP) and many other enterprise applications. Because IDS is easily embeddable, it is often integrated into original equipment manufacturer (OEM) solutions, such as those from Intrado (911 emergency systems), Telelogic (Software Configuration Management) and many others. It is fully compatible with WebSphere Application Server to enable you to build e-business applications quickly. In addition, future releases of IDS will encompass IBM's SMART self-managing concepts—in line with e-business on demand.

Informix Dynamic Server (IDS) is available in two different versions. The first (version 7.x) is built on the relational model and contains the table and index concepts presented earlier, with some variations. IDS version 7 is the most commonly installed version of the IDS family, however, it is a mature product and will not be seeing much enhancement in the future. Instead, IBM recommends that customers use IDS version 9.x which is a fully object-relational engine. IDS version 9 data types can be built-in (standard types such as character, numeric and LOB) or extended, enabling you to use either bundled, non-standard types (e.g. Collections or named row types) or create your own. A structure unique to IDS, called an aggregate, is a function that returns information about a set of query results. For example, the built-in SUM aggregate adds values returned from a query and returns the result.

The partitioning scheme of IDS is similar to that of DB2 for z/OS in that the table is divided up based on user-selected columnar values and portions of it placed on different disk storage (called expression partitioning). IDS supports additional types of partitioning as well. For example simple round-robin partitioning causes every new record to go to the next partition in the sequence.

IDS has a concept called data skip. This allows a complex query that accesses many partitions to skip one that isn't available. The main query completes, and a second query to access the missing data can be issued once the partition has been restored. If data skip is used, a flag is returned to the missing statement that an incomplete set of values was returned. It is up to the developer to trap for this condition and determine the appropriate course of action.

Another concept unique to IDS is that a partitioned table and indexes can be modified using the "alter fragment" command. Two tables with identical structures can be combined into a single fragmented (partitioned) table, called an attached table. Alternatively, a table fragment (partition) can be placed in a new table, called a detached table. This method of attaching and detaching tables can be used when limited disk space necessitates moving outdated data from disk to other forms of storage media.

IDS places this relational structure on top of a parallel database architecture called Dynamic Scalable Architecture (DSA). DSA enables all major database operations, such as I/O, complex queries, index builds, log recovery, and backups and restores to execute in parallel across all available system resources. A configurable pool of database server processes (virtual processors) schedules and manages user requests across multiple CPUs and disks. Like DB2 for z/OS, user requests are represented by a mechanism, called a thread. Each thread can spawn multiple database threads (subtasks) that can be used to speed up the processing of requests such as multi-table joins.

A process called a thread scheduler controls the scheduling of the threads. Threads are spawned, queued and serviced by the first available virtual processor. Each virtual processor can work on multiple threads simultaneously, depending on the work that needs to be done. Like DB2 Universal Database for Multiplatforms, IDS takes advantage of the specific hardware and operating systems that underlie the database.

IDS, Informix verion 9.x is the underlying engine of three functional bundles called Foundation products. Foundation bundles provide additional data management functionality through the use of one or more DataBlades as well as a JVM. The latest Foundation bundle, J/Foundation contains the most requested feature from the larger foundations—a bundled JVM. This foundation allows you to build and execute Java routines, either in the form of stored procedures or JavaBeans, directly in the database engine.

Recoverability is important for all databases, and IDS offers several methods to improve availability as well as provide failover processing. These include simple master/slave copies through High-Availability Data Replication (HDR), configurable, discrete, and bi-directional enterprise-level data replication using Enterprise Replication, as well as automatic client connection with MaxConnect.

HDR works from a concept of primary and secondary copies of the database. These instances can be on the same system or two different systems. (The latter can be useful for disaster recovery preparedness.) HDR copies the IDS transaction log records from the primary instance to the secondary instance as the log records are written. The transaction is not considered complete until the secondary instance receives the transaction records. There is almost no impact to the primary instance in this mode. As a result, HDR provides a real-time, fully synchronous secondary copy of the data. This technology will be built into DB2 Universal Database in the near future, replacing the current DB2 replication technology.

With IDS's enterprise replication technology, data can be replicated asynchronously or synchronously to one or multiple sites. Unlike HDR, data can be replicated bi-directionally. The enterprise replication employs a message-delivery mechanism, which stores data locally and propagates it to the target server(s) as a separate transaction. This insures recoverability should a network failure occur. Target database instances can continue to operate and will be synchronized once network connectivity is restored. While enterprise replication can be configured to replicate data in simple master/slave mode, it is more commonly used for complex operations requiring node and leaf, cascading, forest of trees, or snowflake replication scenarios.

To add to availability of online systems, particularly e-business systems, automatic resizing needs to take place as demand increases or decreases. IDS dynamically adds and releases resources (including memory) as needed during peak periods. Configuration changes for things like CPU changes, disk space and partitioning schemes can be changed online, avoiding system downtime.

Informix DataBlades

Informix DataBlades extend the database to handle complex objects and the methods and operations that surround them. In this way, they are similar to DB2's database extenders. They allow IDS to integrate new data types, operations that process the data and access methods that index the data. Some of the key technologies that Informix developed with DataBlades, such as Rtrees and TimeSeries technology will be implemented into future releases of DB2 Universal Database.

The following DataBlades are available:

- Excalibur Image DataBlade allows you to store, retrieve and search images stored on the database.

- Image Foundation DataBlade provides a base on which new or specialized image types and image processing technologies can be added or changed.

- Video Foundation DataBlade provides an open architecture for video-enabling technologies such as video servers, external control devices, compression codes or cataloging tools.

- Excalibur Text Search DataBlade supports full-text searching of documents.

- Web DataBlade is a collection of tools, functions and examples that eases the development and management of Web-based database applications.

- Spatial DataBlade allows you to manage geo-spatial data and includes a specialized Rtree index to enable high-performance SQL access to spatial data.

- Geodetic DataBlade stores and manipulates four-dimensional objects, particularly useful for managing spatial-temporal data.

- TimeSeries DataBlade supports management and analysis of time series data, such as data that needs to be accessed and processed in chronological order.

- Numeric Algorithms Group (NAG) DataBlade provides numerical analysis functions and formulas. The TimeSeries RealTime Loader works with this DataBlade to achieve greater analytical performance.

- C-ISAM DataBlade stores ISAM data in the database and allows you to access it using C functions.

Informix also provides a DataBlade Development Kit that allows you to create new data types and routines. The development kit manages the packaging, installation and registration of completed DataBlade modules.

OnLine Extended Edition

OnLine Extended Edition is an easy-to-use, embeddable relational database server for low-to-medium workloads. This product replaces Informix OnLine 5 and Informix STAR, although IBM has stated that it will continue to enhance the Informix OnLine products for the new generation of lightweight "Internet appliance" servers with one or two CPUs.

OnLine Extended Edition is specifically designed for UNIX operating systems. To improve performance, it can take advantage of UNIX configurations, or avoid them. For example, it avoids the UNIX file management system and stores data on raw disks so it can take advantage of direct memory access to disk, speeding the time it takes to commit transactions to disk.

The memory is shared between different processes. When data is requested from disk, only one copy of the data is stored in memory, allowing all processes to access and use the same copy, saving expensive trips to disk. This memory is divided into internal tables and buffer pages. Internal tables are used to store data during processing; buffer pages are for data retrieved from disk.

Like DB2 Universal Database, OnLine Extended Edition makes use of a cost-based optimizer as well as other features that make a robust relational database system. This includes locking algorithms for data integrity, mirroring for data availability, and logging for recoverability.

Red Brick Warehouse

Red Brick Warehouse is also built on the relational model, but has been designed and enhanced to be particularly useful for business intelligence applications where little or no maintenance overhead is important. It utilizes a form of star and snowflake schema that has been built for performance. (Star and snowflake schemas were described in Chapter 2.)

IBM will continue to offer enhancements and support for Red Brick, but also plans to integrate key features of Red Brick into DB2 Universal Database. Some of these include the Red Brick style loader enhancements and Red Brick style Star Join optimizations into DB2 Universal Database.

One of the things that Red Brick adds to the relational design is a number of different types of indexes. One of these is a STARindex which accelerates join processing between multiple tables. The Red Brick STARjoin technology leverages referential integrity relationships in a star or snowflake schema and uses these indexes to improve performance. Another type of index is the TARGETindex. This type of index improves performance when queries are looking for data that doesn't have a lot of selectivity. For example, let's imagine a table that has information about 20 million customers, including gender and the state in which they live. A query looking for all the women living in California is going to return a lot of rows. These are the types of queries that TARGETindexes were designed to help.

Informix Extended Parallel Server (XPS)

Informix Extended Parallel Server (XPS) is a product designed for decision support applications built on very large databases. IBM intends to continue to offer enhancements and support of XPS, and will move toward integrating XPS with DB2 business intelligence tools.

XPS takes advantage a shared-nothing architecture in its engine. (Shared-nothing architectures were discussed in Chapter 3.) If you'll recall, one of the advantages of these architectures is their ability to divide queries requiring large answer sets into multiple parts for quicker execution. These types of queries are typical in decision support applications that query data warehouse style databases. XPS is also enhanced for star join optimization.

Each part of the shared nothing architecture is called a node. In XPS each node runs its own instance of XPS and manages its own logging, recovery, locking and buffer management. Each instance is called a co-server. Each co-server owns a set of disks and partitions of the database that reside on these disks.

Different clients can connect to different co-servers. If a co-server determines that the client is requesting information that resides on the disks of another co-server, it interacts and coordinates activities with participating co-servers. Every co-server has a request manager which makes decisions about how a query should be divided and distributed while insuring that the workload is balanced across the nodes. Information about what node has what data (called metadata by XPS) is managed by a metadata manager which also resides on each node. A scheduler also resides on every co-server. Its responsibility is to distribute tasks within the system.

The shared-nothing architecture also lends itself to adjustments for changing workloads, as well as failover solutions for increased availability. It can be rapidly reconfigured so that if a processor fails, one can be switched to take over its workload. In addition, XPS allows processors to be added at times of peak load, simply by restarting the database. A co-server typically can access disks owned by other co-servers for failover purposes.

Tables and indexes are partitioned across the nodes. They can be partitioned through a number of different methods, including simple round-robin (every record goes to the next partition in the sequence); hashed (an algorithm applied to the record key determines its partition number); range (data is divided based on key ranges); and expression (each partition gets a set of records based on their key value).

XPS has several types of indexes, including the DB2 index described earlier. In addition, it can use a bitmap index, popular in many data warehouse implementations. The bitmap index uses a single bit with values of 0 or 1 to indicate that a specific value of a column is, or is not, associated with a particular row. These bits are associated with a B-tree index. For example, if you are looking for a store that has a sports department, you only need to access the rows that have the "sports" bit turned on. XPS also has a generalized key (GK) index. These indexes come in three flavors: GK join indexes, GK virtual column indexes and GK selective indexes. Although they vary in structure, essentially these indexes pre-create an index based on join, expression or subquery.

Like DB2 Universal Database and other Informix products, XPS contains enhanced SQL structures. In the case of XPS, these enhancements are designed to support decision support and business intelligence queries.

Informix Solutions

Informix solutions are suites of products that are packaged together to enable fast development in a particular industry. These products have been previously described. The following solutions, called Foundations, were available at the time of this writing:

- Finance Foundation for Capital Markets contains TimeSeries RealTime Loader, TimeSeries DataBlade, NAG DataBlade and the Informix Dynamic Server.

- Law Enforcement Foundation for Biometrics contains Video Foundation DataBlade, Image Foundation DataBlade, Excalibur Image DataBlade and Informix Dynamic Server.

- Internet Foundation includes Informix Web Database, Excalibur Text Search DataBlade, Office Connect (described later), Object Translator, and Informix Dynamic Server.

U2 Product Family

IBM has separated the Informix products into two main groups: the Informix product line described earlier and the U2 (UniVerse/Unidata) product family, which is what this section is about. UniVerse is an extended-relational (or object-relational) database that supports both direct record I/O as well as standard SQL. UniData is an extended-relational, ODBC-compliant database that supports repeating groups, hierarchies and arrays. IBM is actively enhancing both these databases and many of the supporting tools and add-on products.

UniData

UniData is a small-footprint, embeddable database with a Java technology-based GUI administration tool and automatic table space management. IBM intends to offer enhancements and support for this product as long as customers require. For example, the most recent release provided enhancements to openness, security, robustness and scalability. This included a native JDBC driver as well as support for XML input and output from the database engine. The database supports Secure Socket Layer (SSL) for the HTTP and socket interfaces, as well as Telnet and UniObjects for Java.

UniData is a nested relational database. DB2 Universal Database, Oracle, IDS, XPS and others in this paper are relational databases based on the relational model described in Chapter 2. If you'll recall, a relational database was a construct of tables with keys that related to each other in some way. If all of the relational rules are followed, a database design is said to be normalized. There are varying degrees of normalization, but the one that concerns us here is First Normal Form.

The predominant rule for a database to be in First Normal Form is that there cannot be any repeating groups. For example, if you had a table that contained information about a store's sales, you might first think of a row that had the Store Identification Number and a column for each month's total sales. This table is not in First Normal Form. In order to make it into First Normal Form, you would need to have twelve rows for each store—one for each month.

Another concept we need to explore is that of logical design. Logical design of a relational database is a business activity, with drawings and dictionaries designed to be comprehensible to a business user. During a logical design phase, a connector and phrase is used to connect the tables (Figure 5.9). For example:

Store *contains* products.

Products *exist in* stores.

In order for the database to be built, however, a table has to take the place of this connector. This table consists of a row containing a key from each table. In our example, there would be a row with the key from the Store Table and a key from the Product Table (Figure 5.10).

Using a nested relational database structure, this set of three tables would be collapsed, or denormalized. Repeating fields or groups would be allowed, allowing the association of an amount field with a product (Figure 5.11). One advantage to this structure is that the performance required to develop a report of all the products in a store is vastly reduced. Another is that the schema is easier to maintain with the elimination of relationship tables. In this way, nested relational databases share a similarity with the hierarchical structures discussed in Chapter 3. Of course, this comes with a price as well (nothing's free in data processing). While hierarchical and nested relationships perform extremely well for well identified and consistent processes, they are less flexible than a relational database in terms of structural changes where the process is not as well defined.

Like other relational databases, UniData can have a construct of triggers which allow you to support business rules.

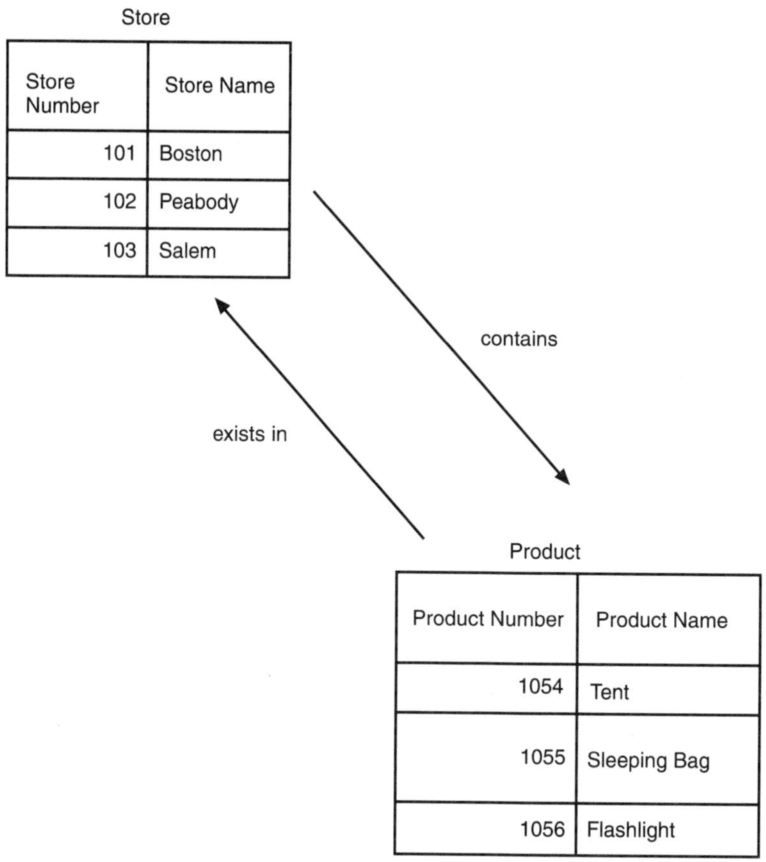

Figure 5.9. Logical database view.

These tables are accessed with a flavor of SQL called UniData SQL. This SQL provides extensions for navigating UniData's nested data structures. With the newest release UniData can output XML from both UniQuery (UniData query language) and UniData SQL. Data is actually accessed using direct I/O, and supports both set-based and record I/O.

The integrated native server-side development environment for UniData is UniBasic. UniBasic compiles to byte-code, similar to that of Java, and allows you to develop and deploy UniData applications across any platform for which a UniData virtual machine is available. This environment has full SQL and C language interfaces. It also supports input of XML via document object model (DOM) handling within UniBasic.

Store

Store Number	Store Name
101	Boston
102	Peabody
103	Salem

Store/Product Table

Store Number	Product Number	Product Amount
101	1054	25
101	1055	300
101	1056	569

Product Table

Product Number	Product Name
1054	Tent
1055	Sleeping Bag
1056	Flashlight

Figure 5.10. Physical relational database view.

Store Number	Product Number	Product Amount	Product Number	Product Amount	Product Number	Product Amount
101	1054	25	1055	300	1056	569
102	1054	0	1055	10	1056	999
103	1054	100	1055	500	1056	10

Figure 5.11. Nested relational view.

UniData provides native support for WebSphere MQ (Chapter 4). A UniBasic API allows UniData to operate as an MQ client or server and perform queue management.

UniData offers a number of file structures, including hashed files for faster file access and dynamic files for automatic file sizing. Tables are implemented using the native files of the operating system. Recovery of a UniData file is done by using automatic roll forward and roll back, journaling, and transaction logging. It also includes data replication functionality based on a publisher/subscriber model. This can be used to support high availability, failover solutions or create report servers to off-load processing on OLTP systems.

UniVerse

Like UniData, UniVerse is an extended-relational database management system that supports both direct record I/O, as well as standard SQL. It also offers ActiveX, ODBC, OLEDB, JDBC and Java interfaces. IBM intends enhancements and support for UniVerse customers as long as required. Recent enhancements include a native JDBC driver, support for XML I/O from the database engine, added support of SSL for the HTTP and socket interfaces and an encryption API in the stored procedure language. Future enhancements will include a native interface to WebSphere MQ, extensions to XML and SSL support, the addition of a SOAP API and some performance improvements.

UniVerse can dynamically vary table space allocation to provide optimum performance and maximum efficiency. This capability also streamlines traditional database monitoring, reconfiguration and maintenance tasks. UniVerse excels at support of multilingual applications by providing support for Unicode for server side programming. (Remember that Unicode doesn't do language translation. It provides a rich character set so that languages' character sets can be properly represented.) It also provides excellent support of client/server or n-tier development using UniVerse middleware and APIs.

The integrated native server-side development environment for UniVerse is UniVerse Basic. UniVerse Basic compiles to byte-code, similar to that of Java, and allows you to develop and deploy UniVerse applications across any platform for which a UniVerse Virtual machine is available. This environment has full SQL and C language interfaces. It also supports input of XML via Document Object Model (DOM) handling within UniVerse Basic. UniVerse supports the use of triggers and stored procedures to support business rules and improve performance in a client/server environment.

UniVerse also supports data replication using a publication and subscription methodology. This allows you to have continuous multi-site, multi-table replication and a hot standby in case of system failure.

RedBack

RedBack is a scalable object-enabling infrastructure solution for N-tier development for the U2 databases. It uses RedBack Business Objects (RBOs) to transform the nested relational database into an object-based client/server or Web application. IBM intends to offer enhancements to RedBack as long as required. Look for this product to have a tighter integration with WebSphere development products.

There are three parts to the RedBack product: the application server, the gateway and development interfaces. A visual tool called RedBack Designer is available to help design and maintain RBOs.

The RedBack Application Server manages and controls connections to the network application server of a Web application. HTTP connections are stateless connections. Once a connection completes a piece of work, whether or not the transaction is complete, information about that connection goes away unless there is something else to manage it. That something else, in this case, is the RedBack Application Server. The server also can be used by developers to maintain the state of any objects they are using while processing the application. The application server also manages the results from a request, whether that request has come from a Java Native Interface (JNI) module, or directly from an HTTP request using XML/SOAP.

RBOs are user-defined objects that contain properties and business rules as method calls. (For more information on object-oriented design and implementation, see Chapter 2.) RBOs can be referenced as stored procedures, or directly as ActiveX Data Objects, JavaBeans, or XML interfaces.

The RedBack Gateway provides the interface between a Web server and the RedBack Application Server. The Gateway Client Requester component resides in the network application server and the Gateway Server Schedule component resides on the same server as the RedBack Application Server. The communication protocol between these two components is based on named pipes and sockets technologies (UNIX) or Windows NT operating system technologies (Figure 5.12).

RedBack Development Interfaces separate the Web design elements from the application development design elements. The application development team focuses on business rules and database implementation. This tool allows the integration of these two layers.

SystemBuilder

SystemBuilder allows developers to build and deploy portable U2 applications quickly using visual development technologies. It integrates with

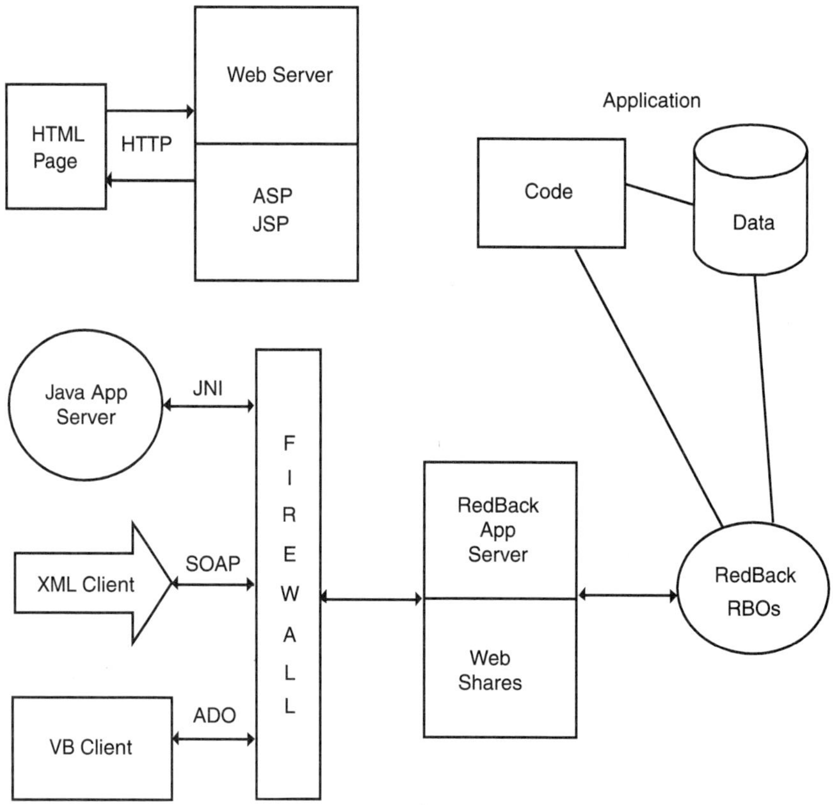

Figure 5.12. RedBack application infrastructure.

RedBack to extend applications with Java technologies and browser-based interfaces. IBM intends to offer enhancements and support for SystemBuilder as long as required.

SystemBuilder is made up of SB+Server, a fourth generation language (4GL) development environment for host-based and client/server development and SBClient which brings GUI features to host-based applications.

The SB+Server resides within the U2 database environment and is comprised of the default development tools, run-time support libraries and server-side execution of client/server functions. The server allows you to create process-oriented server-centric applications using UniData or UniVerse databases. Application sessions can be initiated remotely.

SBClient provides an ActiveX-based GUI environment, as well as data migration between the server and client.

These two components form the basis for rapid application development (RAD) including application functions such as screen design, logical file definition, global dictionary management, process definition, menu design report generation and system documentation. These processes are built from an object-oriented point of view, allowing encapsulation methods and other object components to be built into the application.

The SystemBuilder logical file model reflects organization and relationships of logical business entities. These logical files link to several physical files so that developers can manipulate them as if they were one. SystemBuilder incorporates HyperText Markup Language (HTML) functionality, allowing you to call its processes from HTML, as well as presenting reports generated by SystemBuilder's report writer in HTML format.

wIntegrate

wIntegrate is an advanced terminal emulation and host-based application enhancement tool for multi-valued databases, such as UniData and UniVerse. IBM intends to offer enhancements and support to wIntegrate as long as required.

This product provides high-performance terminal emulation and data transfer, Windows interoperability with character-based applications using supplied host subroutines, a complete GUI interface driven from the host, and the ability to present an existing application as an ActiveX component inside third-party applications such as Visual Basic. wIntegrate may be deployed on an individual PC basis, on a network, or as a thin client.

COBOL Direct Connect

COBOL Direct Connect is a conversion tool and runtime interface for the UniData database. It converts C-ISAM files into UniData tables. IBM intends to enhance and support COBOL Direct Connect as long as required.

Information Movement and Access

In your company data can be sitting in IMS, DB2 Informix, U2, or any other data storage mechanism. However, in order to have a functioning e-business you need to get information from one place to another. Without content, a Web site is just another pretty painting. The whole point of e-business-to-business is moving information from one organization to another, either internally or externally. IBM has incorporated Web ability into several of its products such as DB2 Universal Database and DB2 Connect using a product called Net.Data.

Net.Data gives you the ability to write code that enables your data to be visible to the Web in a fairly efficient manner, serving up dynamic Web pages to the user nearly as fast as static Web pages. It can access DB2 Universal Database natively, taking advantage of dynamic statement caching to speed up queries that are frequently used. It provides XML output, Extensible HyperText Markup Language (XHTML) compatibility, file upload capability, and SQL statement nesting to bring DB2 Universal Database content to the Web.

IBM also has products created for many different types of data movement. This section will discuss these products and how they fit into an e-business environment. The information products to be discussed are the DB2 Connect, and DB2 DataPropagator and IMS Data Propagator.

DB2 Connect

Distributed Relational Database Architecture (DRDA) is a protocol that was developed to facilitate communication between two relational database systems. DRDA consists of two parts: an application request and an application server. Any client that implements the application request portion of the protocol can connect to any server that implements the application server portion. DRDA is the foundation for IBM's communication protocol.

DB2 Connect provides the application request. It can access data on any server that has implemented the DRDA application server, including DB2 for z/OS, DB2 for AS/400 and DB2 for VM/VSE. DB2 Connect can be installed on a client machine to access DRDA-compliant DB2 databases, or placed on a separate machine to act as a gateway for many clients to access DRDA-compliant DB2 Universal Database systems.

Since it is a key component of several packaged applications such as PeopleSoft and Siebel, licensing terms have recently changed to provide the DB2 Connect Application Server Edition.

Informix Connect and Office Connect

Like DB2 Connect, Informix Connect provides the runtime libraries needed by client machines to access Informix servers.

Office Connect allows you to transparently access any DB2 or Informix database servers, as well as any ODBC/OLEDB/JDBC-compliant database or any HTML data source over the Internet. The tool allows you to use Microsoft Excel spreadsheet technology to obtain the reports you want and need. This can be done either through a personal client or Web server.

DataJoiner

Using DB2 DataJoiner, you can access almost any type of data store, including the DB2 Product Family, Oracle, Microsoft SQL Server, Informix, Sybase, and NCR Teradata. This can be done to produce a report reflecting combined data, or to combine data from different data stores and push it on to another data store. For example, DB2 DataJoiner can pull data from many heterogeneous data stores and put it into DB2 Universal Database tables, pull from DB2 Universal Database tables and put out to many heterogeneous data stores, or do any combination thereof (Figure 5.13). This functionality is not limited to character data sets, but also includes multi-media data, such as image, video or spatial data.

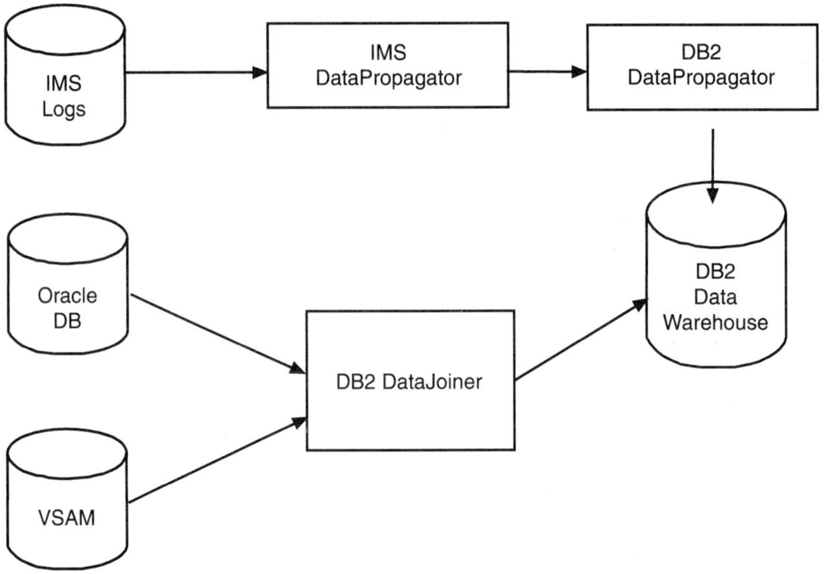

Figure 5.13. DB2 DataJoiner example.

DataJoiner is a product built on a DB2 database. As such, the product retains the ability to store data, as well as the important optimizer benefits that DB2 Universal Database provides.

It performs this magic by creating aliases called nicknames for each data store it needs to access. The user views the entire data structure as one piece and DB2 DataJoiner translates the nicknames to point to the proper storage device. Queries are optimized for the data store they are accessing. For example, a query that accesses an Oracle database is optimized to use Oracle's access methods, not DB2 Universal Database's.

Informix Enterprise Gateway Manager and Informix Gateway with DRDA

Informix Enterprise Gateway manager provides transparent access to a number of non-Informix database management systems, including those offered by IBM, Sybase and Oracle. The gateway translates Informix

SQL requests into ODBC-compliant function calls. It makes the target database appear as an instance of IDS, similar to the function provided in DB2 DataJoiner. One of its nice features is that it allows you to perform a distributed join with Informix, Oracle and Sybase data in a single SQL statement.

The Gateway with DRDA provides access to DB2 Universal Database, using connectivity protocols defined by IBM and described under DB2 Connect.

DB2 DataPropagator

DB2 DataPropagator provides a robust and flexible method for moving data from one DB2 Universal Database table to another. It has three components: Administer, Capture, and Apply. The user defines how the data should be changed (completely overwrite the table or only insert changed data), the source tables, any filter criteria to apply, and the target tables. The request, otherwise known as the registration and subscription process, is stored in the Administration component.

The Capture component of DB2 DataPropagator is used to capture information from the base source table(s) or their log records, depending on the request. The data obtained by Capture can be placed in a staging area for use by other programs, most particularly, the Apply component of DB2 DataPropagator.

The Apply component can either copy information from the staging area and, using an insert process, apply the information to the target tables, or it can perform a complete refresh from the source to target tables.

DB2 DataPropagator is a component of DB2 Universal Database and DB2 DataJoiner in the UNIX, Windows, and OS/2 environments, and is a separately orderable tool or feature in the z/OS (OS/390), z/VM, VSE, and OS/400 environments.

IMS DataPropagator

IMS DataPropagator (formerly DataPropagator Non-Relational) enables you to capture information from IMS data stores and put it either in a corresponding DB2 Universal Database table or a staging table. The

DB2 DataPropagator Apply component can then be used to insert this data into other DB2 Universal Database tables.

In fact, if you combine IMS DataPropagator, DB2 Propagator, and DB2 DataJoiner, you can move data from anywhere to anywhere on a regular basis. In terms of e-business, this may be the only way to get information, on the fly, from heterogeneous data stores for access from the Web.

With the Batch Resource Recovery Service, IMS allows batch programs that use WebSphere MQ to coordinate a commit with DB2 Universal Database, as well as IMS. This support allows disparate database management systems to be included in a single unit of work.

Resource Recovery Service is used by IMS DataPropagator to allow near real-time propagation from IMS to DB2 Universal Database by taking advantage of asynchronous messaging services provided by WebSphere MQ.

6

Managing Your e-business Application

This chapter looks at software and solutions that can help solve several key issues that go across all e-business development initiatives. These include security requirements with the attendant privacy concerns, management of software and data so that it is available and performs within the business criteria specified, and the enormity of the task of configuring and maintaining the coupled components and nested networks that make up today's e-business environments. The chapter will also review Tivoli's contributions to one of IBM's newest initiatives: e-business on demand.

The initial set of products and solutions are divided into four sections—security, storage, performance/availability, and configuration/operations.

Security Software

When software was first developed, the mainframe was king. Most applications were written for the mainframe, and data was accessible only from the mainframe. Security was tight, and 24×7 applications were not imagined. Weekends were for software and hardware upgrades and other data maintenance. Applications and data were not mixed as they are today on multiple platforms with multiple purposes.

During the first attempts at client/server architecture, most of the critical data was still kept on the mainframe. An application might develop a graphical user interface (GUI) front end, but would ultimately need to pass through a security gate to get the information it needed. The wealth of analytical information that was kept on people's personal computers in the form of spreadsheets was generally untapped and unprotected.

As the computer industry moved into a more robust client/server architecture and data moved off the mainframe and on to "server farms" in an effort to save costs, security and management became stepchildren to the process. These items were thought of after the applications were implemented, if they were thought of at all. Initially, third party software vendors made an effort to fill in the hole of management and security software. These products tended to be proprietary and only monitor a particular aspect of a particular server—for instance, a product to monitor DB2 for z/OS. Early efforts at consolidated viewpoints only provided operators with the ability to view the health of a few different systems at one time—a minimal management perspective. Deployment components and security components came later in the evolution of these tools. After the concept of "Web-year" (three months) and pervasive computing became commonplace, software distribution, security, and system availability became more important.

In addition, the pieces of applications became much more complex. No longer was the problem limited to the mainframe, its operating system, and the application, transaction, and data storage systems. There were network considerations, client problems, translation problems, and more. Figuring out exactly where the problem was took a great deal of time. Teams of experts developed for each component, but there were very few ways to look at the system as a whole.

Today IBM believes that security needs to move from an idea of "keeping the bad guys out" to "letting the good guys in." Security should be a company asset that allows your most profitable customers to do business easily. With the right solutions and software, you should be able to enforce a consistent security policy that reduces costs and lets you develop your own products more quickly.

The aim of enforcement of a security policy is to provide a clear, consistent policy for security and privacy that is unerringly followed, no matter what the application or the platform on which it's running. How a person accesses the system—desktop, laptop, cell phone, text, or voice—should have no bearing on whether or not the policy is enforced.

In today's environment of heterogeneous systems in heterogeneous companies, this is a difficult task. Security administration can also be an expensive proposition, particularly if every system must be individually administered at an individual level. This means work must be completed for individuals multiple times as they initiate logon authorizations for each system they access.

This also produces a complexity of administration across different systems. Each type of operating system, network, application, and database has its own method to natively access its structures. Administrators must learn the nuances of every native system of security as well as how to implement the corporate policy within the system. Add to this the consistency of mergers and acquisitions, and the learning curve for a security administrator is constantly on the rise.

Tivoli addresses these business issues by providing role-based policy management software that allows businesses to centrally define a security policy and have that policy consistently enforced across the entire application and system portfolio. This means that rather than doing security at an individual level, although this is still possible, individuals can be assigned to groups and automatically inherit the security rights of a group. It also means that a central, rule-based privacy/security policy can be developed. Rules can be kept in a central data store and changed in this one place as needed. Tivoli security management aids in the development and use of this policy. The Tivoli security methodology also allows use of a single sign-on and implementation of these policies across heterogeneous systems.

These are preventative measures to give people secure access to the information they need to know and no more. Yet, there is a demonstrable need for audit trails and discovery of unauthorized attempts at access. It is helpful if the security system can provide trends for security analysts. What seems an isolated incident can be a serious attempt to breach security when viewed from a historical perspective.

Security Concepts

From the earliest days of secrecy, whenever that may have been, there have been codes. Kids use codes to define the in-group and the out-group, so we are all familiar with them. Codes grew through the Navajo language codes of World War II and forms of code called cryptography. Cryptography requires a key. (If you want an exciting explanation of cryptography and keys, read Ken Follet's *The Key to Rebecca.*) If you do not have the key, you cannot read the message.

Cryptography requires two steps—encryption and decryption—that is, in essence, coding and decoding the messages. There are two main types of encryption—symmetric, or private key encryption systems and asymmetric, or public key encryption. The symmetric keys use the same key for both encryption and decryption. In an asymmetric key system there are two keys—one for encryption and one for decryption. The encryption key can be a public key, but the decryption key needs to be kept private. Security systems follow different types of algorithms to determine these keys.

A digital signature is a way to define who you are. It is a form of message that can be encrypted and decrypted asymmetrically.

A digital certificate contains information about the sender of a document with a digital signature. This information is kept by a certification authority (CA). A CA is like the passport offices of different countries. The passport office issues a passport based on personal information obtained from the applicant. The passport office then puts its authority behind the passport and you are set. Until you stand in front of the customs officer, that is. Then you need authentication.

Authentication is proving that you really are who you say you are. It is answering all the questions for the customs officer. Security products, such as those provided by Tivoli, provide the authorization authentication between clients and servers.

Access control determines who has control to what objects. Within Tivoli access control is determined by policies and rules that are established by a central administrator.

Firewalls are pieces of software that act as a barrier between your private network and the public Internet to secure your information and systems from intruders.

Tivoli covers this range of requirements by offering both security software products and solutions. There are four key areas that need to be developed to transform security into a business asset. Access management helps deploy applications faster. Identity management gets users productive more quickly. Threat management lowers risks from threats and audits. And privacy management consistently enforces privacy policies. We'll look at access management first.

Access Management

Today, many security solutions seem to be piecemeal, requiring a large expenditure of human resources for a system that may be riddled with security holes. An organization needs to control not only who accesses its corporate Web, but also which resources each individual user can access. Users need to access everything they need, but nothing more. The 2002 FBI/CSI (Federal Bureau of Investigation/Crime Scene Investigation) survey reported that 40% of enterprises detected system penetration from outside their organizations in 2001. Ironically, it is not only the hackers outside an organization that cause a problem. If 40% of the attacks are outside, that means 60% of the attacks are from inside an organization. Organizations need a framework for making authorization decisions instead of relying on a custom access control service for each server and application.

In order to insure the safety of your information resources, a few key elements have to be present. First, the identity of an individual wishing access needs to be authenticated. This authentication must be managed from several Web sites that access different portions of your company data. In order to ease the complexity of the process, it is nice to be able to manage all these servers as if they were a single unit. This provides two benefits—the user does not need to remember multiple logons and passwords and the system administrator doesn't need to maintain multiple authentication lists for the same user. This type of access is called single sign-on.

Second, the access privileges for a user need to be determined based on existing security policies. These policies should grant explicit access to resources, not just assume a lowest default value. Third, unauthorized attempts need to be logged so they can be examined for insecurities in the system. Finally, there must be the ability, particularly in large organizations, to be able to delegate the security administration function to multiple people.

Tivoli's access management family of products is an integrated set of products that provide security across a wide range of operating systems and implementations, including Web applications. This allows you to begin to build the structures that you need to implement a comprehensive security authorization policy.

The products use the same set of shared services including a central security policy manager, a central credential directory, and a Web-based administration tool. A single instance of these shared services can support the installation of all three products.

Tivoli Access Manager for e-business

Tivoli Access Manager for e-business supports almost every type of user authentication to almost any type of resource by using a policy-based access control solution. It can store secure user data in a Lightweight Directory Access Protocol (LDAP) directory server built on DB2 Universal Database (see Chapter 5). The software provides support for the following security needs:

- Basic authentication (user ID and password)
- Forms-based authentication
- SecurID Token
- Certificates
- Customer HTTP (HyperText Transfer Protocol) header (like Entrust Proxy header and Nokia Wireless Application Protocol [WAP] Gateway)
- Wireless devices (such as WAP and i-mode protocol devices)
- Customer HTTP header (such as Entrust Proxy header and Nokia WAP Gateway)
- Pluggable authentication for unique authentication requirements (such as biometrics)
- Step-up authentication for select, sensitive resources when additional security is required
- Forced re-authentication for resources or environments where authentication is desired each time a resource is accessed
- Single sign-on (SSO) capabilities, both single- and cross-domain.

and for the following business applications and solutions:

- Trust association interceptor support, for single sign-on to WebSphere environments

- LTPA cookie support for tighter integration and easier administration for WebSphere (see Chapter 4) and Lotus Domino (see Chapter 7) users
- WebSphere Application Server (see Chapter 4)
- WebSphere Edge Server (see Chapter 4)
- WebSphere Portal Server (see Chapter 4)
- WebSphere Everyplace Suite (see Chapter 4)
- Plumtree
- Siebel
- BEA WebLogic.

Tivoli Access Manager for Business Integration

Tivoli Access Manager for Business Integration provides security management for WebSphere MQ (Message Queue) across multiple operating systems and hardware platforms from a single point of control. The product provides application level data protection for WebSphere MQ systems without modification to the existing application. This enhanced security is provided for messages both while they are in transit and while they are waiting in a queue.

When an application makes a call to the WebSphere MQ interface to put a message in the queue, Tivoli Access Manager for Business Integration intercepts and analyzes the call to verify whether the sending application is authorized to access the requested queue. Once the call to WebSphere MQ is authorized, Tivoli Access Manager for Business Integration modifies the call to implement the security policies you have previously defined. For example, the transaction can be digitally signed, signed and encrypted, or passed on unchanged before placing the message in the requested queue.

Tivoli Access Manager for Business Integration uses public key-based credentials for application authorization. It supports public key credentials issued by popular certificate authorities including VeriSign, Entrust, Baltimore, and Netscape. Message encapsulation is performed using the PKCS #7 (Public Key Cryptography Standard) standard. The message can be unwrapped only by a process that has access to the application's private key to which the message was specifically directed. Different encryption strengths are available.

Tivoli Access Manager for Operating Systems

Tivoli Access Manager for Operating Systems is a policy-based access control system for UNIX and Linux operating systems. These systems have a vulnerability in their super user or "root" accounts. Security problems arise due to super user account abuse or a hack that gains access to this account. Tivoli Access Manager for Operating Systems prevents this access.

Identity Management

Identity management helps simplify and manage identities, allowing automation wherever possible, thus freeing up the security administrator for more complex tasks. An important part of identity management is something called a Public Key Infrastructure (PKI). One of the functions that PKI provides is a secure authentication for parties involved in e-business transactions. It does this by providing digital signing to insure that transferred data has not been altered. It also provides you with an audit trail of all your transactions.

Tivoli Identity Management software provides for:

- Certificate management systems. The certificate authority manages the complete life cycle of digital certification. To vouch for the authenticity of a certificate, the CA digitally signs each certificate. It also signs Certificate Revocation Lists (CRLs) to vouch for the fact that a certificate is no longer valid. To further protect its signing key, you can use cryptographic hardware to digitally sign and authenticate each certificate to check validity.

- Registration facilities. The registration authority (RA) handles the administrative tasks behind user registration. The RA can be used to help insure that only certificates that support a company's business activities are issued, and that they are issued only to authorized users. The administrative tasks can be handled through automated processes or human decision making. Policy exits enable application developers to customize the registration processes according to a company's defined policies and procedures.

- Web-based administration. The Web-based enrollment interface makes it easy to obtain certificates for browsers, servers, and other purposes such as virtual private network (VPN) devices, smart cards, and secure e-mail. Web-based administration also allows authorized registrars to approve or reject enrollment requests and administer certificates after they have been issued. A client interface is also available for management without a Web browser.

- Audit subsystem. The audit subsystem maintains audit records, encrypted for security, for important transactions. It computes a message authentication code (MAC) for each audit record. If audit data is altered or deleted after it has been written, the MAC is used to detect intrusions. Audit records may also be signed when archived.

- Data storage. An LDAP-compliant directory is used to store certificates and revoked certificate lists.

Tivoli Identity Manager

Tivoli Identity Manager supports policy-based identity management across legacy and e-business environments. It incorporates a workflow engine as well as the ability to glean information from the data for activities such as audit and reporting. It also coordinates and automates user account creation and provisioning.

Tivoli Identity Manager interacts directly with users and with two external types of systems: identity sources and access control mechanisms. Identity sources deliver authoritative information about the users that need accounts. Tivoli Identity communicates directly with access control systems (such as RACF [Resource Access Control Facility]) to create accounts, supply user information and passwords, and define the entitlements of the account. Changes made to the access control system by an external user are captured and evaluated against the policy before becoming permanent. Data from different identity sources, such as human resource databases and enterprise directories, are automatically reconciled based on pre-defined rules.

Threat Management

Threat management is your insurance against "the bad guys." These products help reduce the risk of invasion from hackers and their kin. While security has been seen primarily as authorizing users, there are also attacks by viruses that have inadvertently been let into the business. These viruses can destroy data or slow down a network enough to prevent companies from meeting their service level agreements, risking fines and loss of customers.

Tivoli Risk Manager

The purpose of Tivoli Risk Manager is to take control of the enterprise and prevent intrusions. These include both threats external to the enterprise and those from within. Like other Tivoli solutions, Tivoli Risk Manager contains an easy-to-use single point to access the monitors. These security monitors help administrators focus on the true invasive problems, eliminating clutter and false intrusions. Tivoli Risk Manager allows the capture and analysis of historical data. This way trends can be analyzed to determine changes that might signal an impending threat. Tivoli Risk Manager can also react to a threat, rebuilding firewalls and eliminating viruses from user workstations. Because it has been built with open standards in mind, Tivoli Risk Manager easily integrates with other Tivoli products as well as other security products that follow the same set of standards.

Policies and policy regions play an important part in Tivoli architecture. Policies are a set of rules for managed resources. These policies can allow the administrator to set up default values for newly created resources (default policies) and can insure that management guidelines are met when managed resources are modified (validation policies). A rule within a policy is a policy method. A default policy method can provide default values through supplying a value or running a program or shell script that computes the value. Most validation policy methods run programs or shell scripts to create the values needed.

Policy regions are a handy way to bring managed resources into groups so they can be managed by the same set of policies.

Tivoli Risk Manager takes advantage of policy regions to allow different administrators to administer the regions. For example, policies can be administered based on the geographical location of the administrator (West Coast) or the role of the administrator (antivirus administrator). Both role- and geographic-based administrators can delegate their authorities.

Risk Manager is integrated with the Tivoli Enterprise Console (TEC). Security managers can use input from the TEC to respond to open events, open trouble tickets, and respond to serious events with specific actions. Alerts received from the TEC from a variety of sources, such as firewalls, routers, intrusion detection systems, antivirus software, servers, and desktops can be grouped for review and action using Tivoli Risk Manager. The product also contains the capability to manage firewall log files, thus insuring more accurate information than was previously available by reviewing and consolidating separate firewall log files. Figure 6.1 shows how the Risk Manager is integrated with the TEC.

Resources such as firewalls produce alerts that are captured in formats native to that resource. A Risk Manager adapter monitors the managed resource and converts the native format to a format that can be securely passed to the TEC. Risk Manager has adapters for firewalls, applications, and intrusion detection systems. Risk Manager supports the Intrusion Detection Exchange Format (IDEF) for its common data

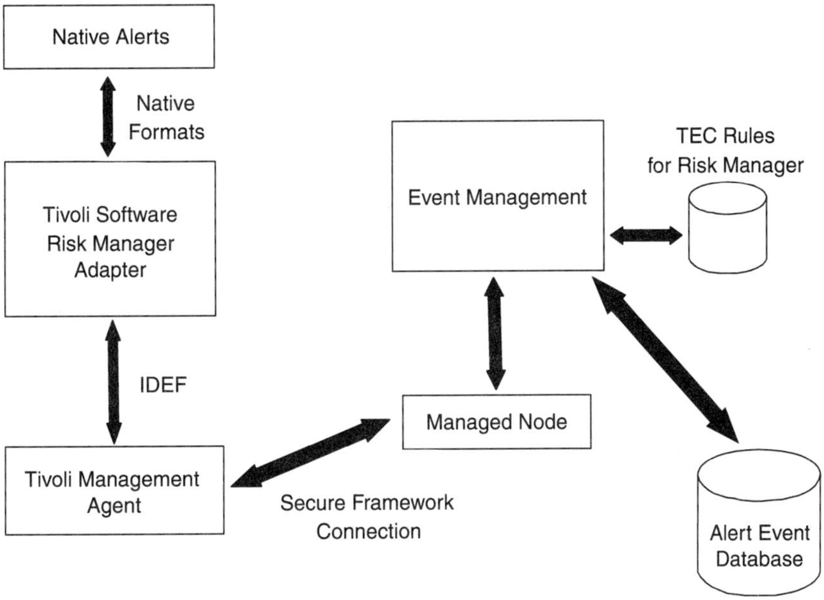

Figure 6.1. Risk Manager adapter and TEC integration.

format. The IDEF formatted data is sent to a Tivoli Management Agent or Endpoint Personal Computer (PC) for eventual routing to the TEC.

Since all Tivoli products are integrated and feed through to a single management console, Risk Manager can be brought to bear on all types of information that comes from Tivoli-ready applications.

The product includes several other IBM software components in addition to TEC: NetView, DB2 Universal Database (see Chapter 5), and Tivoli Enterprise Data Warehouse. Integration between Tivoli Enterprise Console and NetView gives you the capability to drill down to the network topology to see the root cause of the problem. Tivoli Enterprise Data Warehouse provides enterprise reporting capabilities.

Tivoli Risk Manager is part of IBM's self-healing initiatives. It assesses potential security vulnerabilities and then responds with such self-configuring autonomic capabilities as a server reconfiguration or security patch deployment.

Tivoli Intrusion Manager

Tivoli Intrusion Manager is an entry-level security product that provides much of the function of Tivoli Risk Manager for smaller companies. It helps mitigate and manage intrusions as well as protecting the network and Web servers. Like Tivoli Risk Manager, a Java event and problem management console helps the user monitor events and respond to security attacks.

The product collects data from a variety of sources, such as Checkpoint VPN-1/FireWall-1, Microsoft Internet Information Server (IIS), Norton AntiVirus, Cisco Secure PIX Firewall, and Cisco Routers. It consolidates the data and applies business security rules against the data to present the data as security information to the user. The data is also stored in a DB2 database for future report generation using a Crystal Report Generator.

Privacy Management

IBM is very concerned about the protection of people's privacy. It has a published privacy policy that is available from its Web site. Previously, they have stated that the paramount public policy issue is that of privacy—that if we do not act responsibly, we run the risk of choking off e-business.

In order for an e-business transaction to take place, a certain amount of information needs to be gathered. Some of it is gathered through the user's data entry into a form, some through the use of "cookies," small pieces of software that keep client session information persistent and may pass it back to the application server. The general public attitude about gathering information via cookies or surveys has become one of suspicion. While we like the convenience of not having to fill out our entire life's history to order a book, we get concerned that someone is monitoring what we are reading. And they *are* monitoring what we are reading. The question is what they are going to do with the information they gather. Using this information to make suggestions, rather like the librarian who used to tuck away the latest novel by your favorite author, is okay for most people. Selling the information to your insurance provider (have you read a lot of books about a disease that may cause you to be dropped from an insurance plan?) or your employer crosses a boundary. The debate over the use of this information for Homeland Security is still going on at the time of this writing.

Privacy policies are a first step in giving users control over the use of their personal information. If you know that a Web site routinely sells information to telemarketers, you will only give them information if you like having your dinner interrupted. Otherwise, you will move on to another site. Of course, there is the problem of deciphering what the privacy policy is for a particular site. A privacy policy needs to be clear and non-legalistic.

A specification called P3P (Platform for Privacy Preferences) is being developed to provide users some control over the use of personal information on the Web sites they visit. It specifies where privacy policies should be on a Web site and how they should be formatted, and enables users to act on what they see. The P3P format is a machine-readable Extended Markup Language (XML) format for privacy policies. This enables client software to read the policy, compare it against the user's preferences, and give the user a comparison conclusion quickly and simply. The client software can also determine if the site's use of cookies is acceptable to the user.

People who are working with privacy issues on the Web recommend that both the P3P format and a human-readable format be available on the Web site. IBM has a product called the P3P Policy Editor that will produce a human-readable version of a P3P policy. This can be used to review that the P3P policy says what you mean it to say. (P3P

Policy Editor is available from IBM's alphaWorks Web site, discussed in Chapter 9.)

Policy management software, Tivoli Policy Manager for e-business, provides the mechanism to develop and enforce your privacy policy throughout your e-business environment.

Tivoli Policy Manager for e-business

Tivoli Policy Manager for e-business helps you define, enforce, and manage your privacy policies across your enterprise. Because it manages your enterprise policy from one location, any changes to this policy only need to be made in one place.

The software enables you to define a new digital privacy policy, convert an existing written policy to digital form, deploy the policy to applications and systems, record opt-in and opt-out choices, monitor and enforce access according to the policy, and create audit trail reports. The Tivoli Privacy Wizard is the technology used to define privacy policies in a digital format.

Tivoli Solutions

In order to provide integrated solutions to security problems, Tivoli provides two solution packages: Tivoli Identity Management Solution and Tivoli Security Event Solution. This allows the customer the choice of building and integrating a solution of products that vary among companies or purchasing a complete, off-the-shelf solution.

Tivoli Identity Management Solution

Tivoli Identity Management Solution is an integrated package of six key Tivoli products. It provides the user with the ability to perform identity lifecycle management (user self-care, enrollment, and provisioning), identity control (access and privacy control, single sign-on, and auditing), identity federation (sharing user authentication and information between trusted Web services applications), and identity foundation (directory and workflow management).

VeriSign Managed Services

There are four VeriSign Managed services.

- VeriSign Access Management Service is built on the Tivoli Access Management framework (Figure 6.2). It provides four key components of an access management architecture: centralized access control, SSO, delegated administration, and managed service. The Web-based front end provides easy access for administrators.

- IBM-VeriSign Solution for Secure e-business Integration is an enterprise application integration (EAI) solution for trusted

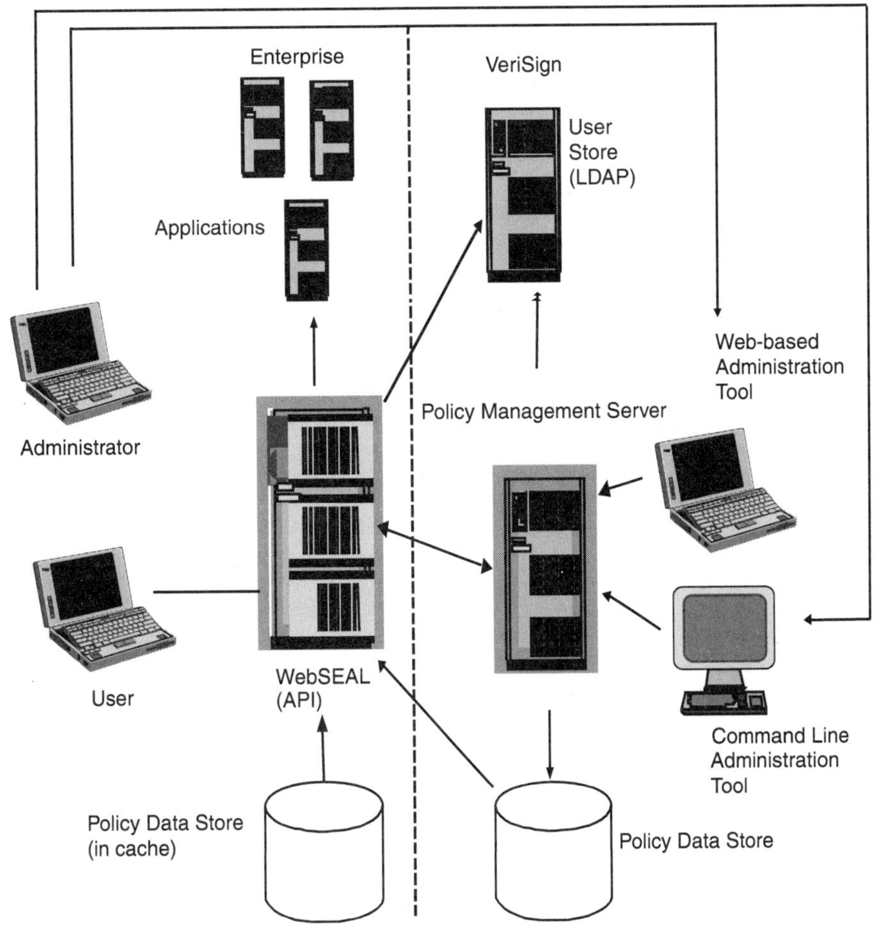

Figure 6.2. VeriSign Access Management Service.

extranets using WebSphere MQ. This helps customers improve collaboration with business partners, suppliers, and preferred customers while mitigating the risks involved.

- VeriSign Managed Public Key Infrastructures is an integrated registration and certification solution that provides applications with the means to authenticate users, insure the accuracy and privacy trusted communications, and establish an appropriate level of trust. It does this by providing digital signing to insure that transferred data has not been altered. It also provides you with an audit trail of all your transactions.

- VeriSign Public Provisioning Infrastructure service is based on Tivoli Identity Manager and provides organizations with the ability to grant the right level of access to the right individuals at the right time for the right length of time.

Tivoli Security Event Solution

Tivoli Security Event Solution is an integrated set of Tivoli products that helps you actively monitor resources and automate responses to security incidents. The products included are:

- Tivoli Risk Manager
- Tivoli Intrusion Manager
- Tivoli Enterprise Console.

Tivoli Enterprise Console

The Tivoli Enterprise Console provides a centralized point of control over your distributed systems, tracking events and alarms that occur from network devices, hardware systems, relational database management systems, and Tivoli partner and customer applications. TEC can view these systems either from an infrastructure view (hardware, software, etc.), or a business process view (the entire set of supply chain management applications).

Storage Software

In addition to these solutions, there are multiple products within the storage arena. Many of these allow you to manage the multiple terabytes and petabytes of data acquired from Web contacts and nontraditional media, such as voice and pictures. Some of these solutions also help you back up and recover data, including the tools necessary to gain off-site recovery.

Content is important in the e-business world—some people might even say vital. As the gathering of information explodes, the chore of managing that data and insuring its availability becomes too big to manage manually. Tivoli offers a comprehensive SAN (Storage Area Network) solution that provides end-to-end data protection, resource sharing, and SAN management for complex storage environments.

Tivoli Storage Network Manager

Tivoli Storage Network Manager provides the interface for managing the SAN infrastructure, including network, disk, file systems, and event reporting. Following IBM's commitment to open standards, the Network Manager supports vendors' components that are standards compliant. It performs SAN topology and disk resource discovery, which provides a visual confirmation of initial SAN architecture and element connectivity. The manager also provides continuous monitoring, problem identification, and resolution techniques to assist in the maintainability of the SAN infrastructure, so that applications can continue to have access to data. Administrators can launch the specific SAN component management software to assist in closure of problems and to perform device configuration and management functions.

Storage allocation, a time-consuming task if done manually, can be handled by the Storage Network Manager's disk management component. This component easily and securely allocates storage resources to the appropriate host systems for application processing. Files are monitored to insure that they are automatically extended to prevent data storage failure.

Tivoli Storage Network Manager can be integrated into Tivoli Enterprise Console, enabling you to view your e-business infrastructure with a single point of control. Network Manager events are captured and forwarded to SNMP (Simple Network Management Protocol) and/or

Tivoli Event Console monitors to report problems to the designated administrator or management console.

Tivoli Storage Manager

Tivoli Storage Manager (both regular and extended edition) utilizes high-performance patented technologies to protect and manage business information in an enterprise-wide SAN and traditional network environment. Combined with Tivoli Storage Manager's host of optional products, Tivoli offers an end-to-end scalable solution spanning palm tops to mainframes on over 35 platforms.

The Storage Manager works to improve processes that are inherent in the e-business world—managing data, moving data, and insuring its availability, including the ability to back up and restore data as needed. Optional software modules allow business-critical applications that must run 24×365 to utilize Storage Manager's centralized data protection with no interruption to their service. It can provide the following functions:

- Automated, unattended incremental backups, high-speed restore, and long-term data archives
- Hierarchical storage management integration
- Disaster recovery enablement integration
- Database and application support integration
- Storage of data on over 250 different types of storage devices
- Checksum capability for improved data integrity guarantees
- LAN (Local Area Network)-free disk to tape over a SAN for data movement
- Server-to-server communication
- Open API (Application Programming Interface) for applications to build access to Tivoli Storage Manager

- Java-enabled Web browser administration for central administration
- Enterprise reporting mechanisms
- Enterprise configuration and policy management.

Tivoli Storage Manager uses the Adaptive Differencing Technology to transfer data by byte, block, or file level based on the data size. This type of data transfer is designed for mobile computer users and other users with a need to minimize the amount of data transmitted over a network. Another technique that is inherent in the Storage Manager approach is to diminish the use of LANs for routine tasks such as backup and recovery by defining a SAN path for the data. This path is used for communication between a client and the Storage Manager.

The next few paragraphs cover the other members of the Tivoli Storage Manager family.

Tivoli Storage Manager for Application Servers is a software module that works with Tivoli Storage Manager to protect the infrastructure and application data and improve the availability of WebSphere Application Servers (see Chapter 4). These modules allow for automated online backups of the WebSphere Application Server environment, including the WebSphere administration database, configuration data, and deployed application program files.

Tivoli Storage Manager for Databases is a software module that works with Tivoli Storage Manager to protect data stored in Oracle, Microsoft SQL Server, and Informix. These modules allow for high-speed backups of the data stored in data objects such as tables and table spaces, as well as data required to recover the surrounding infrastructure, such as log files.

Tivoli Storage Manager for Enterprise Resource Planning (ERP) is an SAP-certified software module to provide an integrated backup mechanism for SAP R/3 environments. The product is capable of supporting heterogeneous environments (including multiple database servers), large-volume data backups, data recovery, data cloning, and disaster recovery of multiple SAP R/3 servers.

Tivoli Storage Manager for Hardware integrates the Tivoli Storage Manager software with the hardware capabilities of more advanced data stores such as the IBM Enterprise Storage Server (ESS—also known as Shark). This integration improves the speed of data backups by using the FlashCopy hardware function of ESS or the EMC Symmetrix TimeFinder with the software. This software works with DB2 Universal Database, Oracle, and SAP R/3 databases.

Tivoli Storage Manager for Mail is a software module that provides backup and recovery mechanisms for Lotus Domino or Microsoft Exchange mail servers.

Tivoli Storage Manager for Space Management automatically moves infrequently used data to less expensive offline or near-line storage, freeing up expensive disk space and potentially improving performance. We've been collecting data for over three decades; there's a chance that a good portion of it doesn't need to be online all the time.

Tivoli Storage Manager for Storage Area Networks is a high-performance alternative to LAN usage for transferring the large amounts of data required for data backup/restore and archive/retrieve processes. This reduces central processing unit (CPU) utilization on both client and server.

Tivoli Storage Resource Manager

Tivoli Storage Resource Manager is a part of IBM's new set of products geared toward helping systems be self-reliant, self-healing, and autonomous. A great deal of time and effort can be spent by humans trying to determine the state of their storage. Even as the information is collected, it changes. This product helps in two ways.

First, it requires the business to produce a set of policies. These policies are set up from a business perspective, requiring end users to determine the costs and benefits of data storage and accessibility. Second, it allows these policies to be used in an automated fashion to handle data growth, data analysis for deletion or movement to less expensive storage devices, and data analysis of storage outages.

Using a Web and Java-based solution, Tivoli Storage Resource Manager provides reporting and notification capabilities to alert you when constraints have been exceeded or quotas exceeded. A series of reports allows you to determine where problems are happening in a repetitive fashion and where there are holes in your data protection schemes.

Tivoli Storage Resource Manager for Chargeback shows users what their data processing and data storage efforts are costing them on a departmental, group, or user level. Used intelligently, the chargeback report can allow businesses to determine if the cost of service is being met by a corresponding amount of revenue.

Tivoli Storage Resource Manager for Databases helps the database administrator or storage administrator look at the database from a storage utilization viewpoint rather than a database viewpoint. This helps pinpoint potential trouble spots within the storage arena prior to an outage, rather than reacting to an outage.

Tivoli SANergy

Tivoli SANergy is patented software that runs on the computers connected to a SAN to provide high-performance LAN, disk volume, and file sharing between multiple computers running multiple operating systems connected to a SAN. The product is implemented as a file system extension and leverages the distributed data sharing capabilities embedded within the Windows, UNIX, Linux, and Apple Macintosh operating systems. By redirecting the data portion of standard network file I/O (input/output) off the LAN and onto the SAN, it insures that the data flows at much higher bandwidth over the SAN.

The product manages this by using a Windows NT or UNIX server as a Metadata Controller (MDC) for shared storage. The MDC manages access to common shared storage by providing the necessary file system metadata when requested by the host computers. There can be multiple MDCs within the system that manage the SAN disk volumes using a high-performance network.

Tivoli Storage Solutions

Tivoli storage solutions are integrated products that can be purchased as a suite to provide an integrated result to a business problem. These solutions are:

- Tivoli Storage Resource Management Solution, which helps manage storage resources across your enterprise environments.

- Backup and recovery solutions provide a centralized, comprehensive method to make backups and restores as fast, flexible, and low impact as possible. The products support more than a dozen operating systems, a variety of network connectors and more than 500 offline storage devices.

- Tivoli Application Protection solution supports a wide variety of business-critical applications—such as databases, ERP, and mail and application servers—that must remain available 24×7.
- Disaster preparedness solutions are designed to get critical business systems up quickly after any type of disaster that affects on-site storage.
- Managed archives allow you to back up data through a policy-automation engine and retrieve it when necessary, allowing you to manage storage more effectively.

Performance and Availability Software

The performance and availability software from Tivoli consists of software products and solutions that monitor the different components of your e-business infrastructure. Based on policy set up, the products can send an alert, perform an action, or, in some cases, analyze, determine, and act on the information it receives without human intervention. The last is a demonstration of the self-healing and self-optimizing software that IBM is evolving over the next set of releases of its product families.

This software group also includes the Tivoli Enterprise Console described earlier.

Tivoli Analyzer for Lotus Domino

Tivoli Analyzer for Lotus Domino provides the ability to monitor Lotus Domino statistics and activity measurements while running smoothly inside the Domino Administrator (Chapter 7). This provides the Lotus Domino administrator with the knowledge to understand the health of the server, perform predictive analysis about growth patterns, and perform workload balancing.

Tivoli Business Systems Manager

Tivoli Business Systems Manager allows you to manage distributed systems as one management group, allowing you to manage groups of related applications that form critical business components. The components can be purchased applications, like many ERP or CRM (Customer Relationship Management) applications, component-built e-business applications, computer systems, middleware, network devices, and storage devices. Because many of these systems are built with a component-based architecture, managing them provides a significant challenge. Problems can occur on any component of the distributed system and anywhere in between them. Business Systems Manager integrates these disparate systems into a single point of view and management scope.

Tivoli Business Systems Manager also enables the prioritization of resource problems based on the business impact of the various problems.

Tivoli Business Systems Manager for z/OS extends the capabilities of Tivoli to manage OS/390 and z/OS host systems as well as distributed systems.

Tivoli Monitoring

Tivoli Monitoring works from the principles of automating best practices. The gray-haired mavens of the computing world carry around with them many ideas and thoughts that have served them well as they built and maintained systems. Some codify these practices and write books. Others become consultants. Software companies like IBM capture these best practices and create products. Tivoli Monitoring is such a product.

With Tivoli Monitoring, resources are tuned autonomically to give you the transactional characteristics that you desire (greater number of users, faster transactions, etc.). Tivoli software insures the economic performance of data processing resources by insuring the economic performance of data processing services.

The Tivoli Monitoring Active Directory Option provides a set of pre-configured, out-of-the-box automated best practices that proactively manage an active distributed directory by monitoring essential resources and detecting potential problems for components such as domain controllers, replication services, Domain Name Systems (DNS) and Dynamic Host Configuration Protocol (DHCP). It also provides the ability for you to add best practices using Proactive Analysis Components (PACs) for managing hardware and software that form the basis of middleware, applications, and databases.

Tivoli Monitoring is extended to several other products.

- Tivoli Monitoring for Applications extends this monitoring to two pre-built applications: mySAP.com and Siebel e-business applications. The mySAP.com component allows you to monitor SAP structures such as SAP Business Warehouse and SAP Customer Relationship Management (Infrastructure). You can also automatically discover and centrally manage all infrastructure components such as application servers and Internet transaction servers. Finally, it allows you to determine performance information on a server, user, transaction, or resource level. The Siebel component discovers and monitors the health of Siebel application servers, gateway name servers, and connection brokers. In case of a failure, the software provides automated recovery capability. In-depth and best practices monitoring is provided down to the Siebel component and task level within each Siebel server instance.

- Tivoli Monitoring for Business Integration works on WebSphere MQ and WebSphere MQ Integrator (see Chapter 4). It monitors the status of key MQ components, such as queue managers, queues, channels, and message flows; identifies problems in real time; and notifies administrators by providing local correlation, root cause analysis, and corrective action capabilities for problem resolution.

- Tivoli Monitoring for Databases monitors DB2 Universal Database, Informix, and Oracle databases, allowing you to manage all three types of databases from a single place. The monitor checks the health of key database objects, such as user data tables, replication services, logging, and recovery ability.

- Tivoli Monitoring for Messaging and Collaboration identifies Lotus Domino server (see Chapter 7) and system problems in real time, notifies administrators, and takes automated actions to resolve problems.

- Tivoli Monitoring for Network Performance is a combination of two products, Tivoli NetView for Transmission Control Protocol/Internet Protocol (TCP/IP) Performance and Tivoli NetView Performance Monitor, that allow you to monitor both Systems Network Architecture (SNA) and TCP/IP networks and applications. They provide a visible heartbeat of network performance, allowing trouble spots to become visible more quickly.
- Tivoli Monitoring for Web Infrastructure monitors the health of Web application servers, such as WebSphere Application Server (see Chapter 4) and associated Web servers, providing the same health analysis and automated actions as other Tivoli Monitoring software products.
- Tivoli Monitoring for Transaction Performance provides an end-to-end monitoring tool, allowing you to monitor the performance and availability of e-business and enterprise transactions based on pre-defined service level objectives.

Tivoli NetView

The mainland United States is connected by superhighways. We've even built city bypasses to avoid the complexities of urban life. Yet, anyone who has ever had the pleasure of being on one of those interstate highways during the "rush hour" knows what it's like to be sitting in six lanes of traffic not going anywhere. Helicopters hover overhead, feeding the radio station with the facts we already know—we are stuck.

Throw too much data through a network pipeline and the same situation occurs. The data gets stuck, the Web page doesn't appear, and our potential customer moves on to the next site.

The purpose of the Tivoli NetView set of products is to move the traffic before it gets stuck. Tivoli NetView discovers TCP/IP networks, displays network topologies, correlates and manages events and SNMP traps, monitors network health, and gathers performance data. The product is your helicopter over your network, identifying the "overturned tractor trailer" that's causing the slowdown or failure of your network. Reports can be developed so that you can build a new highway and bring it online when it's needed, not after the fact.

Tivoli NetView is extended to several other products:

- Tivoli NetView for TCP/IP Performance provides detailed information about TCP/IP performance from a host perspective as well as network connection information to selected critical distributed systems.
- Tivoli NetView for z/OS manages TCP/IP networks that connect to any application on OS/390 or z/OS and provides support for Dynamic Virtual IP Addressing (DVIPA).
- Tivoli NetView Performance Manager monitors SNA-based networked applications, reporting communications network performance and utilization in a VTAM (Virtual Telecommunications Access Method) environment.

Tivoli Switch Analyzer

Tivoli Switch Analyzer is another product to help you determine the root cause of any network slowdown. It provides automated Layer-2 discovery and identifies the relationship between devices. Even during a network event storm, it can identify the root cause of a problem without human intervention. Combined with the Tivoli NetView products described above, it extends problem resolution to include Layer-2 or LAN switch analysis.

Tivoli Performance Modeler for z/OS

Tivoli Performance Modeler for z/OS is one of those crystal ball tools that helps you do performance modeling and capacity planning for applications that run on OS/390 or z/OS. As with all of these types of tools, the issue is never so much the tool as it is obtaining the information to feed into it. If you've grown up in an era of "slap it on the computer and do it over until it works," this tool will help you understand the planning necessary to make a system that eats petabytes of data and crushes millions of transactions work.

Once you've shaken the information loose from business analysts, the tool provides reports and charts to do iterative "what if" analysis—

modeling on an Intel computer is much cheaper than ordering the wrong amount of mainframe processors and disk storage.

Tivoli Service Level Advisor

A service level agreement is a critical item of work that's often overlooked. It documents the agreement between the business leaders of a company and the information technicians as to what constitutes good service. Is a subsecond response time for an online transaction acceptable? How fast does an application need to be available in case of a failure? Company system design and development is always a trade-off—dollars versus desire.

Tivoli Service Level Advisor allows you to define services from a user perspective, including response time, availability, security, and configuration metrics. Based on these agreements, the product can evaluate service level agreements and receive alerts for when violations occur. Reports can be provided that give facts of service level performance, relieving you from the user's gut feeling that the system is always slow.

Tivoli System Automation for OS/390

Tivoli System Automation for OS/390 provides you with Parallel Sysplex management integrated systems and network management and automation capabilities. It can manage host operations, remote processor operations, and I/O operations from one place. The information can be made available to TEC and Tivoli Business Systems Manager, consolidating one more portion of the availability puzzle into the picture.

Tivoli Web Site Analyzer (formerly WebSphere Site Analyzer)

One of the critical areas for e-business is the difficulty of getting feedback from the sites. How many people are visiting? Are they finding it easy to navigate your site? Do people "click on through" your site to another? Do they spend time at your site and utilize it effectively? Do all the links work correctly?

You can put a customer survey on your Web site, and your customers may fill it out and may actually fill it out correctly. This gives you some information, but just ask a statistical analyst how much information that really gives you. There is also a lot of software that will help you count the number of times someone clicks on a page, but even this only provides one part of the picture.

Tivoli Web Site Analyzer provides detailed statistical information about your Web site. Some of the information that can be provided with this tool includes the ability to:

- Track the progression of users across your Web site (including most frequently visited sites, pages, and campaigns)
- Determine site traffic volume
- Identify site traffic sources (where the users came from)
- Manage site integrity (do the links work correctly?)
- Categorize and aggregate statistics about groups of information
- Save the data in a DB2 Universal Database for trend analysis.

IBM CICS Performance Monitor for OS/390

CICS (Customer Information Control System) Performance Monitor (PM) for OS/390 provides monitoring tools to capture information about CICS transactions as they occur. The reports can be analyzed after the fact, or in real time, using a Windows workstation and GUI graphics to pinpoint problems and analyze trends.

CICS PM works with other tools within the CICS performance suite: CICS Performance Analyzer, CICS Online Transmission Time Optimizer, and CICS Interdependency Analyzer.

WebSphere Studio Application Monitor for OS/390 and z/OS

WebSphere Studio Application Monitor for OS/390 and z/OS is another tool designed to improve performance within an individual component of an e-business application—in this case J2EE (Java 2, Enterprise Edition) applications running on WebSphere Application Server for z/OS and OS/390 (see Chapter 4). Like CICS and DB2 PM products, the tool captures information during a running transaction. Reports or real-time screens can be used to analyze the information and improve transactional performance.

Tivoli Performance and Availability Management Solutions

Tivoli Performance and Availability Management Solutions are integrated products that can be purchased as a suite to provide an integrated result to a business problem. These solutions are:

- Business Impact Management, which helps align daily operations management with business priorities, set and meet service level commitments, and implement predictive management capabilities across your e-business infrastructure.
- Event Correlation and Automation helps companies make sense of your business environments by consolidating and correlating event data across networks and systems to identify the true root cause of a problem.
- Systems and Applications Monitoring enables you to deploy a single monitoring solution for most or all of the resources in your environment, allowing your system monitors to share a common reporting engine, graphical user interface, and data repository.
- Web Management solution allows you to go beyond firewalls without compromising security to insure a high level of performance, availability and customer service. This solution has been extended to include emerging technologies, such as Web Services.

Configuration and Operations Management Software

One of the realities of today's host and distributed applications is that the management of hardware and software components has become more complex. Even if a piece of software works with another, it may be dependent on the version of the other software. How do you keep track of these complexities? How do you insure that the right individuals or systems have the software they need to perform their role for the business? Indeed, how do you even remember what version of what you have where? And how do you efficiently track and deploy software across your environment?

The purpose of Tivoli's configuration and management software suite is to help you do just that—manage and configure your software wherever it is found and wherever it needs to be.

Tivoli Configuration Manager

Tivoli Configuration Manager provides the software to effectively manage software distribution over servers, desktops, laptops, and other multiple devices, including pervasive devices such as Palm OS, PocketPC, and Nokia Communicator devices. This software solution includes a directory of software, level, and location (where your software is today), as well as the ability to subset this directory into different groups (where the software needs to go tomorrow) across heterogeneous operating system platforms. It can also securely manage software distribution outside of multiple firewalls.

Tivoli License Manager

Software is a product that is governed less by the purchase of the medium on which it is installed than by its licensing for use. (In parts of Silicon Valley, used software CDs make excellent scarecrows.) Insuring proper licensing is important legally and ethically; paying for licenses you aren't using isn't good business sense.

Tivoli License Manager provides the ability to insure compliance with software license terms and conditions. The reporting capabilities allow companies to insure that license usage matches licenses owned so they can identify whether they are overdeployed or underdeployed according to their licensing. This way they can adjust their contract to avoid penalty fees or excessive license costs.

Tivoli Point-of-Sale Manager

Have you ever stood in a line at a busy store, hard-won purchase in hand, pressing the bounds of your lunch hour? You get up to the front of the line, hand over your credit card and merchandise, and tap your finger nervously, only to have the clerk start frantically punching buttons and looking around for a supervisor. You know it's only moments before the dreaded words are spoken, "I'm sorry, my system is down. You'll have to go to another register." Of course, you don't have time, so you leave the item and the sale is lost.

Tivoli Point-of-Sale Manager helps store owners manage this problem and cut down on the incidence of lost sales due to inoperative machines. The software monitors IBM's 4690 point-of-sale terminals and corrects problems before they result in a lost sale.

The software also interacts with the Tivoli Enterprise Console so that staff that is familiar with the console layout for managing back-end systems doesn't need any further training. It can also integrate with Tivoli Configuration Manager for automatic software distribution and inventory management.

Tivoli Remote Control

Tivoli Remote Control allows a technician to take control of a remote computer for the purpose of debugging and fixing problems. It shortens the length of time that the user is offline and improves communication of the problem because the technician can see what's going on with the problem machine without having to get to the office that contains the machine. With remote service often in a different state, this product makes outsourcing of technical services a reality.

The software provides five management functions: take control of the remote machine (active state), view the remote workstation (monitor state), reboot the workstation, chat with the workstation, and send or receive files and directories. Tivoli Remote Control can dramatically lower the manual labor costs involved in repairing systems.

Tivoli Workload Scheduler

Tivoli Workload Scheduler is another software product that allows you to schedule, coordinate, and automate application execution across the enterprise based on business policies, rather than reacting to the crisis of the moment. This insures consistent and reliable operations. From a single point of control, the product analyzes the status of the production work and drives the processing of the workload. It supports a multiple-end-user environment, enabling distributed processing and control across sites and departments within your enterprise.

Tivoli Workload Scheduler for Applications extends these management capabilities to interact with the workload capabilities of Oracle e-business Suite, PeopleSoft 8, SAP R/3, and SAP Business Warehouse.

Tivoli Workload Scheduler for z/OS handles the management of production workloads on mainframe servers and integrates well with the distributed product to form an end-to-end scheduling solution.

Tivoli Data Exchange

Frequently, you need to get data from one operating system to another, a process that can be cumbersome at best and error-prone at worst. Although File Transfer Protocol (FTP) does provide an answer for this problem, Tivoli Data Exchange enhances that solution by leveraging WebSphere MQ (see Chapter 4) to provide secure guaranteed transfer of multiple types of data. This data can be transferred across many types of operating systems, even if the receiving system isn't operational when the transfer begins. Compression is used to keep the size of transferred data as small as possible.

Tivoli Configuration and Operations Management Solutions

Tivoli configuration and operations management solutions are integrated products that can be purchased as a suite to provide an integrated result to help customers reduce costs, gain automated control of an e-business infrastructure, and improve organization productivity.

- The Job Scheduling solution coordinates and automates application execution across host and distributed systems and is extensible to purchased applications such as Siebel.

- The Tivoli Change and Configuration Management solution automates tasks such as software distribution, asset inventory, and remote system control.

7

Lotus

Lotus was a key purchase for IBM in the early 1990s. With the purchase, IBM expanded into the developing collaborative world, as well as purchasing well-known applications for small businesses, such as Lotus 1-2-3 (a spreadsheet product). Lotus has continued its emphasis on collaborative products and provides the ability for global teamwork, global meetings, and global learning.

This chapter focuses on five major Lotus products (Lotus Notes, Lotus Domino, Lotus Sametime, Lotus Team Workplace [formerly QuickPlace], and Lotus LearningSpace) that support collaboration in the e-business world.

Many of the concepts that underlie Lotus products, such as Web application servers, connectors, development studios, and the like, have been discussed in earlier chapters, primarily Chapter 4. This chapter will tell you what distinguishes the Lotus products and how these products help position IBM for a global e-business.

Lotus Notes

Lotus Notes is one of the most commonly known Lotus software products. It provides a messaging and collaboration platform to enable e-business teamwork across the globe. In format, Lotus Notes provides a portal (portals were discussed in Chapter 4) that allows you to work on e-mail, calendaring, scheduling, journal, to-do lists, Web pages, and Lotus Notes databases at the same time.

The Notes database is used as the basis for all the applications—including e-mail. This database can be manipulated through a programming language to present different views, rather like sorting the information in a variety of ways. The table can be presented as a document, with each field available for data entry. Allowable values can be associated with each field and made available to the user via a pull-down screen. (These databases will be discussed further under the Lotus Domino section.)

Notes works in a client/server environment, with Lotus Domino as the server. This allows you to take advantage of Domino's security capabilities such as smart card support, single sign-on, and support for S/MIME (Multipurpose Internet Mail Extensions). The databases stored on the server can be downloaded as a local copy for use offline from the server and then replicated back to the server. Support is also provided for the roving remote user. By capturing relevant files that provide personalization and security information, a user can log on to any computer that has a Lotus client, see his or her own personal portal, and have secure access to his or her e-mail, schedule, databases, etc.

Replication and other background tasks are an important feature of Lotus Notes. When I work from home, which is as often as I can, I like to have the machines in my house working in the background as I work. For example, I have written several chapters in this book and done laundry at the same time. The laundry is a background task that requires me to throw in the clothes and walk away. Notes perform background tasks in a similar fashion. All you need to do is start the task and then you can go back to something else that requires your full attention. With Notes you can detach documents, run non-interactive agents, replace or refresh a database design, poll for new mail, replicate, monitor alarms, and queue print jobs in the background—all while writing a politically correct e-mail.

The most difficult and interesting problem with Lotus Notes is not the technology, but rather the people that use it. Moving from an e-mail environment to a virtual team environment is a tough transition for many people to make. It's easier for most people to reply to all the people on an e-mail list than take the trouble to go to a Notes database and enter the information there. Yet, if you can achieve the cultural shift, the benefits are amazing. The database serves as a repository for a group history, a reference, and a place for virtual discussions as well as the more mundane "to-do" list.

Lotus Domino

The Lotus Domino Server Family is an integrated messaging and Web application software platform. It includes the following:

- Domino Server: Web application server for Lotus clients (more information below).

- Domino Everyplace: With Mobile Notes, users can access Domino-based information from wireless and hand-held devices (more information below).

- Domino Designer: Allows you to build Lotus Notes and Lotus Domino collaborative applications.

- Enterprise Integrator for Domino: Allows you to exchange data between Lotus Domino and host and relational data systems such as DB2 Universal Database, Oracle, Sybase, Microsoft SQL Server (through OLE DB (Object Linking and Embedding Database), Microsoft Access (through OLE DB) and ODBC (Open Database Connectivity) data sources. You can also use Enterprise Integrator for Domino to connect to ERP (Enterprise Resource Planning) and transaction-processing systems such as SAP R/3, PeopleSoft, and Oracle Applications.

- Domino Application Studio: A suite of tools to design and deploy Web applications. It contains Domino Designer, VisualAge for Java (see Chapter 4), Macromedia Fireworks, Macromedia Dreamweaver UltraDev, Domino Server, WebSphere Application Server (see Chapter 4), and Lotus Developer Network Pro Membership Toolkit.

- Domino Connectors: Connect, authenticate, and translate data between Domino and external relational databases and applications such as DB2 Universal Database, Oracle, Microsoft SQL Server, any ODBC-ready database, SAP, PeopleSoft, and Oracle Applications.

- Enterprise Solution Builder: Development and runtime service that provides the ability to build applications that integrate your existing Web application server with Domino applications, external data, transactions, and reporting capabilities.

- Domino Unified Communications Service (DUCS): Provides the convergence of voice, e-mail, and fax messages so they are stored in a single location and can be accessed from a variety of devices, including telephones, PCs (Personal Computers), mobile phones, pagers, PDAs (Personal Digital Assistants), and browsers (more information below).

Lotus Domino Server

Lotus Domino Server has many abilities that enable it to become an integral part of a company's e-business structure. These include:

- Application server functions with the ability to design applications in CORBA (Common Object Request Broker Architecture), Java, or Java Script

- Mail functions, including the ability to perform messaging with Web browsers and Internet mail clients

- A relational database to hold the content required.

As we discussed under Lotus Notes, Lotus database structures bring another meaning to the term "database." If you will recall from earlier discussions in this chapter, relational theory positions all data stores and results in a tabular structure made up of rows and columns called tables. In DB2 Universal Database, tables were grouped into table spaces and then into databases. Lotus only has databases. These databases look like DB2 Universal Database tables in that they have rows and columns. These large (up to 64-gigabyte [GB]) structures in a tabular format are ideal for storing unstructured data such as large text blocks. If you have ever run a Lotus Notes application, you have seen a Domino table, with the actual e-mail fitting into one of the columns within the table. The physical structure of Lotus database keeps pointers to provide physical access to data, similar to an index structure in DB2 Universal Database.

Domino takes advantage of transaction logging to allow for 24×7 online server backup and recovery support. A transaction log provides a sequential record of every operation that occurs and helps to insure complete data integrity for updates in case of a failure. Logs can then be used to reapply all the changes made and bring databases up to date when needed. Like IMS and DB2 Universal Database, Domino logging occurs at a unit-of-work level, insuring that only completed transactions are logged. This logging can be used to record and measure server use by user and application. This activity logging can serve as input to Tivoli Analyzer for Lotus Domino (see Chapter 6), which helps you make informed decisions about your future hardware and software requirements. Third party products provide backup and recovery tools, and Domino has recently added support for online database backup and media recovery, including point-in-time media recovery, via API (Application Programming Interface) functions.

An important application server function is the notion of client failover. This is the ability for an application server to maintain a copy of its database on another server via replication. Should a server be unavailable or have too high a load, the client machine is automatically redirected to the alternate server. In Domino this task is handled by the Internet Cluster Manager (ICM) server component. The ICM acts as an intermediary between the Web client and the server's cluster. Web clients direct requests for databases to the ICM, and then the ICM determines the best server to receive the request based on the server availability and workload. This failover handling is automatic.

By definition, an application server provides the ability to manipulate data as well as store it. Domino embraces Internet models of programming including JavaScript, Java, HTML 4.0, and LotusScript to create applications. It also supports CORBA and Internet Inter-ORB Protocol (IIOP) to allow you to create client/server Web applications that take advantage of Domino objects and application services.

The Object Request Broker (ORB) technology and Java allow you to create client applications that are dynamically loaded from the Domino server, primarily through Java applets or applications. For example, you can place a custom Java applet on an input form. The form can then be accessed by a Notes client or a Web browser. During the input process, the applet is triggered. From the Notes client, the local Java interface processes the required objects. From the browser, CORBA objects are accessed. The applet uses IIOP to connect back to the ORB on the server.

Domino includes the ability to access data from relational databases, using Domino Enterprise Connection Services (DECS) to build live links between Domino pages and forms to relational data. The DECS template is used to identify forms and the fields that will contain external source data. The template is also used to define the real-time connections to DB2 Universal Database, Oracle, Sybase, EDA/SQL, or ODBC. A Domino server add-in task then passes the real-time connection instructions to the Domino Extension Manager. When events are intercepted (such as a query for data), the Extension Manager handles the request for data and return of results.

For running your Web applications, Domino includes an HTTP (HyperText Transfer Protocol) engine. An HTTP server provides the function of receiving a request for a Web page, creating that page, and passing it back to the requesting browser. If there are embedded instructions within the requested page, such as a Java applet, the HTTP engine passes those instructions back to the appropriate business logic engine for further processing. In this case the business logic engine is on the Domino Server. Alternatively, Domino can run on top of Microsoft Internet Information Servers (IIS) in order to combine Domino's application services with the HTTP services of IIS.

Like DB2 Universal Database's Control Center, Domino has an administrative tool (Domino Administrator) to manage the maintenance of the database, security functions, and the like.

Like other IBM software, Domino is being enhanced to provide more ease of use, more automation, and less-people-intensive features. With Domino you can deploy client upgrades to your end users from the server. Policy-based management lets you centrally manage and control end user settings and configurations for individuals, groups, or the entire organization. Policies also help you centrally manage user registration defaults, client configurations, password and security controls, and e-mail file archiving.

Multiple-client support is provided from a single server, including industry-standard protocol support for mail clients and browsers such as Internet Message Access Protocol (IMAP), POP3 (Post Office Protocol), LDAP (Lightweight Directory Access Protocol), SMTP (Simple Mail Transfer Protocol), HTTP, IIOP and Extensible Server Pages (XSPs). Support for Domino Off-Line Services is also provided.

Lotus Domino Everyplace

The Lotus Domino Everyplace family of products extends the Lotus applications to wireless and hand-held devices. The family includes three products:

- Domino Everyplace Access provides wireless access to e-mail, calendars, directories, and WAP-enabled (Wireless Application Protocol) Domino applications. If Mobile Notes is added to the configuration, you have access to full service PIM (Personal Information Management) capabilities and access to business applications such as sales force automation (SFA), field service, and Customer Relationship Management (CRM).

- Domino Everyplace Enterprise server provides wireless and wired synchronous solutions to mobile workers. The application development environment can be used to extend business applications to devices on Palm, Windows Pocket PC, and EPOC platforms.

- Lotus Domino Everyplace SMS (Short Message Service) allows applications to automatically send e-mail messages, alerts, and notifications to pagers, mobile phones, and other SMS devices. It can also receive short messages from pagers and SMS devices, and receive instant e-mail notifications and alerts from any Domino application.

Domino Unified Communications Services

Domino Unified Communications Services (DUCS) provide the ability to consolidate messaging in a central location, provide access from multiple devices, and provide notification based on message content and characteristics. For example, users can program the system to be paged when they receive a message from their manager and called when they get a message from their customers.

The entire process involves software from IBM's business partners (Figure 7.1), but DUCS controls the interactions and the data is stored on a Domino server. The flow is as follows:

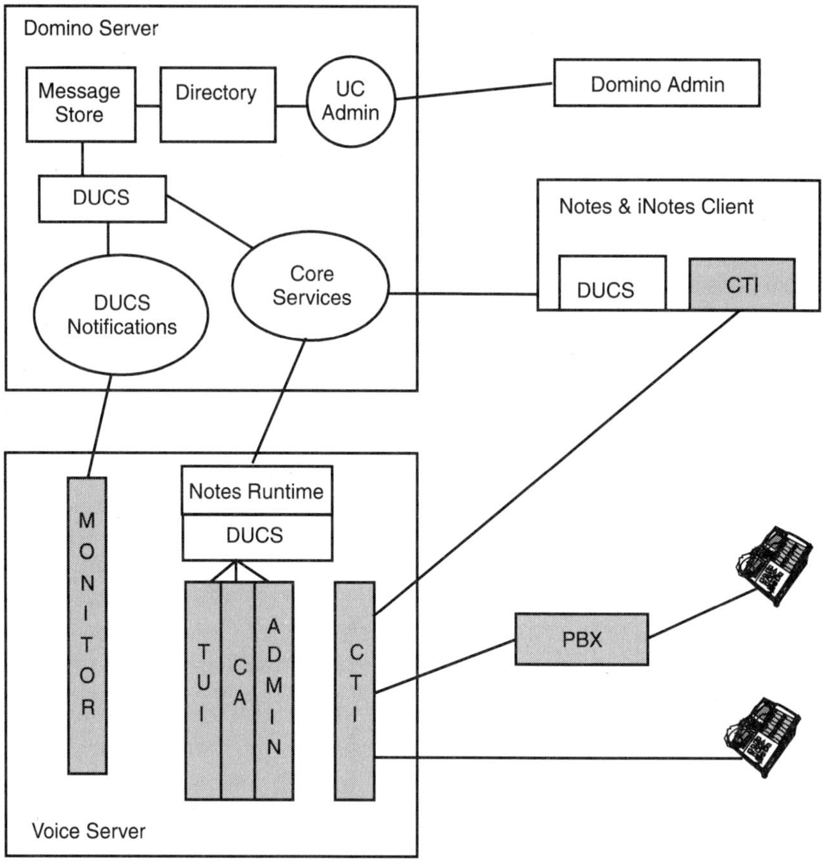

Figure 7.1. Domino Unified Communications Services.

- When an incoming call is unanswered, the call goes to the voice server via the Call Answering (CA) function. The voice server determines subscriber information from the voice server database or directory and streams the message via the Telephone User Interface (TUI) function. The streamed message along with other information (urgency, privacy, etc.) is stored in the subscriber's mail file. DUCS categorizes the voice message and then generates an alert or a message waiting indicator, based on the subscriber's personal preferences. The subscriber can then access this information from a telephone or, using the Computer

Telephony Interface (CTI), the subscriber can access information from Lotus Notes or iNotes.

Lotus Sametime

The ads for Lotus Sametime tell you, "This is not your teenager's instant messaging." And it's not, although there is some surface resemblance.

Lotus Sametime is a complete collaboration and messaging tool. It does contain an instant chat feature, which is wonderful for getting that quick question answered. However, it also contains a facility to share documents during a meeting, which is very convenient when the person who needs to draw on the board to explain something is 3,000 miles away. Another nice feature of the product family is the ability to transfer control of a PC to another person, say a person at a help desk, so you can demonstrate exactly what is wrong.

The Sametime family includes three main components: the server, the client, and developer toolkits. The server provides the platform that manages the flow of information between the clients, including text messaging, streaming audio and video, a shared whiteboard, and shared applications. The client provides the ability to exchange ideas and present information through instant messaging. (Alternatively, a browser application can be used as the client.) The developer toolkits give companies a way to embed real-time collaboration into a wide range of Web- and Windows-based applications.

In addition, there are three components that help companies move beyond the local area network (LAN). The Enterprise Meeting Server allows companies to host and administer enterprise-wide Web conferencing. (In fact, IBM uses this technology a lot to inform customers about the company's products, including new releases.) Sametime Everyplace extends these technologies to users with mobile phones and wireless PDAs that have WAP- and SMS-enabled devices.

As with most IBM technology families, the abilities of Sametime expand when they are integrated with other Lotus products such as Notes, Team Workplace, or Domino. For example, when an e-meeting is scheduled via Notes, the reminder contains a URL (Uniform Resource Locator) link that brings you quickly to the e-meeting site.

Applications can move to real time. With a Notes client or browser, you can see who is working in a team space and exchange instant messages with them. This ability to import presence awareness to applications is an important feature of Sametime. IBM is leveraging this technology in many of its own applications, such as Team Workplace and WebSphere Portal. Acknowledging that some people don't want to be interrupt-driven, Sametime allows users to post an electronic "Do Not Disturb" sign.

In terms of security, users are authenticated when they access Sametime. Online meetings can be protected by passwords and restricted invitee lists. Data is encrypted to protect meeting content from unauthorized viewing. Chat data is also encrypted as it's transmitted. The server supports Session Initiation Protocol (SIP) for instant messaging and presence-leveraging extensions for the Sametime IM (Instant Messaging) Gateway to securely transmit information. The Sametime IM Gateway gives companies a way to securely connect to other instant messaging communities, such as AOL IM, although it is most useful when two companies merge and want to be able to communicate easily. Directories (either Domino's or any LDAP) are used to control who can and cannot access the environment.

External users can access the server if Sametime is put in a spot in your network that allows them access without compromising network security. Clients support proxies such as HTTP, HTTPS (HyperText Transfer Protocol Secure), SOCKS4 and SOCKS5. HTTP tunneling enables Sametime clients that have restrictive firewalls and operate in corporate networks to connect to a Sametime server on the Internet.

Lotus Team Workplace (formerly QuickPlace)

Lotus Team Workplace is a Web-based collaborative team workspace that integrates with existing applications such as Lotus Notes, Sametime, and Microsoft Office XP. The tool helps users schedule meetings, manage tasks, communicate in real time, present ideas, and create and edit documents. Similar in concept to a Yahoo or MSN "group," Team Workplace provides a group environment for teamwork called a "place." Users have the ability to search across all the places in which they are members, or restrict the search to a single place. Users can work offline when disconnected from the network using Domino Off-Line Services.

Team Workplace is customizable, so Web designers and developers can customize its look and features. It can be integrated in a Web portal using the Team Workplace Java/SML API. But the best news about Team Workplace is that it is easy to install and use, providing self-service to all business users.

IBM Mindspan Solutions and Lotus LearningSpace

In the heyday of the computing industry in the mid-1990s, conferences abounded, people flew to go to classes, and accountants accepted training as a legitimate expense. To add to that, people actually had time to take a week-long class. No more. Classes are held locally, and if you can get away for one or two days, you count yourself lucky.

Sometimes a classroom experience is the only way to truly learn a new skill. However, many new technologies can be learned relatively quickly online if the course is constructed well, exercises are interactive, and the help system is robust. IBM's Mindspan Solutions using Lotus LearningSpace, IBM's e-learning software, helps you build these types of classes.

Mindspan Solutions is a combination of services, technologies, and the collaborative expertise of Lotus that provides an end-to-end e-learning solution. Its resources include more than 3,400 services practitioners, as well as a global content development community with 15 Mindspan Custom Content Development sites around the world.

Mindspan Solutions builds e-learning classes using the LearningSpace family of products. There are two separate products: Lotus LearningSpace Forum and Lotus LearningSpace.

LearningSpace Forum consists of five interdependent Domino databases that contain information about scheduling; a repository for learning media; a course room for discussions and document sharing; a database of profiles; and a repository for instructors and course developers to build and catalog a variety of questions and assessments. This forum provides the ability for instructors and training participants to take their classes with them and participate any time or any place. Similar to Notes, LearningSpace Forum allows you to replicate databases, share documents and discussions, and collaborate on content authoring and management.

On the other hand, Lotus LearningSpace is a Web-based application and doesn't need a Domino infrastructure. There are two modules within LearningSpace: The Core Module and the Collaboration Module.

The Core Module uses active server page technology and relational databases (such as DB2, Oracle, or Microsoft SQLServer) to support the delivery and tracking of learning content. Management information (course descriptions, schedules, assignments, user profiles, permissions, and enrollment records) and student information (status, tracking, and assessment records) are stored in a relational database with ODBC access. Curriculum materials and activities can be stored in a file system or Web server. LearningSpace stores a pointer such as a URL or UNC (Universal Naming Convention) path to the content, rather than storing the content itself. There is also a built-in assessment authoring tool for question and test building.

The Collaboration Module extends the Core Module to allow collaborative learning capabilities using discussion databases or real-time, virtual classrooms. The Collaborative Module is supported by the Domino and Sametime technologies described earlier.

8

Application Accelerators

There are more IBM e-business software products than you can easily count, and new ones occur all the time. Companies need to move rapidly into the e-business age. Without experienced Web architects, it can be a risky business. If your company is small to medium in size, you probably do not have the people to develop the applications that you need. That is where application accelerators come in.

Application accelerators are anything that can help you get your e-business up and running as quickly as possible. They range from "out-of-the-box" software that you can install and run to fully architected solutions for specific business needs provided by application vendors. IBM has created a few applications but is more heavily invested in working with partners (including IBM Global Services) to create solutions that its customers need.

This chapter covers a range of these application accelerators. If you'll recall from Chapter 4, we delayed exploration of WebSphere's commerce solutions (part of the Reach and User Experience part of WebSphere Software Platform) until this chapter. This group of products provides an "out-of-the-box" solution for various types of e-commerce applications—the company just beginning e-business, a company that wants to expand its e-business offering, an e-marketplace company, and a service provider of e-commerce services.

We will take a look at Patterns for e-business. These are sets of reusable, proven guidelines formed from the experience IBM has gained from more than 20,000 e-business engagements. They provide Web application architects and development firms with a set of methodologies to build consistent and workable Web applications. Finally, we will look at IBM's relationships with its e-business partners, including its partnerships with large Enterprise Resource Planning (ERP) and Customer Relationship Management (CRM) firms. So, let's begin with a look at WebSphere Commerce Suite.

WebSphere Commerce Solutions

Why should you care about e-commerce? Some estimates say business-to-business (B2B) e-commerce sales will reach $8.5 trillion by 2005. Businesses that extend their reach to the Web in a meaningful way will reap a huge part of that demand. As reviewed in Chapter 1, IBM is getting behind the e-business phenomenon by offering "e-business on demand." It's an important way to get involved in e-business in a way that's effective but not draining for your business.

WebSphere Commerce solutions support your entry into e-business. There are many different types of e-commerce solutions, designed to fit what you need. However, it's important to remember that taking time to determine what you need before you begin will save you a lot of heartache (and money) later.

To give you an idea of the rapid development possible with WebSphere e-commerce, consider that you can have a production-ready retail Web site up and running within 60 days using IBM MerchantReach e-commerce Services Solution for Retail.

WebSphere Commerce software allows you to establish e-commerce sites in B2B, business-to-customer (B2C), private, or public trading hubs and application service provider environments. The software is based on an open, industry-standard architecture employing Java technology and Extended Markup Language (XML)-based solutions. It is built to leverage Web services, including UDDI (Universal Description, Discovery, Integration), SOAP (Services-Oriented Architectural Protocol), XML (Extended Markup Language), and WSDL (Web Services Description Language), to provide flexible solutions.

WebSphere Catalog Manager allows you to create, update, and manage product information. In addition, the software provides all types of services, including payment processing (WebSphere Payment Manager) and integration with current business systems.

Combining commerce software with other WebSphere products allows you to extend these applications to wireless users. WebSphere Commerce contains support for mobile commerce (m-commerce), allowing you to use cellular phones, pagers, personal digital assistants (PDAs) and the like. Many protocols are supported including HTTP (HyperText Transfer Protocol) and WAP (Wireless Access Protocol). Use of WebSphere Everyplace and WebSphere Transcoding Publisher with these products means you can automate the tasks of sending information to these different types of devices.

Content can be varied in these solutions. WebSphere Commerce for Digital Media allows you to store, search, view, manage, collaborate, purchase, sell, and download digital assets via the Internet.

WebSphere Commerce also integrates e-commerce technology with collaborative technology (Lotus Sametime and Lotus QuickPlace—described in Chapter 7) to enable trading partners and customers to communicate with you.

Once your commerce site is built, it can't be static. You need to figure out what works and what doesn't. Products like WebSphere Commerce Analyzer can help you report and analyze customer statistics. The WebSphere Commerce Accelerator component of WebSphere Commerce extends the analysis capability to managers to allow them to monitor, analyze, and understand customer behavior.

WebSphere Commerce

The basic building block for the WebSphere Commerce solutions is WebSphere Commerce. We'll discuss three editions:

- Professional Entry Edition for companies that want to get an initial Web site up and running
- Professional Edition for enhanced e-commerce
- Business Edition for a robust business solution with a Web front end.

WebSphere Commerce Professional Entry Edition

The Professional Entry Edition allows you to create and manage online catalog information, including marketing and reporting tools that help you decide which promotions are working and which aren't. With this entry-level product, you can manage inventory and orders 24 hours a day. WebSphere Commerce Professional Entry Edition is the same product as WebSphere Commerce Professional Edition except the license limits you to one processor, one store, and one server for production, Lotus Sametime is not included, and its support is limited to the Windows NT or Windows 2000 operating systems, DB2 Universal Database Extended Edition (EE) as a database and IBM HTTP Server.

WebSphere Commerce Professional Edition

The Professional Edition is the next step up the ladder from the entry edition. In addition to doing what the entry edition does, it provides advanced order management capabilities, dynamic collaborative technology with Lotus Sametime for live-help reference applications, portal add-on capabilities, and multicultural support for global customers. It includes WebSphere Commerce Accelerator, WebSphere Catalog Manager, and WebSphere Commerce Payments. This edition is built on a foundation that includes WebSphere Application Server (see Chapter 4), IBM HTTP Server, and DB2 Universal Database.

WebSphere Commerce Business Edition

The Business Edition extends beyond the traditional Web storefront to enable you to build a robust integrated process that uses the Web as its front end. In addition to the abilities contained in the Professional Edition, the Business Edition helps you personalize your B2B relationships in order to serve your trading partners better. It provides assisted selling technology to walk customers and partners through the requirements gathering and product selection process. It also includes contract management to support complex contracts and business policies.

Like the Professional Edition, the Business Edition is built on WebSphere Application Server, IBM HTTP Server, and DB2 Universal Database. It takes full advantage of an open standards infrastructure in a pure Java environment, including technologies such as Enterprise JavaBeans (EJBs), JavaServer Pages (JSPs), XML, Secure Electronic Transaction (SET), HTTP, and Wireless Markup Language (WML).

WebSphere Catalog Manager

With newer versions of WebSphere Commerce, WebSphere Catalog Manager is included with the WebSphere Commerce products noted above. The functionality included is described here.

WebSphere Catalog Manager is a set of tools for catalog development and management using standards-based Java and XML technologies. Catalogs can be easily updated for product changes, price changes, and personalization. Users can log on to the Web and see your catalog in their language. XML data exchange insures that your metadata will always ride along with your data. The Catalog Manager provides several types of clients as well as a server. The clients include workstation clients, Web browser clients, and spreadsheet clients.

WebSphere Catalog Manager workstation client provides end user tools to manage the build-time process of electronic catalog creation. You can create product definition templates that define the base information required for each product. This allows you to give a consistent message to your customers. If you wish, you can create a hierarchical structure of product entries as well as bundling and packaging products together in different manners. So, if you want to create a Web site that has only long-sleeve blouses and then subclass them by color, the Catalog Manager can do that. Alternatively, you can bundle the same black belt with dresses, pants, and skirts. The created catalog pages can then be exported in an XML format, ready to be imported into the WebSphere Catalog Manager server.

WebSphere Catalog Manager Web browser client provides the means for users to create and update data through a Web browser interface. This allows you to take advantage of the "thin"-client model of client/server and access and update your catalog from any location. The Catalog Manager generates and maps the Web interface to the targeted catalog data store. Spreadsheet clients can convert spreadsheet data into specific XML formats for input to the Catalog Manager server or WebSphere Commerce Suite environments.

The Catalog Manager is also available to the e-marketplace hub operators or distributors. These organizations need the ability to aggregate different content from multiple sources. Our old friend XML comes in handy in this application as well. The Catalog Manager enables the XML-based information from multiple sources into a Catalog Manager server. This can be done as a complete refresh or by importing catalog data in an incremental manner. The data can then be extracted at a selective level for target audiences or systems, improving your ability to do target marketing.

If the data is not already in XML format, the Catalog Manager server provides tools that enable the conversion of spreadsheet ASCII (American Standard Code for Information Interchange) files into XML format or map data in XML files from one catalog structure to another. It also provides the means to remap data in XML files between different XML formats. While it does not provide its own XML editor, Catalog Manager allows you to use any generic XML editor to create files in the needed formats for the Catalog Manager or Commerce Suite servers.

WebSphere Commerce Payments (formerly WebSphere Payment Manager)

WebSphere Commerce Payments is now a component of the WebSphere Commerce editions described earlier. The information here allows you to understand its functionality. Before we go into its functionality and components, let's take a look at SET (Secure Electronic Transfer).

SET is an open specification developed by Visa and Mastercard to establish secure payment card transactions over the Internet. In December 1997, SET Secure Electronic Transaction LLC (SETCo) was formed to oversee compliance testing and adoption of SET as a global payment standard. IBM is part of the technology advisors to SET and is approved for use of the standard.

SET uses digital certificates (described in Chapter 6) to verify that the cardholder and the merchant are who they say they are. The data is encrypted, and public and private keys are used for verification and decryption. All IBM payment processing products are intended to work with any other SET certified product.

WebSphere Commerce Payments is composed of multiple components. In addition to the basic product, it uses Payment Registry and Payment Gateway. It also integrates with NewGenPay's Valuto system to provide a wireless end-to-end payment solution.

WebSphere Commerce Payments is used to support multiple payment protocols. The Payment Server uses the Multi-Payment Framework

(MPF) to allow buyers, sellers, and financial institutions to accept multiple types of payments over the Internet. The reason that it is necessary to accept multiple payment types is the globalization of the Internet world. Instead of only accepting the four or so methods you are used to as a brick and mortar merchant (cash, check, ATM, or credit card), there are new payment processes and new global buyers that you want as your customers. The Multi-Payment Framework allows you to do this.

MPF separates payment management (the framework) from particular payment process by using payment cassettes to support the different payment types such as Secure Sockets Location (SSL), SET, or Merchant Initiated Authorization (MIA). The general structure of an Internet payment (Figure 8.1) is complex, with many possibilities of payment outcomes. For example, what happens if a customer has insufficient funds? Or, as happened frequently in the 2002 holiday season, what if a customer returns an item? MPF seeks to simplify that process by combining WebSphere Commerce Payment with the other components to simplify the process (Figure 8.2).

The MPF framework components (Figure 8.3) follow the general format of the Internet components we discussed in Chapter 1. It con-

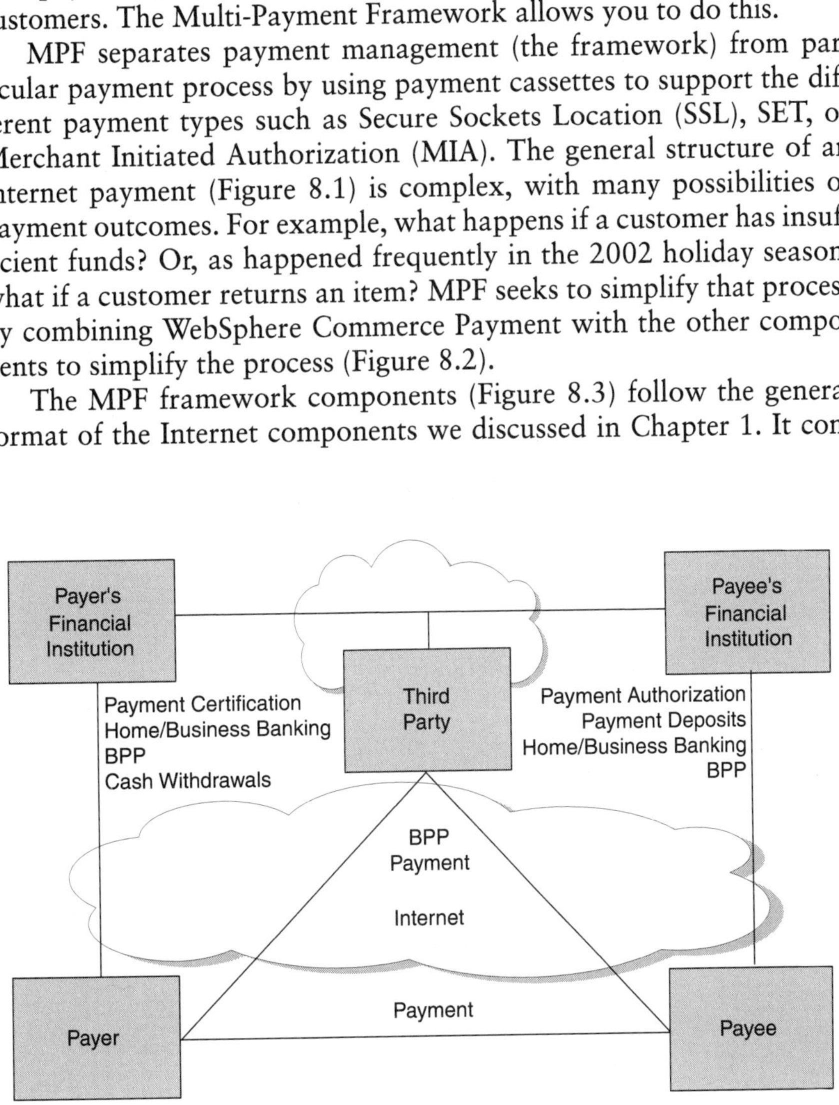

Figure 8.1. Internet payment structure.

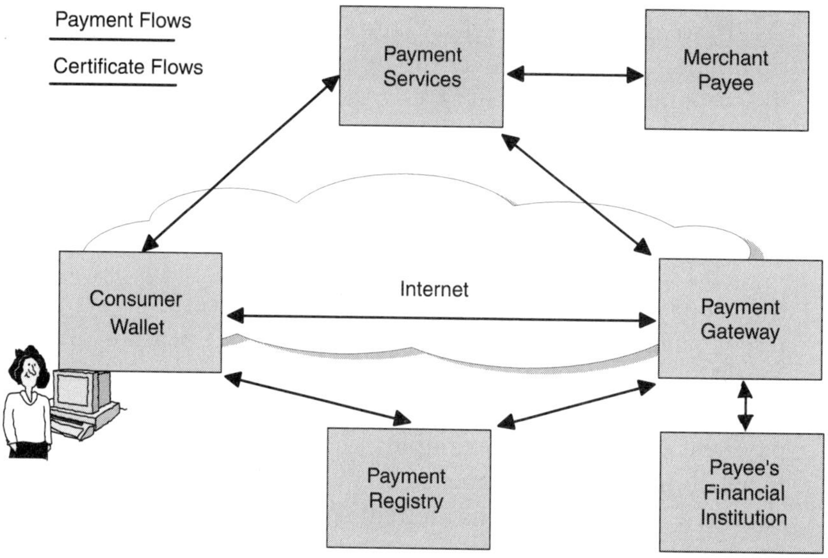

Figure 8.2. WebSphere Commerce Payment.

tains a user interface, connectors, APIs (Application Programming Interfaces), and components for communication, message routing, and persistent storage. The APIs provide standard interfaces to external services to access and send information about payments, payees, and payers. The communications component is an HTTP server that receives the request from the user interface. The message routing component is in charge of receiving and routing payments using the different payment cassettes supplied with WebSphere Commerce Payment and interacting with the different databases to retrieve and store pertinent information. The configuration database stores configuration data, such as the payment cassettes that are installed. The payment database provides persistence for payment transactions that pass through WebSphere Commerce Payment. The cryptography component provides software encryption services for payment cassettes written in C, C++, or Java. Alternatively, hardware encryption can be accessed using the hardware access component. The Service Provider Interface (SPI) provides the communication services between the payment cassettes and WebSphere Commerce Payment.

IBM Payment Registry is a SET approved component that manages and stores digital certificates in a relational database such as DB2 Uni-

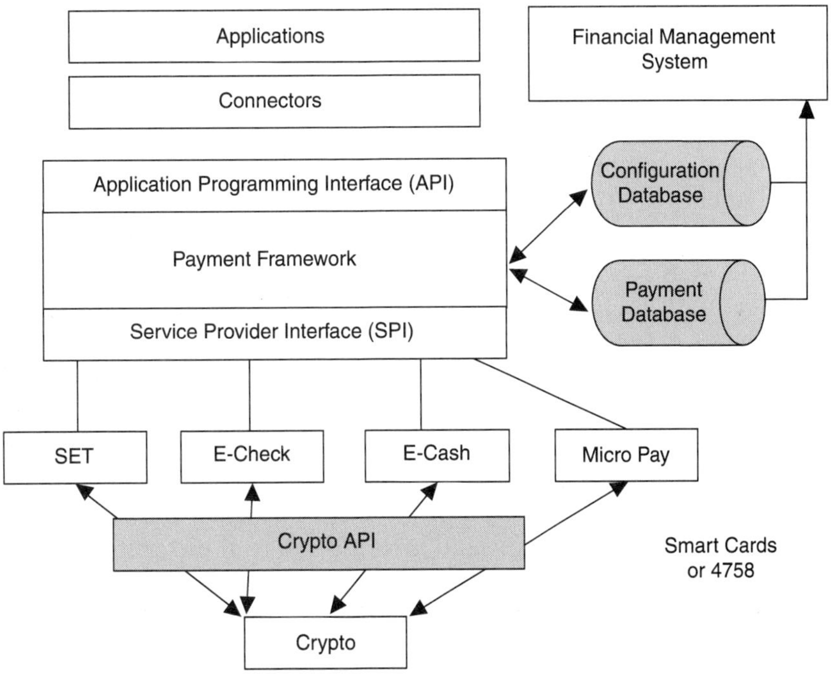

Figure 8.3. Multi-payment Framework components.

versal Database. It offers both automated and manual approval processes for certification. For encryption, the Payment Registry uses the IBM 4758 Cryptographic Adapter. The Payment Registry is itself broken down into four components:

- The SET certificate authority server processes the certificate requests, signing and issuing the request online or offline, depending on its configuration. The transaction information for cardholder, merchant, acquirer, approver, and administrator functions is encrypted and stored in a relational database.

- The approver module allows the user to review information provided, approve/reject requests, or revoke issued certificates using a GUI (Graphical User Interface) interface.

- The administrator module provides operational server management for the SET certificate authority server over encrypted channels.

- The certificate management module manages certificate and key databases along with any offline certificate requests.

IBM Payment Gateways is a SET approved component that gives credit card authorizations either by extending existing point-of-sale (POS) payment networks to the Internet or adding credit card authorizations to e-commerce applications. A gateway is a type of router that can send requests to the appropriate client or server. The Payment Gateway allows financial institutions, payment processors, and network providers to manage the acceptance and authorization of payment messages over the Internet. You can accept your customer's credit card and pass it to the Payment Gateway using SSL encryption technology. The gateway, in turn, passes it to the appropriate financial institution or payment processor. The Payment Gateway is aware of the formats that the particular financial institution or payment processor may require. Because of this, the gateway can send information to these units using flat files, Open Database Connectivity (ODBC) connections, DB2 Universal Database, or Oracle to produce standard formats such as International Standards Organization (ISO)–8583. Once the correct format is complete, the message is encrypted and safely sent to the financial institution or payment processor.

The Payment Gateway comes with a set of APIs that can be used to extend the development of customized formats or to use as external services for back-end payment systems. The AIX (Advanced Interactive eXecutive) version can use the 4758 Cryptographic Adapter for support of hardware encryption.

The Payment Gateway transaction manager component routes payment messages between applications, regardless of platform. This transaction manager is equipped to handle UNIX connections, Transmission Control Protocol/Internet Protocol (TCP/IP), Systems Network Architecture (SNA), and X.25 protocols (X.25 is available only on AIX). The secure application component handles encryption and description, certificate validation, cryptographic signing, PIN (Personal Identification Number) processing, certificate management, and other security functions for the gateway.

WebSphere Commerce Analyzer Advanced Edition

WebSphere Commerce Analyzer Advanced Edition provides tools for creating and maintaining an online store. It generates business reports that help you manage the success of the store. Data mining features of this product allow you to do in-depth analysis and discover patterns that improve your sales success. This product extends the analytical capabilities provided in the WebSphere Commerce package.

Report data is stored in DB2 Universal Database (see Chapter 5) on the WebSphere Commerce Analyzer server. Other tools include Business Object software for Web analytical reporting and DB2 Intelligent Miner for Data to do in-depth analysis. Business reports can be generated dynamically or on a scheduled basis. WebSphere Commerce Analyzer provides the ability to extract, transform, move, and load the raw report data, providing the ability to do summarized reports.

Websphere Commerce Analyzer contains three main components, an IBM Business Intelligence (BI) component, an IBM site analyzer component, and a Business Objects component. The IBM BI component provides the database for storage and manipulation of data, combining DB2 Universal Database, DB2 Warehouse Manager, DB2 Intelligent Miner for Data, and IBM HTTP server. Site analysis is obtained through Tivoli Site Analyzer (formerly WebSphere Site Analyzer, described in Chapter 6). End user Web analytical reporting is supplied through Business Objects products, including WebIntelligence, InfoView, Broadcast Agent, Supervisor, and Business Objects Commerce Tracker.

WebSphere Commerce Portal

WebSphere Commerce Portal is a portal solution that fully integrates with the WebSphere Commerce family of products. This portal allows you to integrate your e-commerce Web site with highly personalized content to unify and streamline online information and business applications. The product is build on WebSphere Commerce and WebSphere Portal (Chapter 4) software, and includes everything you need to create an e-commerce portal, including security through an LDAP (Lightweight Directory Access Protocol) directory and single sign-on.

Patterns for e-business

As Web applications are developed there is a certain sameness to the development process. As previously discussed, most companies face similar business issues—Sales Force Automation (SFA), payroll, general ledger, Supply Chain Management (SCM), and the like. These similarities have enabled companies such as SAP and Siebel to sell their applications to many companies, allowing for some customization for each customer.

The other approach to company similarities is to provide application development tools and methodologies to produce individual applications built on previously proven best practices. This is frequently the lot of consulting and contracting firms. If they have built an e-commerce application before, they will probably use the same methodology to build one for you, changing the design as needed to accommodate your specific needs.

This second approach forms the basis for Patterns for e-business. The main objective of these patterns is to provide reuse of designs and implementations that have proven successful in the past while allowing modifications for particular business implementations. The patterns are sets of reusable, proven guidelines formed from the experience IBM has gained from more than 20,000 e-business engagements. They are the best-practice implementations of e-business.

These patterns provide multi-tier e-business architectures, designs, and product mappings from IBM software, including the design and some code for implementation of a particular pattern. The Patterns for e-business Web site (available through the Companion Web Site listed on page xx) provides a rich set of references and methodology to use these patterns. The procedure to use these mappings is to begin where all good design begins—in analyzing the business problem that needs to be solved, including existing data and processing as well as business rules, whether captured in existing systems or not. The next step is to compare the results of this analysis to the current patterns of business interaction contained in the Patterns for e-business. Specifically, the site recommends five steps:

- Select a business pattern to meet the needs of the application you're developing.

- Select an application pattern that can implement the application's specific functionality.

- Review runtime patterns, and select a pattern that satisfies the system requirements of the solution.

- Review product mappings to determine which products have been successfully used for the runtime pattern selected in Step 3.

- Review guidelines and related links for the application pattern and product mapping you selected in Steps 2 and 4.

There are five main groupings of patterns:

- Business patterns identify the interaction between users, business, and data, and are used to create simple, end-to-end e-business applications. There are four business patterns: Self-Service, Collaboration, Information Aggregation, and Extended Enterprise.

- Integration patterns connect other business patterns together to create advanced e-business applications. The two integration patterns are access integration and application integration.

- Composite patterns are combinations of business patterns and integration patterns for advanced e-business applications. Composite patterns are Electronic Commerce, e-Marketplace, Portals, and Account Access.

- Custom designs are similar to composite patterns but haven't been implemented to the extent of composite patterns. They are developed to solve e-business problems of a small number of companies.

- Application and runtime patterns are driven by the customer's requirements to shape applications and supporting runtime for the e-business application. An application pattern describes how the application logic and data are partitioned and how they interact. Runtime patterns use nodes to group functional requirements. The nodes are then interconnected to solve a business problem. A set of conceptual layouts composed of application patterns and runtime patterns compose a logical pattern.

Product mappings based on proven implementations are used to populate the solution. Guidelines are available for the design, development, deployment, and management of e-business applications.

e-business Partner Solutions

IBM has partnered with thousands of businesses to offer solutions to get you started with e-business. From the IBM solutions page, you can browse these solutions by using selection criteria to narrow your search. Some of the ways you can view these solutions are:

- e-Commerce
- e-Business Infrastructure
- Business Intelligence
- Customer Relationship Management (CRM)
- Supply Chain Management (SCM).

For example, if you look in Supply Chain Management, you will find solutions such as:

- Ariba Buyer Solution to automate an employee-based purchasing and approval system for nonproduction goods and services.
- i2's Intelligent eBusiness Solutions for procurement solutions such as Supply Chain Management, Factory Planner, Demand Planner, and Supply Chain Strategist.
- IBM Infrastructure and J.D. Edwards to combine J.D. Edwards' collaborative business applications with IBM's infrastructure and industry expertise.

Alternatively, you can view the list by industries:

- Automotive
- Banking, Finance, and Securities
- Consumer Packaged Goods
- Distribution

- Education
- Government
- Healthcare/Pharmaceuticals
- Insurance
- Internet Service Providers
- Manufacturing/Process
- Media and Entertainment
- Retail
- Services
- Telecommunications
- Travel and Transportation
- Utilities/Energy.

Again, if you look under Retail, you will find solutions such as:

- Customer Loyalty Program to help increase sales and customer loyalty.
- The IBS e-Business Suite to enable distributors, online retailers, and resellers to conduct real-time e-business transacting.
- retail.dot.commerce for CommercialWare Customers, which manages all aspects of a retail enterprise across a seamless, scalable platform.

Interested in becoming an IBM e-business partner? Then check out the PartnerWorld for Developers Web site (link on the Companion Web Site listed on page xx), which gives information about a worldwide program supporting developers who build solutions using IBM technologies.

Recent features included:

- IBM develops heart rate monitor that calls cell phone for help
- e-business infrastructure co-marketing
- Revolving Creditline for Resellers
- Webcasts
- IBM e-business Hosting Services
- PartnerWorld 2003 Conference.

There are links from the main Web site to Business Partners, marketing and sales, education, conferences, video clips—in short, everything that a business partner needs to do business as a value-added reseller (VAR) with IBM.

Business Solutions

IBM has developed relationships with several large ISVs (Independent Software Vendors) to make applications available that today's e-business customers need. These are broken down to several areas: Enterprise Resource Planning (ERP), Customer Relationship Management (CRM), Supply Chain Management (SCM), and e-marketplaces.

Enterprise Resource Planning and Customer Relationship Management

ERP and CRM are two big areas that have been ripe for outside application developers. However, they have also been stumbling blocks for many companies during their implementation. The reason that this has happened is not due to the software—but to the culture. Lou Gerstner has indicated that for e-business to work, companies that have invested in their pipeline organizational model are going to have to make significant changes to become an integrated e-business. This was also true when ERP applications were first implemented. All of a sudden people needed to do things in a similar manner. Data, process, and business rules needed to be the same, and, most often, they needed to comply to the manner of the purchased solution.

Much of that pain is in the past, and companies that have implemented these solutions are taking advantage of the business knowledge they have gained by building data warehouses and implementing data mining search algorithms. Many solutions are also being externalized to Web clients.

IBM has partnered closely with a few of these solution providers, most notably SAP, Baan, PeopleSoft (ERP providers), and Siebel (a CRM provider). These companies provide application solutions, not data stores or data movement techniques. Many of them use DB2 Universal as a data store and work with connecting technologies such as DB2 Connect and WebSphere MQ (Message Queue). Some are also working with Tivoli to build management interfaces so that their customers can monitor the ERP or CRM solution along with the rest of their applications. Lotus is available for collaborative portions of these applications.

The significant point of this relationship is just that, the relationship. IBM works closely with these companies as each puts out a new release, communicating and testing to insure that performance, reliability, and availability are incorporated into the solutions that they provide their customers.

9

An Approach to e-business

This chapter is the summing it up chapter. It is also the chapter that goes through the steps that you might take if you are architecting an e-business solution. The purpose of this book is to help you, the architect or designer of an e-business application, understand IBM's e-business strategy, the history of computing that lives in your company, and IBM products that can help you get from where you are to where you want to be. I am hopeful that this book will be a reference book during your development efforts, helping you understand which IBM solution is going to solve your problem.

The previous chapters of the book may have overwhelmed you with the number of choices of software products that IBM has available to implement your solution. And yet, as we have gone through those sections, you have probably thought that there are other things you would like to see in the IBM portfolio, such as the following:

1. This book does not cover all the software products that IBM offers—even e-business products. One could reasonably argue that all software products enable e-business, but this book has focused on those associated with the major brand initiatives, such as WebSphere Software Platform. Even then, we have not covered all the products. Many of them are niche products or are incorporated into suites of products already mentioned. Rather than overwhelm you altogether, we limited the scope.

2. IBM has deliberately left some areas of software development to its business partners. With few exceptions, it has decided not to enter the application market, choosing instead to support application builders with foundation software products. For example, we discussed major application builders such as SAP and Siebel in Chapter 8. IBM works closely with these vendors, testing the applications with IBM products to insure compatibility and performance excellence of these applications.

3. This book is a snapshot in time. Even while the book was being written, IBM was making announcements regarding new software products, renaming solutions, and repositioning and including products in new offerings. This is the state of e-business today. Things change at a very rapid pace, and with book lead times, everything can't be included up to the minute. That is what the Web is for.

What this book has given you is a foundation in the world of IBM's e-business, including an introduction to IBM's new strategic direction of e-business on demand.

By understanding the historical influences on software architectures, you now have a base of knowledge that will help you understand how to make your business a successful e-business. The hodgepodge of hardware, architectures, and applications is no longer an impossible barrier to e-business, but an external service of e-business on demand. IBM has the hardware, software, and services to get you where you need to go.

So where do you begin? A good way to start is to figure out where you are, where you want to go, and what you want to gain from e-business. Then you need to find out where you are and how you are going to get from one place to another. Let us look at the possible places you might want to go.

Where Do You Want to Go?

There are many different types of Web sites. Some are static, changing rarely, presenting content that is updated by an HTML (Hypertext Markup Language) script and hosted by an ISP (Internet Service Provider). You probably do not need a fancy solution for that—the content and the updating of the content take higher priority than the mechanisms that keep it going.

But you probably want your application to be more interactive than a static Web page. What, exactly, does that mean? The best way to look at the situation is from a business perspective. There are several different reasons for getting a Web application up and running. One of the most common reasons is to reduce costs. Just as ATMs make banking transactions cheaper than dealing with a human, Web transactions save money. Another frequent reason is to improve customer satisfaction and loyalty. It is common knowledge that the cost of getting a customer is much higher than the cost of keeping one. How personalized do you want your Web site to be?

Depending on your answer, you can begin to look at how much you are willing to spend and how long you want to wait for your return on investment. As Gerstner has stated, the laws of business still exist in an Internet world. You can pour money into your Web application for a very long time, but if there is no return on investment, you will eventually go bankrupt.

So you know why you want to go on the Internet and what you expect to gain from it. You have a good idea of how long you can wait for a return on investment. This is when you begin to think about the business model that you want to develop.

Chapter 1, as well as the IBM Web site, can help you with ideas for understanding the possibilities for e-business. So can browsing the Internet to see what other companies are doing. Primarily, though, there are a few essential types of e-business—e-commerce, externalizing your back-end systems to the Web, business-to-business electronic computing, and connecting to pervasive devices. Each of these will dictate the components you need. Of course, you may eventually need to do all of these types of e-business in order to provide end-to-end computing.

You can break any one of these primary types of e-business into components. As you work with the programming model described in Chapter 1, you can see that there are three major breakdowns to determining how to break down your business model:

- Presentation: Who (or what) is your end user? If it is a human, how will he or she interact with your system? As we saw in Chapter 4, IBM provides many ways that the presentation layer can be displayed—using WebSphere Transcoding Publisher to provide the same image to many types of devices and WebSphere

Voice Server for voice presentation, as well as WebSphere Portal Server and WebSphere Personalization for specific formats of presentation on a Web site. IBM can also provide connectivity to the Web application server for pervasive devices that meet open standards.

- Web application servers: This is a rather large concept that contains such things as business logic, runtime environments, and persistent data stores. The bulk of the material was covered in Chapter 4 with the discussion of WebSphere Application Server; Chapter 5 regarding DB2 Universal Database, IMS, Informix, and U2; and Chapter 7 with Lotus Domino Server, and DB2 Universal Database. Security and management, discussed in Chapter 6, fit into this space as well, although they are implemented with and around the server.

- External services: This includes all the existing systems that you happen to have just lying around your company that you want to make accessible to e-business with a minimum of fuss. They are also services that link to other companies, be they co-marketers in your e-marketplace, regulatory agencies with whom you must comply, or financial institutions that provide authorization for your customer's purchase.

For example, let us imagine that we are developing a banking application for our best bank customers. We have two intentions—to provide better service at a lower cost for these customers and to keep them as loyal customers. We want to make it easy for them to access all our services via the Internet, including having a personal relationship with one of the customer service representatives. We want them to be able to maximize their return, sweeping funds from one account to another at will. We want them to be able to import their data into another financial application that they would like to use, such as Quicken or Microsoft Money, send a file to their accountant, or use it as the basis for an IRS audit. Finally, we would like to send them an e-mail, alerting them to changes in the markets that might affect their portfolio. And they should be able to do this all from a personalized Web portal. Because they are our best customers, we want to make sure all of their transactions are very secure. Our dream application looks like Figure 9.1.

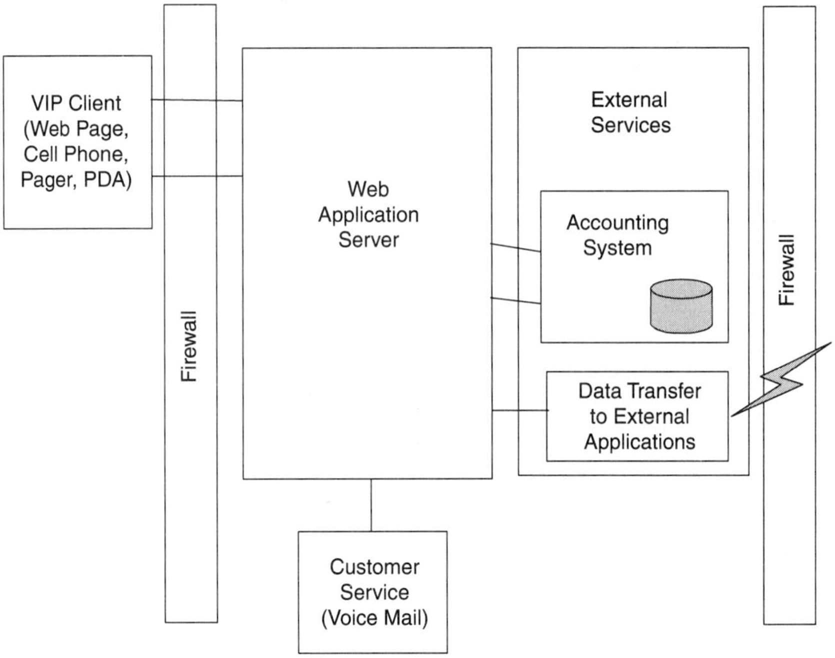

Figure 9.1. Application component example.

Our presentation layer includes interacting with our client's Web browser (in a personalized way), cell phone, and pager. Our Web application server contains the business logic and rules to service this very important customer. Security and manageability are important adjuncts to this server. Finally, there are a few external services that we need to include: an interface to our company's voice mailbox, access to our existing banking account system, and communication with financial packages and the IRS.

At this point the e-business developer can make a decision to turn the whole project over to a team of experts, possibly working with Patterns of e-business. Or he or she can look through the solutions directory on the IBM Web site to see if there are any solutions from IBM business partners to meet their needs.

You will need to find out if the decision is to go further in your application development.

Where You Are

There are many questions to answer about your current situation. The most obvious aspect is current applications. Where are these applications, and what runs them—hardware, operating systems, application code, and communication systems? Are these proprietary systems or open systems? Where is the data kept? What is used to run the process and enforce the business rules? Is this a component architecture or one built with the open standards of Java, XML, and the like? Is it a distributed system or one that is centralized?

But it is more than that. Where exactly are the applications that you would like to use? Are they remote to the applications? External to your organization or internal? What kind of formats are required for the external organizations? What kind of security is there in your applications? What kind of management do they have so you can insure the constant availability of your applications?

Do you need to build a new part of your application, or do you just want to put a pretty face on an application that you already have? Do you want to have your business rules centralized?

And, perhaps most important, what kind of skill level do you have in your organization? Are there skills to implement a Web application of the complexity that you are planning? If you are planning on building your own application, do you have the skills you need in Java development and programming as well as security management and network design?

Looking at the same three layers (presentation, Web application server, and external services), you can take the information that you know and begin to understand the gaps between what you have and what you need.

- Presentation: If you have a company Web site already, you probably have the structure needed to accept requests and return them. The same goes if you have done previous work in small devices such as PDAs (Personal Digital Assistants). If you have programmed in these presentation layers, then you have those types of skills as well. However, is there a design that is consistent on every Web site? Can this be expanded to other types of devices? Do you have a privacy policy and understand how it is to be implemented across your presentation layers? Is your security built in—both for your protection and your clients? How does the client request get through your firewall, assuming you have one? How do you insure that access to your Web application server is always available?

- Web application server: This is component technology at its best. It is a good idea at this point to take a look at the components you already have with an eye toward reuse. Do you have development and deployment tools for the components? What languages do you use? Is there an understanding of open technology such as Java, Linux, Web services, and XML? How are business rules implemented? If you are like most companies, business rules are implemented across many applications. What is your current security setup; management setup? Are there components already in existence to get information from back-end systems, authorize credit card use, and accept personal information from a Web site?

- External services: This tends to be where the rubber meets the road. Although building something from scratch sounds more difficult, in reality it is much simpler than trying to interface with systems that have been around forever that no one truly understands. What types of applications do you have and what hardware and software do they sit on? Who knows what they do and how they do it? What formats are required to send information to applications that are external to your organization?

In our imaginary scenario, we discover that we have got a good deal of knowledge of VisualAge for Java programming, but the mainframe-based skills are low. We have a Web site that tells about our bank and accepts prospect information. The prospect information is subsequently sent through our WebSphere Application Server on Windows 2000 to a DB2 Universal Database on Windows 2000. Our existing customer banking application is an IMS application that services our ATMs. We currently have the ability to send information to both Quicken and Microsoft Money. IRS audits require Electronic Data Interchange (EDI) files from our bank, but those are in place as well. We do not have a mechanism to send information to our voice mail from anyplace within our technical structure. Figure 9.2 has some of this information plugged in.

Armed with this knowledge—where we are and where we want to go—we begin the research to fill in the gaps. Along with this book,

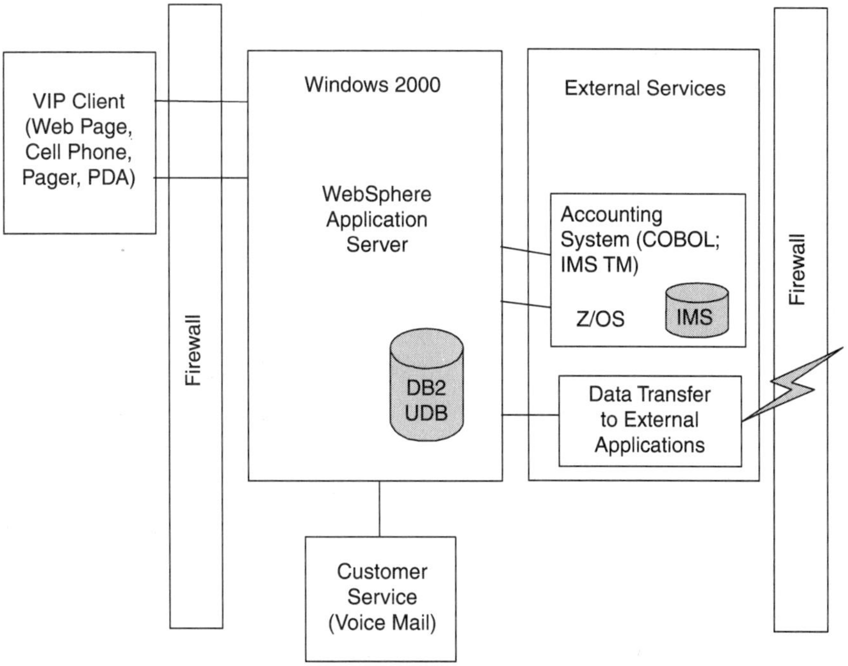

Figure 9.2. Application components and existing systems.

there are a few other places to go for information—the IBM Sales Team and the IBM Web site.

IBM Sales Team

With this information in hand, we can begin to speak with the IBM Client Representative or Software Account Manager (SAM). The IBM sales structure can seem complicated to the outsider, but it allows salespeople to have different areas of expertise. For example, IBM often has small teams focused on particular applications, such as a Business Intelligence sales representative and a Data Management sales representative, who have overlapping sales portfolios. However, as you may have gathered from this book, IBM produces a great deal of software and no one person can understand it all.

The IBM Client Representative is in charge of your account if you are a large business. These representatives usually deal at the executive level, selling IBM hardware, software, and services to your company. Predominantly, however, their role is to help you find the solutions for your business problems, such as the one we are discussing here. Then, based on a determination of what your business need is, the Client Representative will pull together the IBM account team to come up with a proposal that can solve your problem.

The sales team is also a good source to obtain white papers and detailed brochures that demonstrate what others have done to solve the same type of problem that you are facing.

If you are a small or medium-size company, you probably do not have your own Client Representative. There is probably a representative that is assigned to your company, or one may be looking for your company to help you become aware of IBM's solutions. If you have not heard from anyone, the best place to start is the IBM Web site—after all, we are talking e-business here, aren't we?

IBM Web Sites

From the Web site, you can look at IBM's e-business solutions. These solutions are presented in business terms, not technology terms, so you can begin with the problem as you understand it. Many of these pages reference case studies so that you can see how others have used IBM's e-business software. Most IBM Web pages have a link that allows you to contact a sales representative. When you find the page that appeals to you most, that is the time to send off your question.

Two sites are worth an additional mention—developerWorks and alphaWorks. Both of these links are on the Companion Web Site (see page xx), as is a link to the IBM Redbook site. Another important Web site is IBM's Web site for Business Partners, covered in Chapter 8.

developerWorks

developerWorks is full of information for people who want to work with the latest technologies that IBM is developing as well as get information on new open source initiatives. Like most sites, it's divided into several different areas.

Technology zones cover the major open source areas of interest: Linux, Java technologies, XML, Web services, wireless, and the like. A quick glance under Web services shows a link to an education piece on using mobile devices with the WSTK and articles on Web services security and accelerating your Web services with caching.

Product domains cover information about software brands and eServers: WebSphere, DB2, Tivoli, and Lotus, as well as IBM developer solutions. A quick glance under DB2 shows tutorials on SQL/XML (Structured Query Language/Extended Markup Language) publishing and SQLJ and JDBC (Java Database Connectivity), an interview with DB2 expert Susan Malaika, and an article on building a Net client that uses Web services.

The rest of the page is devoted to new news, as well as links to other sites, including alphaWorks.

alphaWorks

alphaWorks is a Web site that is dedicated to speeding IBM technology to early adopter developers. Its mission states that:

> *alphaWorks' mission is to provide early adopter developers direct access to IBM's emerging "alpha-coder" technologies. We are dedicated to surfacing the latest software technologies for you to download and evaluate. alphaWorks is redefining the way IBM conducts new product development by involving you in the earliest stages, before new developments are integrated into products or become licensing opportunities. If you are an innovative developer or technology decision-maker, this is your chance to work directly with IBM's researchers and developers through our discussion forum, and influence the earliest phases of IBM's new product development. Check out the latest innovations from IBM research and development—then tell us what you think.*

This is a pretty bold statement for a company that originally held proprietary knowledge of its systems close to its chest. If you are at all interested in some of the technologies that IBM is reviewing in its lab, this is a good place to start. The site has had topics such as:

- IP (Internet Protocol) Security Validation
- XML Wrapper Generator
- XML Parser for Java
- Fundamentals of Grid Computing
- Killer Combo: Mixins, Jam, and Unit Testing
- Web Services Toolkit for Mobile Devices.

Tutorials are available from the site on such topics as HTTP (HyperText Transfer Protocol), Java servlets, and XML for programmers. There's even a method to access alphaWorks from your PDA.

Putting the Pieces Together

With the information gathered, a solution can be determined and a plan for implementation laid out. At each level of the application presentation, Web application server and the interface to external services, the decision to build or buy can be made. It doesn't have to be an all or nothing proposition. For example, WebSphere Commerce Suite can be used for the bulk of your e-commerce application, but you can use WebSphere MQ (Message Queue) to send messages to your accounting department regarding income from your Web application.

Remember, even with the speed of Web development, old rules apply. You need to walk before you can run and you need to apply good business sense. It doesn't make sense to have a return on investment so far out that you can't see it. If it means implementing your designs a component at a time, then that does work. Keeping to open standards allows you to constantly build and improve your e-business applications. IBM solutions are built on these standards, giving you the flexibility to implement the solution that you need, when you need it.

Appendix A: Rational Software

In December 2002, IBM announced its decision to purchase Rational Software. Rational makes tools used to build, test, and manage software projects, allowing developers to build models of their software applications before they write the code. Ninety-eight of the Fortune 100 use Rational tools and services. Since IBM and Rational have been industry partners for 15 years, they decided to merge to exploit the fact that enterprise customers want to buy technology packaged as cohesive solutions to business problems.

Unlike other purchases it has made in the past few years (Informix, for example), IBM has also announced that it intends to make Rational a separate brand, alongside Tivoli, WebSphere, DB2, and Lotus. At the time of this writing, strategies haven't been finalized. How the brand will look and who will run it is still under discussion.

The purpose of this chapter is to review some of the products of the existing Rational company, with the understanding that some of these products may be re-branded and re-packaged once the transition is complete. For the most up-to-date information, check the companion Web site (see page xx) on a periodic basis.

Rational Software has been around for over 20 years and focuses its solutions in three core areas: best practices, tools, and services to help automate the software engineering practice.

Best Practices

Rational Software has developed best practices based on years of customer work and experience in project management. The umbrella ideas of best practices include:

- Iterative development to identify and eliminate risks before they threaten the project

- Requirements management to insure change is managed correctly

- Component architectures to make the architecture tangible to all practitioners
- Visual modeling for high-quality architectures
- Quality verification throughout the project

In addition, Rational has developed a process platform to help companies put these practices to work for them.

Rational Unified Process (RUP)

Rational Unified Process (RUP) is a software development process based on an iterative model. There are eight main components:

- The Business Modeling component defines the existing environment, including business vision, processes, rules, glossary, entities, and objects. It also develops a business architecture and defines how processes use objects. Finally, this component helps you identify what automation is necessary.
- The Requirements component helps you define the business problem to be solved, capture stakeholder concerns, and manage the scope of the system.
- The Analysis and Design component helps you build a theoretical architecture, test the architecture, and design the database.
- The end result of the Implementation component is the group of developed and tested components that make up the architecture required for the business problem solution.
- The Test component allows you to define what is going to be tested, how you are going to test it, and how you are going to know when you're done testing.
- The Deployment component completes the fulfillment cycle for software development, including acceptance testing, production, and moving completed software to media for customer use.

- The Configuration and Change Management component carries throughout the product life cycle to insure that change proposals are complete and that their impact is measured.

- The Project Management component is another cross-project component that helps manage the software project.

- The Environment component helps you prepare and manage the software environment for all phases of the project development life cycle.

Tools

In addition to RUP, Rational Software has developed tools to aid developers throughout the life cycle process. These tools can assist you with:

- Requirements Management
- Visual Modeling and Development
- Automated Testing
- Project Management
- Software Configuration Management.

Services

Rational also has a services division that helps companies implement their software development best practices. It does this by providing training, professional services, technical support, an online developers network and development accelerators. The development accelerators are similar in concept to IBM's Patterns for e-business discussed in Chapter 9.

Appendix B: Glossary

- 4GL (Fourth Generation Language) is a programming language that was developed after COBOL (a third generation language).
- 2PKDP (Two-Party Key Distribution Protocol) is a security protocol that combines bi-directional authentication with key distribution.
- ASCII (American Standard Code for Information Interchange) is the character set used for representing English characters as numbers.
- ADFs (Application Description Files) provide necessary information about a distributed client/server application.
- AFP (AppleTalk Filing Protocol) is a file sharing protocol used in Apple networks.
- AIFF (Audio Interchange File Format) is a format for transmitting sampled sound.
- AIX (Advanced Interactive eXecutive) is a UNIX-style operating system that works with RS/6000 hardware.
- ALCS is an application server that provides online transaction management for mission-critical applications.
- AMPS (Advance Mobile Phone Service) is a communication system that divides a geographic region into areas called cells.
- AMS (Application Management Specification) is a formal specification for that communication based on MIF.
- ANR (Automatic Network Routing) provides a connectionless routing mechanism for moving packets through the network on a predetermined path.

- ANSI (American National Standards Institute).

- API (Application Programming Interface) is a set of routines, protocols, and tools that can serve as building blocks for application development.

- APPC (Advanced Program-to-Program Communications) is a protocol for distributed computing that's the basis of SNA networking. Also known as LU6.2.

- Applet is a program that can be executed from another application, but not from an operating system. Applets are small in size, cross-platform compatible, and highly secure. Web browsers that are equipped with Java virtual machines can interpret applets they obtain from Web servers.

- APPN (Advanced Peer-to-Peer Networking) is a network protocol that is an alternative to TCP/IP.

- ATM (Asynchronous Transfer Mode) is a network technology that transfers data in packets of a fixed size—generally small. Alternatively (Automated Teller Machine), a machine designed to perform basic bank teller transactions without human assistance.

- AVI (Audio Video Interleave) is the file format for Windows Video files.

- B2B (Business-to-Business) is the selling of goods and services between businesses.

- B2C (Business-to-Customer) is the selling of goods and services from a business to a customer.

- B2E (Business-to-Employee) is communication between a business and its employees.

- BPM (Business Process Management) is a set of applications that helps businesses manage their processes.

- BPP (Bill Presentation and Payment) is a service provided by financial institutions to access and pay bills.

- CA (Certificate Authority) is a trusted third party organization that issues a certificate that guarantees that someone is who they say they are.

- CAE (Client Application Enabler) is a piece of software that sits on a client that allows it to communicate with a server.

- CCI (Common Client Interface) manages the flow of data between the application and the connected system without being aware of any business logic on the application server or within a container.

- CDF (Component Description File) describes the management characteristics of a part of the application on a particular platform.

- CDMA (Code-Division Multiple Access) is a digital cellular technology that makes the full available spectrum of digital channels available to a cellular user.

- CDPD (Cellular Digital Packet Data) is a digital cellular technology that is an enhancement to an existing analog network.

- CGI (Common Gateway Interface) is a server-side specification that allows the transfer of information between a Web server and a program that conforms to the CGI specification.

- CHAP (Challenge-Handshake Authentication Protocol) is a security authentication that uses a key to encrypt the client's user name and password for transmission.

- cHTML (compact HTML) is a version of HTML used for small devices such as personal digital assistants (PDAs).

- CICS (Customer Information Control System) is a transaction management system.

- CIM (Common Information Module) is the database on a client containing information about a user.

- CLDC (Connected, Limited Device Configuration) is the J2ME configuration for small devices such as cell phones.
- CLI (Call Level Interface) is the interface that an application program can use to submit SQL statements for processing.
- CMOS (Complementary Metal Oxide Semiconductor) is a semiconductor used in computers that requires less energy than other types of semiconductors.
- CMS (Conversational Monitor System) is a virtual machine operating system that only operates under the control of VM.
- COBOL (COmmon Business Oriented Language) is a computer language developed in the 1950s to manipulate data and processes.
- CORBA (Common Object Request Broker Architecture) is an architecture developed by OMG that is based on object-oriented theories.
- CP (Central Processor) is a shortened name for CPU.
- CPI-C is a port used for communication.
- CPU (Central Processing Unit) is the heart of the computer, giving it the ability to function.
- CRL (Certificate Revocation List) is a list of revoked security certificates.
- CRM (Customer Relationship Management) is a set of applications that helps businesses manage their customer relationships by tracking customers' histories and managing the customer in a coordinated way through all the company's sales channels.
- CSS (Cascading Style Sheets) is an HTML feature that gives control over how pages are displayed.

- CWMI (Common Warehouse Metadata Interchange) is a standard for exchanging metadata developed by OMG.
- DADX (Document Access Data eXtension) specifies a Web Service using a set of operations that are defined by SQL statements or XML Extender Document Access Definition documents.
- DASD (Direct Access Storage Device) is a disk storage device.
- DataTAC is a proprietary packet radio protocol for wireless technology and messaging.
- DBMS (DataBase Management System) is a set of programs that manages the storage, integrity and recoverability of data.
- DCE (Distributed Computer Environment) is a suite of tools to develop distributed applications based on open standards.
- DCM (Desk Client Manager) monitors networked PCs and workstations for trouble.
- DHCP (Dynamic Host Configuration Protocol) is a protocol to assign dynamic IP addresses on a network.
- DHTML (Dynamic HTML) can be a page of Web content that changes each time it is viewed, depending on items such as time of day and the profile of the reader.
- DIAL is the method of connecting a client device to a network via a modem and a public telephone network.
- DMTF (Desktop Management Task Force) is a cooperative, industry-wide consortium formed in 1992 to develop and deliver standards for building easily managed PC systems.
- DNS (Domain Name Service or System) translates domain names such as *www.IBM.com* into an IP address such as 123.456.789.1.

- DOM (Document Object Model) specifies how objects in a Web page should be displayed.
- DOS (Disk Operating System) is shorthand for MS-DOS—Microsoft's pre-Windows operating system.
- DRDA (Distributed Relational Database Architecture) is a method of requesting information from a client to a server.
- DSLs (Digital Subscriber Lines) are lines that use a modulation scheme to pack data onto copper wires and are traditionally able to transmit more data more rapidly than traditional telephone lines.
- DTD (Document Type Definition) is a file that contains definitions of valid XML tags used in a particular document or set of documents.
- DTMF (Dual Tone MultiFrequency) is the use of number keys on the telephone to create client requests.
- DTXA is a method to connect to telephones.
- DVIPA (Dynamic Virtual IP Addressing) is the ability to assign IP addresses on the fly.
- E2E (Exchange to Exchange) is the exchange of transactions or information between Web sites. Alternatively, (Employee-to-Employee), indicating transactions between employees.
- EAI (Enterprise Application Integration) is the unrestricted sharing of data and processes through networked computers.
- ECML (Electronic Commerce Markup Language) is a standard for merchant field data collection.
- EDI (Electronic Data Interchange) is a tool to exchange data and support transactions from like platform to like platform.

- EJB (Enterprise JavaBean) is a component of J2EE that contains business logic.

- EHLLAPI is a group of routines that allows a PC to emulate a mainframe.

- EOCF/2 (Extended Operations Console Facility/2) is a TPF systems console solution.

- EPOC is an operating system designed for mobile devices.

- ERP (Enterprise Resource Planning) is a set of applications that automates the business of businesses—predominantly in areas such as finance, human resources, order processing and production scheduling.

- ESCON is a channel-to-channel connection to transmit data between hardware resources.

- ESS (Enterprise Storage Server), code named Shark, is an IBM RAID storage device.

- Ethernet is a LAN protocol that supports data transfer rates of 10 MBps (megabits per second).

- Extranet is an intranet that can be accessible to trusted users outside the firewall. Extranets are common means for business partners to exchange information.

- Fast Ethernet is a newer version of Ethernet that supports data transfer rates of 100 MBps.

- FDDI (Fiber Distributed Data Interface) is a set of protocols to send digital data over fiber optic cable and support data transfer rates of 100 MBps.

- Firewall is a piece of software that shields an organization's network from exposure to hackers and other unauthorized users via the Internet.

- FIX (Financial Information Exchange) Protocol is a standardized message system for security transactions.
- FTP (File Transfer Protocol) is the protocol used on the Internet to send files.
- GDF (Global Description File) describes the overall application.
- GIF (Graphics Interchange Format) is a bit-mapped graphics format to capture graphic objects such as photos.
- Gigabit Ethernet is the newest version of Ethernet that supports data transfer rates of 1 gigabit per second.
- GPRS (General Packet Radio Service) is a wireless digital standard that transmits information in short bursts.
- GSM (Global System for Mobile communications) is a digital cellular technology that assigns eight simultaneous calls to the same radio frequency.
- GUI (Graphical User Interface) is a way to use graphics to interface between program and user rather than character commands.
- HACMP (High-Availability Cluster Multi-Processing) is an application service that allows RS/6000 to access data in parallel.
- HDML (Handheld Device Markup Language) is used to format content for Web-enabled mobile phones that use phone.com browsers.
- HPR (High Performance Routing), an extension to APPN, improved the performance and flexibility and employed ANR and RTP.
- HTML (HyperText Markup Language) is a language associated with Web page content that tells the browser how that item is to be displayed on the screen.

- Internet is a global network connecting millions of independent computers.
- I/O (Input/Output) is any device that is used to move data to and from a computer.
- IP (Internet Protocol) specifies the type of packet that is transmitted over the Internet.
- IPX (Internetwork Packet Exchange) is a connectionless protocol used by the Novell NetWare operating systems that run on top of IP.
- ISDN (Integrated Services Digital Network) is an international standard for sending data over regular telephone lines.
- ISO (International Standards Organization) is an international standards board.
- ISP (Internet Service Provider) is a company that provides access to the Internet.
- IIS (Microsoft Internet Information Server) is Microsoft's Web application server.
- IVR (Interactive Voice Response) allows a touch-tone phone to be used to retrieve information from a database.
- J2EE (Java 2, Enterprise Edition) is a standard for mutli-tiered programming built on the Java programming base and developed by a consortium of software vendors.
- J2ME (Java2 MicroEdition) is a set of configurations and profiles for development of wireless device applications.
- JAAS (Java Authentication and Authorization Service) is a piece of software that allows programmers to integrate authentication, authorization, and security in Java.
- Java is an object-oriented language developed by Sun Microsystems that can run on most computers using a Java virtual machine.

- JavaBean is a piece of software code that can be used as a component in a Web application.
- JCA (Java Connector Architecture) defines a standard programming interface that can be used to connect Java applications to different types of systems, such as IMS, CICS, or DB2.
- JDBC (Java Database Connectivity) is a Java API that allows Java programs to access SQL-compliant databases.
- JIT (Just-in-Time) is a compiler for Java byte-code.
- JPEG (Joint Photographic Experts Group) is a compression technique for graphic objects.
- JMS (Java Messaging Service) implements the transfer of asynchronous messages among J2EE components and legacy applications that allow messaging.
- JMX (Java Management Extensions) records and logs statistics on usage and resources for Java application monitoring and management.
- JSP (Java Server Page) is an HTML extension for doing server-side scripting in Web pages.
- JVM (Java Virtual Machine) is a Java interpreter and runtime environment that can run on most operating systems.
- LAN (Local Area Network) is a network connecting computer nodes in a relatively small area such as a building, or a small group of buildings on a business campus.
- LDAP (Lightweight Directory Access Protocol) is a set of protocols to enable the access of information directories such as security directories.
- LOB (Large OBject) is a piece of data that is exponentially larger than common data types of variable length character or graphic data types.

- LPAR (Logical PARtitioning Region) is a section of a z/OS computer that can be treated as if it were a separate mainframe.
- MIA (Merchant Initiated Authorization) is a SET extension that can be used by merchants to accept credit card information from consumers using any method other than SET.
- MICR (Magnetic Ink Character Recognition) is used in banks to print special characters with magnetic ink.
- MIF (Management Information Format) is a syntax for describing management information for a manageable component.
- MIME (Multipurpose Internet Mail Extensions) is a specification that formats content such as graphics, audio, and video files so they can be sent over the Internet.
- Mobilex is a packet radio network for transmission of data over wireless networks.
- MOM (Message Oriented Middleware) is a set of programs that allows applications from different operating systems, hardware, and programming languages to communicate reliably and securely.
- MP3 is a file extension for MPEG.
- MPEG (Moving Picture Experts Group) comes in MPEG-1, MPEG-2, MPEG-4, and is a standard for video compression.
- MPP (Massively Parallel Processor) is a hardware architecture in which the memory, I/O and processors are not shared, but connected to each other through a high-speed communication device.
- MPTN (MultiProtocol Transport Networking) is a communications protocol.
- MVS (Multiple Virtual Storage) was introduced in 1974 for the S/390 computer.

- NFS (Network File System) allows networked users on different types of hardware to share files.
- NUMA (Non-Uniform Memory Access) is a computer that allows a large number of processors to operate as a single system.
- OAGIS (Open Applications Group Integration Specification) contains a large set of XML Document Type Definitions.
- OCR (Optical Character Recognition) is the ability to read text from paper and translate it into machine-readable language.
- ODBC (Open DataBase Connectivity) is a program layer that translates application requests into commands that can be understood by a database that is ODBC-compliant.
- ODMA (Open Document Management API) is a program layer that translates application requests into commands that can be understood by a database that is ODBC-compliant.
- OEM (Original Equipment Manufacturer) is a company that supplies a basic piece of hardware or software that is used in the creation of another separate object.
- OLE (Object Linking and Embedding) is a standard method to link created objects between one application and another.
- OLTP (OnLine Transaction Processing) is processing of a single complete unit of work using an online mechanism.
- OMG (Object Management Group) is a group of about 700 companies whose goal is to provide standards for developing object-oriented applications.
- OO (Object-Oriented) is a design methodology that embraces the idea that content has certain properties and can only be acted upon in certain ways.
- The Open Group is an international consortium of computer and software manufacturers and users formed in February 1996

by merging two previously independent groups—the Open Software Foundation (OSF) and X/Open Company Ltd. to promote open systems.

- ORB (Object Request Broker) is a component in the CORBA programming model that acts as the middleware between clients and servers. The ORB passes the request to the business application (service) that is required. If the service lies on another server, the ORB gets the information from that server. After the information is received, the ORB passes the information back to the client.
- OS (Operating System) is the software that runs a hardware computer.
- OTMA (Open Transaction Management Access) provides connections to TCP/IP.
- P3P (Platform for Privacy Preferences) is a simple, automated way for users to gain more control over the use of personal information on the Web sites they visit.
- PABX (Private Automatic Branch Exchange) is a telephone system.
- PAP (Password Authentication Protocol) is a form of security authentication which receives an unencrypted user name and password to compare to a table for authorization.
- PC (Personal Computer) is a computer used in an office or home.
- PCL (Printer Control Language) is a method for computers to communicate with printers.
- PDA (Personal Digital Assistant) is a handheld device that can be used for computing, as a telephone and fax sender or receiver that contains the ability to be part of a network.
- PDC (Personal Digital Cellular) is a Japanese digital cellular network.

- PHPS (Personal Handy Phone System) is a Japanese digital cellular network.

- PIM (Personal Information Manager) allows users to organize small bits of information.

- PIX (Private Internet eXchange) is a type of firewall software.

- PKCS (Public Key Cryptography Standard) is a standard for encryption.

- PKI (Public Key Infrastructure) is a system of identification for security purposes.

- PNG (Portable Network Graphics) is a file system to map graphics.

- POP (Post Office Protocol) is a protocol to retrieve e-mail from a server.

- Proxy Server is a server between a client application and its server. The proxy server intercepts all requests and attempts to fulfill them before passing them on to the destination server.

- PSTN (Public Switched Telephone Network) is the copper-wired analog international telephone system.

- RACF (Resource Access Control Facility) provides the ability for clients to sign on to a host machine using a secure password.

- RAD (Rapid Application Development) was a type of development that came about in the 1980s that promised faster code development using specific methodologies. RAD is not so different from normal development today.

- RAID (Redundant Array of Independent [or Inexpensive] Disks) is a data storage device that provides duplicate storage in case of problems with the primary storage.

- RADIUS (Remote Authentication Dial-In User Service) is an authentication service generally used by Internet Service Providers.

- RAM (Random Access Memory) is a type of computer memory that can be accessed randomly.
- RISC (Reduced Instruction Set Computing) is a computer with a simplified range of instructions used to perform tasks.
- RMI (Remote Method Interface) is a set of protocols that allows Java objects to communicate remotely with other Java objects.
- RPC (Remote Procedure Call) is a protocol that allows a program on one computer to execute a program on another.
- RTOS (Real-Time Operating System) is an operating system that guarantees something will happen within a certain amount of time.
- RTP (Routing Transport Protocol) is the mechanism used by the nodes to establish a connection as needed.
- SAN (Storage Area Network) is a group of storage devices networked together with high speed connections.
- SCM (Supply Chain Management) is a set of applications that helps businesses manage their supply chain, including managing warehouses, tracking inventory and distributing goods.
- Servlet is an applet that runs on a server—the Java alternative to a CGI program.
- SDK (Software Development Kit) is a programming package for a specific software application.
- SET (Secure Electronic Transaction) is an industry-standard transport and messaging protocol using encrypted certificates for highly secure payment processing.
- SGML (Standardized General Markup Language) is one of the oldest tag languages and is the forerunner to HTML and XML.

- SLIC (System Licensed Internal Code) is a set of highly specialized programs that are imbedded deep within the AS/400 computing hardware.

- SMF (System Management Facility) is a method of automatically allocating storage as needed.

- SMP (Symmetric MultiProcessing) is a computer architecture that allows multiple processors to work at the same time.

- SMS (Short Messaging Support), a service that sends short messages to mobile phones. Alternatively, (System Managed Storage) is a method of automatically allocating storage as needed.

- SMTP (Simple Mail Transfer Protocol) is a protocol that is used to send e-mail messages from one server to another or a client to a server.

- SNA (Systems Network Architecture) is a set of network protocols that was introduced in 1974 to support system communication.

- SNMP (Simple Network Management Protocol) is a protocol used for managing complex networks.

- SOAP (Services-Oriented Architectural Protocol) is a method to wrap a message in a common technology for transference.

- SOCKS is a protocol for handling TCP traffic through a proxy server.

- SQL (Structured Query Language) is a query language that was developed by IBM 1974 and 1975. It has been standardized, but there are different dialects of the language.

- SSL (Secure Sockets Layer) protocol was developed by Netscape to transmit secure documents over the Internet.

- TCP/IP (Transmission Control Protocol/Internet Protocol) is a connectivity protocol that allows dissimilar devices to communicate with each other.

- TDMA (Time Division Multiple Access) is a digital technology that divides a radio frequency into time slots and allocates the time slots to multiple calls. It is used by GSM.

- TELNET is a program that connects a PC to a server.

- TM (Transaction Monitor) is a piece of software that can watch transactions for problems.

- Token Ring is a network in which all the computers are arranged in a ring. A token is passed around the ring, picking up and delivering messages as it goes.

- TPF (Transaction Processing Facility) is a system designed to optimize communication between computer and database.

- TPI (Tracks per Inch) measures density of data storage on disk devices.

- TSO (Time Sharing Option) is a mainframe programming environment that allows multiple users to share the same resources.

- TTS (Text-To-Speech) is a method to translate machine-readable data to a synthesized voice.

- TWAIN is the interface standard for scanners.

- UDDI (Universal Description, Discovery, Integration) is a project designed to provide the registry portion of Web services.

- UDF (User Defined Function) is a method that can be defined on a particular object.

- UML (Unified Modeling Language) is a notational language for specifying logical designs of OO projects.

- UDP (User Datagram Protocol) is a connectionless protocol that runs on top of IP networks.

- UNIX is a multi-user, multitasking operating system developed at Bell Labs in the early 1970s.

- UOW (Unit of Work) is the total of events that must occur if a transaction is to be considered complete.

- URL (Uniform Resource Locator) is the World Wide Web's addressing scheme for Web sites.

- UDT (User-Defined Type) is a data type that can be defined by the user based on a pre-existing data type.

- VM (Virtual Machine) is an operating system that makes each user feel they are running their own operating system.

- VoiceXML (Voice eXtensible Markup Language) is an XML standard geared to building voice-response systems for speech-to-text and text-to-speech applications.

- VoIP (Voice over Internet Protocol) is a specification that allows the transmission of telephone calls over the Internet.

- VPN (Virtual Private Network) is a network that uses encryption and other security mechanisms to use the Internet as a private network.

- VSE (Virtual Storage Extended) is an operating system developed for the smaller models of the System/360 computer architecture.

- VT (Virtual Terminal) is a shared terminal using underlying resources that looks like a single terminal to the user.

- VTAM (Virtual Telecommunications Access Method) controls communication in an SNA environment.

- W3C (World Wide Web Consortium) is an organization founded by Tim Berners-Lee, the inventor of the World Wide Web, to promote common protocol specifications for the evolution of the Web.

- WAN (Wide Area Network) is a network that spans a large geographical area.
- WAP (Wireless Application Protocol) is the specification used to transmit data over wireless devices.
- WAS (WebSphere Application Server) is the IBM Web application server.
- WAV is a format for storing audio files.
- WBMP (Wireless Bitmap) is a graphic format optimized for mobile computing devices.
- WfMC (Workflow Management Coalition) was founded in August 1993 to promote and develop the use of workflow applications through the development of standards.
- WinHLLAPI provides a protocol for file transfers and interactive communications from Windows operating systems.
- WLM (WorkLoad Manager) is a component of the z/OS operating system that manages the work based on business goals.
- WMF (Windows Metafile Format) is a file format used to store graphic data.
- WML (Wireless Markup Language) is an XML language for WAP devices.
- WSDL (Web Services Description Language) is an XML extension to describe service interfaces.
- WSP (Wireless Server Provider) is company that offers transmission services (similar to an Internet Service Provider), but for wireless devices. Alternatively, (Wireless Session Protocol), the protocol used for wireless devices.

- WTLS (WAP Transport Layer Security) is a secure sockets system (SSL) used between a wireless WAP device and a WAP gateway server.

- WYSIWYG (What You See Is What You Get) is a method that shows you on a computer screen what will be formatted when the page is printed.

- WWW (World Wide Web) is a group of networked servers (Internet) that supports specially formatted documents.

- XHTML (eXtensible Hypertext Markup Language) is a hybrid between HTML and XML that is specifically designed to display on pervasive devices.

- XML (eXtended Markup Language) is a standardized way to define the meaning of a piece of content.

- XSL (eXtended Style Language) is an XML language for reformatting and presentation.

- YODA (Your Own Data Access) is a Java applet that allows the use of XML and XSL to create EDI files.

Index

2PKDP (Two-Party Key Distribution Protocol), 109
64-bit architecture, 50, 54, 56, 57, 59

A

access connectors, EIP, 98–99
access control lists, WAS, 75
access management, 205–208. *See also* security software; Tivoli Access Manager
  access privileges, 205
  authentication, 205
  DB2 Universal Database and, 206
  delegation of security functions, 205
  identity management mechanisms, 209
  Lightweight Directory Access Protocol (LDAP) directory server, 206
  public key-based credentials, 207–208
  single sign-on, 205
  unauthorized attempts, 205
  WebSEAL component of Tivoli Access Manager, 75
  WebSphere MQ and, 207
access methods
  DB2 Universal Database, 158
  Information Management System (IMS), 150–151
action business rules, 97
ActiveX, 74, 88, 130
Adaptive Differencing Technology, 219
address spaces, DB2 Universal Database, 162
Administer component of DB2 Data Propagator, 199
Administrator, IBM Screen Customizer, 89
advanced ("black box") components of WSBCC, 141
Advanced Edition, WAS, 94
Advanced Interactive eXecutive (AIX), 35, 59–60, 254
Advanced Peer-to-Peer Networking (APPN), 68, 90
Advanced Program-to-Program Communications (APPC), 88
Advanced Workflow service, EIP, 100
aggregates, Informix, 181
ahead-of-time (AOT) compiling, 85
AIX (Advanced Interactive eXecutive), 35, 59–60, 254
alphaWorks, 271–272
alter fragment command, Informix, 181–182
Amazon.com, 4, 96
American Express, 5
American National Standards Institute (ANSI), 157–158
American Standard Code for Information Interchange (ASCII) conversion, WebSphere, 250
AMI (Application Messaging Interface), 124, 125
annotation feature of WebSphere Transcoding Publisher, 114
ANR (Automatic Network Routing), 68
ANSI (American National Standards Institute), 157–158
AOT (ahead-of-time) compiling, 85
API (application programming interface), 22, 176
APPC (Advanced Program-to-Program Communications), 88
Apple Computer, 52
applets (Java programs), 20, 21
application accelerators, 245–261. *See also* Patterns for e-business; WebSphere; WebSphere Commerce
  business solutions, 260
  Customer Relationship Management (CRM), 260–261
  e-business partner solutions, 246, 258–260, 263
  Enterprise Resource Planning (ERP), 260–261
  IBM MerchantReach e-commerce Services Solution for Retail, 246
  independent software vendors (ISVs), 5, 12, 260
  "out-of-the-box" solutions, 245
  overview of, 5, 245
  partner solutions, 246, 258–260, 263
Application Connectors, IBM CrossWorlds Connectors, 119

Application Developer Integration Edition, WebSphere Studio, 82
application development. *See also* WebSphere Studio
  DB2 Universal Database, 161
  WebSphere Application Server (WAS), 75
application integration, 121–128. *See also* WebSphere Business Integration
  Application Messaging Interface (AMI), 124, 125
  Customer Relationship Management (CRM) applications, 127
  Enterprise Resource Planning (ERP) applications, 127
  Human Resources (HR) application, 127
  Java Messaging Service (JMS), 124–125
  Mainframe Adapters, 127
  Message Oriented Middleware (MOM), 121
  Message Queuing Interface (MQI), 123–125
  object-oriented philosophy, 121–122
  Queue Manager Clusters of WebSphere MQ, 124
  Queue Managers of WebSphere MQ, 122–124
  security and WebSphere MQ, 123–124
  Supply Chain Management (SCM) applications, 127
  WebSphere Data Interchange, 126–127
  WebSphere e-business Adapters, 127
  WebSphere MQ (Message Queue), 121–128
application layer
  architectures pre-dating e-business, 36, 37
  networks, 64
application management
  Tivoli Application Protection, 222
  Tivoli Monitoring for Applications, 224
  Tivoli Storage Manager for Application Servers, 219
  Tivoli Workload Scheduler for Applications, 232
Application Messaging Interface (AMI), 124, 125
application patterns, 256, 257
application program interaction, DB2 Universal Database, 158–159
application programming interface (API), 22, 176
application programming languages, IMS, 151
application requester functionality, DB2 Universal Database, 168
application server. *See* WAS (WebSphere Application Server)
application sharing, 95
applications pre-dating e-business, 47–48
Apply component of DB2 Data Propagator, 199
APPN (Advanced Peer-to-Peer Networking), 68, 90
architectural structure, IMS, 151–152
architectures pre-dating e-business, 24–48. *See also* business intelligence (data warehouses); databases
  application layer, 36, 37
  applications, 47–48
  availability, 29
  base 16 numbers, 25
  batch, 6, 25–27, 28, 30, 32, 33
  bits, 25
  characters, 26
  client/server architecture, 6, 36–37
  codes (data), 25–26
  Common Object Request Broker Architecture (CORBA), 42–43
  component broker architecture, 42–43
  Customer Information Control System (CICS), 29–30, 71
  data integrity, 27
  data layer, 36
  data quality, 27–28
  distributed architectures, 35–37
  Distributed Common Object Model (DCOM), 42
  "dumb" terminals, 26
  electronic file structures (flat files), 26–27, 32, 43
  Electronic Numerical Integrator And Computer (ENIAC), 25, 50, 52
  "fat" clients, 36
  fields, 26
  field types, 26
  files, 26
  fixed-length records and fields, 26
  flat files (electronic file structures), 26–27, 32, 43
  Graphical User Interface (GUI), 36
  indexes, 27
  Information Management System (IMS), 30, 32–33, 71

journaling, 29
latency, 36
legacy systems, 24
logging capability, 29
Object Linking and Embedding (OLE), 42
Object Management Group (OMG), 42
online transaction processing (OLTP), 6, 28–31, 33, 43, 44
Open Database Connectivity (ODBC), 42
personal computers (PCs), 6, 35
positional information, 25–26
presentation layer, 36, 37
punch cards, 25
records, 26
recovery capability, 29
reuse, 27
"screen scraper" technology, 36
"sneaker net," 36
syncpoints, 29, 30
System Object Model (SOM), 42
"thin" clients, 37, 249
transaction management, 28–31
unit of work (UOW), 29, 152
variable-length records and fields, 26
Virtual Storage Architecture (VSAM), 24, 27–28, 43
archive management, 222
ARPANET, 1
AS/400 family, 51, 55, 59, 60, 171, 173
ASCII (American Standard Code for Information Interchange) conversion, WebSphere, 250
attached tables, Informix, 182
audio files supported, WebSphere Studio, 80
audit subsystem, identity management, 208, 209
authentication, 204, 205
automated attendant of WebSphere Voice Response, 103
Automatic Network Routing (ANR), 68
auto-tuning software, WAS, 76–77
availability. *See also* performance and availability software
architectures pre-dating e-business, 29
DB2 Universal Database, 160, 164–165
Information Management System (IMS), 152, 154
Informix, 182–183, 187

B
B2B (business-to-business), 5–6, 93
B2C (business-to-customer), 93
B2E (business-to-employee), 93
Baan, 261
background tasks, Lotus, 234
backup. *See* recovery
Baltimore, 207
bank teller business components, WebSphere, 141, 142
base 16 numbers, 25
base control program (BCP), 57
base ("white box") components of WSBCC, 140–141
basic business practices for e-business, 5
batch, 6, 25–27, 28, 30, 32, 33
Batch Resource Recovery Service, 200
BCP (base control program), 57
best practices automation, 223–224
binding business rules, 97
bitmap index, Informix, 187
bits, 25
"black box" (advanced) components of WSBCC, 141
BPM (Business Process Management), 116–121
browser thin client, DB2 Content Manager, 175
buffer pages, Informix, 185
Business Edition, WebSphere Commerce, 247, 248–250
Business Impact Management (Tivoli solution), 229
Business Integration (WebSphere), 70, 116–128. *See also* application integration; process integration
business intelligence (data warehouses), 43–47. *See also* architectures pre-dating e-business
cleansing data, 46
data mining, 47
detailed data, 44, 46
dimension tables, 44, 45
"dirty" data, 46
"fact" table, 44, 45
fourth-generation languages, 43
latency of data, 44
metadata, 44, 46
OnLine Analytic Process (OLAP) databases, 47
presentation layers, 46
replication, 44
spreadsheets and, 46–47

star schema, 44, 45
summarized data, 44
transformation, 46
business logic beans, WAS, 73
Business Logic Container, WAS, 72–73
business model, 264–265, 272
business patterns, 256, 257
Business Process Management (BPM), 116–121
business rule engines, 97
business rules, WebSphere Studio, 82, 86
business solutions, application accelerators, 260
business-to-business (B2B), 5–6, 93
business-to-customer (B2C), 93
business-to-employee (B2E), 93

C
CA (Call Answering) function of DUCS, 240
CA (certification authority), 204, 208
cache, 54, 159
Call Answering (CA) function of DUCS, 240
Call Level Interface (CLI), 159, 170
Capture component of DB2 Data Propagator, 199
Cascading Style Sheet (CSS), 79
catalog manager, WebSphere Commerce, 247, 248, 249–250
categorization capability, EIP, 98, 99
Categorization Engine of WebSphere Text Analyzer Business Components, 143
C/C++
Information Management System (IMS) and, 154
OS/390 and, 131
WebSphere Application Server (WAS) and, 74
z/OS and, 131
CCI (Common Client Interface) of JCA, 23
cellular network support, EIP, 107
central nodes, networks, 67
Central Processing Units (CPUs), 54, 55
Central Processors (CPs), 54
central storage, 54
certificate management systems, identity management, 208
Certificate Revocation Lists (CRLs), 208
certification authority (CA), 204, 208
CF (Coupling Facility), 58, 165–166
CGI (Common Gateway Interface) script, 72
challenge-handshake authentication protocol (CHAP), 109
Change and Configuration Management (Tivoli solution), 232
CHAP (challenge-handshake authentication protocol), 109
characters, 26
Charles Schwab, 5
child, IMS, 149
cHTML (compact HTML), 106
CICS (Customer Information Control System), 29–30, 71
CICS (Customer Information Control System) Monitor for OS/390, 228
CICS (Customer Information Control System) Transaction Gateway, 130
CICS (Customer Information Control System) Transaction Server, 130–131
C-ISAM DataBlade, 184
Cisco Voice over Internet Protocol (VoIP), 101, 102–105
classes (building), Lotus, 243–244
classes of objects (parent, superclass), 38, 39
classifier business rules, 97
class libraries support, EIP, 115
cleansing data, 46
CLI (Call Level Interface), 159, 170
client component of Lotus Sametime, 241
client failover, Lotus, 237
Client Runtime, IBM Screen Customizer, 89
client/server architecture, 6, 36–37, 202
client/server environment, Lotus, 234
clusters
hardware architectures, 55–56, 58, 62
WebSphere Application Server (WAS), 76
CMOS (Complementary Metal Oxide Semiconductor) technology, 53
CMS (Conversational Monitor System), 56
COBOL (COmmon Business Oriented Language), 6, 24, 133
COBOL Direct Connect, 196
Codd, E.F., 33, 47
codes (data), 25–26
Collaboration Module of Lotus LearningSpace, 244
Collaborative Portals, 92
commitment to e-business, 1–2
commit process, databases, 152–153
COmmon Business Oriented Language (COBOL), 6, 24, 133

Common Client Interface (CCI) of JCA, 23
Common Gateway Interface (CGI) script, 72
Common Object Request Broker Architecture. *See* CORBA
Common Security Interoperability (CSI), 75
Common Warehouse Metadata Interchange (CWMI) standard, 99
communications, IMS, 154
communications server, WebSphere Host Integration, 90–91
communication stack, 63, 64
compact HTML (cHTML), 106
Companion Web site for e-business, xix
Complementary Metal Oxide Semiconductor (CMOS) technology, 53
complex data types, 38
complexity of object, 39
Component Broker
  architectures pre-dating e-business, 42–43
  WebSphere Application Server (WAS), 74
component servers, WAS, 74–75
components (J2EE), 22
composite patterns, 257
Computer Telephony Interface (CTI) of DUCS, 240–241
Conference Expo, 3
configuration and operations management software, 229–232. *See also* Tivoli
  Change and Configuration Management (Tivoli solution), 232
  data exchange, 232
  Job Scheduling (Tivoli solution), 232
  license manager, 230
  point-of-sale manager, 230–231
  remote control, 231
  Tivoli Workload Scheduler, 231–232
  WebSphere MQ and, 232
  workload scheduler, 231–232
  z/OS and, 232
connection-oriented transport, 67
connection pooling, WAS, 76
Connection Services, WAS, 74
Connector Builder Component, WebSphere Studio, 83
connectors, IMS, 155
connectors (J2EE), 22
constraints, DB2 Universal Database, 41
containers, DB2 Universal Database, 169–170
containers (J2EE), 22
content accuracy, 17, 18
content adaptation services of WebSphere Everyplace Access, 106–107
Control Center, DB2 Universal Database, 170
Conversational Monitor System (CMS), 56
cookies for privacy management, 213
CORBA (Common Object Request Broker Architecture)
  architectures pre-dating e-business, 42–43
  Information Management System (IMS), 154
  Lotus, 237, 238
  WebSphere Application Server (WAS), 73, 74
Core Module of Lotus LearningSpace, 244
corporate portals, 92
co-servers, Informix, 186–187
cost-based optimizers, 160, 185
cost efficiency of e-business, 2–3, 264
costs, hardware architectures, 53
Coupling Facility (CF), 58, 165–166
CPs (Central Processors), 54
CPUs (Central Processing Units), 54, 55
Credit Function Group of WebSphere Order Capture Business Component, 144
CRLs (Certificate Revocation Lists), 208
CRM (Customer Relationship Management)
  application accelerators, 260–261
  application integration, 127
  e-business and IBM, 5, 48, 264
  Informix, 181
  Reach and User Experience (WebSphere), 94
cross-systems communication facility/cross-systems extended services (XCF/XES), 58
CrossWorlds. *See* IBM CrossWorlds
cryptography, 204
Crystal Report Generator, 212
CSI (Common Security Interoperability), 75
CSS (Cascading Style Sheet), 79
CTI (Computer Telephony Interface) of DUCS, 240–241
custom data connectors, EIP, 99
custom designs, patterns for e-business, 257
custom environment, EIP, 115
Customer Information Control System (CICS), 29–30, 71
Customer Information Control System (CICS) Monitor for OS/390, 228

Customer Information Control System (CICS) Transaction Gateway, 130
Customer Information Control System (CICS) Transaction Server, 130–131
Customer Relationship Management. *See* CRM
customization of Java Beans, 21
Customization Studio, IBM Screen Customizer, 89
CWMI (Common Warehouse Metadata Interchange) standard, 99

D

DADX (Web Services Document Access Definition Extension) Group Configuration, 81
database connectivity, WebSphere Studio, 82
Database Descriptors (DBDs), IMS, 150, 151
Database Management System (DBMS), 40
Database Recovery Control, IMS, 152
databases, 31–35, 37–42. *See also* architectures pre-dating e-business; DB2 Universal Database; IMS (Information Management System) family; information movement and access; Informix; U2 (UniVerse/Unidata) family
- classes of objects (parent, superclass), 38, 39
- complex data types, 38
- complexity of object, 39
- Database Management System (DBMS), 40
- encapsulation of objects, 38
- First Normal Form, 189
- hierarchical databases, 32–33, 149
- hybrid database management systems, 40–42
- identity of object, 39
- inheritance, 38
- instances of classes, 38–39
- intersection tables, 33–34
- logical design, 189, 190
- methods allowed on objects, 38, 39
- network databases, 31–32
- normalization, 189
- object complexity, 39
- object identity, 39
- object-oriented databases, 37–40
- object persistence, 39
- objects, 38, 39
- OnLine Analytic Process (OLAP) databases, 47
- parent-child data relationships, 33
- persistence of object, 39
- pointers, 32, 33
- properties of objects, 38
- records, 32
- relational databases, 33–34, 37, 38, 40, 189
- repeating groups, 189
- reuse of code, 38
- segments of data, 31–32, 33
- subclasses, 38, 39
- tables, 33–34, 189, 191
- Tivoli Monitoring for Databases, 224
- Tivoli Storage Manager for Databases, 219
- Tivoli Storage Resource Manager for Databases, 221
- WebSphere Application Server (WAS) and, 73, 74–75

Data Entry Database (DEDB), IMS, 151, 153
data exchange, 232
data integrity, 27, 160, 166
Data Language/One (DL/1), IMS, 151
data layer, 36
data link layer, networks, 64, 65
Data Management (DB2), 147–148. *See also* DB2 Universal Database; IMS (Information Management System) family; information movement and access; Informix; U2 (UniVerse/Unidata) family
data mining, 47, 255
data quality, 27–28
data replication, 193
data sharing, 152, 154, 165–166, 169
data skip, 181
data storage
- Enterprise Information Portal (EIP), 98–99
- identity management, 209
- WebSphere Application Server (WAS), 74–75

data warehouses, 43. *See also* business intelligence
DB2 Audio, Image, Video (AIV), 172
DB2 Connect, 196–197
DB2 Content Manager, 173–180. *See also* DB2 Universal Database
- application programming interfaces supported, 176

AS/400 and, 173
browser thin client, 175
desktop client, 175
document capture applications, 175–176
document indexing, 176
document routing capabilities, 174
eClient, 175
Electronic Media Management System (EMMS), 177–178
Enterprise Customer Service for Call Centers and, 178
Enterprise Information Portal (EIP) and, 99, 100, 176
fax solutions, 175
"fill-in-the-blank" queries, 180
Folder Application Facility, 176
IBM eRecords Solution and, 179
Intelligent Character Recognition (ICR), 176
library server of, 174–175
MessagePlus/Open and, 175, 179
multiplatforms, 173, 174
Object Access Method, 174, 176
Object Distribution Manager, 176
object server of, 174
Optical Character Recognition (OCR), 175–176
OS/390 and, 173, 174, 176
overview of, 173, 174
process integration and, 118
Reach and User Experience (WebSphere), 95
resource managers and, 174
scanning, 175–176
search capability, 175
Structured Query Language (SQL) queries, 175
templates, 175
Tivoli Storage Manager and, 174
video, 176–177
Web-exploiting broker, 174
WebSphere Portal and, 178
workflow, 174, 175
DB2 Content Manager CommonStore, 179
DB2 Content Manager for AS/400, 173
DB2 Content Manager for Financial institutions, 179
DB2 Content Manager for Multiplatforms, 74, 1731
DB2 Content Manager for OS/390, 173
DB2 Content Manager ImagePlus for OS/390, 176
DB2 Content Manager OnDemand, 179–180
DB2 Content Manager Solutions, 178–179
DB2 Content Manager VideoCharger, 176–177
DB2 DataJoiner, 99, 197–198, 199, 200
DB2 (Data Management), 147–148. *See also* DB2 Universal Database; IMS (Information Management System) family; information movement and access; Informix; U2 (UniVerse/ Unidata) family
DB2 DataPropagator, 199, 200
DB2 Developer Domain, 156
DB2 Everyplace, 171–173
DB2 Everyplace Mobile Application Builder, 172
DB2 Everyplace Sync Server, 171, 172
DB2 Extenders, 172–173
DB2 Information Catalog, 99
DB2 Server for VSE and VM, 166–167
DB2 Spatial Extender, 173
DB2 Universal Database, 156–173. *See also* DB2 Content Manager
access management, 206
access methods, 158
address spaces, 162
application development, 161
application program interaction, 158–159
application requester functionality, 168
availability, 160, 164–165
cache, 159
Call Level Interface (CLI), 159, 170
commit process, 152–153
constraints, 41
containers, 169–170
Control Center, 170
cost-based optimizer, 160
Coupling Facility (CF), 165–166
data integrity, 160, 166
data sharing, 165–166, 169
data warehouses, 43
Deferred Embedded SQL, 159, 170
Distributed Relational Database Architecture (DRDA), 167, 168
DSNZPARM, 162
dynamic Structured Query Language (SQL), 158, 159, 170
Enterprise Extended Edition (EE), 168–169
Enterprise Information Portal (EIP) and, 99
Extended Edition (EE), 168

eXtended Markup Language (XML) and, 161
hardware platforms supported, 156–157
IBM DB2 Universal Database SQL Reference for Cross-Platform Development, 161
IBM Resource Lock Manager (IRLM), 152, 160
image copies, 165
indexes, 157, 164, 170
instances of, 169–170
Inter-Partition Parallelism, 168, 169
iSeries computers and, 156
Java 2MicroEdition (J2ME) and, 172
Java Database Connectivity (JDBC), 159–160
Java Stored Procedures, 153
Large Objects (LOBs), 41, 164
Linux and, 156, 169
locking, 152, 160
logging capability, 160, 165, 170
Logical Partitions (LPARs), 162
Massively Parallel Processing (MPP), 168, 169
Microsoft Back Office certification, 147
multiplatforms, 94, 167–170
Net Search Extender, 172
non-partitioned index (NPI), 164
object-relational extensions, 40–42
Open Database Connectivity (ODBC), 159
open standards and, 171
operating systems supported, 156–157
optimizers, 160–161, 169
OS/390 and, 156, 161–166
overview of, 33, 34–35
parallelism, 163
Parallel Sysplex, 166
partitioned table space, 162–164, 170
Personal Edition (PE), 167
pervasive solutions, 103
pointers, 157, 164
process integration, 118
recovery capability, 160, 164–165, 165
Redundant Array of Independent (of Inexpensive) Disks (RAID), 163–164
relational database, 156
Resource Access Control Facility (RACF), 166
security, 160, 166, 170
SQL99 standard, 158
Starburst optimizer, 161
static SQL for Java (SQLJ), 159, 160
static Structured Query Language (SQL), 158, 159, 170
stored procedures, 41
Structured Query Language (SQL), 156, 157–158, 159, 170
Symmetric Multi-Processor (SMP), 162
synchronization capability with Information Management System (IMS), 154
Sysplex technology and, 165–166, 169
system catalog, 164
System R and, 33, 161
table data, 157
tables, 157, 160, 162–163, 170
table space partitioning, 162–164
table spaces, 157, 162, 163, 169–170
Text Extender, 172
Text Information Extender, 172
threat management, 212
Tivoli Monitoring for Databases, 224
transaction management, 160
triggers, 41
type pointer, 164
UNIX and, 156, 169
User-Defined Functions (UDFs), 40–41
User-Defined Types (UDTs), 40
view, 160
Virtual Machine (VM) and, 166–167
Virtual Storage Extended (VSE) and, 166–167
Web Services and, 161
WebSphere Application Server (WAS) and, 74, 75
WebSphere Business Components and, 144
WebSphere Commerce and, 248, 255
WebSphere Studio and, 82, 83, 86
Windows and, 156
Workgroup Edition (WE), 167
Workload Manager (WLM), 166
z/OS and, 156, 161–166, 169, 170
DB2 Universal Database for iSeries, 171
DB2 Universal Database for Multiplatforms, 94, 167–170
DB2 Universal Database for z/OS and OS/390, 156, 161–166
DB2 XML Extender, 172
DBDs (Database Descriptors), IMS, 150, 151
DBMS (Database Management System), 40
DCE (Distributed Computer Environment), 60, 131–132

DCOM (Distributed Common Object Model), 42
debugging applications, WebSphere Studio, 82
decision support, Informix, 181
deck fragmentation of WebSphere Transcoding Publisher, 114
DECS (Domino Enterprise Connection Services), 238
DEDB (Data Entry Database), IMS, 151, 153
default policies, threat management, 210
Deferred Embedded SQL, DB2 Universal Database, 159, 170
Dell, 52
demand to delivery integration, 7–8
desktop client, DB2 Content Manager, 175
detached tables, Informix, 182
detailed data, data warehouses, 44, 46
developers and WAS, 77
developer toolkits of Lotus Sametime, 241
development environments, WebSphere Studio, 81
developWorks, 270–271
Device Developer (VisualAge Micro Edition), WebSphere Studio, 85–86, 91, 100, 115
device profiles of WebSphere Transcoding Publisher, 114
device-side client, WebSphere Everyplace Suite Embedded Edition, 109–110
digital certificates
  Enterprise Information Portal (EIP), 108–109
  identity management, 208
  security, 204
  WebSphere Commerce, 250, 252
  WebSphere Host Integration, 87
digital signatures, 204
digital signing, identity management, 208
Digital Subscriber Line (DSL), 50, 67, 107
Digital Trunk Extended Adapter (DTXA), 103
dimension tables, data warehouses, 44, 45
direct dependent segment of DEDB, 153
direct storage, IMS, 150–151
DirectTalk technology, 103
"dirty" data, 46
disaster preparedness, 222
disk mirroring, IMS, 152
Disk Operating System (DOS), 57
disk resource discovery, 217
distributed architectures, 35–37
Distributed Common Object Model (DCOM), 42
Distributed Computer Environment (DCE), 60, 131–132
distributed computers, 52–53
Distributed Relational Database Architecture (DRDA), 167, 168, 196–197
distributed systems management, 223
DL/1 (Data Language/One), IMS, 151
document capture applications, DB2 Content Manager, 175–176
Document Object Model (DOM), 190, 192–193
document routing capabilities, DB2 Content Manager, 174
document type definition (DTD), 20
DOM (Document Object Model), 190, 192–193
Domino, 235–238. *See also* Lotus
Domino Administrator, 238
Domino Application Studio, 235
Domino Connectors, 235–236
Domino Designer, 235
Domino Enterprise Connection Services (DECS), 238
Domino Everyplace, 108, 235, 239
Domino Everyplace Access, 239
Domino Everyplace Enterprise server, 239
Domino Everyplace Short Message Service (SMS), 239
Domino Server, 235, 236–239
Domino Unified Communications Service (DUCS), 236, 239–241
DOS (Disk Operating System), 57
dot-coms businesses, 3
download times, 50
DRDA (Distributed Relational Database Architecture), 167, 168, 196–197
DSA (Dynamic Scalable Architecture), 182
DSL (Digital Subscriber Line), 50, 67, 107
DSNZPARM, 162
DTD (document type definition), 20
DTMF (Dual Tone MultiFrequency), 102
DTXA (Digital Trunk Extended Adapter), 103
Dual Tone MultiFrequency (DTMF), 102
DUCS (Domino Unified Communications Service), 236, 239–241
"dumb" terminals, 26

Dun and Bradstreet, 5, 99
DVIPA (Dynamic Virtual IP Addressing), 226
dynamic content services, WAS, 73
Dynamic Scalable Architecture (DSA), 182
dynamic Structured Query Language (SQL), 158, 159, 170
Dynamic Virtual IP Addressing (DVIPA), 226

E
E2E (employee-to-employee) portals, 93
EAI (enterprise application integration), 215–216
eBay, 5, 8
e-business and IBM, 1–23. *See also* application accelerators; architectures pre-dating e-business; configuration and operations management software; DB2 (Data Management); e-business approach; e-business concepts; hardware architectures; information technology; Lotus; networks; OSs (operating systems); performance and availability software; security software; storage software; WebSphere products
  application accelerators, 5
  basic business practices for, 5
  business-to-business (B2B), 5–6, 93
  commitment to, 1–2
  Companion Web site for, xix
  cost efficiency of e-business, 2–3, 264
  Customer Relationship Management (CRM) applications, 5, 48, 264
  dot-coms businesses, 3
  e-business on demand, 15–16
  e-commerce, 4–5
  end-to-end infrastructure for, 4, 10
  Enterprise Resource Planning (ERP) applications, 5, 48
  focus of e-business on demand, 16
  HyperText Markup Language (HTML), 1, 18–19
  importance of e-business, 2–3
  independent software vendors (ISVs), 5, 12, 260
  infrastructure for, 3, 4, 10–11
  integration of business systems for, 3–4, 9–10
  Internet impact on, 1, 2–3, 53
  open standards for, 4, 8–9, 10, 272
  pervasive e-business, 4
  resiliency of e-business of demand, 16
  responsiveness of e-business on demand, 15
  return on investment (ROI), 3, 264
  self-configuration infrastructure for, 14, 15, 63
  self-healing infrastructure for, 4, 10, 14, 15, 63
  self-optimization infrastructure for, 14, 15, 63
  self-protection infrastructure for, 14, 15, 63
  standard communications protocol, 1
  Supply Chain Management (SCM) applications, 5
  Transmission Control Protocol/Internet Protocol (TCP/IP), 1, 20
  variability of e-business on demand, 15–16
  Web site for, xix
  wireless devices, 2–3
  World Wide Web, 1, 37
e-business approach, 262–272
  alphaWorks, 271–272
  business model, 264–265, 272
  current applications and operations, 267–269
  developWorks, 270–271
  example, 265–266
  external services of business model, 265, 267, 268, 272
  goals for business, 263–266
  help with, 269–272
  IBM Client Representative, 269, 270
  IBM Sales Team, 269–270
  IBM Web sites, 270–272
  open standards importance, 4, 8–9, 10, 272
  presentation layer of business model, 264–265, 267–268, 272
  Web application servers of business model, 265, 267, 268, 272
e-business concepts, 16–23. *See also* e-business and IBM; Java
  applets (Java programs), 20, 21
  application programming interface (API), 22
  Common Client Interface (CCI) of JCA, 23
  components (J2EE), 22
  connectors (J2EE), 22
  containers (J2EE), 22
  content accuracy, 17, 18
  customization of Java Beans, 21
  document type definition (DTD), 20

Electronic Data Interchange (EDI), 19, 126–127
Enterprise JavaBeans (EJBs), 22
eXtended Markup Language (XML), 9, 19–20
eXtensible Style Language (XSL), 20
HyperText Markup Language (HTML), 1, 18–19
introspection from Java Beans, 21
J2EE Connector Architecture (JCA), 23, 74, 82
keywords, 18
parsers, 18
persistence of Java Beans, 22
platform dependent computer programs, 20
portability of computer programs, 20–21
properties of Java Beans, 22
scalability, 17
self-learning transactions, 17
servlet (Java), 21
Standardized General Markup Language (SGML), 18
tag languages, 18–20
transaction persistence, 17
transaction security, 17
Transmission Control Protocol/Internet Protocol (TCP/IP), 1, 20
unstructured documents, 19
wrappering components (J2EE), 22
write once, run anywhere (computer programs), 20, 21, 60, 154
e-business connectors, IBM CrossWorlds Connectors, 119–120
e-business on demand, 15–16
e-business partner solutions, 246, 258–260, 263
ECI (external call interface) of CICS Transaction Server, 131
eClient, 175
e-commerce, 4–5. *See also* WebSphere Commerce
EDI (Electronic Data Interchange), 19, 126–127
EE (Enterprise Extended Edition), DB2 Universal Database, 168–169
EE (Extended Edition), DB2 Universal Database, 168
EGL (Enterprise Generation Language), 78, 83
EHLLAPI (Emulator High-Level Language Applications Programming Interface), 88
EIP (Enterprise Information Portal), 98–115. *See also* pervasive solutions; WebSphere Everyplace
access connectors, 98–99
Advanced Workflow service, 100
annotation feature of WebSphere Transcoding Publisher, 114
categorization capability, 98, 99
cellular network support, 107
challenge-handshake authentication protocol (CHAP), 109
class libraries support, 115
Common Warehouse Metadata Interchange (CWMI) standard, 99
compact HTML (cHTML), 106
content adaptation services of WebSphere Everyplace Access, 106–107
custom data connectors, 99
custom environment, 115
data stores, access to, 98–99
DB2 Content Manager and, 99, 100, 176
DB2 DataJoiner and, 99
DB2 Information Catalog and, 99
DB2 Universal Database and, 99
deck fragmentation of WebSphere Transcoding Publisher, 114
deployment of WebSphere Transcoding Publisher content, 114
device profiles of WebSphere Transcoding Publisher, 114
device-side client, WebSphere Everyplace Suite Embedded Edition, 109–110
digital certificates, 108–109
Everyplace Wireless Client, 106, 110
Everyplace Wireless Gatekeeper, 106, 110
eXtended HyperText Markup Language (XHTML), 106
federated data stores, 99
File Transfer Protocol (FTP) collections, 99
HyperText Markup Language (HTML) and, 112, 113
IBM Business Intelligence Information Catalog, 98
IBM Everyplace Synchronization Manager, 108
IBM J9 Virtual Machine (J9) support, 115
IBM Service Management Framework (SMF) and, 110
images and WebSphere Transcoding Publisher, 114
Information Access Layer functions, 98

J2ME "Java-powered" platform, 115
Java Database Connectivity (JDBC), 99
Lightweight Directory Access Protocol (LDAP) and, 110, 114
Lotus data and, 99
Lotus Domino Everyplace, 108
metadata, 98
micro environment, 115
mobile application platforms, 105–112
network profiles of WebSphere Transcoding Publisher, 114
overview of, 92, 95, 98–100
packet radio network support, 107
password authentication protocol (PAP), 109
Point-to-Point Protocol over Ethernet (PPPoE), 111
portlet applications (prepackaged) of WebSphere Everyplace Access, 107
push technology, 108
real-time operating system (RTOS) of WebSphere Everyplace Suite Embedded Edition, 109–110
Remote Authentication Dial-In User Service (RADIUS), 112
satellite network support, 107
search capability, 98, 99
security, 99, 108–109, 110–111
Server Provider Offering, WebSphere Everyplace Server, 107–109
service offerings management, 111–112
Short Messaging Support (SMS), 108
streamlining content by WebSphere Transcoding Publisher, 113–114
synchronization manager, 108
synchronization services of WebSphere Everyplace Access, 106
"talking" software, 109–110
text clipping feature of WebSphere Transcoding Publisher, 114
Tivoli Access Manager and, 109
Tivoli Personalized Service Manager and, 109
transcoding Web data, 112–114
Two-Party Key Distribution Protocol (2PKDP), 109
Unified Content API, 99
Web content browsing (offline) of WebSphere Everyplace Access, 107
Web crawler, 99
Web data adaptation for pervasive computing, 112–114
WebSphere Application Server (WAS) and, 112
WebSphere Custom Environment, 115
WebSphere Edge Server, 112, 145
WebSphere Micro Environment, 115
WebSphere MQSeries Everyplace, 108
WebSphere MQ Workflow and, 100
WebSphere Studio Device Developer and, 110
WebSphere Transcoding Publisher, 108, 112–114
Wireless Application Protocol (WAP) support, 106, 110–111
wireless environments and, 107
Wireless Markup Language (WML), 106
Wireless Session Protocol (WSP) support, 111
workflow service, 100
EJBs (Enterprise JavaBeans)
overview of, 22
Reach and User Experience (WebSphere), 98
WebSphere Application Server (WAS), 73, 74
WebSphere Host Integration, 87, 88, 130
WebSphere Studio, 82
e-learning, Lotus, 243–244
Electronic Data Interchange (EDI), 19, 126–127
electronic file structures (flat files), 26–27, 32, 43
Electronic Media Management System (EMMS), 177–178
Electronic Numerical Integrator And Computer (ENIAC), 25, 50, 52
eLiza (IBM Autonomic Computing Initiative), 14–15, 62–63
e-mail, Lotus, 234
e-meetings, Reach and User Experience (WebSphere), 95
EMMS (Electronic Media Management System), 177–178
employee-to-employee (E2E) portals, 93
Emulator High-Level Language Applications Programming Interface (EHLLAPI), 88
encapsulation of objects, 38
Encina product family, 131–132
encryption, 204
end nodes, networks, 68

end-to-end infrastructure for e-business and IBM, 4, 10
end-to-end integration, 7–8
ENIAC (Electronic Numerical Integrator And Computer), 25, 50, 52
enterprise application integration (EAI), 215–216
Enterprise Customer Service for Call Centers and DB2 Content Manager, 178
Enterprise Edition, WAS, 77
Enterprise Extended Edition (EE), DB2 Universal Database, 168–169
Enterprise Generation Language (EGL), 78, 83
Enterprise Information Portal. *See* EIP
Enterprise Integrator for Domino, 235
Enterprise JavaBeans. *See* EJBs
Enterprise Meeting Server of Lotus Sametime, 241
Enterprise Modernization, 128–130
Enterprise Resource Planning. *See* ERP
Enterprise Solution Builder, Lotus, 235–236
Enterprise Storage Server (ESS), 219–220
Enterprise System Architecture/390 (ESA/390), 51
Entrust, 207
ERP (Enterprise Resource Planning)
  application accelerators, 260–261
  application integration, 127
  e-business and IBM, 5, 48
  Informix, 181
  Reach and User Experience (WebSphere), 94
  Tivoli Storage Manager for, 219
  WebSphere Application Server (WAS), 74
ESA/390 (Enterprise System Architecture/390), 51
e-servers, 54–55
ESS (IBM Enterprise Storage Server), 219–220
Ethernet LAN, 65
Event Correlation and Automation (Tivoli solution), 229
Everyplace Wireless Client, 106, 110
Everyplace Wireless Gatekeeper, 106, 110
Everyplace Wireless Gateway, 146. *See also* WECM (WebSphere Everyplace Connection Manager)
Excalibur Image DataBlade, 183
Excalibur Text Search DataBlade, 184
Expertise Portals, 92
Exploring IBM Technology, Products, and Services (Hoskins), xvi, 9, 50
expression partitioning, Informix, 187
Extended Edition (EE), DB2 Universal Database, 168
eXtended HyperText Markup Language (XHTML), 106, 196
eXtended Markup Language. *See* XML
extended-relational (object-relational) database, 188, 192
eXtended Remote Copy (XRC), IMS, 154
eXtensible Style Language (XSL), 20
external call interface (ECI) of CICS Transaction Server, 131
external services of business model, 265, 267, 268, 272

F
"fact" table, 44, 45
failover processing, operating systems, 58–59
Fast Path database, 151, 153
"fat" clients, 36
fax solutions, DB2 Content Manager, 175
FBI/CSI (Federal Bureau of Investigation/Crime Scene Investigation), 205
FDDI (Fiber Distributed Data Interface), 65
FDL (Flow Definition Language), 118
Federal Bureau of Investigation/Crime Scene Investigation (FBI/CSI), 205
federated data stores, EIP, 99
Fiber Distributed Data Interface (FDDI), 65
fields
  architectures pre-dating e-business, 26
  segments, fields within (IMS), 149
field types, 26
files
  architectures pre-dating e-business, 26
  flat files (electronic file structures), 26–27, 32, 43
  UniVerse/Unidata (U2) family, 192
File Transfer, WebSphere Studio, 80
File Transfer Protocol (FTP) collections, 99
file upload capability, 196
"fill-in-the-blank" queries, DB2 Content Manager, 180
Finance Foundation for Capital Markets, Informix, 188
firewalls, 204
First Normal Form, 189
fixed-length records and fields, 26
flat files (electronic file structures), 26–27, 32, 43
Flow Definition Language (FDL), 118

Focus (fourth-generation language), 43
focus of e-business on demand, 16
Folder Application Facility, DB2 Content Manager, 176
Follet, Ken, 204
"footprint," WebSphere Studio, 85
Forrester Research, 91
Foundation and Tools (WebSphere), 71–91, 128–138. *See also* Transaction processing; WAS (WebSphere Application Server); WebSphere Host Integration; WebSphere Studio
  Customer Information Control System (CICS) Transaction Gateway, 130
  Enterprise Modernization, 128–130
  eXtended Markup Language (XML), 71
  Java, 71
  Java 2, Enterprise Edition (J2EE) support, 130
  legacy applications and, 71
  open standards, 71
  overview of, 70
  Web services, 71
Foundation products, Informix, 182, 187–188
fourth-generation languages, 43
frame relay routers, 66
frames, networks, 65
FTP (File Transfer Protocol) collections, 99
Fulfillment Function Group of WebSphere Order Capture Business Component, 144
functional automation wave (1960s-1970s), 6. *See also* architectures pre-dating e-business

G
Gartner Group, 8
Gateway, 52
Gateway Client Requester, UniVerse/Unidata family, 193
Gateway Server of WAS, 136–137
generalized key (GK) index, Informix, 187
Geodetic DataBlade, 184
geographic-based administrators, threat management, 210–211
Gerstner, Lou, xviii, 3, 4, 10, 11–12, 260–261, 264
GIF (Graphics Interchange Format) conversion, WebSphere Studio, 79
Gigabit Ethernet, 65
GK (generalized key) index, Informix, 187
Globus Project, 14
glossary, 276–295
goals for business, 263–266
Graphical User Interface (GUI), 36
Graphics Interchange Format (GIF) conversion, WebSphere Studio, 79
"green screens," 88–89, 134–135
grid computing, 14, 62
grouping profiles, 98
GUI (Graphical User Interface), 36

H
hacker attacks, 210
HACLs (Host Access Class Libraries), 88, 89, 130
HACMP (High Availability Cluster Multi-Processing), 60
hand-held device application development, WebSphere Studio, 85–86
hardware architectures, 49–56. *See also* architectures pre-dating e-business; OSs (operating systems)
  64-bit architecture, 50, 54, 56, 57, 59
  AS/400 family, 51, 55, 59, 60, 171
  cache, 54
  Central Processing Units (CPUs), 54, 55
  Central Processors (CPs), 54
  central storage, 54
  clusters, 55–56, 58, 62
  Complementary Metal Oxide Semiconductor (CMOS) technology, 53
  costs, 53
  distributed computers, 52–53
  Electronic Numerical Integrator And Computer (ENIAC), 25, 50, 52
  Enterprise System Architecture/390 (ESA/390), 51
  e-servers, 54–55
  grid computing, 14, 62
  IBM and, 50
  IBM Autonomic Computing Initiative (project eLiza), 14–15, 62–63
  "IBM compatible," 52
  IBM PCs, 52, 59
  Intel microprocessors, 52
  Internet impact on, 53
  I/O processors, 54
  iSeries computers, 50, 51, 54, 60
  mainframes, 51, 52–53

main storage, 54
Massively Parallel Processing (MPP), 55, 168, 169
memory (storage), 54
microcode, 50
microprocessors, 54, 55
multiprocessing, 55
Netfinity family, 55
nodes, 55
operating systems and, 52, 60–61
platform, 49
proprietary systems, 53
pSeries computers, 50, 54
Random Access Memory (RAM), 54
Reduced Instruction Set Computing (RISC), 51–52, 59
RS/6000 family, 52, 54, 55, 59
S/390 family, 56, 61
Scalable POWER parallel (SP), 55
servers, multiple, 53
shared-nothing architectures, 55, 186, 187
software blending with, 60–61
software context, 50
supercomputer, 54
Symmetric Multi-Processor (SMP), 54, 55, 162
System/3X computers, 51
System/360 (S/360) family, 50–51
System/370 (S/370) family, 51
system processors, 54
Tivoli Storage Manager for Hardware, 219–220
uniprocessing, 55
vacuum tubes, 50
xSeries computers, 50, 52, 54
zSeries computers, 50, 51, 53, 54, 61
hardware blending with OSs (operating systems), 60–61
hashed partitioning, Informix, 187
HDAM (Hierarchical Direct), 151, 153
HDR (High-Availability Data Replication), 182–183
help with e-business, 269–272
heterogeneous systems and security software, 202–203
HIDAM (Hierarchical Indexed Direct), 151
hierarchical databases, 32–33, 149
Hierarchical Direct (HDAM), 151, 153
Hierarchical Indexed Direct (HIDAM), 151
Hierarchical Indexed Sequential (HISAM), 150
Hierarchical Sequential (HSAM), 150
High Availability Cluster Multi-Processing (HACMP), 60
High-Availability Data Replication (HDR), 182–183
High Performance Routing (HPR), 68, 88
HiperSockets, 61
HISAM (Hierarchical Indexed Sequential), 150
historical data analysis, threat management, 210
Holosofx Business Process Management (BPM) Suite, 116–117, 120–121
Holosofx Business Process Management Monitor, 120
Holosofx Business Process Management Server, 120–121
Holosofx Business Process Management Workbench, 120
homepage building, WebSphere Studio, 78–80
hop (movement segment), networks, 63
Hoskins, Jim, xvi, 9, 50
Host Access Beans for Java, 88, 89, 130
Host Access Class Libraries (HACLs), 88, 89, 130
host-based application enhancement tool, UniVerse/Unidata family, 195–196
host (legacy) applications. *See* WebSphere Host Integration
HPR (High Performance Routing), 68, 88
HR (Human Resources) application, 127
HSAM (Hierarchical Sequential), 150
HTML (HyperText Markup Language)
e-business and, 1, 18–19
Enterprise Information Portal (EIP), 112, 113
Lotus, 237
overview of, 1, 18–19
UniVerse/Unidata (U2) family, 195
WebSphere Application Server (WAS), 72, 73
WebSphere Host Integration, 90
WebSphere Studio, 79
HTTP (HyperText Transfer Protocol)
Lotus, 238
WebSphere Application Server (WAS), 30–31, 72, 73
WebSphere Commerce, 247, 249
HTTPS (HyperText Transfer Protocol Secure), 73
hub (shared) routing, networks, 66

Human Resources (HR) application, 127
hybrid database management systems, 40–42. *See also* DB2 Universal Database
HyperText Markup Language. *See* HTML
HyperText Transfer Protocol. *See* HTTP
HyperText Transfer Protocol Secure (HTTPS), 73

I
IBM Autonomic Computing Initiative (project eLiza), 14–15, 62–63
IBM Business Intelligence Information Catalog, 98
IBM Client Representative, 269, 270
IBM Communications Server, 87, 90–91, 128, 130
"IBM compatible" hardware, 52
IBM CrossWorlds, 116, 117, 119–120
IBM CrossWorlds Collaborations, 120
IBM CrossWorlds Connectors, 119–120
IBM CrossWorlds InterChange Server, 119
IBM DB2 Universal Database SQL Reference for Cross-Platform Development, 161
IBM Enterprise Storage Server (ESS, Shark), 219–220
IBM eRecords Solution and DB2 Content Manager, 179
IBM Everyplace Synchronization Manager, 108
IBM Firewall, 87
IBM Intelligent Miner, 47
IBM J9 Virtual Machine (J9), 115
IBM Language Environment, 151
IBM MerchantReach e-commerce Services Solution for Retail, 246
IBM Mindspan Solutions and Lotus LearningSpace, 243–244
IBM Payment Gateway, 254
IBM Payment Registry, 252–254
IBM PCs, 52, 59
IBM Personal Communications, 87, 88
IBM Research, 33
IBM Resource Lock Manager (IRLM), 152, 160
IBM Sales Team, 269–270
IBM SanFrancisco, 145
IBM Screen Customizer, 87, 89
IBM Service Management Framework (SMF), 110
IBM Software Group, 11
IBM-VeriSign Solution for Secure e-business Integration, 215–216
IBM Web sites, 270–272
ICM (Internet Cluster Manager), 237
ICR (Intelligent Character Recognition), 176
ICSF (Integrated Cryptographic Service Facility), 57
IDC, 2, 13, 91
IDEF (Intrusion Detection Exchange Format), 211–212
identity management, 208–209. *See also* security software
  access control mechanisms, 209
  audit subsystem, 208, 209
  certificate management systems, 208
  Certificate Revocation Lists (CRLs), 208
  certification authority (CA), 204, 208
  data storage, 209
  digital certificates, 208
  digital signing, 208
  identity sources, 209
  Lightweight Directory Access Protocol (LDAP)-compliant directory, 209
  message authentication code (MAC), 209
  policy-based identity management, 209
  Public Key Infrastructure (PKI), 208
  registration authority (RA), 208–209
  Tivoli Identity Management, 208–209, 214
  Tivoli Identity Manager, 209
  Web-based administration, 209
identity of object, databases, 39
IDS (Informix Dynamic Server), 181–183
IFX (Interactive Financial Exchange), 144
IIOP (Internet Inter-ORB Protocol), 73, 237, 238
Image Foundation DataBlade, 184
images
  conversion, WebSphere Studio, 79
  copies, DB2 Universal Database, 165
  files, WebSphere Studio, 80
  WebSphere Transcoding Publisher, 114
Image Tools, WebSphere Studio, 79
IMS Connect, 155–156
IMS Connector for Java, 155–156
IMS DataPropagator (DataPropagator Non-Relational), 199–200
IMS/DB2 Coordinated Disaster Recovery, 154
IMS (Information Management System) family, 148–156
  access methods, 150–151
  application programming languages, 151

architectural structure, 151–152
architectures pre-dating e-business, 30, 32–33, 71
availability, 152, 154
C/C++ and, 154
child, 149
commit process, 152–153
Common Object Request Broker Architecture (CORBA) and, 154
communications, 154
connectors, 155
Database Descriptors (DBDs), 150, 151
Database Recovery Control, 152
Data Entry Database (DEDB), 151, 153
Data Language/One (DL/1), 151
data sharing, 152, 154
direct dependent segment of DEDB, 153
direct storage, 150–151
disk mirroring, 152
eXtended Markup Language (XML) and, 149, 155
eXtended Remote Copy (XRC), 154
Fast Path database, 151, 153
fields within segments, 149
hierarchical database, 149
Hierarchical Direct (HDAM), 151, 153
Hierarchical Indexed Direct (HIDAM), 151
Hierarchical Indexed Sequential (HISAM), 150
Hierarchical Sequential (HSAM), 150
IBM Language Environment, 151
IBM Resource Lock Manager (IRLM), 152
indexes, 151
Java Database Connectivity (JDBC), 153
Java Dependent Regions, 154
Java support, 149, 154
Java Virtual Machines (JVMs), 154
legacy processing and, 148–149
locking, 152
logging capability, 152
logical view, 150
Multiple Virtual Storage (MVS) and, 151–152
MVS Cross Coupling Facility (XCF), 155
Open Database Access (ODBA)-compliant programs and, 154
Open Transaction Management Access (OTMA), 154, 155
parents, 149
physical view, 150
Program Specification Blocks (PSBs), 150, 151
recovery capability, 152
regions of Multiple Virtual Storage (MVS), 151–152, 155
restart capabilities, 152
secondary indexes, 151
security, 153–154
segments (records) of tree structures, 149
sequential dependent segment of DEDB, 153
sequential storage, 150–151
storage methods, 150–151
synchronization capability with DB2 Universal Database, 154
Sysplex technology and, 152, 154
System Log Data Sets, 152
Transmission Control Protocol/Internet Protocol (TCP/IP) and, 154
tree structures, 149–150
IMS/TM (IMS Transaction Manager), 153, 155
independent software vendors (ISVs), 5, 12, 260
indexes
architectures pre-dating e-business, 27
DB2 Universal Database, 157, 164, 170
Information Management System (IMS), 151
Informix, 187
Information Access Layer functions, EIP, 98
Information Management System family. *See* IMS
information movement and access, 196–200
Administer component of DB2 Data Propagator, 199
Apply component of DB2 Data Propagator, 199
Batch Resource Recovery Service, 200
Capture component of DB2 Data Propagator, 199
DB2 Connect, 196–197
DB2 DataJoiner, 99, 197–198, 199, 200
DB2 DataPropagator, 199, 200
Distributed Relational Database Architecture (DRDA), 167, 168, 196–197
eXtended HyperText Markup Language (XHTML), 106, 196
eXtended Markup Language (XML), 196
file upload capability, 196

IMS DataPropagator (DataPropagator Non-Relational), 199–200
Informix Connect, 197
Informix Enterprise Gateway Manager, 198–199
Informix Gateway with DRDA, 198, 199
Net.Data, 196
Office Connect, 197
Open Database Connectivity (ODBC)-compliant function calls, 199
Structured Query Language (SQL) statement nesting, 196
Web ability, 196
information technology, 6–15. *See also* architectures pre-dating e-business; e-business and IBM
client/server architecture, 6, 36–37, 202
demand to delivery integration, 7–8
end-to-end infrastructure for, 4, 10
end-to-end integration, 7–8
functional automation wave (1960s-1970s), 6
grid computing, 14, 62
IBM Autonomic Computing Initiative (project eLiza), 14–15, 62–63
independent software vendors (ISVs), 5, 12, 260
infrastructure for, 3, 4, 10–11
innovation in software, 11–15
integration of business systems for, 3–4, 9–10
network computing wave (1990s), 6
open standards for, 4, 8–9, 10
patented research, 12
personal computers (PCs) wave (1970s-1980s), 6, 35
process- and event-driven systems wave (21st century), 6–7
self-configuration infrastructure for, 14, 15, 63
self-healing infrastructure for, 4, 10, 14, 15, 63
self-optimization infrastructure for, 14, 15, 63
self-protection infrastructure for, 14, 15, 63
service broker, 12, 13
service provider, 12, 13
service requester, 12, 13
Services-Oriented Architectural Protocol (SOAP), 12, 13, 246
Universal Description, Discovery, Integration (UDDI), 12, 13, 81, 246
waves of, 6–8
Web Services Description Language (WSDL), 12–13, 246
Web services innovations, 12–14
Informix, 180–188. *See also* U2 (UniVerse/Unidata) family
aggregates, 181
alter fragment command, 181–182
attached tables, 182
availability, 182–183, 187
bitmap index, 187
buffer pages, 185
C-ISAM DataBlade, 184
co-servers, 186–187
cost-based optimizer, 185
Customer Relationship Management (CRM) applications, 181
data skip, 181
decision support, 181
detached tables, 182
Dynamic Scalable Architecture (DSA), 182
Enterprise Resource Planning (ERP) applications, 181
Excalibur Image DataBlade, 183
Excalibur Text Search DataBlade, 184
expression partitioning, 187
Finance Foundation for Capital Markets, 188
Foundation products, 182, 187–188
generalized key (GK) index, 187
Geodetic DataBlade, 184
hashed partitioning, 187
High-Availability Data Replication (HDR), 182–183
Image Foundation DataBlade, 184
indexes, 187
internal tables, 185
Internet Foundation, 188
Java Virtual Machine (JVM), 182
Law Enforcement Foundation for Biometrics, 188
metadata, 186
nodes, 186
Numeric Algorithms Group (NAG) DataBlade, 184
object-relational database, 181
OnLine Extended Edition, 185
online transaction processing (OLTP), 181

original equipment manufacturer (OEM) solutions, 181
overview of, 74, 82, 131, 180
partitioning, 181, 187
range partitioning, 187
Red Brick Warehouse, 185–186
relational database, 181
replicated data, 183
resizing, automatic, 183
round-robin partitioning, 187
schedulers, 186–187
shared-nothing architecture, 186, 187
Spatial DataBlade, 184
STARindex, 185–186
STARjoin technology, 186
Structured Query Language (SQL) structures, 187
tables, 187
TARGETindex, 186
thread scheduler, 182
TimeSeries DataBlade, 184
Tivoli Monitoring for Databases, 224
UNIX and, 185
Video Foundation DataBlade, 184
Web DataBlade, 184
WebSphere Application Server (WAS) and, 181
Informix Connect, 197
Informix DataBlades, 182, 183–184
Informix Dynamic Server (IDS), 181–183
Informix Enterprise Gateway Manager, 198–199
Informix Extended Parallel Server (XPS), 186–187
Informix Gateway with DRDA, 198, 199
infrastructure for e-business, 3, 4, 10–11. *See also* DB2; Lotus; Tivoli; WebSphere
inheritance, databases, 38
innovation in software, 11–15
instances of classes, databases, 38–39
instances of DB2 Universal Database, 169–170
Instant Messaging feature of Lotus Sametime, 241, 242
Integrated Cryptographic Service Facility (ICSF), 57
Integrate Interwoven TeamSite, 98
integration of business systems, 3–4, 9–10. *See also* e-business approach; Patterns for e-business
integration patterns, 257
Intel Dialogic, 101, 102
Intelligent Character Recognition (ICR), 176
Intel microprocessors, 52
Interaction Controller of VisualAge Generator, 136
Interactive Financial Exchange (IFX), 144
Interactive Test Facility of VisualAge Generator, 137
interactive voice response (IVR), 103
internal tables, Informix, 185
International Organization for Standardization (ISO), 157–158
Internet Cluster Manager (ICM), 237
Internet Foundation, Informix, 188
Internet impact on e-business, 1, 2–3, 53
Internet Inter-ORB Protocol (IIOP), 73, 237, 238
Internet network, 65
Inter-Partition Parallelism, DB2 Universal Database, 168, 169
intersection tables, 33–34
Intrado, 181
intranets, 65
introspection from Java Beans, 21
Intrusion Detection Exchange Format (IDEF), 211–212
inventory process, WebSphere Studio, 83
I/O processors, 54
i-Photo Builder, WebSphere Studio, 80
IRLM (IBM Resource Lock Manager), 152, 160
ISDN support, pervasive solutions, 103
iSeries computers, 50, 51, 54, 60, 156
ISO (International Organization for Standardization), 157–158
ISVs (independent software vendors), 5, 12, 260
IVR (interactive voice response), 103

J

J2EE Connector Architecture (JCA), 23, 74, 82
J2EE (Java 2, Enterprise Edition)
Foundation and Tools (WebSphere), 130
overview of, 22
WebSphere Application Server (WAS), 8, 71, 74, 75
J2ME (Java 2MicroEdition), 172
J2ME "Java-powered" platform, EIP, 115
J9 (IBM J9 Virtual Machine), 115
JAAS (Java Authentication and Authorization Service), 23, 76

Java
Foundation and Tools (WebSphere), 71
Information Management System (IMS) and, 149, 154
Lotus and, 237
overview of, 20–23
WebSphere Application Server (WAS), 74
WebSphere Commerce and, 246, 249
Java 2, Enterprise Edition. *See* J2EE
Java 2MicroEdition (J2ME), 172
Java Authentication and Authorization Service (JAAS), 23, 76
JavaBeans, 21–22, 136, 137
Java Cryptography Extension (JCE), 76
Java Database Connectivity. *See* JDBC
Java Dependent Regions, IMS, 154
Java Management Extensions (JMX), 23, 76–77
Java Messaging Service. *See* JMS
JavaScript, WebSphere Host Integration, 89
Java Servlet Pages. *See* JSPs
Java Stored Procedures, DB2 Universal Database, 153
Java Virtual Machine. *See* JVM
JCA (J2EE Connector Architecture), 23, 74, 82
JCE (Java Cryptography Extension), 76
JDBC (Java Database Connectivity)
DB2 Universal Database, 159–160
Enterprise Information Portal (EIP), 99
Information Management System (IMS), 153
overview of, 23
UniVerse/Unidata (U2) family, 188, 192
WebSphere Application Server (WAS), 73
WebSphere Host Integration, 90
JIT (just-in-time) compiling, 85
JMS (Java Messaging Service)
application integration, 124–125
overview of, 23
WebSphere Application Server (WAS), 73
JMX (Java Management Extensions), 23, 76–77
Jobs, Steven, 52
Job Scheduling (Tivoli solution), 232
Joint Photographic Experts Group (JPEG) conversion, WebSphere Studio, 79
journaling, 29
JPEG (Joint Photographic Experts Group) conversion, WebSphere Studio, 79
JSPs (Java Servlet Pages)
Reach and User Experience (WebSphere), 97
transaction processing, 136, 137
WebSphere Application Server (WAS), 73
WebSphere Host Integration, 87, 88, 90, 130
WebSphere Studio, 83
just-in-time (JIT) compiling, 85
JVM (Java Virtual Machine)
Information Management System (IMS), 154
Informix, 182
overview of, 21
WebSphere Application Server (WAS), 76

K
Kennedy Consulting Summit, 14
Kerberos, 57, 75
Key to Rebecca, The (Follet), 204
keywords, 18
Knowledge Portals, 92

L
language translation, pervasive solutions, 104–105
LANs (Local Area Networks)
Lotus and, 241
networks, 65, 90, 145
WebSphere Host Integration and, 90
Large Objects (LOBs), 41, 164
Law Enforcement Foundation for Biometrics, 188
LDAP (Lightweight Directory Access Protocol)
access management, 206
Enterprise Information Portal (EIP), 110, 114
identity management, 209
operating systems (OSs), 57
Reach and User Experience (WebSphere), 94, 98, 99
WebSphere Application Server (WAS) user directories, 75
legacy information. *See also* Foundation and Tools (WebSphere); WebSphere Host Integration
architectures pre-dating e-business, 24
Information Management System (IMS), 148–149
library server of DB2 Content Manager, 174–175

license manager, 230
Lightweight Directory Access Protocol. *See* LDAP
Linux
  DB2 Universal Database and, 156, 169
  growth of, 12
  open standards operating system, 8–9, 60–61
  overview of, 8–9, 12, 56, 60–61
  Tivoli Access Manager for Operating Systems, 208
L.L. Bean, 4
LOBs (Large Objects), 41, 164
Local Area Networks. *See* LANs
locking capability
  databases, 152, 160
  operating systems (OSs), 58
logging capability
  architectures pre-dating e-business, 29
  DB2 Universal Database, 160, 165, 170
  Information Management System (IMS), 152
  Lotus, 237
logical design of databases, 150, 189, 190
Logical Partitions (LPARs), 58, 61, 162
Lotus, 233–244
  background tasks, 234
  backup/recovery, 237
  browsers support, 238
  Call Answering (CA) function of DUCS, 240
  classes, building, 243–244
  client component of Lotus Sametime, 241
  client failover, 237
  client/server environment, 234
  Collaboration Module of Lotus LearningSpace, 244
  Common Object Request Broker Architecture (CORBA) support, 237, 238
  Computer Telephony Interface (CTI) of DUCS, 240–241
  Core Module of Lotus LearningSpace, 244
  developer toolkits of Lotus Sametime, 241
  Domino Administrator, 238
  Domino Enterprise Connection Services (DECS), 238
  Domino Everyplace Access, 239
  Domino Everyplace Enterprise server, 239
  Domino Unified Communications Service (DUCS), 236, 239–241
  e-learning, 243–244
  e-mail, 234
  Enterprise Information Portal (EIP) and, 99
  Enterprise Integrator for Domino, 235
  Enterprise Meeting Server of Lotus Sametime, 241
  Enterprise Solution Builder, 235–236
  HyperText Markup Language (HTML) and, 237
  HyperText Transfer Protocol (HTTP) support, 238
  IBM Mindspan Solutions and Lotus LearningSpace, 243–244
  Instant Messaging feature of Lotus Sametime, 241, 242
  Internet Cluster Manager (ICM), 237
  Internet Inter-ORB Protocol (IIOP) support, 237, 238
  Java and, 237
  Local Area Networks (LANs) and, 241
  logging capability, 237
  mail functions, 236
  message consolidation, 236, 239–241
  messaging tool, 241–242
  multiple-client support, 238
  Object Request Broker (ORB) technology, 237–238
  pointers, 237
  policy-based management, 238
  presence awareness of Lotus Sametime, 242
  relational database, 236
  replication, 234
  security, 234
  security of Lotus Sametime, 242
  server component of Lotus Sametime, 241
  Session Initiation Protocol (SIP) support, 242
  tables, 236–237
  team workspace, 242–243
  Telephone User Interface (TUI) function of DUCS, 240
  Tivoli Analyzer for Lotus Domino, 222, 237
  Tivoli Monitoring for Messaging and Collaboration, 224
  Tivoli Storage Manager for Mail, 220
  virtual team environment, 234–235
  Web applications, 238
  wireless support, 239
Lotus Collaborative Components, 94
Lotus Collaborative Places, 94

Lotus Domino, 235–238
Lotus Domino Administrator, 238
Lotus Domino Application Studio, 235
Lotus Domino Connectors, 235–236
Lotus Domino Designer, 235
Lotus Domino Enterprise Connection Services (DECS), 238
Lotus Domino Everyplace, 108, 235, 239
Lotus Domino Everyplace Access, 239
Lotus Domino Everyplace Enterprise server, 239
Lotus Domino Everyplace Short Message Service (SMS), 239
Lotus Domino Server, 235, 236–239
Lotus Domino Unified Communications Service (DUCS), 236, 239–241
Lotus Extended Search, 95
Lotus LearningSpace, 243–244
Lotus LearningSpace Forum, 243
Lotus Notes, 233–235
Lotus QuickPlace, 95
Lotus QuickPlace and WebSphere Commerce, 247
Lotus Sametime, 95, 241–242, 247
LotusScript, 237
Lotus Team Workplace (QuickPlace), 242–243
LPARs (Logical Partitions), 58, 61, 162

M
Macintosh computers, 52
MAC (message authentication code), 209
Macromedia ColdFusion MX for WebSphere, 86
mail functions, Lotus, 236
mail servers, Tivoli Storage Manager for Mail, 220
Mainframe Adapters, 127
mainframe connectors, IBM CrossWorlds Connectors, 120
mainframes
  hardware, 51, 52–53
  operating systems, 56–59
  security software, 201–202
main storage, 54
Maintenance Function Group of WebSphere Order Capture Business Component, 143–144
Malaika, Susan, 271
management functions, WebSphere products, 69
managing e-business application, 201. *See also* configuration and operations management software; performance and availability software; security software; storage software
Massively Parallel Processing (MPP), 55, 168, 169
matchmaking, Reach and User Experience (WebSphere), 97
Maximum Press Web site, xix
m-commerce (mobile commerce), WebSphere Commerce, 247
MDC (Metadata Controller), 221
"Members Only" Web site, xix
memory (storage), 54
Merchant Initiated Authorization (MIA), 251
message authentication code (MAC), 209
message consolidation, Lotus, 236, 239–241
Message Oriented Middleware (MOM), 121
MessagePlus/Open and DB2 Content Manager, 175, 179
Message Queue Everyplace (MQe), 85–86, 125
Message Queuing Interface (MQI), 123–125
messaging tool, Lotus, 241–242
metadata, 44, 46, 98, 186
Metadata Controller (MDC), 221
methods allowed on objects, 38, 39
MIA (Merchant Initiated Authorization), 251
microcode, 50
micro environment, EIP, 115
microprocessors, 54, 55
Microsoft, 147
Microsoft Back Office certification of DB2 Universal Database, 147
Microsoft SQLServer, 74, 82, 131
mobile application platforms, EIP, 105–112. *See also* WebSphere Everyplace
mobile commerce (m-commerce), WebSphere Commerce, 247
model-view-controller (MVC) architecture, 83
MOM (Message Oriented Middleware), 121
monitor environments, transaction processing, 131
monitoring tools, WebSphere Studio, 83–84
MPF (Multi-Payment Framework), 250–252, 253
MPP (Massively Parallel Processing), 55, 168, 169
MPTN (MultiProtocol Transport Networking), 90–91

MQe (Message Queue Everyplace), 85–86, 125
MQI (Message Queuing Interface), 123–125
MQSeries Integrator, 118. *See also* WebSphere MQ Integrator Broker
MQSeries Messaging. *See* WebSphere MQ (Message Queue)
MQSeries messaging software, transaction processing, 131
Multi-Payment Framework (MPF), 250–252, 253
multiplatforms
  DB2 Content Manager, 173, 174
  DB2 Universal Database, 94, 167–170
  WebSphere Portal for Multiplatforms, 92–96
multiple-client support, Lotus, 238
Multiple Virtual Storage (MVS), 151–152
Multiple Virtual Storage (MVS/ESA), 57
multiprocessing, 55
MultiProtocol Transport Networking (MPTN), 90–91
MVC (model-view-controller) architecture, 83
MVS Cross Coupling Facility (XCF), 155
MVS/ESA (Multiple Virtual Storage), 57
MVS (Multiple Virtual Storage), 151–152
mySAP.com, 224
MySQL, 82

N
NAG (Numeric Algorithms Group) DataBlade, 184
NCT Teradata, 197
nested relational database, 188–189, 189, 191
Net.Data, 196
Netfinity family, 55
Netscape, 207
Net Search Extender, DB2 Universal Database, 172
network computing wave (1990s), 6
network databases, 31–32
network (IP) layer, 64
network nodes, 68
network profiles of WebSphere Transcoding Publisher, 114
networks, 63–68. *See also* LANs (Local Area Networks); TCP/IP (Transmission Control Protocol/ Internet Protocol)
  Advanced Peer-to-Peer Networking (APPN), 68, 90
  application layer, 64
  Automatic Network Routing (ANR), 68
  central nodes, 67
  communication stack, 63, 64
  connection-oriented transport, 67
  data link layer, 64, 65
  Digital Subscriber Line (DSL), 50, 67, 107
  download times, 50
  end nodes, 68
  Ethernet LAN, 65
  Fiber Distributed Data Interface (FDDI), 65
  frame relay routers, 66
  frames, 65
  Gigabit Ethernet, 65
  High Performance Routing (HPR), 68
  hop (movement segment), 63
  hub (shared) routing, 66
  Internet, 65
  intranets, 65
  network (IP) layer, 64
  network nodes, 68
  physical layer, 64, 65
  presentation layer, 64
  protocols, 66–68
  routers, 63, 65–66
  Routing Transport Protocol (RTP), 68
  session layer, 64
  sources, 63
  switches, 63, 65–66
  Systems Network Architecture (SNA), 67–68
  targets, 63
  Tivoli Monitoring for Network Performance, 225
  Tivoli Storage Manager for Storage Area Networks, 220
  Tivoli Switch Analyzer, 226
  Token Ring LAN, 65
  "transport pipe," 68
  transport (TCP) layer, 64
  WebSphere Application Server (WAS) and, 77
  Wide Area Networks (WANs), 65, 90, 145
  wrapped packets, 64, 65
nodes, hardware, 55
nodes, Informix, 186
non-mainframe operating systems, 59–60
non-partitioned index (NPI), DB2 Universal Database, 164

normalization, databases, 189
NPI (non-partitioned index), DB2 Universal Database, 164
Numeric Algorithms Group (NAG) DataBlade, 184

O

OAGIS (Open Applications Group Interface Specification), 143
Object Access Method, DB2 Content Manager, 174, 176
object complexity, databases, 39
Object Distribution Manager, DB2 Content Manager, 176
object-enabling infrastructure for N-tier development, 193–194
object identity, databases, 39
Object Linking and Embedding (OLE), 42
Object Management Group (OMG), 42
object-oriented
  application integration, 121–122
  databases, 37–40
object persistence, databases, 39
object-relational database, 181
object-relational (extended-relational) database, 188, 192
object-relational extensions, 40–42
Object Request Broker (ORB), 73, 237–238
objects, databases, 38, 39
object server of DB2 Content Manager, 174
OCR (Optical Character Recognition), 175–176
ODBA (Open Database Access)-compliant programs, 154
ODBC (Open Database Connectivity)
  architectures pre-dating e-business, 42
  DB2 Universal Database, 159
  information movement and access, 199
  UniVerse/Unidata (U2) family, 188
OEM (original equipment manufacturer) solutions, 181
Office Connect, 197
OGSA (Open Grid Services Architecture), 14
OLAP (OnLine Analytic Process) databases, 47
OLE (Object Linking and Embedding), 42
OLTP (online transaction processing)
  architectures pre-dating e-business, 6, 28–31, 33, 43, 44
  Informix, 181
OMG (Object Management Group), 42
on-demand business. *See* e-business on demand
OnLine Analytic Process (OLAP) databases, 47
OnLine Extended Edition, Informix, 185
online transaction processing. *See* OLTP
Open Applications Group Interface Specification (OAGIS), 143
Open Database Access (ODBA)-compliant programs, 154
Open Database Connectivity. *See* ODBC
Open Grid Services Architecture (OGSA), 14
Open Services Gateway Initiative (OSGi), 110
Open Software Foundation (OSF), 60, 131
open standards
  Data Management (DB2), 147
  DB2 Universal Database, 171
  e-business, 4, 8–9, 10, 272
  Foundation and Tools (WebSphere), 71
Open Transaction Management Access (OTMA), 154, 155
operating systems. *See* OSs
Optical Character Recognition (OCR), 175–176
optimizers, DB2 Universal Database, 160–161, 169
Oracle
  data management, 147
  Enterprise Information Portal (EIP), 99
  Foundation and Tools (WebSphere), 74, 75, 82
  information movement and access, 197, 198
  performance and availability software, 224
  transaction processing, 131
  UniVerse/Unidata (U2) family, 188
  WebSphere Business Components, 144
ORB (Object Request Broker), 73, 237–238
Order Capture Group of WebSphere Order Capture Business Component, 144
original equipment manufacturer (OEM) solutions, 181
OS/2 Warp, 59
OS/390
  DB2 Content Manager and, 173, 174, 176
  DB2 Universal Database and, 156, 161–166
  overview of, 56, 57
  performance and availability software, 223, 226–227, 228–229
  WebSphere Studio and, 83–85, 228–229
OS/400, 59, 60
OSF (Open Software Foundation), 60, 131

OSGi (Open Services Gateway Initiative), 110
OSs (operating systems), 56–60. *See also* hardware architectures; Linux; OS/390; UNIX; z/OS
  64-bit architecture, 50, 54, 56, 57, 59
  Advanced Interactive eXecutive (AIX), 35, 59–60, 254
  base control program (BCP), 57
  clusters, 55–56, 58, 62
  Conversational Monitor System (CMS), 56
  Coupling Facility (CF), 58
  cross-systems communication facility/cross-systems extended services (XCF/XES), 58
  DB2 Universal Database support, 156–157
  Disk Operating System (DOS), 57
  failover processing, 58–59
  grid computing, 14, 62
  hardware architectures and, 52, 60–61
  High Availability Cluster Multi-Processing (HACMP), 60
  HiperSockets, 61
  IBM Autonomic Computing Initiative (project eLiza), 14–15, 62–63
  Integrated Cryptographic Service Facility (ICSF), 57
  Kerberos, 57
  Lightweight Directory Access Protocol (LDAP), 57
  locking information, 58
  Logical Partitions (LPARs), 58, 61
  mainframe operating systems, 56–59
  Multiple Virtual Storage (MVS/ESA), 57
  non-mainframe operating systems, 59–60
  OS/2 Warp, 59
  OS/400, 59, 60
  Parallel Sysplex technology, 58–59, 62, 166
  Public Key Infrastructure (PKI), 57
  Secure Sockets Layer (SSL) support, 56, 57
  Symmetric Processors (SPs), 60
  System Licensed Internal Code (SLIC), 60
  Tivoli Access Manager for Operating Systems, 208
  Transaction Processing Facility (TPF), 56
  Transmission Control Procotol/Internet Protocol (TCP/IP) and, 56, 57
  Virtual Machine (VM), 56
  Virtual Storage Extended (VSE), 57
  VSE/ESA, 56
  Workload Manager (WLM), 57, 58
  zSeries computers, 57
  z/VM, 56
OTMA (Open Transaction Management Access), 154, 155
"out-of-the-box" solutions, 245. *See also* application accelerators

P
P3P (Platform for Privacy Preferences), 213–214
P3P Policy Editor, 213–214
packet radio network support, 107
PACs (Proactive Analysis Components), 224
Page Editor Homepage Builder, WebSphere Studio, 79
Palmisano, Sam, xviii, 6
PAP (password authentication protocol), 109
parallelism, DB2 Universal Database, 163
Parallel Sysplex technology, 58–59, 62, 166
parent-child data relationships, 33
parents, IMS, 149
parsers, 18
partitioned table space, DB2 Universal Database, 162–164, 170
partitioning, Informix, 181, 187
partner solutions, 246, 258–260, 263
password authentication protocol (PAP), 109
patented research, 12
Patterns for e-business, 255–257. *See also* application accelerators
  application patterns, 256, 257
  business patterns, 256, 257
  composite patterns, 257
  custom designs, 257
  guidelines, 257
  integration patterns, 257
  overview of, 246, 256
  product mappings, 257
  runtime patterns, 256, 257
  selection of, 256–257
  Web site for, 256
payment manager, WebSphere Commerce, 247, 248, 250–254
PCs (personal computers) wave (1970s-1980s), 6, 35. *See also* architectures pre-dating e-business
PeopleSoft, 198, 261
PE (Personal Edition), DB2 Universal Database, 167
performance and availability software, 222–229
  best practices automation, 223–224

Business Impact Management (Tivoli solution), 229
Customer Information Control System (CICS) Monitor for OS/390, 228
distributed systems management, 223
Dynamic Virtual IP Addressing (DVIPA), 226
Event Correlation and Automation (Tivoli solution), 229
OS/390 and, 223, 226–227, 228–229
Proactive Analysis Components (PACs), 224
Systems and Applications Monitoring (Tivoli solution), 229
Systems Network Architecture (SNA) and, 225, 226
Tivoli Monitoring, 223–225
Tivoli NetView, 225–226
Tivoli Web Site Analyzer (WebSphere Site Analyzer), 95, 98, 146, 227–228
Virtual Telecommunications Access Method (VTAM), 226
Web Management (Tivoli solution), 229
Web site analyzer, 95, 98, 146, 227–228
WebSphere MQ and, 224
WebSphere Studio Application Monitor for OS/390 and z/OS, 83–84, 228–229
z/OS and, 223, 226–227, 228–229
performance management, WAS, 76–77
persistence of Java Beans, 22
persistence of object, databases, 39
persistent storage, WAS, 74
Personal Communications of WebSphere Host Integration Solution, 128
personal computers (PCs) wave (1970s-1980s), 6, 35. *See also* architectures pre-dating e-business
Personal Edition (PE), DB2 Universal Database, 167
personalization of portals, 96–98
personalization technologies, 93, 265
perspectives, WebSphere Studio, 81, 82
pervasive device support, Reach and User Experience (WebSphere), 93
pervasive solutions, 100–105. *See also* EIP (Enterprise Information Portal); WebSphere Voice
automated attendant of WebSphere Voice Response, 103
DB2 Universal Database and, 103
Digital Trunk Extended Adapter (DTXA), 103
DirectTalk technology, 103
Dual Tone MultiFrequency (DTMF), 102
e-business and, 4
interactive voice response (IVR), 103
ISDN support, 103
language translation, 104–105
Signaling System #7 (SS7) support, 103
speech recognition of WebSphere Voice Server, 101
telephony platforms, 101, 102
Text-to-Speech engine of WebSphere Voice Server, 101–102
Touch-Tone, 102
transcription, 103–104
voice application development tools, 102
Voice over Internet Protocol (VoIP), 101, 102–105
VoiceXML technology, 102
WebSphere Translation Server, 104–105
physical layer, networks, 64, 65
physical view, IMS, 150
PKI (Public Key Infrastructure)
identity management, 208
operating systems (OSs), 57
WebSphere Host Integration, 87
platform, 49
platform dependent computer programs, 20
Platform for Privacy Preferences (P3P), 213–214
pointers, databases
DB2 Universal Database, 157, 164
Lotus, 237
overview of, 32, 33
point-of-sale manager, 230–231
Point-to-Point Protocol over Ethernet (PPPoE), 111
policies
privacy, 213
security, 202–203
storage, 220
threat management, 210
policy-based identity management, 209
policy-based management, Lotus, 238
policy regions, threat management, 210–211
portability of computer programs, 20–21
portable U2 applications, 194–195
portal solutions. *See also* EIP (Enterprise Information Portal)

Reach and User Experience (WebSphere), 91–92
WebSphere Commerce Portal, 255
portlet applications (prepackaged) of WebSphere Everyplace Access, 107
positional information, 25–26
PPPoE (Point-to-Point Protocol over Ethernet), 111
presence awareness of Lotus Sametime, 242
presentation layer
architectures pre-dating e-business, 36, 37
business intelligence (data warehouses), 46
business model, 264–265, 267–268, 272
networks, 64
privacy management, 212–216. *See also* security software; VeriSign
cookies for, 213
enterprise application integration (EAI) solution, 215–216
IBM-VeriSign Solution for Secure e-business Integration, 215–216
overview of, 5, 17
P3P Policy Editor, 213–214
Platform for Privacy Preferences (P3P), 213–214
policies, 213
Tivoli Identity Management Solution, 208–209, 214
Tivoli Policy Manager for e-business, 214
Tivoli Security Event Solution, 216
VeriSign Managed Services, 207, 214–216
WebSphere MQ and, 216
private key (symmetric) encryption, 204
Proactive Analysis Components (PACs), 224
process- and event-driven systems wave (21st century), 6–7
process integration, 116–121. *See also* Business Integration (WebSphere)
Application Connectors, IBM CrossWorlds Connectors, 119
Business Process Management (BPM), 116–121
DB2 Content Manager and, 118
DB2 Universal Database and, 118
e-business connectors, IBM CrossWorlds Connectors, 119–120
Flow Definition Language (FDL), 118
Holosofx Business Process Management (BPM) Suite, 116–117, 120–121
IBM CrossWorlds, 116, 117, 119–120
mainframe connectors, IBM CrossWorlds Connectors, 120
MQSeries Integrator, 118
WebSphere MQSeries Messaging, 118
WebSphere MQSeries Workflow, 116, 117, 118–119
workflow management, 116, 117, 118–119
product mappings, patterns for e-business, 257
Professional Edition, WebSphere Commerce, 247, 248
Professional Entry Edition, WebSphere Commerce, 247, 248
profiles of users, 97
Program Specification Blocks (PSBs), 150, 151
Project Eclipse, 78
Project eLiza (IBM Autonomic Computing Initiative), 14–15, 62–63
properties of Java Beans, 22
properties of objects, 38
proprietary systems, 53
protocols, 66–68. *See also* networks
PSBs (Program Specification Blocks), 150, 151
pSeries computers, 50, 54
public key-based credentials, 207–208
public key encryption, 204
Public Key Infrastructure. *See* PKI
public portals, 92
punch cards, 25
push technology, EIP, 108

Q
Queue Manager Clusters of WebSphere MQ, 124
Queue Managers of WebSphere MQ, 122–124
QuickPlace (Lotus Team Workplace), 242–243

R
RACF (Resource Access Control Facility), 87, 129, 166
RADIUS (Remote Authentication Dial-In User Service), 112
RAD (Rapid Application Development), 137, 195
RAID (Redundant Array of Independent (of Inexpensive) Disks), 163–164
Ramis (fourth-generation language), 43
RAM (Random Access Memory), 54
range partitioning, Informix, 187

Rapid Application Development (RAD), 137, 195
RA (registration authority), 208–209
Rational ClearCase LT, 82
Rational Rose, 137
Rational Software, 11, 273–275
RBOs (RedBack Business Objects), 193
Reach and User Experience (WebSphere), 91–98. *See also* EIP (Enterprise Information Portal); WebSphere Commerce; WebSphere Portal
  action business rules, 97
  application sharing, 95
  binding business rules, 97
  business rule engines, 97
  business-to-business (B2B) portals, 93
  business-to-customer (B2C) portals, 93
  business-to-employee (B2E) portals, 93
  classifier business rules, 97
  Collaborative Portals, 92
  corporate portals, 92
  Customer Relationship Management (CRM) application access, 94
  DB2 Content Manager, 95
  DB2 Universal Database for Multiplatforms, 94
  e-meetings, 95
  employee-to-employee (E2E) portals, 93
  Enterprise JavaBeans (EJBs), 98
  Enterprise Resource Planning (ERP) applications, 94
  Expertise Portals, 92
  grouping profiles, 98
  Java Servlet Pages (JSPs), 97
  Knowledge Portals, 92
  Lightweight Directory Access Protocol (LDAP) support, 94, 98, 99
  Lotus Collaborative Components, 94
  Lotus Collaborative Places, 94
  Lotus Extended Search, 95
  Lotus QuickPlace, 95
  Lotus Sametime, 95
  matchmaking, 97
  overview of, 70, 91
  personalization of portals, 96–98
  personalization technologies, 93, 265
  pervasive device support, 93
  portal solutions, 91–92
  profiles of users, 97
  public portals, 92
  recommendation engines, 97
  Resource Engine of WebSphere Personalization, 97–98
  rules-based filter, 93
  search facility, 93–94, 94
  security, 94, 95
  statistical models and matching techniques, 93
  Supply Chain Management (SCM) application access, 94
  team rooms, 94, 95, 96
  Tivoli Access Manager (Tivoli Policy Director), 95
  Tivoli SecureWay Directory, 94
  Tivoli Web Site Analyzer (WebSphere Site Analyzer), 95, 98, 146, 227–228
  Web Content Publisher, 94, 95
  WebSphere Application Server (WAS) Advanced Edition, 94
  WebSphere Personalization, 94, 96–98
  WebSphere Studio Application (WAS) Developer, 94
  WebSphere Studio Device Developer (VisualAge Micro Edition), 85–86, 91, 100, 110, 115
  Wireless Application Protocol (WAP) support, 95, 106, 110–111
real-time operating system (RTOS) of WebSphere Everyplace Suite Embedded Edition, 109–110
recommendation engines, 97
records
  architectures pre-dating e-business, 26
  databases, 32
recovery capability
  architectures pre-dating e-business, 29
  DB2 Universal Database, 160, 164–165
  Information Management System (IMS), 152
  Lotus, 237
  storage software, 221–222
  UniVerse/Unidata (U2) family, 192
RedBack, 193–194
RedBack Application Server, 193
RedBack Business Objects (RBOs), 193
RedBack Gateway, 193–194
Red Brick Warehouse, 185–186
Reduced Instruction Set Computing (RISC), 51–52, 59
Redundant Array of Independent (of Inexpensive) Disks (RAID), 163–164
reengineering. *See* Business Integration (WebSphere)

regions of Multiple Virtual Storage (MVS), 151–152, 155
registration authority (RA), 208–209
relational databases
  DB2 Universal Database, 156
  Distributed Relational Database Architecture (DRDA), 167, 168, 196–197
  Informix, 181
  Lotus, 236
  nested relational database, 188–189, 189, 191
  object-relational database, 181
  overview of, 33–34, 37, 38, 40, 189
  UniVerse/Unidata (U2) family, 188–189, 189, 191
Remote Authentication Dial-In User Service (RADIUS), 112
remote control, operations management, 231
Remote Method Interface (RMI), 73
repeating groups, databases, 189
replicated data, Informix, 183
replication, business intelligence, 44
replication, Lotus, 234
resiliency of e-business of demand, 16
resizing (automatic), Informix, 183
Resource Access Control Facility (RACF), 87, 129, 166
Resource Engine of WebSphere Personalization, 97–98
resource managers and DB2 Content Manager, 174
responsiveness of e-business on demand, 15
restart capabilities, IMS, 152
return on investment (ROI), 3, 264
reuse
  architectures pre-dating e-business, 27
  databases, 38
  WebSphere products, 69
RISC (Reduced Instruction Set Computing), 51–52, 59
RMI (Remote Method Interface), 73
ROI (return on investment), 3, 264
role-based administrators, threat management, 210–211
role-based policy management, security, 203
round-robin partitioning, Informix, 187
routers, 63, 65–66
Routing Transport Protocol (RTP), 68
RS/6000 family, 52, 54, 55, 59
RTOS (real-time operating system) of WebSphere Everyplace Suite Embedded Edition, 109–110
RTP (Routing Transport Protocol), 68
rules-based filter, 93
runtime environment provided by WAS, 71–72, 74
runtime patterns, 256, 257

S
S/360 (System/360) family, 50–51
S/370 (System/370) family, 51
S/390 (System/390) family, 56, 61
SAN (Storage Area Network) solution, 217, 219
SAP, 47–48, 94, 139, 219, 256, 261
satellite network support, EIP, 107
SB+Server, 195
SBClient, 195
scalability, 17
Scalable POWER parallel (SP), 55
scanning, DB2 Content Manager, 175–176
schedulers, Informix, 186–187
SCI (Socket Communication Interface), 138
SCM (Supply Chain Management)
  application integration, 127
  e-business and IBM, 5
  Reach and User Experience (WebSphere), 94
screen customizer, WebSphere Host Integration, 89
"screen scraper" technology, 36
search capability
  DB2 Content Manager, 175
  EIP (Enterprise Information Portal), 98, 99
  Reach and User Experience (WebSphere), 93–94, 94
secondary indexes, IMS, 151
Secure Electronic Transaction (SET), 249, 250, 251, 252, 253, 254
Secure Sockets Layer. *See* SSL
security software, 201–216. *See also* access management; identity management; privacy management; threat management
  access control, 204
  authentication, 204, 205
  certification authority (CA), 204, 208
  client/server architectures and, 202
  cryptography, 204
  DB2 Universal Database, 160, 166, 170
  digital certificates, 204

digital signatures, 204
encryption, 204
Enterprise Information Portal (EIP), 99, 108–109, 110–111
firewalls, 204
heterogeneous systems and, 202–203
Information Management System (IMS), 153–154
Lotus, 234
Lotus Sametime, 242
mainframes and, 201–202
policies, 202–203
public key encryption, 204
Reach and User Experience (WebSphere), 94, 95
role-based policy management, 203
server farms, 202
symmetric (private key) encryption, 204
Tivoli and, 203, 204
Tivoli Enterprise Console (TEC) and, 211, 212, 216
transaction processing, 138
WebSphere Application Server (WAS), 75–76
WebSphere Host Integration, 87–88, 129–130
WebSphere MQ, 123–124
WebSphere products and, 69
"Web-year" and, 202
segments of data, 31–32, 33
segments (records) of tree structures, IMS, 149
self-configuration infrastructure for e-business, 14, 15, 63
self-healing infrastructure for e-business, 4, 10, 14, 15, 63
self-learning transactions, 17
self-optimization infrastructure e-business, 14, 15, 63
self-protection infrastructure e-business, 14, 15, 63
Selinger, Pat, 161
sequential dependent segment of DEDB, 153
sequential storage, IMS, 150–151
server component of Lotus Sametime, 241
server farms, security, 202
Server Provider Offering, WebSphere Everyplace Server, 107–109
servers, multiple, 53
service broker, 12, 13
Service Management Framework (SMF), 110
service offerings management, EIP, 111–112
service provider, 12, 13
service requester, 12, 13
Services-Oriented Architectural Protocol (SOAP), 12, 13, 246
servlets (Java), 21, 73, 87, 88
Session Initiation Protocol (SIP), 242
session layer, networks, 64
SETCo (SET Secure Electronic Transaction LLC), 250
SET (Secure Electronic Transaction), 249, 250, 251, 252, 253, 254
SGML (Standardized General Markup Language), 18
shared-nothing architectures, 55, 186, 187
shared work areas, WAS, 73–74
Shark (Enterprise Storage Server), 219–220
Short Messaging Support (SMS), 108
Siebel, 94, 139, 145, 198, 224, 256, 261
Signaling System #7 (SS7), 103
single sign-on, 205
SIP (Session Initiation Protocol), 242
site development, WebSphere Studio, 75, 80–81
Site Management/Site Gallery View, WebSphere Studio, 80
Site Style Wizard, WebSphere Studio, 80
64-bit architecture, 50, 54, 56, 57, 59
SLIC (System Licensed Internal Code), 60
SMF (IBM Service Management Framework), 110
SMP (Symmetric Multi-processor), 54, 55, 162
SMS (Domino Everyplace Short Message Service), 239
SMS (Short Messaging Support), 108
SNA (Systems Network Architecture)
networks, 67–68
performance and availability software, 225, 226
WebSphere Host Integration, 88, 90, 91
"sneaker net," 36
SOAP (Services-Oriented Architectural Protocol), 12, 13, 246
Socket Communication Interface (SCI), 138
software. *See also* application
blending with hardware architectures, 60–61
context for hardware, 50
SOM (System Object Model), 42
sources, networks, 63

Spatial DataBlade, 184
speech recognition of WebSphere Voice Server, 101
spreadsheets and data warehouses, 46–47
SP (Scalable POWER parallel), 55
SPs (Symmetric Processors), 60
SQL99 standard, 158
SQLJ (static SQL for Java), 159, 160
SQL (Structured Query Language)
  DB2 Content Manager, 175
  DB2 Universal Database, 156, 157–158, 159, 170
  Informix, 187
  statement nesting, 196
SS7 (Signaling System #7), 103
SSL (Secure Sockets Layer)
  operating systems (OSs), 56, 57
  transaction processing, 138
  UniVerse/Unidata (U2) family, 188, 192
  WebSphere Application Server (WAS), 73
  WebSphere Commerce, 251, 254
  WebSphere Host Integration, 87, 129
standard communications protocol, 1
Standardized General Markup Language (SGML), 18
Starburst optimizer, 161
STARindex, 185–186
STARjoin technology, 186
star schema, 44, 45
static SQL for Java (SQLJ), 159, 160
static Structured Query Language (SQL), 158, 159, 170
statistical models and matching techniques, 93
storage allocation, 217
Storage Area Network (SAN) solution, 217, 219
storage methods, IMS, 150–151
storage software, 217–222
  Adaptive Differencing Technology, 219
  archive management, 222
  backup/recovery, 221–222
  disaster preparedness, 222
  disk resource discovery, 217
  IBM Enterprise Storage Server (ESS, Shark), 219–220
  Metadata Controller (MDC), 221
  policies, 220
  storage allocation, 217
  Storage Area Network (SAN) solution, 217, 219
  Tivoli Application Protection, 222
  Tivoli Enterprise Console (TEC) and, 216–217
  Tivoli SANergy, 221
  Tivoli Storage Manager, 218–220
stored procedures, 41, 75
stores online. *See* WebSphere Commerce
streamlining content by WebSphere Transcoding Publisher, 113–114
Structured Query Language. *See* SQL
"Struts," WebSphere Studio, 83
subclasses, databases, 38, 39
summarized data, data warehouses, 44
Sun Microsystems, 21
supercomputer, 54
Supply Chain Management. *See* SCM
switches, 63, 65–66
Sybase, 74, 82, 131, 197, 198
Symmetric Multi-processor (SMP), 54, 55, 162
symmetric (private key) encryption, 204
Symmetric Processors (SPs), 60
synchronization capability
  databases, 154
  Enterprise Information Portal (EIP), 108
  WebSphere Everyplace Access, 106
syncpoints, 29, 30
Sysplex technology
  DB2 Universal Database, 165–166, 169
  Information Management System (IMS), 152, 154
System/3X computers, 51
System/360 (S/360) family, 50–51
System/370 (S/370) family, 51
System/390 (S/390) family, 56, 61
SystemBuilder, UniVerse/Unidata family, 194–195
system catalog, DB2 Universal Database, 164
System Licensed Internal Code (SLIC), 60
System Log Data Sets, IMS, 152
System Object Model (SOM), 42
system processors, 54
System R and DB2 Universal Database, 33, 161
Systems and Applications Monitoring (Tivoli solution), 229
Systems Network Architecture. *See* SNA

T

table data, DB2 Universal Database, 157
tables, databases

DB2 Universal Database, 157, 160, 162–163, 170
Informix, 187
Lotus, 236–237
overview of, 33–34, 189, 191
table spaces
allocation, UniVerse/Unidata family, 192
DB2 Universal Database, 157, 162, 163, 169–170
partitioning, DB2 Universal Database, 162–164
tag languages, 18–20
"talking" software, EIP, 109–110
TARGETindex, Informix, 186
targets, networks, 63
TCP/IP (Transmission Control Protocol/ Internet Protocol)
e-business and, 1, 20
Information Management System (IMS), 154
networks and, 64, 66–67, 68
operating systems (OSs) and, 56, 57
overview of, 1, 20
Tivoli NetView for Transmission Control Protocol/Internet Protocol, 225, 226
WebSphere Host Integration, 88, 90, 91
TCP (transport) layer, networks, 64
teaming structures, WebSphere Studio, 81, 82
team rooms, Reach and User Experience (WebSphere), 94, 95, 96
team workspace, Lotus, 242–243
TEC (Tivoli Enterprise Console)
configuration and operations management, 231
security, 211, 212, 216
storage software, 216–217
threat management, 211, 212, 216
Telelogic, 181
Telephone User Interface (TUI) function of DUCS, 240
telephony platforms, 101, 102
Telnet client traffic conversion, WebSphere Host Integration, 90–91
templates
customizer program of VisualAge Generator, 135–136
DB2 Content Manager, 175
Page Editor Template Wizard, WebSphere Studio, 79
terminal emulation, UniVerse/Unidata family, 195–196
testing and debugging applications, WebSphere Studio, 82
text analyzer business components, WebSphere, 141, 143
text clipping feature of WebSphere Transcoding Publisher, 114
Text Extender, DB2 Universal Database, 172
Text Information Extender, DB2 Universal Database, 172
Text-to-Speech engine of WebSphere Voice Server, 101–102
"thin" clients, 37, 249
thread scheduler, Informix, 182
threat management, 210–212. *See also* security software
Crystal Report Generator, 212
DB2 Universal Database and, 212
default policies, 210
geographic-based administrators, 210–211
hacker attacks, 210
historical data analysis, 210
Intrusion Detection Exchange Format (IDEF), 211–212
policies, 210
policy regions, 210–211
role-based administrators, 210–211
self-healing initiative, 212
Tivoli Enterprise Console (TEC) and, 211, 212, 216
Tivoli Enterprise Data Warehouse and, 212
Tivoli Intrusion Manager, 212, 216
Tivoli NetView and, 212
Tivoli Risk Manager, 210–212, 216
validation policies, 210
virus attacks, 210
TimeSeries DataBlade, 184
Tivoli Access Manager for Business Integration, 75, 207–208, 215
Tivoli Access Manager for Operating Systems, 208
Tivoli Access Manager (Tivoli Policy Director)
e-business and, 206–207
Enterprise Information Portal (EIP) and, 109
Reach and User Experience (WebSphere), 95
Tivoli Analyzer for Lotus Domino, 222, 237
Tivoli and security, 203, 204
Tivoli Application Protection, 222
Tivoli Business Systems Manager, 223
Tivoli Configuration Manager, 230

Tivoli Data Exchange, 232
Tivoli Enterprise Console. *See* TEC
Tivoli Enterprise Data Warehouse, 212
Tivoli Identity Management, 208–209, 214
Tivoli Internet Services Manager. *See* WESM (WebSphere Everyplace Subscription Manager)
Tivoli Intrusion Manager, 212, 216
Tivoli License Manager, 230
Tivoli Monitoring, 223–225
Tivoli Monitoring Active Directory Option, 223–224
Tivoli Monitoring for Applications, 224
Tivoli Monitoring for Business Integration, 224
Tivoli Monitoring for Databases, 224
Tivoli Monitoring for Messaging and Collaboration, 224
Tivoli Monitoring for Network Performance, 225
Tivoli Monitoring for Transaction Performance, 225
Tivoli Monitoring for Web Infrastructure, 225
Tivoli NetView, 212, 225–226
Tivoli NetView for Transmission Control Protocol/Internet Protocol, 225, 226
Tivoli NetView for z/OS and OS/390, 226
Tivoli NetView Performance Monitor, 225, 226
Tivoli Performance Modeler for z/OS and OS/390, 226–227
Tivoli Performance Viewer, 76–77
Tivoli Personalized Service Manager and EIP, 109
Tivoli Point-of-Sale Manager, 230–231
Tivoli Policy Director. *See* Tivoli Access Manager
Tivoli Policy Manager for e-business, 214
Tivoli Remote Control, 231
Tivoli Risk Manager, 210–212, 216
Tivoli SANergy, 221
Tivoli SecureWay and WebSphere Host Integration, 87, 130
Tivoli SecureWay Directory, 94
Tivoli Security Event Solution, 216
Tivoli Storage Manager, 218–220
Tivoli Storage Manager and DB2 Content Manager, 174
Tivoli Storage Manager for Application Servers, 219
Tivoli Storage Manager for Databases, 219
Tivoli Storage Manager for ERP, 219
Tivoli Storage Manager for Hardware, 219–220
Tivoli Storage Manager for Mail, 220
Tivoli Storage Manager for Space Management, 220
Tivoli Storage Manager for Storage Area Networks, 220
Tivoli Storage Network Manager, 217–218
Tivoli Storage Resource Manager, 220–221
Tivoli Storage Resource Manager for Chargeback, 220–221
Tivoli Storage Resource Manager for Databases, 221
Tivoli Switch Analyzer, 226
Tivoli Web Site Analyzer (WebSphere Site Analyzer), 95, 98, 146, 227–228
Tivoli Workload Scheduler, 231–232
Tivoli Workload Scheduler for Applications, 232
Tivoli Workload Scheduler for z/OS, 232
Token Ring LAN, 65
Torvalds, Linus, 60–61
Touch-Tone, 102
TPF (Transaction Processing Facility), 56, 133
Training Tool of WebSphere Text Analyzer Business Components, 143
transactional Application Programming Interfaces (APIs), WAS, 74
transaction flow, WAS, 72–73
transaction management
  architectures pre-dating e-business, 28–31
  DB2 Universal Database, 160
transaction persistence, 17
transaction processing, 130–138. *See also* Foundation and Tools (WebSphere)
  C/C++ for OS/390 and z/OS, 131
  COmmon Business Oriented Language (COBOL), 6, 24, 133
  Customer Information Control System (CICS) Transaction Server, 130–131
  Distributed Computer Environment (DCE), 60, 131–132
  Encina product family, 131–132
  external call interface (ECI) of CICS Transaction Server, 131
  Gateway Server of WebSphere Application Server (WAS), 136–137
  "green screens" support, 88–89, 134–135
  Interaction Controller of VisualAge Generator, 136

Interactive Test Facility of VisualAge Generator, 137
JavaBeans, 136, 137
Java Servlet Pages (JSPs), 136, 137
monitor environments, 131
MQSeries messaging software, 131
programming languages supported, 131
Rapid Application Development (RAD), 137, 195
Secure Sockets Layer (SSL) support, 138
security, 138
Socket Communication Interface (SCI), 138
templates customizer program of VisualAge Generator, 135–136
Transaction Servers and Tools (WebSphere), 70
TXSeries, 74, 131–132
Unified Modeling Language (UML), 137
User Interface (UI) record of VisualAge Generator, 136, 137
VisualAge (VA) Generator, 134–137, 138
Web services support, 138
WebSphere Studio and, 136
Transaction Processing Facility (TPF), 56, 133
transaction security, 17
Transaction Servers and Tools (WebSphere), 70
transcoding Web data, EIP, 112–114
transcription, 103–104
transformation, data warehouses, 46
Transmission Control Protocol/Internet Protocol. *See* TCP/IP
"transport pipe," networks, 68
transport (TCP) layer, networks, 64
tree structures, IMS, 149–150
triggers, DB2 Universal Database, 41
TUI (Telephone User Interface) function of DUCS, 240
TWAIN 32-compliant devices, 79
2PKDP (Two-Party Key Distribution Protocol), 109
Two-Party Key Distribution Protocol (2PKDP), 109
TXSeries, 74, 131–132
type pointer, DB2 Universal Database, 164

U

U2 (UniVerse/Unidata) family, 188–196. *See also* Informix
COBOL Direct Connect, 196
data replication, 193
Document Object Model (DOM) handling, 190, 192–193
eXtended Markup Language (XML), 188, 190, 192
extended-relational (object-relational) database, 188, 192
file structures, 192
Gateway Client Requester, 193
host-based application enhancement tool, 195–196
HyperText Markup Language (HTML) functionality, 195
Java Database Connectivity (JDBC), 188, 192
nested relational database, 188–189, 189, 191
object-enabling infrastructure for N-tier development, 193–194
Open Database Connectivity (ODBC)-compliant database, 188
portable U2 applications, 194–195
Rapid Application Development (RAD), 195
recovery capability, 192
RedBack, 193–194
repeating groups, 189
SB+Server, 195
SBClient, 195
Secure Socket Layer (SSL) support, 192
Secure Sockets Layer (SSL) support, 188
SystemBuilder, 194–195
table space allocation, 192
terminal emulation, 195–196
UniBasic, 190, 192
Unicode support, 192
UniData, 188–192
Unidata SQL, 190
UniQuery, 190
UniVerse Basic, 192–193
Web server and, 193
WebSphere MQ and, 192
wIntegrate, 195–196
UDDI (Universal Description, Discovery, Integration), 12, 13, 81, 246
UDFs (User-Defined Functions), 40–41
UDTs (User-Defined Types), 40
UI (User Interface) record of VisualAge Generator, 136, 137
UK National Grid, 14
UML (Unified Modeling Language), 137
unauthorized attempts, 205

UniBasic, 190, 192
Unicode support, 192
UniData, 188–192
Unidata SQL, 190
Unified Content API, 99
Unified Modeling Language (UML), 137
uniprocessing, 55
UniQuery, 190
unit of work (UOW), 29, 152
Universal Description, Discovery, Integration (UDDI), 12, 13, 81, 246
UniVerse Basic, 192–193
UniVerse/Unidata family. *See* U2
University of Pennsylvania, 50
UNIX
  DB2 Universal Database and, 156, 169
  Informix and, 185
  overview of, 57
  Tivoli Access Manager for Operating Systems, 208
unstructured documents, 19
UOW (unit of work), 29, 152
U.S. Department of Defense, 1
U.S. Department of Energy
User-Defined Functions (UDFs), 40–41
User-Defined Types (UDTs), 40
User Interface (UI) record of VisualAge Generator, 136, 137

V
vacuum tubes, 50
validation policies, threat management, 210
value-added resellers (VARs), 260
variability of e-business on demand, 15–16
variable-length records and fields, 26
VARs (value-added resellers), 260
VA (VisualAge) Generator, 134–137, 138
VeriSign Access Management Service, 215
VeriSign Managed Public Key Infrastructures, 216
VeriSign Managed Services, 207, 214–216
VeriSign Public Provisioning Infrastructure, 216
Versata Logic Suite for WebSphere, 86
video
  DB2 Content Manager, 176–177
  editing features, WebSphere Studio, 80
Video Foundation DataBlade, 184
Virtual Machine (VM), 56, 166–167
virtual private network (VPN), 87–88, 130
Virtual Storage Architecture (VSAM), 24, 27–28, 43
Virtual Storage Extended (VSE), 57, 166–167
virtual team environment, Lotus, 234–235
Virtual Telecommunications Access Method (VTAM), 226
virus attacks, 210
VisualAge Enterprise Suite, 137
VisualAge for Java, 133–134. *See also* WebSphere Studio
VisualAge Generator Customizer Program, 136
VisualAge Micro Edition (WebSphere Studio Device Developer), 85–86, 91, 100, 110, 115
VisualAge Pacbase, 137
VisualAge Smalltalk, 138
VisualAge (VA) Generator, 134–137, 138
VM (Virtual Machine), 56, 166–167
voice application development tools, 102
Voice over Internet Protocol (VoIP), 101, 102–105
VoiceXML technology, 102
VoIP (Voice over Internet Protocol), 101, 102–105
VPN (virtual private network), 87–88, 130
VSAM (Virtual Storage Architecture), 24, 27–28, 43
VSE/ESA, 56
VSE (Virtual Storage Extended), 57, 166–167
VTAM (Virtual Telecommunications Access Method), 226

W
WANs (Wide Area Networks), 65, 90, 145
WAP (Wireless Application Protocol), 95, 106, 110–111, 247
WAS (WebSphere Application Server), 71–77. *See also* Foundation and Tools (WebSphere)
  access control lists, 75
  ActiveX bridge, 74
  application development tools, 75
  applications, access to, 73–75
  applications supported by, 71
  auto-tuning software, 76–77
  business logic beans, 73
  Business Logic Container, 72–73
  C++ applications, 74
  clustering, 76

Common Gateway Interface (CGI) script, 72
Common Object Request Broker Architecture (CORBA), 73, 74
Common Security Interoperability (CSI), 75
Component Broker, 74
component servers, 74–75
connection pooling, 76
Connection Services, 74
databases and, 73, 74–75
data stores and, 74–75
DB2 Universal Database and, 74, 75
developers and, 77
dynamic content services, 73
Enterprise Edition, 77
Enterprise Information Portal (EIP) and, 112
Enterprise JavaBeans (EJBs), 73, 74
Enterprise Resource Planning (ERP) applications, 74
eXtended Markup Language (XML) support, 73, 75, 81
failover capacity, 76
HyperText Markup Language (HTML), 72, 73
HyperText Transfer Protocol (HTTP), 30–31, 72, 73
HyperText Transfer Protocol Secure (HTTPS), 73
Informix and, 181
Internet Inter-ORB Protocol (IIOP) support, 73
J2EE Connector Architecture (JCA), 74
Java, 74
Java 2, Enterprise Edition (J2EE) support, 8, 71, 74, 75
Java Authentication and Authorization Service (JAAS), 76
Java Cryptography Extension (JCE), 76
Java Database Connectivity (JDBC), 73
Java Management Extensions (JMX), 76–77
Java Messaging Service (JMS), 73
Java Servlet Pages (JSPs), 73
Java Virtual Machine (JVM), 76
Kerberos tokens, 75
Lightweight Directory Access Protocol (LDAP)-based user directories, 75
Lotus Domino and, 76
network deployment and, 77
Object Request Broker (ORB), 73
overview of, 71–72
performance management, 76–77
persistent storage, 74
Remote Method Interface (RMI), 73
runtime environment provided by, 71–72, 74
Secure Sockets Layer (SSL) support, 73
security, 75–76
servlets (Java), 73
shared work areas, 73–74
stored procedures development tools, 75
Tivoli Monitoring for Web Infrastructure, 225
Tivoli Performance Viewer, 76–77
transactional Application Programming Interfaces (APIs), 74
transaction flow, 72–73
TXSeries, 74
Web browser, 72, 73
Web Container, 72, 73
WebSEAL component of Tivoli Access Manager, 75
Web services, 73, 75
Web Services Gateway, 76
WebSphere Commerce and, 248
WebSphere Host Integration and, 87, 128
workload balancing, 76
WAS (WebSphere Application Server) Advanced Edition, 94
WAS (WebSphere Application Server)-Express, 77
WAS (WebSphere Application Server) for Developers, 77
WAS (WebSphere Application Server) Network Deployment, 77
WAS (WebSphere Studio Application) Developer, 94, 110
waves of information technology, 6–8
Web ability, information movement and access, 196
Web Animator, 80
Web applications, Lotus, 238
Web application servers of business model, 265, 267, 268, 272. *See also* DB2 Universal Database; IMS (Information Management System); Informix; Lotus Domino Server; U2 (UniVerse/Unidata) family; WAS (WebSphere Application Server)

WebArt Designer, 79
Web-based administration, identity management, 209
Web browser and WAS (WebSphere Application Server), 72, 73
Web Container, 72, 73
Web content browsing (offline) of WebSphere Everyplace Access, 107
Web Content Publisher, 94, 95
Web crawler, EIP, 99
Web data adaptation for pervasive computing, 112–114
Web DataBlade, 184
Web-exploiting broker, DB2 Content Manager, 174
Web Management (Tivoli solution), 229
WebSEAL component of Tivoli Access Manager, 75
Web server and UniVerse/Unidata family, 193
Web services
  DB2 Universal Database, 161
  Foundation and Tools (WebSphere), 71
  innovations, 12–14
  transaction processing, 138
  WebSphere Application Server (WAS), 73, 75
Web Services Client, WebSphere Studio, 81
Web Services Description Language (WSDL), 12–13, 246
Web Services Document Access Definition Extension (DADX) Group Configuration, 81
Web Services Gateway, 76
Web site analyzer, 95, 98, 146, 227–228
Web sites
  for e-business and IBM, xix
  for IBM, 270–272
  for Patterns for e-business, 256
WebSphere Application Server. *See* WAS
WebSphere Asset Analyzer, 128
WebSphere Bank Teller Business Components, 141, 142
WebSphere Business Components, 138–145
  advanced ("black box") components of WebSphere Business Components Composer (WSBCC), 141
  bank teller business components, 141, 142
  base ("white box") components of WebSphere Business Components Composer (WSBCC), 140–141
  Categorization Engine of WebSphere Text Analyzer Business Components, 143
  Credit Function Group of WebSphere Order Capture Business Component, 144
  DB2 Universal Database and, 144
  Fulfillment Function Group of WebSphere Order Capture Business Component, 144
  Interactive Financial Exchange (IFX), 144
  Maintenance Function Group of WebSphere Order Capture Business Component, 143–144
  Order Capture Group of WebSphere Order Capture Business Component, 144
  overview of, 138–139
  text analyzer business components, 141, 143
  Training Tool of WebSphere Text Analyzer Business Components, 143
  WebSphere Order Capture Business Component, 143–144
  WebSphere Software MultiChannel Banking Solution, 142, 144–145
  WebSphere Text Analyzer Business Components, 141, 143
WebSphere Business Components Composer (WSBCC), 140–141
WebSphere Business Components Studio, 141, 144
WebSphere Business Integration Adapter Development Kit, 127
WebSphere Business Integration Adapters, 127–128
WebSphere Business Integration Application Adapters, 127
WebSphere Business Integration Technology Adapters, 127–128
WebSphere Catalog Manager, 247, 248, 249–250
WebSphere Commerce, 246–255. *See also* application accelerators
  American Standard Code for Information Interchange (ASCII) conversion, 250
  Business Edition, 247, 248–250
  catalog manager, 247, 248, 249–250
  data mining, 255
  DB2 Universal Database and, 248, 255
  digital certificates, 250, 252

eXtended Markup Language (XML) and, 246, 249, 250
HyperText Transfer Protocol (HTTP) support, 247, 249
IBM Payment Gateway, 254
IBM Payment Registry, 252–254
Java environment, 249
Java technology, 246
Lotus QuickPlace and, 247
Lotus Sametime and, 247
management of stores, 254–255
Merchant Initiated Authorization (MIA), 251
mobile commerce (m-commerce), 247
Multi-Payment Framework (MPF) support, 250–252, 253
payment manager, 247, 248, 250–254
Professional Edition, 247, 248
Professional Entry Edition, 247, 248
Secure Electronic Transaction (SET), 249, 250, 251, 252, 253, 254
Secure Sockets Layer (SSL) support, 251, 254
Services-Oriented Architectural Protocol (SOAP) support, 246
Universal Description, Discovery, Integration (UDDI), 246
Web Services Description Language (WSDL), 246
WebSphere Application Server (WAS) and, 248
WebSphere Catalog Manager, 247, 248, 249–250
WebSphere Commerce Accelerator, 248
WebSphere Everyplace and, 247
WebSphere Transcoding Publisher and, 247
Wireless Application Protocol (WAP), 247
Wireless Markup Language (WML) support, 249
wireless users, 247
WebSphere Commerce Accelerator, 248
WebSphere Commerce Analyzer, 247
WebSphere Commerce Analyzer Advanced Edition, 254–255
WebSphere Commerce for Digital Media, 247
WebSphere Commerce Payments (WebSphere Payment Manager), 247, 248, 250–254
WebSphere Commerce Portal, 255. *See also* application accelerators
WebSphere Custom Environment, 86, 115
WebSphere Data Interchange, 126–127
WebSphere e-business Adapters, 127
WebSphere Edge Server, 112, 145
WebSphere Everyplace Access, 105–106
WebSphere Everyplace and WebSphere Commerce, 247
WebSphere Everyplace Connection Manager (WECM), 110–111, 146
WebSphere Everyplace Server, Service Provider Offering, 107–109
WebSphere Everyplace Subscription Manager (WESM), 111–112
WebSphere Everyplace Suite Embedded Edition, 109–110
WebSphere Everyplace Toolkit, 107
WebSphere Homepage Builder, 78–80
WebSphere Host Integration, 86–91. *See also* Foundation and Tools (WebSphere)
ActiveX, 88, 130
Administrator, IBM Screen Customizer, 89
Advanced Peer-to-Peer Networking (APPN), 90
Advanced Program-to-Program Communications (APPC), 88
Client Runtime, IBM Screen Customizer, 89
communications server, 90–91
Customization Studio, IBM Screen Customizer, 89
digital certificates, 87
Emulator High-Level Language Applications Programming Interface (EHLLAPI), 88
Enterprise JavaBeans (EJBs), 87, 88, 130
Enterprise Modernization, 128–129
eXtended Markup Language (XML) support, 87, 88, 130
"green screens" support, 88–89, 134–135
High Performance Routing (HPR), 88
Host Access Beans for Java, 88, 89, 130
Host Access Class Libraries (HACLs), 88, 89, 130
HyperText Markup Language (HTML), 90
IBM Communications Server, 87, 90–91, 128, 130
IBM Firewall, 87
IBM Personal Communications, 87, 88
IBM Screen Customizer, 87, 89
Java Database Connectivity (JDBC), 90
JavaScript, 89

Java Servlet Pages (JSPs), 87, 88, 90, 130
Local Area Networks (LANs) and, 90
MultiProtocol Transport Networking (MPTN), 90–91
Personal Communications of WebSphere Host Integration Solution, 128
Public Key Infrastructure (PKI), 87
Resource Access Control Facility (RACF), 87, 129
screen customizer, 89
Secure Sockets Layer (SSL) support, 87, 129
security, 875–88, 129–130
servlets (Java), 87, 88
Systems Network Architecture (SNA), 88, 90, 91
Telnet client traffic conversion, 90–91
Tivoli SecureWay and, 87, 130
Transmission Control Protocol/Internet Protocol (TCP/IP), 88, 90, 91
virtual private network (VPN), 87–88, 130
WebSphere Application Server and, 87
WebSphere Application Server (WAS), 128
WebSphere Asset Analyzer, 128
WebSphere Studio and, 87, 128
WebSphere Studio Enterprise Developer, 128
WebSphere Transcoding Publisher, 128
Wide Area Networks (WANs) and, 90
Windows High-Level Language Applications Programming Interface (WinHLLAPI), 88
WebSphere Host Integration Solution, 128–129
WebSphere Host On-Demand, 87, 88–89, 128
WebSphere Host Publisher, 87, 89–90, 128
WebSphere Micro Environment, 85–86, 115
WebSphere MQ Event Broker, 125–126
WebSphere MQ Everyplace, 85–86, 125
WebSphere MQ Integrator Broker, 126
WebSphere MQ (Message Queue)
access management, 207
application integration, 121–128
configuration and operations management software, 232
performance and availability software, 224
privacy management, 216
UniVerse/Unidata (U2) family, 192
WebSphere MQSeries Everyplace, 108
WebSphere MQSeries Messaging, 118
WebSphere MQSeries Workflow, 116, 117, 118–119
WebSphere MQ Workflow and Enterprise Information Portal (EIP), 100
WebSphere Order Capture Business Component, 143–144
WebSphere Payment Manager (WebSphere Commerce Payments), 247, 248, 250–254
WebSphere Personalization, 94, 96–98
WebSphere Portal and DB2 Content Manager, 178
WebSphere Portal Enable, 93–94
WebSphere Portal Experience, 95
WebSphere Portal Express, 96–98
WebSphere Portal Express Plus, 96
WebSphere Portal Extend, 94–95
WebSphere Portal for Multiplatforms, 92–96
WebSphere products, 69–146. *See also* Business Integration; Foundation and Tools; Reach and User Experience; Transaction Servers and Tools; WebSphere Business Components
IBM SanFrancisco, 145
management functions, 69
overview of, 69–70
reuse of building blocks, 69
security and, 69
WebSphere Software MultiChannel Banking Solution, 142, 144–145
WebSphere Studio, 77–86. *See also* Foundation and Tools (WebSphere); Reach and User Experience
ahead-of-time (AOT) compiling, 85
Application Developer Integration Edition, 82
application development, 75, 81–82
audio files supported, 80
business rules, 82, 86
Cascading Style Sheet (CSS) support, 79
Connector Builder Component, 83
database connectivity, 82
DB2 Universal Database and, 82, 83, 86
development environments, 81
Device Developer (VisualAge Micro Edition), 85–86, 91, 100, 115
Enterprise Generation Language (EGL), 78, 83
Enterprise JavaBeans (EJBs), 82
File Transfer, 80

"footprint," 85
Graphics Interchange Format (GIF) conversion, 79
hand-held devices, application development, 85–86
homepage building, 78–80
HyperText Markup Language (HTML) editing, 79
image conversion, 79
image file supported, 80
Image Tools, 79
inventory process, 83
i-Photo Builder, 80
J2EE Connector Architecture (JCA), 82
Java Servlet Pages (JSPs), 83
Joint Photographic Experts Group (JPEG) conversion, 79
just-in-time (JIT) compiling, 85
Macromedia ColdFusion MX for WebSphere, 86
Message Queue Everyplace (MQe), 85–86, 125
model-view-controller (MVC) architecture, 83
monitoring tools, 83–84
OS/390 and, 83–85, 228–229
overview of, 77–78
Page Editor Homepage Builder, 79
Page Editor Template Wizard, 79
perspectives, 81, 82
Project Eclipse, 78
Rational ClearCase LT, 82
site development, 75, 80–81
Site Management/Site Gallery View, 80
Site Style Wizard, 80
"Struts," 83
teaming structures, 81, 82
testing and debugging applications, 82
transaction processing, 136
TWAIN 32-compliant devices, 79
Universal Description, Discovery, Integration (UDDI), 81
Versata Logic Suite for WebSphere, 86
video editing features, 80
Web Animator, 80
WebArt Designer, 79
Web Services Client, 81
Web Services Document Access Definition Extension (DADX) Group Configuration, 81
WebSphere Custom Environment, 86
WebSphere Homepage Builder, 78–80
WebSphere Host Integration and, 87, 128
WebSphere Micro Environment, 85–86
What You See Is What You Get (WYSIWYG) editor, 79
workload simulator, 85
z/OS and, 83–85, 228–229
WebSphere Studio Application Developer, 75, 81–82
WebSphere Studio Application Monitor for OS/390 and z/OS, 83–84, 228–229
WebSphere Studio Application (WAS) Developer, 94
WebSphere Studio Assess Analyzer for Multiplatforms, 83, 84
WebSphere Studio Device Developer (VisualAge Micro Edition), 85–86, 91, 100, 110, 115
WebSphere Studio Enterprise Developer, 82–83, 128
WebSphere Studio Site Developer, 75, 80–81
WebSphere Studio Workbench, 78
WebSphere Studio Workload Simulator for z/OS and OS/390, 85
WebSphere Text Analyzer Business Components, 141, 143
WebSphere Transcoding Publisher, 108, 112–114, 128, 247
WebSphere Translation Server, 104–105
WebSphere Voice Response, 101, 102, 103
WebSphere Voice Server, 100–102
WebSphere Voice Server for Transcription, 103–104
WebSphere Voice Server SDK, 102
WebSphere Voice Toolkit, 102
"Web-year" and security, 202
WECM (WebSphere Everyplace Connection Manager), 110–111, 146
WESM (WebSphere Everyplace Subscription Manager), 111–112
WE (Workgroup Edition), DB2 Universal Database, 167
WfMC (Workflow Management Coalition), 118
What You See Is What You Get (WYSIWYG) editor, 79
"white box" (base) components of WSBCC, 140–141

Who Says Elephants Can't Dance? (Gerstner), 12
Wide Area Networks (WANs), 65, 90, 145
Windows and DB2 Universal Database, 156
wIntegrate, UniVerse/Unidata family, 195–196
Wireless Application Protocol (WAP), 95, 106, 110–111, 247
wireless devices, 2–3. *See also* EIP (Enterprise Information Portal); pervasive solutions
Wireless Markup Language (WML), 106, 249
Wireless Session Protocol (WSP), 111
wireless support, Lotus, 239
wireless users, WebSphere Commerce, 247
Wladawsky-Berger, Irving, 14
WLM (Workload Manager), 57, 58, 166
WML (Wireless Markup Language), 106, 249
workflow management
  DB2 Content Manager, 174, 175
  Enterprise Information Portal (EIP), 100
  process integration, 116, 117, 118–119
  WebSphere Application Server (WAS), 76
Workflow Management Coalition (WfMC), 118
Workgroup Edition (WE), DB2 Universal Database, 167
Workload Manager (WLM), 57, 58, 166
workload scheduler, 231–232
workload simulator, WebSphere Studio, 85
World Wide Web, 1, 37
Wozniak, Steven, 52
wrapped packets, 64, 65
wrappering components (J2EE), 22
write once, run anywhere (computer programs), 20, 21, 60, 154
WSBCC (WebSphere Business Components Composer), 140–141
WSDL (Web Services Description Language), 12–13, 246
WSP (Wireless Session Protocol), 111
WYSIWYG (What You See Is What You Get) editor, 79

X
XCF (MVS Cross Coupling Facility), 155
XCF/XES (cross-systems communication facility/cross-systems extended services), 58
XHTML (eXtended HyperText Markup Language), 106, 196
XML (eXtended Markup Language)
  DB2 Universal Database, 161
  Foundation and Tools (WebSphere), 71
  Information Management System (IMS), 149, 155
  information movement and access, 196
  metadata and, 46
  open standards software, 9
  overview of, 9, 19–20
  UniVerse/Unidata (U2) family, 188, 190, 192
  WebSphere Application Server (WAS), 73, 75, 81
  WebSphere Commerce, 246, 249, 250
  WebSphere Host Integration, 87, 88, 130
XPS (Informix Extended Parallel Server), 186–187
XRC (eXtended Remote Copy), IMS, 154
xSeries computers, 50, 52, 54
XSL (eXtensible Style Language), 20

Z
z/OS
  configuration and operations management software, 232
  DB2 Universal Database and, 156, 161–166, 169, 170
  overview of, 57–57
  performance and availability software, 223, 226–227, 228–229
  WebSphere Studio and, 83–85, 228–229
zSeries computers, 50, 51, 53, 54, 57, 61
z/VM, 56

Reader Feedback Sheet

Your comments and suggestions are very important in shaping future publications. Please e-mail us at *moreinfo@maxpress.com* or photocopy this page, jot down your thoughts, and fax it to (850) 934-9981 or mail it to:

Maximum Press

Attn: Jim Hoskins

605 Silverthorn Road

Gulf Breeze, FL 32561

Exploring IBM
***@server** pSeries,*
Eleventh Edition
by Jim Hoskins
and Robert Bluethman
344 pages
$54.95
ISBN: 1-885068-81-6

Exploring IBM
***@server** iSeries,*
Eleventh Edition
by Jim Hoskins and
Roger Dimmick
386 pages
$54.95
ISBN: 1-885068-92-1

*Exploring IBM **@server***
zSeries and S/390
Servers,
Eighth Edition
by Jim Hoskins
and Bob Frank
464 pages
$59.95
ISBN: 1-885068-91-3

Exploring IBM
***@server** xSeries,*
Twelfth Edition
by Jim Hoskins, Bill
Wilson, and Ray Winkel
208 pages
$49.95
ISBN: 1-885068-83-2

Exploring IBM
e-business Software,
Second Edition
by Casey Young
360 pages
$49.95
ISBN: 1-931644-00-4

Exploring IBM
Technology, Products
& Services,
Fifth Edition
edited by Jim Hoskins
272 pages
$54.95
ISBN: 1-885068-82-4

Building Intranets
with Lotus Notes &
Domino 5.0,
Third Edition
by Steve Krantz
320 pages
$39.95
ISBN: 1-885068-41-7

Internet Marketing
for Information
Technology
Companies,
Second Edition
by Barry Silverstein
464 pages
$29.95
ISBN: 1-885068-67-0

To purchase a Maximum Press book, visit your local bookstore
or call 1-800-989-6733 (US/Canada) or 1-850-934-4583 (International)
online ordering available at ***www.maxpress.com***